O. Hood Phillips'
First Book of English Law

AUSTRALIA AND NEW ZEALAND
The Law Book Company Ltd.
Sydney : Melbourne : Perth

CANADA AND U.S.A.
The Carswell Company Ltd.
Agincourt, Ontario

INDIA
N. M. Tripathi Private Ltd.
Bombay
and
Eastern Law House
Calcutta and Delhi
M.P.P. House
Bangalore

ISRAEL
Steimatzky's Agency Ltd.
Jerusalem : Tel-Aviv : Haifa

O. Hood Phillips' First Book of English Law

EIGHTH EDITION

by

THE LATE O. HOOD PHILLIPS,
Q.C., D.C.L., M.A.(OXON), J.P.
*Formerly Emeritus Professor of Jurisprudence
and sometime Dean of the Faculty of Law in the University of Birmingham*

and

A. H. HUDSON,
M.A., LL.B. (CANTAB.), PH.D.(MANCH.)
*Of Lincoln's Inn, Barrister;
Professor of Common Law in the University of Liverpool*

LONDON
SWEET & MAXWELL
1988

First Edition 1948
Second Impression 1949
Second Edition 1953
Third Edition 1955
Second Impression 1957
Fourth Edition 1960
Second Impression 1962
Third Impression 1964
Fifth Edition 1965
Sixth Edition 1970
Seventh Edition 1977
Eighth Edition 1988

Published in 1988 by
Sweet & Maxwell Limited
11, New Fetter Lane, London
Laserset by P.B. Computer Typesetting, Pickering, N. Yorks.
Printed in Great Britain by Hazell Watson and Viney Ltd.
Member of BPCC plc, Aylesbury, Bucks.

British Library Cataloguing in Publication Data

Phillips, O. Hood
    O. Hood Phillips' first book of English
    law. — 8th ed.
    1. Law — England
    I. Title   II. Hudson, A. H.
    III. Phillips, O. Hood. first book of
    English law
    344.2   KD532.Z9

    ISBN 0–421–39360–2
    ISBN 0–421–39370–X Pbk

PREFACE TO THE EIGHTH EDITION

This is the first edition in the forty years since the book first appeared for which Professor Hood Phillips has not been wholly or in part responsible. He had hoped to participate in the preparation of this edition but illness and death sadly prevented him doing so.[1] The sadness of this has been brought home the more by the fact that his great distinciton in the field of public law has been recognised by the citation of his textbook on constitutional law, together with Glanvill, Blackstone, Dicey and Holdsworth, by the Court of Appeal in R. v. *Secretary of State for the Home Department Ex p. Northumbria Police Authority* [1988] 2 W.L.R. 590, which was fortunately reported in time for inclusion in Chapter 15 of this book on Books of Authority. Such citation in such company renders any further tribute not only superfluous but presumptuous.

In the preface to the First Edition Professor Hood Phillips said this book was intended to serve as an elementary introduction for those about to embark, for whatever purpose on the study of English Law. No attempt has been made in this edition to depart from that overriding aim, though in the years which have elapsed since the last edition much has occurred that has required inclusion and both the legal profession and the legal system seem to be poised on the brink of changes which will radically change the face of any further editions. Again, the emphasis of the book has always been on the historical evolution of both rules and institutions, and once again, no attempt has been made to set a different course, though demands of space have led to the exclusion of some more detailed material and some slight re-arrangement has been effected elsewhere in order to highlight topics of growing

---

[1] For a biographical note see O. Hood Phillips and Jackson, *O. Hood Phillips' Constitutional and Administrative Law* (7th ed.) pp. ix–xi.

importance. Otherwise the scope and plan of the book remain very much as the author designed them for the last edition.

Problems of timing have meant that two important pieces of forthcoming legislation, the Legal Aid Bill and the Criminal Justice Bill, have had to be referred to in their unenacted form, but the likelihood of change in those parts of the Bills mentioned in the text seemed small. Moreover, there seems to be a steady growth in the number of cases of interest which are reported in newspapers such as *The Times*, *The Daily Telegraph*, *The Independent* and *The Financial Times* which do not later find a place in a regular series of reports, and this has been reflected by more frequent citation of such cases.

Finally, it would be wrong to conclude without a word of gratitude to the publisher's staff for their generous help. In particular they have undertaken their usual responsiblity for the preparation of the Tables of Cases and Statutes and the Index.

March 1988   A. H. HUDSON
                                                     Faculty of Law,
                                            University of Liverpool

CONTENTS

PART III: The Sources of English Law

PART IV: Main Branches of English Law

TABLE OF CASES

PART I

Introduction

CHAPTER 1

Introduction

1. THE CHARACTERISTICS OF ENGLISH LAW

The Law of England

"English Law" means the law of England. England (which includes Wales) is a smaller unit than the United Kingdom. The latter is a parliamentary union which supplies England with her legislature, and which is the State for international and most constitutional purposes. England is a smaller unit even than Great Britain, which is a union of the kingdoms of England and Scotland and may be said to form the British "nation." Scotland retained her own system of private law after the union of 1707. Scots law has a history quite distinct from English law, and has been much more under the influence of Roman and continental ideas. In recent times, however, various factors such as the sharing of a common legislature and a common court of final appeal for civil cases have tended to make Scots law resemble English rather than continental law, especially in its practical application. The differences in administrative law have become less marked as a result of the Crown Proceedings Act 1947.

A continental observer would find the distinguishing characteristics of English law to be its antiquity and continuity, its predominantly judicial character and the absence of codification, the survival of feudal conceptions and the comparatively slight influence of Roman law.[1]

[1] Lévy-Ullmann, *The English Legal Tradition*, pp. xlvi–liii.

3

Antiquity and Continuity

The present law of most continental countries is separated from the law of the past by revolution, declaration of independence or codification. English law has a continuous history which can be traced back to Ethelbert, who was King of Kent from the year 560 to 616, though the Norman Conquest may be taken for most purposes as its starting point, owing to the scanty materials for a knowledge of Anglo-Saxon law. The origins of English law appear to have been primarily Teutonic, the result of successive invasions of Angles and Saxons. A Norse or Scandinavian element was introduced by the Danes, and Frankish elements were first borrowed by the Anglo-Saxons and then introduced by the Normans. There is no evidence that Roman law, any more than the Roman language or religion, survived in this country after the Romans left, nor are there vestigial remains of Celtic (British) laws surviving the Roman and Anglo-Saxon invasions. Traces of Romanic law in Anglo-Saxon laws are either ecclesiastical, appearing after St. Augustine re-introduced Christianity, or else they are borrowings from the Franks. The idea of written law, such as the Laws of Ethelbert, was Roman. Norman law was Frankish, not Scandinavian, and primarily feudal in content, though showing Roman influence in form. English law was not greatly affected for some time by the Norman Conquest, William I's most important change being to separate the civil from the ecclesiastical jurisdiction. Strong central government supported the custom or practice of the King's Courts, and this under the Plantagenets fostered the development of the English Common Law. Thus John Selden likened English law to "the ship that by often mending had no piece of the first materials or . . . the house that is so often repaired *ut nihil ex pristina materia supersit* which yet (by the civil law) is to be accounted the same still."

English law is remarkable in that its rules do not cease to be binding merely by disuse, for however long a time. Thus it was possible for the defendant in *Ashford* v. *Thornton*[2] to claim trial by battle, to the consternation of the court as well as of his unwarlike opponent. Wager of battle was introduced soon after the Norman Conquest, but had been virtually superseded by the Grand Assize (recognition by a jury of knights) introduced as an alternative by Henry II, probably in 1179. In 1963 it was thought expedient to enact that persons should no longer be

---

[2] (1818) 1 B. & Ald. 405. Wager of battle was abolished by Parliament as a result of this case.

liable to suffer imprisonment in consequence of being excommunicated.[3]

The work of the Law Commission[4] in revising the statute law more systematically than hitherto, is leading to the repeal by Parliament of a large number of statutory provisions that are obsolete or spent or superseded by modern law. A large number of these are scheduled to the Statute Law (Repeals) Act 1969, including the whole or parts of the residue of the Statutes of Westminster the First (1275) and Second (1285), statutes of Edward I and Edward III confirming Magna Carta (but preserving the famous declaration of liberties), various remnants of the ecclesiastical legislation of Henry VIII, Elizabeth I and Charles II, the Ship Money Act 1640, the Parliament Act and Tenures Abolition Act both of 1660, and some of the seventeenth-century Sunday Observance Acts.[5]

Uncodified

English law is not codified, whereas the law of continental countries is. This statement must be modified to the extent that, though continental States have a series of Codes of the most important branches of law, not all their law (for example, administrative law in France) is codified; while on the other hand various topics in English law (for example, the sale of goods and theft) have been codified from time to time. Gradual codification is one of the aims of the Law Commission, but revision and reform are necessary prerequisites.[6]

The absence of a Code renders the arrangement of an exposition of English law a matter of convenience. The main branches—criminal law, the law of property, the law of tort and the law of contract—are briefly described in Part IV of this book.

Judicial Character

A corollary of the uncodified nature of English law is its predominantly judicial character. The creative activity of the superior English courts, whose records and reports go back to the thirteenth century, is not paralleled in modern continental courts, whose judges are regarded primarily as interpreters of statute law. The formative influence of the courts on English law makes it necessary for one who studies the development of

---

[3] Ecclesiastical Jurisdiction Measure 1963, s.82(4).
[4] Set up by the Law Commissions Act 1965.
[5] There have been several further Statute Law (Repeals) Acts.
[6] A Draft Criminal Code has now appeared.

English law to know something of the jurisdictions of the different courts at various times. It reveals itself also in the doctrine of binding judicial precedents. The growth of English law, therefore, has been conditioned to a great extent by the political, economic and intellectual environment of the judges.

Influence of Procedure

A striking feature of the Common Law in medieval times was the importance of procedure, emphasis being placed on remedies rather than rights. By this we mean that, though right and remedy must be correlative terms, the common lawyers argued from the remedy to the right rather than vice versa. Litigation in the royal courts had to be commenced by one of a limited number of writs, and it was the absence of a sufficient variety of writs that induced injured parties to seek the aid of the Lord Chancellor, and so led to the establishment and growth of the equitable jurisdiction of the Court of Chancery. Each common law writ set in motion a particular form of action; and it was the existence of more than one form of action to cover the same case, or the invention of an alternative form of action, that enabled the common law to develop empirically within these limits.

Feudal Survivals

English law still contains some feudal elements. Until recently these were especially marked in the land law, but the Law of Property Acts 1922–25, and the Administration of Estates Act 1925, have done away with most of the survivals of feudalism. The doctrine of tenure has practically disappeared, the doctrine of estates has been greatly simplified, while primogeniture and the old law of inheritance have given way to rules of succession more in consonance with reason and fairness. But still in theory the Sovereign is the ultimate lord of all land in England, and a subject cannot be more than a tenant of a fee—conceptions which are extinct on the continent.

No Reception of Roman Law

Continental law, at least of Western Europe excluding Scandinavia, has been described as the heir of Roman law, from which it received the classifications and institutions and many of the rules of private law which it still preserves. The extent of the influence of Roman law on English law at various periods in its history is a subject of controversy, but at least we may say that

English law has not been romanised. By the fifteenth and sixteenth centuries it had pursued its own line and methods of development for so long that there was no "reception" of Roman law in England as there was generally at that time on the continent. "We have received Roman law," says Holdsworth,[7] "but we have received it in small homoeopathic doses, at different periods as and when required. It has acted as a tonic to our native legal system, and not as a drug or poison."

Extension of English Law Overseas

As a result of settlement, cession or conquest, English law provides the basis of the legal systems of many countries throughout the world, not only Northern Ireland and the Republic of Ireland, but also many parts of the Commonwealth and the United States of America. The rule is that *British* settlers in hitherto unoccupied territory take with them the system of *English* common law, and existing statute law so far as it is applicable to the new environment[8]; while ceded or conquered territories retain their own law unless and until it is altered by legislation of the Crown or Parliament.[9] How much of English law obtains in other countries therefore depends on the history of each—the time and circumstances of settlement, cession or conquest, and the effect of subsequent legislation. Thus the basis of the law in the Province of Quebec is the French law of the Code Napoléon; that of South Africa is Roman-Dutch law, a modernised form of Roman law taken there by Dutch settlers; and French law is the basis of the law in the state of Louisiana. The inhabitants of India and Pakistan are mainly subject to Hindu or Islamic law with regard to their personal and family relations, but codes of land law, contract law, criminal law, procedure and evidence based on English law have been introduced into those countries, and the English common law of torts is also applied.

In so far as English law is said to obtain throughout the Commonwealth and the United States of America, this refers not so much to substantive rules as to the traditions and technique of English lawyers. These general principles and the traditional technique by which they are applied are sometimes called "Anglo-American law" or "the common law" in its

---

[7] *History of English Law*, IV 293.
[8] *Pictou Municipality* v. *Geldert* [1893] A.C. 524; *Cooper* v. *Stuart* (1889) 14 App.Cas. 286.
[9] *Campbell* v. *Hall* (1774) 1 Cowp. 204; Lofft 655; *Sammut* v. *Strickland* [1938] A.C. 678.

widest sense. In this manner their common basis is distinguished from that of many European States and their present and former dependencies, including the Spanish- and Portuguese-speaking States of South America, which is Roman Law. Other countries also have borrowed from the continental Codes which are modernised Roman law—Japan from the German, and Turkey from the Swiss, Italian and German. If we except the personal allegiance of many millions to Islamic and Hindu law, we may say that the nations of the non-communist world are governed either by English law or by Roman law.

Ingredients of English Law

The English legal system is a mixture compounded of three systems of law formerly administered in different courts with separate jurisdictions, together with the recent addition of European Community law. Although competing jurisdictions were abolished and a unified system of central courts established by the Judicature Acts 1873–75, to administer all branches of the law,[10] there are still echoes of former differences in terminology, principles, remedies and procedure, and in the Divisions of the High Court traces of the former separate jurisdictions.

First, there is the *Common Law,* being that part of the law which was developed and formerly administered by the "Common Law Courts." The common law was a unification of the customs of the English, welded together by the practice of the royal courts.

Secondly, there is *Equity,* being that part of the law which was developed and formerly administered by the Court of Chancery and minor Courts of Equity. The Court of Chancery worked on the principles of conscience and fairness, and the early Chancellors, being ecclesiastics, probably borrowed something from canon law. It will be seen that "Equity," as meaning the principles formerly applied in the Court of Chancery, is a part of English law, while "equity" in the sense of conscience or fairness is one of the sources of English law—equity is a source of Equity.

Thirdly, there is that part of English law which was largely derived from Roman law, whether civil or canon, namely, *Admiralty Law and Ecclesiastical Law.* Advocates in the Admiralty and Ecclesiastical Courts before 1857 had to be doctors

[10] See now, Supreme Court Act 1981.

of civil law.[11] Their headquarters were not at Westminster, but at Doctors' Commons in the City of London.

2. COMMON LAW

The expression "Common Law" has several different meanings according to its context.

Common Law and Statute Law

The term "Common Law" was in use in the time of Edward I to describe that part of the law common to the whole of England which was not statutory, in contrast to statute law, local custom and royal prerogative. "Common Law" often means that part of English law (including Equity) which is unenacted, especially that contained in the decisions of the courts as opposed to Acts of Parliament and subordinate legislation. Although the common law in general has a customary origin, it is not quite accurate to describe it as equivalent to "the custom of the Realm," for it includes some principles which originated in legislation or the practice of the royal courts, but whose origin has long since been forgotten.

It follows from the legislative supremacy of Parliament that where common law and statute law conflict the latter prevails. A judge cannot refuse to apply an Act of Parliament on the ground that it is contrary to a fundamental principle of the common law, or that a common law development has rendered the statute obsolete. On the other hand Parliament can abolish well-established rules of common law, and in modern times it quite frequently does so, as with the immunity of the Crown in tort,[12] the rules of intestate succession to land[13] and the liability of a husband to be sued for his wife's torts.[14]

Common Law and Equity

The term "Common Law" often refers to those principles of English law which were evolved in the common law courts, as opposed to the principles which were applied in the Chancery, Admiralty and Ecclesiastical courts. The courts of common law

---

[11] Before the Reformation, practitioners in the Ecclesiastical Courts would be canonists. "Civil Law" here means Roman Law. In other contexts it may mean non-criminal law as in "Court of Appeal (Civil Division)" or non-military law. Practitioners of Roman Law were known as "civilians."

[12] Crown Proceedings Act 1947.

[13] Administration of Estates Act 1925.

[14] Law Reform (Married Women and Tortfeasors) Act 1935.

before the passing of the Judicature Acts 1873–75, were the three royal courts of Queen's Bench, Common Pleas or Common Bench, and Exchequer, which had emerged from the King's Council (*Curia Regis*) as separate courts by the end of the thirteenth century.

Common Law is more particularly contrasted with Equity. By "Equity" English lawyers mean, not that which is morally just and fair, but those principles of law which were administered before 1875 by the Courts of Equity (mainly the Court of Chancery). So the members of the "Common Law Bar" practise mainly in cases of contract, tort and crime, while members of the "Chancery Bar" practise mainly in matters of conveyancing and trusts.

The Old Forms of Action

We have already referred to the importance of the system of writs and forms of action at common law before the nineteenth century. It is necessary now to explain shortly what writs and forms of action were.

Writs

A writ addressed to a royal officer was commonly the way of initiating administrative and judicial acts in the Middle Ages. No action could be brought in the royal courts unless a writ was first obtained. For judicial purposes a writ was a sealed letter issued in the name of the King commanding some person, whether the sheriff of a county or the lord of a manor or the defendant, to do what was specified in the writ. The writ of right, which commenced an action for the recovery of land, commanded L (the lord of the manor) without delay to do full right to A (the demandant or plaintiff) in respect of certain land which A claimed to hold of L by free services and of which he claimed that X (the tenant or defendant) was depriving him, and declared that if L did not do this the sheriff of the county (a royal officer) would, in order that there should be no further complaint for want of justice. The writ of trespass, for many centuries the most important writ by which an action for damages for injury to person or property was commenced, commanded the sheriff of the county in which the matter arose to take security from X (the defendant) to appear before the King's justices on a specified day to show wherefore with force of arms (*vi et armis*) he had assaulted and beaten A (the plaintiff)—or had broken into A's land, or had taken and carried away A's chattels, as the case might be—and had inflicted other enormities on him to the serious damage of the said A and against the King's peace.

Writs were bought from the Chancery writ office, the department of State where they were drafted. The power to issue writs was held in check by the courts, for there comes a point when the creation of remedies amounts to law-making, and that is the province of Parliament.

Forms of Action

We have said that each writ gave rise to "a form of action." A form of action included—besides a particular writ for commencing the action—particular rules of pleading and proof, a particular form of judgment and a particular method of executing judgment.

From the fourteenth century onwards new writs, ostensibly similar to those already existing, gradually came to be allowed by the courts.[15] These new writs gave rise to "actions on the case," so called because the plaintiff inserted into the framework of an existing type of writ the special facts of his case instead of its usual formula. The most important actions on the case were those commenced by modifications of the writ of trespass. Most of the law of torts (*e.g.*, trover and conversion, nuisance and negligence from trespass on the case; deceit, slander, malicious prosecution, conspiracy and vicarious liability from other actions of case), the whole law of simple contract (trespass on the case in *assumpsit*, trespass and deceit on the case in *indebitatus assumpsit*, and the incorporation of the law merchant by the action on the case on the custom of merchants), and a large part of the law of personal property (by means of the action of trover), were developed over the course of several centuries by means of actions on the case.

The main effects of the forms of action on the modern common law lie in the distinction between real and personal property;[16] the differences between the various kinds of torts, in particular between those actions in tort which do and those which do not require proof of special damage, that is, actual pecuniary or other material loss; and (perhaps) in the limits upon the kinds of actionable wrongs; and in the existence of a unified law of simple contract.[17]

---

[15] This was not associated, as was once thought with the statute *In Consimili Casu* 1285. See Baker, *An Introduction to English Legal History* (2nd ed., 1979) pp. 58–59.
[16] Chap. 17.
[17] Chap. 19.

Abolition of Forms of Action

If the plaintiff brought the wrong form of action and was non-suited before the jury had given their verdict, he could begin again at the expense of time and money; but if the verdict had been given, the action was irretrievably lost. The forms of action were finally abolished by the Judicature Acts 1873–75, after piecemeal reforms in the early nineteenth century, and a uniform procedure was provided for all ordinary actions in the High Court. An action in the High Court is now usually commenced by a writ of summons,[18] which is issued on payment of a fee from the Central Office of the Supreme Court or District Registry. It notifies the defendant of the plaintiff's claim, which is endorsed on the writ in simple language to suit the facts of the case, and requires the defendant either to satisfy the claim or return the accompanying acknowledgment of service, failure to do so rendering him liable to judgment in default. The Judicature Acts still required the plaintiff to have a *cause* of action, *e.g.*, in an action for negligence he must show that the defendant owed him a duty of care, but it is no longer necessary to frame the action in technical terms.[19]

3. EQUITY

Origin and Development

By the end of the thirteenth century the kinds of available writs and their appropriate forms of action had become fixed, through conservatism of mind or fear of the Council on the part of the common law courts. However, the increasing complexity of social and commercial life created an urgent need for new remedies. There was always the Council, in which the residue of the royal justice was to be found, and so, in many cases where the common law courts would not give any remedy or where they could not enforce the remedy owing to the relative strength or position of the parties, informal petitions were addressed to the Council, which frequently ordered specific relief on grounds of justice. The petitions were later passed on to the Lord Chancellor, whose Court of Chancery became distinct from the Council some time in the fifteenth century.

The Chancellor acted on the conscience of the parties and against the person of the defendant, issuing writs of attendance,

---

[18] Some proceedings in the Chancery Division and the Family Division are commenced in other ways, *e.g.*, petition, summons or motion; see Chap. 21.

[19] But it may be very desirable to do so: *Sterman* v. *Moore* [1970] 1 Q.B. 596.

hearing evidence on oath, and decreeing relief under pain of fine and imprisonment. This process was well under way in certain types of cases before the common law courts developed actions on the case.

The creative energy of a long line of able Chancellors built up a body of equitable principles supplementing the deficiencies of the common law, though from the Restoration onwards the increasing tendency to rely on Chancery precedents and practice led to the formation of a system of equitable doctrine as definite as the common law, and sometimes even more rigid.[20]

The circumstances of its origin and growth, however, indicate that Equity is not a self-sufficient system but presupposes the existence of the common law. If all Equity were abolished we should still have a coherent though inequitable common law, but if the common law were abolished we should be left with a number of unrelated equitable principles suspended in mid-air.

Equity is, of course, inferior to statute law, and from time to time Acts of Parliament displace or modify equitable doctrines.[21]

Former Threefold Jurisdiction in Chancery

Text-writers of the nineteenth century classified into three branches the jurisdiction of the Court of Chancery in relation to the common law.

The court had an *exclusive* jurisdiction in certain cases where the common law gave no relief, as in the enforcement of trusts and the protection of those who borrowed on the security of their land (mortgagors). Here both the right and the remedy were equitable.

The Court of Chancery had a *concurrent* jurisdiction in cases where the common law recognised the right but did not grant an adequate remedy, as in breaches of contracts for the sale or lease of land and the actual or threatened commission of a tort such as nuisance. In the former cases the court might grant specific performance, that is, issue a decree ordering a party to carry out the contract according to its terms; in the latter cases it might grant an injunction, that is, issue a decree ordering a party to refrain from committing or continuing the nuisance. As a general rule the only remedy which the common law courts could order in such cases was a money payment (damages), and then only when the harm was already done.

---

[20] This came to be embodied in a number of "maxims of Equity" such as "he who seeks Equity must come with clean hands," "equality is Equity," "Equity looks on that as done which ought to be done," originating with R. Francis 1727. See *Baker, op. cit.*, pp. 94–95.

[21] *e.g.*, Law of Property Act 1925; Trustee Act 1925.

The Court of Chancery had an *auxiliary* jurisdiction in cases where the common law recognised the right and gave an adequate remedy, but was unable owing to defective process to enforce it. The Chancellor could, for example, compel "discovery" of documents, that is, order the defendant to produce for the plaintiff's inspection documents relating to the case which were in his possession.

The Contribution of Equity

The chief contributions of Equity to English law have been the conception of equitable property, particularly that created by means of a trust, and the remedies of specific performance of contracts and injunction restraining the commission of torts.

The most important institution developed by the Court of Chancery was the trust, which is peculiar to Anglo-American law, although it has analogies in other legal systems. A trust arises where property is conveyed to or vested in T (called the trustee) in such circumstances that Equity will compel him to administer the property for the benefit of B (called the *cestui que trust* or beneficiary) or for some particular purpose. Trusts are most commonly employed in wills and family settlements and to endow charities. Trusts survived the attempt made by the Statute of Uses 1535, to suppress them in the interests of the King's feudal revenues. The statute was interpreted as not applying where the trustee held copyholds, leaseholds, or pure personalty, or where he had active duties to perform. The resurgence of trusts of freeholds in the early seventeenth century was due to the ingenuity of conveyancers.

It should be noticed that equitable remedies were never granted as of right. They are at the discretion of the court, though in course of time that discretion has come to be exercised judicially according to precedent.

Effect of Judicature Acts 1873–75, on relation between Equity and Common Law

When the Judicature Acts created a single system of central courts with jurisdiction to administer both Common Law and Equity, so that a plaintiff could now bring his action in the same court whether the relief he sought was legal or equitable, it was necessary for Parliament to say what was to happen when the rules of Common Law and Equity conflicted. Section 25 of the Judicature Act 1873, therefore provided for certain specific cases of variance, notably in subsection (6), which allowed the assignee of a debt or other legal chose in action to sue the debtor in his own name. Choses in action[22] were not assignable at Common Law, though they were assignable under certain conditions in Equity. The Common Law had had exclusive jurisdiction in the recovery of debts, and Equity was therefore unable to enforce recovery in its own courts in the name of the assignee. A compromise was worked out whereby the assignee first brought a suit in Equity against the assignor to prove the validity of the assignment; Equity then compelled the assignor to sue for the recovery of the debt in the Common Law courts, and to hold the sum recovered for the benefit of the assignee. This multiplicity of actions involved expense and delay, and was the reason for the change introduced by section 25(6) of the Judicature Act 1873.[23] Subsection (11) of section 25 then declared that in all other matters not specifically mentioned in the section, where the rules of Common Law and Equity were in conflict or at variance with regard to the same matter, the rules of Equity were to prevail. This provision was repealed and re-enacted by the Judicature (Consolidation) Act 1925, and again repealed and re-enacted in section 49 of the Supreme Court Act 1981.[24]

The relation between Common Law and Equity had not as a matter of fact been one of conflict or rivalry for the previous two centuries, but rather one of co-operation. Thus, where the legal estate in land was vested in T (trustee) in trust for B (beneficiary), the Court of Chancery compelled T personally to carry out the trust, but it did not deny his legal ownership of the property. Indeed, unless T had the estate there would be nothing for him to administer.

The effect of this section, therefore, has not been so far-reaching as it might appear at first sight, though a few cases have come before the courts since 1875 in which the rules of Common Law and Equity were actually at variance. An executor was liable at Common Law for loss of those of the testator's assets which had once come into his hands, but he was not liable in Equity unless the loss was due to his wilful default; and so it was decided that in such cases wilful default must be proved.[25] Another important case is *Walsh* v. *Lonsdale*[26] where instead of the deed required for a legal lease, there was a written

---

[22] Intangible items of property *e.g.* a debt, copyright, patent, over which rights may only be asserted by action in court as distinct from choses in possession, tangible movables which may be taken into possession.

[23] Assignments are now governed by the Law of Property Act 1925, s.136(1).

[24] The rule goes back to the *Earl of Oxford's Case* (1615) 1 Rep.Ch. 1.

[25] *Job* v. *Job* (1877) 6 Ch.D. 562.

[26] (1882) 21 Ch.D. 9.

agreement for a lease between A and X, one of the terms of which was that a deed should be executed containing a covenant to pay one year's rent in advance. X went into possession under the agreement and paid rent for some time, though not in advance. Later A claimed rent in advance. It was held that as the agreement to execute a deed would be specifically enforceable in Equity, and as "Equity looks on that as done which ought to be done," and as the Judicature Act said that the principles of Equity were to prevail, A was entitled at law as well as in Equity to claim the rent in advance.

The Judicature Acts also provided that, apart from cases of conflict, the rules of Common Law and Equity were to continue to be applied respectively in accordance with the same principles as when they were administered in separate courts. Thus damages are still granted for the infringement of legal rights in accordance with legal principles, while specific performance and injunction are granted to enforce equitable duties in accordance with equitable principles. The general scope of Equity remains the same as that outlined above. The effect of the Judicature Acts, then, was to convert the "exclusive" jurisdiction of Equity into a concurrent jurisdiction, and to abolish its "auxiliary" jurisdiction; for a party in the Queen's Bench Division of the High Court does not need to go for help to the Chancery Division, let alone to a separate Court of Chancery.

The view has been generally held that the Judicature Acts merely fused the administration of Common Law and Equity, not the substantive principles themselves. Nevertheless they have been administered together for so long that they have interacted on each other, and it may now be true to say that the systems of Common Law and Equity are fused, though for purposes of study Equity may still be treated as a separate whole.

4. ADMIRALTY LAW, MERCANTILE LAW AND ECCLESIASTICAL LAW

Medieval Law Merchant and Maritime Law

In the Middle Ages the *Lex Mercatoria* was a body of international customs regulating transactions between masters of ships on the one hand and mariners and cargo-owners on the other (maritime law), and other transactions between merchants ("law merchant" in the narrow sense). Various European ports had codes of maritime customs, derived from late Roman law through medieval editions of the Rhodian Sea Law. The most important of these codes were the *Consolato del Mare* of the Mediterranean ports, the Laws of Wisby regulating trade between Baltic and other ports, and the Laws of Oleron, an island off the west coast of France.

It was the Laws of Oleron that were borrowed from the ports of Normandy and Brittany by English mariners. Following the medieval European practice, these maritime customs with local variations were administered by the courts of seaport towns; but in the course of time their jurisdiction was encroached upon with increasing success by the Court of Admiralty, which appeared in the fourteenth century, and later by the courts of common law.

Meanwhile, the common law courts were also filching jurisdiction from the courts attached to markets and fairs, which administered local varieties of European mercantile customs, and many of which were in the hands of boroughs. The common law courts were able to do this by conniving at the procedural fictions inserted in writs in order to take advantage of the superior process of the central courts, and by issuing prohibitions.

English Mercantile Law and Admiralty Law

The local courts had practically disappeared by the eighteenth century. Mercantile law and a substantial part of maritime law had been incorporated into the common law; while the rest of maritime law, which was administered by the Court of Admiralty, had become anglicised as English Admiralty law.

The effect of the Judicature Acts 1873–75, which abolished the Court of Admiralty and gave a general jurisdiction to the new High Court, was to assign Admiralty matters to the Probate, Divorce and Admiralty Division, and the other matters we have mentioned to the Queen's Bench Division. The only vestige of the Privy Council's former appellate jurisdiction in such matters is that appeals in Prize Cases,[27] in which international law is applied, go to the Judicial Committee of the Privy Council instead of the Court of Appeal.

Ecclesiastical Law and the Reformation

The creation of a system of Ecclesiastical Courts was one of the most important immediate effects of the Norman Conquest. There has been a controversy among historians on the question whether the Church Courts in England before the Reformation

---

[27] These relate to enemy ships and cargoes captured in war.

considered Roman Canon Law to be binding as such, except for those matters which were taken out of their jurisdiction by English statutes; or whether they merely allowed Canon Law to be of great persuasive authority, but not binding unless received by English custom and practice. Maitland maintained the former view in answer to Bishop Stubb's expression of the latter, and the weight of historical opinion is on the side of Maitland.[28]

However that may be, a result of the Reformation has been the development of an English Ecclesiastical Law. Among its sources, apart from Roman Canon Law (decrees of General Councils and papal decretals), are the Legatine Constitutions of Cardinals Otho and Ottobon promulgated in national synods in the reign of Henry III; the Provincial Constitutions of the synods of Canterbury from Henry III to Henry V; Acts of Parliament, such as the Submission of the Clergy Act 1533, which asserted the legislative supremacy of Parliament in ecclesiastical matters, and the Act of Uniformity 1662, which enacted the Book of Common Prayer and the Thirty-Nine Articles; Measures of the Church of England Assembly set up by the Church of England Assembly (Powers) Act 1919; and pre-Reformation customs which have been continued and recognised and acted upon in England since the Reformation.[29]

The significance of the Ecclesiastical Courts in the development of English law is that, apart from their jurisdiction over clergy for ecclesiastical offences, their jurisdiction over all men for moral offences meant that they were concerned with questions of marriage and legitimacy; and also that they came to interest themselves in wills of personal property and the administration of the estates of deceased persons.

Modern Statutory Reorganisation

By the middle of the nineteenth century many of these matters had been taken over by the Court of Chancery as having more highly developed principles of equity and a more effective process; and when the High Court displaced the Court of Chancery under the Judicature Acts, these were assigned to the Chancery Division. The remainder, which had been transferred by statute in 1857 to two new courts, were assigned in 1875 to the Probate, Divorce and Admiralty Division of the High Court.

[28] H. W. C. Davis, "The Canon Law in England," in *H. W. C. Davis 1874–1928* (ed. Weaver & Lane Poole), Pt. II, Chap. 4. See also, E. Garth Moore *An Introduction to Canon Law.*
[29] *Bishop of Exeter* v. *Marshall* (1868) L.R. 3 H.L. 17, 53–54.

The Administration of Justice Act 1970, replaced the Probate, Divorce and Admiralty Division of the High Court by the Family Division, to deal with matrimonial difficulties and the protection of children, and allocated Admiralty law to the Queen's Bench Division.

The Ecclesiastical Courts of the Church of England, as reorganised by statute,[30] remain to deal according to English Ecclesiastical Law with disciplinary and moral offences committed by clergy of the Church of England and certain other minor matters, with appeal in some cases to the Judicial Committee of the Privy Council.

5. EUROPEAN COMMUNITY LAW

Membership of the European Economic Community

The European Communities Act 1972, gave legal effect in this country to the executive act[31] whereby the United Kingdom adhered to the Treaties constituting the European Communities, notably the European Economic Community (EEC).[32] The Act came into effect from January 1, 1973. Community laws become law in the United Kingdom if: (a) (i) they are "directly applicable" to individuals as distinct from the State,[33] and (ii) the rights and duties arise out of a matter with a "European element"; and (b) the laws are either (i) "self-executing," or (ii) implemented by Statutory Instrument under section 2(2) of the Act, or (iii) implemented by any other Act of Parliament.[34]

Section 2(1) of the European Communities Act gives general effect to rights and obligations created or arising under the Treaties, *i.e.*, created by the Treaties themselves and by existing and future Community Regulations which take effect directly in the member States. Community Regulations are known as European secondary legislation. It was a constitutional

---

[30] See now, Ecclesiastical Jurisdiction Measure 1963, Ecclesiastical Jurisdiction (Amendment) Measure 1974.

[31] The Crown cannot make law for the realm, except by means of Act of Parliament: *Case of Proclamations* (1610) 12 Co.Rep. 74; *Rustomjee* v. *The Queen* (1876) 2 Q.B.D. 69, *per* Lord Coleridge C.J.; *Blackburn* v. *Attorney-General* [1971] 1 W.L.R. 1037 (C.A.), *per* Lord Denning M.R.

[32] The other Communities are the European Coal and Steel Community (ECSC) and the European Atomic Energy Community (EURATOM).

[33] See *R.* v. *Saunders* [1980] Q.B. 72 for Community Law binding the State only.

[34] See also the European Communities (Amendment) Act 1986 which includes in the definition of "The Treaties" certain provisions of the Single European Act. It makes provision for a court of first instance to be associated with the present European Court.

innovation to give effect to future Community Regulations, which constitute a new kind of secondary legislation in this country. Directly enforceable rights and remedies under section 2(1) are called "enforceable Community rights."

Section 2(2) of the Act gives power to make delegated legislation (by Order in Council or Ministerial regulation) to implement future Community obligations, *viz.* to give effect to Community Directives, which set out the objects to be achieved but leave it to each member State to decide the method of achieving them.[35] This power is subject to Schedule 2, which provides, first, that the power of delegated legislation does not extend to taxation, retrospective lawmaking, sub-delegation of legislative power (other than rules of court), or the creation of criminal offences punishable by imprisonment or fines beyond certain maxima; and secondly, that such delegated legislation shall be by Statutory Instrument,[36] which (if made without a draft having been approved by resolution of each House) shall be subject to annulment by resolution of either House. Section 2(4) provides that the power to make Statutory Instruments under section 2(2), and subject to Schedule 2, includes power to amend Acts of Parliament, in order to avoid possible conflicts between Community law and future Acts.

Community Law

The courts have power under Article 177 of the EEC Treaty to request the Court of Justice of the European Communities (the "European Court[37]") to give a preliminary ruling on the interpretation of the Treaty. For the purpose of legal proceedings section 3 of the Act provides that the meaning of the Treaties, and the validity or meaning of any Community Instrument, are questions of law which, if not referred to the European Court, are to be determined in accordance with the principles laid down by, and any relevant decision of, that Court. Judicial notice is to be taken of Community law, *i.e.*, it does not have to be proved (as fact) by expert witnesses as if it were foreign law.

Community law is mainly concerned with customs duties, agriculture, free movement of labour, services and capital; transport; restrictive trade practices; and regulation of coal, steel

---

[35] The Consumer Protection Act 1987 is an example of a statute employed to give effect to a Directive.

[36] Below p. 126.

[37] It sits at Luxembourg. See Brown and Jacobs, *The Court of Justice of the European Communities* (2nd ed. 1983) and see below, p. 101.

and nuclear energy industries. Most of our domestic law remains unaffected, *e.g.*, criminal law, contract, tort, land law and family law.[38]

Community law overrides our domestic law where they are inconsistent with each other.[39] Parliament has a duty (under international treaty law) to refrain from passing legislation inconsistent with Community law for the time being in force; and it may be presumed that, so long as the United Kingdom remains a member of the EEC and the European Communities Act remains in force,[40] it will not intentionally do so. This presumption affects the judicial interpretation of Acts of Parliament passed after the European Communities Act came into force. With regard to English law existing at January 1, 1973, notably company law, Parliament in that Act included a number of provisions to bring our existing law into line with Community law. In *H.P. Bulmer* v. *J. Bollinger SA*[41] the Court of Appeal held that an English judge has a complete discretion whether to refer to the European Court a question of the interpretation of the Treaty.[42] The point must be conclusive, *i.e.*, one that, whichever way it may be decided, will be conclusive of the case; and it is usually better to decide the facts first. Only the House of Lords, as the final appeal court, is bound to make such reference if it considers that the determination of the point is necessary to enable it to give judgment.[43] The European Court has no jurisdiction to declare national law invalid or to reverse decisions of national courts: its function is to interpret the Community Treaties and to expound the principles of

---

[38] But see Consumer Protection Act 1987.

[39] See *McCarthys* v. *Smith* [1981] Q.B. 180 where the Court of Appeal held that Art. 119 prevailed over an English statute. But the European Communities Act 1972 does not constrain a British court "to distort the meaning of a British statute in order to enforce against an individual a Community directive which has no direct effect between individuals. s.2(4) applies and only applies where Community provisions are directly applicable". *Duke* v. *Reliance Systems* [1988] 2 W.L.R. 359, 371.

[40] While it would be a breach of international obligation for the United Kingdom to withdraw from membership of the EEC without the agreement of the other members, Parliament retains the constitutional power to repeal or amend the European Communities Act 1972. The holding of the referendum under the Referendum Act 1975 presupposed that the United Kingdom would withdraw from the Community if the majority voted against continued membership, and that the European Communities Act would be repealed.

[41] [1974] Ch. 401. cf. *R.* v. *Fishing Dept. ex p. Agegate* [1987] 3 C.M.L.R. 939.

[42] The Court may apply Community Law without reference if its meaning appears clear.

[43] Other courts against whose decision there is no judicial remedy such as the Court of Appeal when it is the final court, may be under this obligation.

Community law[44]; and in *Bulmer* v. *Bollinger* Lord Denning M.R. drew a clear distinction between interpreting the Treaty and applying it. The first reference from an English court to the European Court was in *Van Duyn* v. *Home Office*,[45] where the European Court ruled[46] that the Treaty and a Council Directive on the movement and residence of foreign nationals confer on individuals *rights* (qualified by the Directive) which national courts must protect; but that a member State may impose restrictions justified on the grounds of public policy, and may take into account the conduct of the individual concerned and his or her association with some organisation (in this case, the Church of Scientology) which the State considers socially harmful, although such organisation is not unlawful and no similar restriction is placed on its own nationals against taking employment with it.

The Court of Appeal in *Schorsch Meier GmbH* v. *Hennin*[47] held that the common law rule requiring judgment for a sum of money to be awarded only in sterling had been superseded by the Treaty, which requires that a creditor in one member State shall receive payment for goods in the currency of the country in which he resides; but the House of Lords in *Miliangos* v. *George Frank (Textiles) Ltd.*[48] doubted whether Article 106 was "directly applicable," and gave a decision to the same effect as the Court of Appeal in the previous case but on different grounds, *i.e.*, the recent change in the condition of the foreign exchange and in the position of sterling. In *Application des Gaz SA* v. *Falks Veritas Ltd.*[49] the Court of Appeal considered for the first time the effect of the Treaty on English substantive law, *viz.* the law of copyright in relation to the restriction of competition within the Common Market. "In any transaction which contains a European element," said Lord Denning M.R., "we must look to the Treaty. . . . For the Treaty is part of our law. It is equal in force to any statute. It must be applied by our courts."[50] In *R.* v. *Secchi*[51]

---

[44] *Costa* v. *ENEL* [1964] C.M.L.R. 425 (E.C.J.).
[45] [1974] 1 W.L.R. 1107; [1974] C.M.L.R. 347 (Pennycuick V.-C.).
[46] [1975] Ch. 358 (E.C.J.).
[47] [1975] Q.B. 416.
[48] [1976] A.C. 443.
[49] [1974] Ch. 381.
[50] *Cf.* European Convention on Human Rights: "I would dispute altogether that the Convention is part of our law. Treaties and declarations do not become part of our law until they are made law by Parliament:" *R.* v. *Chief Immigration Officer, Heathrow Airport, ex p. Salamat* [1976] 1 W.L.R. 979 (C.A.), *per* Lord Denning M.R., at pp. 984–985. Breach of duty created by Community Law may ground an action for breach of statutory duty: *Garden Cottage Foods* v. *Milk Marketing Board* [1984] A.C. 130.
[51] [1975] 1 C.M.L.R. 383.

it was held that the Community law relating to freedom of movement of workers among EEC countries did not prevent the Home Secretary from deporting an EEC migrant worker who had been convicted of imprisonable offences.

European Convention on Human Rights

The United Kingdom is a party to this Convention (The Convention for Human Rights and Fundamental Freedoms 1950) which establishes a European Commission and European Court of Human Rights. Rights and freedoms protected include the right to life, not to be subjected to torture or degrading punishment, to liberty of person, to respect for family life and home, to freedom of religion, conscience, thought, expression, assembly and association and to free elections. A complainant must first exhaust all remedies in his home state and may then apply to the Commission who will endeavour to arrive at a settlement. If this is not achieved the Commission may then refer the matter to the European Court of Human Rights at Strasbourg for decision. The Commission will not refer claims lacking substance. The Court may order "just satisfaction," including costs and damages, to a successful claimant. Though attempts have been made to secure the enactment of the Convention as a Bill of Rights it is not part of English law and does not create rights directly enforceable in English courts. The Court of Appeal has however, said that it will "have regard" to the Convention in arriving at its decisions.[52] If a Member State does not give effect to the decisions of the Court it will be in breach of its international obligations under the Convention and the sanction would be expulsion from the Council of Europe. Applications under the Convention have led to important changes in English law *e.g.* in regard to corporal punishment, prisoners' letters and in regard to contempt of court.[53]

6. LAW REFORM

There are various methods of initiating and preparing the ground for reforms in the law. Royal Commissions and Departmental Committees are set up from time to time by the Government or individual Ministers to examine the state of some branch of the law and to recommend desirable changes.

---

[52] *Ahmad* v. *I.L.E.A.* [1978] Q.B. 36; see also, *Att.-Gen* v. *B.B.C.* [1981] A.C. 303; *R.* v. *Chief Immigration Officer, Heathrow Airport, ex p. Salamat Bibi* [1976] 1 W.L.R. 979. *Re K.D. (A Minor)* [1988] 2 W.L.R. 398 below, p. 164.
[53] See Contempt of Court Act 1981 below, p. 36.

Private Members' Bills account for some legal reforms, but they face the problems of lack of Parliamentary time, the inability of private Members to propose the expenditure of public money, and the technical difficulty of drafting. Not much can be expected of the Judges in this direction, because in the first place it is the function of the higher courts to develop the law along existing lines, not to change it, and, in the second place, many of the defects in the law are themselves due to judicial decisions.

Ministerial responsibility for supervising the administration and improvement of the law is somewhat anomalously divided between the Lord Chancellor and the Home Secretary. The Lord Chancellor is concerned with the composition of the civil and criminal courts, the civil law and its administration, parts of criminal procedure, and the administration of the courts (other than magistrates' courts). The Home Secretary, on the other hand, is concerned with the criminal law, parts of criminal procedure, the police, the treatment of offenders, and the administration of magistrates' courts. For these purposes the Lord Chancellor has the assistance of the Law Commission set up by the Law Commissions Act 1965, and several standing committees. The Law Reform Committee, replacing the pre-war Law Revision Committee, reviews such legal doctrines as are referred to it, mainly judicial decisions on the common law. The others were the Statute Law Committee, concerned with the form of statute law which is now one of the matters within the Law Commission's terms of reference; and the Committee on Private International Law. Recent additions are the Civil Justice Review and the Standing Commission on Efficiency in the Courts.

The Law Commissions Act 1965, constituted the Law Commission, consisting of a Chairman (a High Court judge) and four other full-time Commissioners appointed by the Lord Chancellor as suitably qualified by the holding of judicial office or by experience as barristers, solicitors or university law teachers. The duty of the Commission is to keep under review all the law with a view to its systematic development and reform, including in particular the codification of the law, the elimination of anomalies, the repeal of obsolete and unnecessary enactments, consolidation, and generally the simplification and modernisation of the law. One of the functions of the Commission is to prepare draft Bills for giving effect to their proposals. The Lord Chancellor is required to lay before Parliament any programmes prepared by the Commission and approved by him, and any proposals for reform formulated by the Commission. The Commission is required to make an annual report to the Lord

Chancellor, who is to lay it before Parliament with his comments.[54]

Matters relating to the operation and reform of the legal system are from time to time referred to Royal Commissions appointed to examine specific areas of law. Examples are the Royal Commission on Assizes and Quarter Sessions (the Beeching Commission) whose report led to the Courts Act 1971 and the creation of the Crown Court,[55] the Royal Commission on Civil Liability and Compensation for Personal Injuries (the Pearson Commission) which investigated aspects of the law of tort, the Royal Commission on Legal Services (the Benson Commission) and the Royal Commission on Criminal Procedure whose report resulted in the Police and Criminal Evidence Act 1984.[56]

The establishment of the Law Commission appears to have laid to rest, at least for the time being, the proposal initiated more than forty years ago for the establishment of a Ministry of Justice such as exists in most other countries.[57] Lord Chancellors Birkenhead, Gardiner and Hailsham of St. Marylebone have expressed opinions against a Ministry of Justice.

[54] See further, J. H. Farrar, *Law Reform and the Law Commission* (1974); A. L. Diamond, "The Work of the Law Commission" (1976) 10 L.Teach. 11. See Oulton, *Law Reform: Obstacles and Opportunities* (1988) 7 C.J.Q. 32; North (1985) 101 L.Q.R. 338; Cretney (1985) 48 M.L.R. 493.

[55] See below, Chap. 4.

[56] See below, Chap. 18.

[57] See Farrar, *op. cit.*, Chap. 2; *What's Wrong with the Law?* (ed. M. Zander, 1970). See below, Chap. 21.

PART II
The Courts

CHAPTER 2

The Administration of Justice

The Organisation of the Courts

The superior English courts are the House of Lords, the Judicial Committee of the Privy Council, the Supreme Court comprising the Court of Appeal, High Court and Crown Court, the Courts-Martial Appeal Court, the Restrictive Practices Court, and the Employment Appeal Tribunal. The inferior courts include county courts, magistrates' courts and coroners' courts. The distinction between superior courts and inferior courts lies chiefly in the scope of their jurisdiction, and in the power of the High Court to supervise the exercise of their jurisdiction by the latter. There are also miscellaneous courts, including anomalous survivals of local courts, courts of special jurisdiction administering military and ecclesiastical law, and administrative tribunals of various kinds. These are discussed in the following chapters.

1. THE ROYAL PREROGATIVE AND THE ADMINISTRATION OF JUSTICE

The administration of justice is one of the prerogatives of the Crown, but it is a prerogative that has long been exercisable only through duly appointed courts and judges. In earlier times the King himself might sit in court, and he was presumed to be present in the King's Bench, though judgment was given by the court. Henry IV and even Edward IV occasionally sat in court;

29

by the end of the fourteenth century, however, the opinion prevailed that though the King might be present with his judges he could not himself give judgment.

Chief Justice Coke relates that he "greatly offended" James I, when that monarch wished to revive the earlier practice, by saying:

> "The King in his own person cannot adjudge any case ... but this ought to be determined and adjudged in some Court of Justice, according to the law and custom of England.... True it was that God had endowed His Majesty with excellent science, and great endowments of nature; but His Majesty was not learned in the laws of his realm of England, and causes which concern the life, or inheritance, or goods, or fortunes of his subjects, are not to be decided by natural reason but by the artificial reason and judgment of law, which law is an art which requires long study and experience, before that a man can attain to the cognisance of it."[1]

Coke's language—a true statement of fact, though not a sound argument—had the desired effect.

The composition and jurisdiction of the various courts at the present day are regulated by statute, but the superior courts are styled the Queen's Courts,[2] and they are staffed by Her Majesty's judges. The Queen has no control over civil justice, but judgment is executed in her name.[3] Criminal proceedings, whether initiated by the Crown or by a private individual, are conducted on behalf of the Crown[4] and, if indictable,[5] in the Queen's name, and Her Majesty's Attorney-General may put an end to proceedings on indictment by entering a *nolle prosequi*.

The prerogative of mercy (much reduced in importance after the abolition of the death penalty for murder) and pardon after conviction is a remnant of the Royal prerogative in the administration of justice, though it is exercised in England through the Home Secretary.

---

[1] *Prohibitions del Roy* (1607) 12 Co.Rep. 63.

[2] The Employment Appeal Tribunal is an exception.

[3] Since 1979 the writ no longer takes the form of a royal command though the Royal Arms appear.

[4] The Prosecution of Offences Act 1985 created the Crown Prosecution Service to handle prosecutions hitherto undertaken by the police and local authorities.

[5] Below, pp. 44, 265.

2. THE APPOINTMENT AND POSITION OF JUDGES

Appointment

The Queen appoints the Lord Chancellor, the Lord Chief Justice, the Master of the Rolls, the Vice-Chancellor, the President of the Family Division, the Lords of Appeal in Ordinary and the Lords Justices of Appeal by convention on the advice of the Prime Minister, who consults the Lord Chancellor; and she appoints the puisne judges of the High Court, Circuit judges and Recorders (part-time judges of the Crown Court) and stipendiary magistrates, on the recommendation of the Lord Chancellor.[6]

Lay magistrates are appointed to the Commission of the Peace in the name of the Queen by the Lord Chancellor or, in appropriate cases, the Chancellor of the Duchy of Lancaster.[7]

Most countries have a Judicial Services Commission to advise the head of state on the appointment of the judiciary, and it has been suggested that there should be a Consultative Committee to assist the Lord Chancellor in the exercise of this function.[8]

Tenure of Judicial Office

The justices of the Royal Courts, which grew up in Norman and Plantagenet times, were the King's servants, and down to the time of the Stuarts they usually held office during his pleasure. It was part of the Revolution settlement of 1688 to free the judges from the royal control which had been exercised over them by the Stuarts. The Act of Settlement 1700, accordingly provided that "Judges' commissions be made *quamdiu se bene gesserint*, and their salaries ascertained and established; but upon an address of both Houses of Parliament it may be lawful to remove them." Three points are involved here: (i) removal by the Crown on an address by both Houses; (ii) removal by the Crown of its own motion; and (iii) establishment of salaries.

As regards (i) and (ii), the statutory provisions now in force are the Supreme Court Act 1981 s.11(3):

"A person appointed to an office to which this section applies (any judge of the Supreme Court except the Lord

---

[6] Supreme Court Act 1981 s.10; Appellate Jurisdiction Act 1876; Courts Act 1971; Administration of Justice Act 1973.

[7] Justices of the Peace Act 1979, ss.6 and 68.

[8] *The Judiciary*: Report of Justice Sub-Committee (1972).

Chancellor[9]) shall hold that office during good behaviour, subject to a power of removal by Her Majesty on an address presented to her by both Houses of Parliament."

and the Appellate Jurisdiction Act 1876, s.6, *viz.*: "Every Lord of Appeal in Ordinary shall hold his office during good behaviour ... but he may be removed from such office on the address of both Houses of Parliament." Thus (i) the Crown may (and presumably would) remove a judge who has been guilty of what the two Houses, acting quasi-judicially in a manner similar to an impeachment, consider to be misbehaviour; and (ii) the Crown may remove without an address for official misconduct, neglect of official duties, or (probably) conviction for a serious offence.[10] In fact, no judge of a superior court in England has been removed from office since the Act of Settlement.

As regards (iii), ascertainment and establishment of salaries apart from the Lord Chancellor, the custom is by permanent Acts to define them and charge them on the Consolidated Fund. These salaries, therefore, do not come up for annual review by the House of Commons as do most of the estimates for national expenditure. These salaries may now be increased, but not reduced, and are charged on and paid out of the Consolidated Fund.[11]

Where the Lord Chancellor is satisfied by means of a medical certificate that a Lord of Appeal in Ordinary or judge of the Supreme Court is disabled by permanent infirmity from the performance of his duties, but is for the time being incapacitated from resigning, the Lord Chancellor with the concurrence of senior judges may declare that person's office to have been vacated.[12]

Circuit judges may be removed by the Lord Chancellor on the ground of incapacity or misbehaviour; and the Lord Chancellor may terminate the appointment of a Recorder on these grounds or failure to comply with the terms of his appointment as to the frequency and duration of his availability (Courts Act 1971).[13]

---

[9] Being also a Minister, the Lord Chancellor holds office at the Queen's pleasure in accordance with the constitutional conventions applicable to other members of the Government.

[10] *Earl of Shrewsbury's Case*, 9 Co.Rep. 42a, 50.

[11] Supreme Court Act 1981, s.12.

[12] Supreme Court Act 1981, s.11(8)(9).

[13] It has been suggested that a Judicial Commission should be established with powers to investigate complaints about the behaviour of judges and to make recommendations to remove a judge for incapacity or misconduct: *The Judiciary*: Report of Justice Sub-Committee, above.

There is a retiring age of seventy-five for Lords of Appeal in Ordinary and judges of the Court of Appeal and High Court appointed after 1959[14]; and Circuit judges are subject to a retiring age of seventy-two, except that the Lord Chancellor may in the public interest continue them in office up to the age of seventy-five.[15]

Justices of the peace may be removed from the commission by the Lord Chancellor if he thinks fit,[16] though by convention he does not remove them except for good cause, such as refusal to administer the law because the justice does not agree with it. The Justices of the Peace Act 1949, required the Lord Chancellor to keep a Supplemental List of justices who are no longer entitled to exercise judicial functions. The Lord Chancellor can direct that the name of a justice be put on the Supplemental List on the ground of "age or infirmity or other like cause," or if he "declines or neglects" his judicial functions. A justice may ask to be put on the Supplemental List, and in any case he will be put on it when he reaches the retiring age of seventy[17] although, if authorised by the Lord Chancellor, he may act as a judge of the Crown Court until the age of seventy-two years.[18]

Judicial Immunity

If the law is to be administered freely and without fear, it is essential that judges should be to a greater or less extent immune from actions in respect of the discharge of their functions. The extent of this judicial immunity was formerly held to vary according to the status of the judge, and was not free from uncertainty in some cases.

All the previous cases were reviewed by the Court of Appeal in *Sirros* v. *Moore*,[19] a case involving a Circuit judge. It was held that no civil action for damages lay against a judge, whether of a superior court of record or of an inferior court (*e.g.* county court or magistrates' court), for acts done in his judicial capacity in good faith, even though the judge acted mistakenly and made an invalid order. Every judge from the highest to the lowest, said Lord Denning M.R., should be protected to the same

---

[14] Judicial Pensions Act 1959.
[15] Courts Act 1971.
[16] Justices of the Peace Act 1979, s.6.
[17] Justices of the Peace Act 1979.
[18] Administration of Justice Act 1973, s.1; and see below, Chap. 4.
[19] [1975] Q.B. 118, affirming Michael Davies J. The law of defamation accords absolute privilege to persons taking part in judicial proceedings: *Law* v. *Llewellyn* [1906] 1 K.B. 487.

degree, and liable to the same degree. So long as he honestly believed it was within his jurisdiction he was not liable whether he was mistaken in fact or ignorant in law. He was only liable if he was not acting judicially, knowing that he had no jurisdiction to do it.

Lord Denning said this principle should cover justices of the peace also but this was rejected by the House of Lords in *McC.* v. *Mullan*[20] where it was held that justices could be sued if they acted outside their jurisdiction. The House of Lords also doubted whether the distinction between superior and inferior courts had ceased to exist, saying that perhaps only legislation could remove it. If so, a judge of an inferior court is not liable for things said or done, even maliciously, within his jurisdiction,[21] but it is for him to prove that he was within his jurisdiction.[22] It would be a good defence for him to prove that he was misled by some false allegation of fact which, if true, would have given him jurisdiction and as to which he had no knowledge which he should have used[23] but in principle he is liable for acts done without jurisdiction.[24]

The liability of justices of the peace (magistrates) in respect of both their judicial and administrative functions is now covered by the Justices of the Peace Act 1979, Part V. It is provided in section 44 that malice and special damage must be proved in an action for an act done within jurisdiction. In *McC.* v. *Mullan* two members of the House of Lords thought this action was obsolete. Under section 45 malice is not required in an action for acts outside or in excess of jurisdiction and section 47 confers an immunity in respect of discretionary powers as do sections 46 and 49 in respect of certain warrants issued as a result of some initial irregularity for which the justice was not responsible. Section 53 provides for the indemnification of justices and their clerks against costs and damages incurred in respect of the exercise or purported exercise of their office.

Immunity of Other Participants

A general immunity against civil proceedings attaches also to other persons taking part in judicial proceedings as regards

---

[20] [1985] A.C. 528.
[21] *Scott* v. *Stansfield* (1868) L.R. 3 Ex. 220.
[22] *Heddon* v. *Evans* (1919) 35. T.L.R. 642.
[23] *Peacock* v. *Bell* (1667) 2 Mod. 218.
[24] *Calder* v. *Halket* (1839) 3 Moo. P.C.C. 28, *Houlden* v. *Smith* (1850) 14 Q.B. 841.

things said or done by them in that capacity, *e.g.*, jurymen,[25] parties,[26] witnesses[27] and advocates.[28]

Contempt of Court

Criminal contempt of court is a common law offence, punishable by fine or imprisonment. It consists of acts hindering the administration of justice, such as: insulting the judge in court; interfering with jurors, parties or witnesses, or publishing comments on a pending case that are calculated to prejudice a fair trial; or publishing scurrilous abuse of a judge with reference to remarks made by him in a judicial proceeding. Thus in the *Thalidomide case*,[29] where the *Sunday Times* was restrained by injunction from publishing an article on the question whether Distillers were negligent to put thalidomide on the market, the House of Lords said it was a contempt of court to hold a "trial by newspaper" of the issues in a pending case. Students supporting the Welsh Language Society committed a contempt in staging a demonstration in the High Court[30]; and it was a contempt to publish the names of the victims of blackmail during a trial in defiance of the judge's directions.[31] A criminal cause remains *sub judice* until an appeal has been determined or the time within which notice of appeal may be given has elapsed; but innocent publication or distribution may be a defence.[32]

Judges are not immune from criticism of their judicial conduct, provided it is made in good faith and does not impute improper motives to those taking part in the administration or justice. "Justice is not a cloistered virtue," said Lord Atkin, "she must be allowed to suffer the scrutiny and respectful, though outspoken, comments of ordinary men."[33] On this ground it was held that Mr. Quintin Hogg, Q.C., M.P., was not guilty of contempt in publishing an

---

[25] *Bushell's Case* (1670) Vaughan 135.
[26] *Astley* v. *Younge* (1759) 2 Burr. 807.
[27] *Seaman* v. *Netherclift* (1877) 2 C.P.D. 53. But a witness may incur criminal liability for perjury.
[28] *Munster* v. *Lamb* (1883) 11 Q.B.D. 588. And see below, p. 40, with regard to negligence.
[29] *Attorney-General* v. *Times Newspapers* [1974] A.C. 273; *Att.-Gen.* v. *News Group Newspapers, The Times*, February 20, 1988.
[30] *Morris* v. *Crown Office* [1970] 2 Q.B. 114 (C.A.).
[31] *R.* v. *Socialist Worker Printers & Publishers* [1975] Q.B. 637 (D.C.).
[32] Contempt of Court Act 1981, s.3.
[33] *Ambard* v. *Att.-Gen. for Trinidad and Tobago* [1936] A.C. 323, 335.

article in *Punch* criticising certain decisions of the Court of Appeal, even though it was in bad taste.[34]

Superior courts may punish for contempt summarily by committal to prison, and any court of record can punish contempt committed in face of the court by immediate fine and imprisonment, though this should never be done unless justice really requires it.[35] Under the Contempt of Court Act 1981 a magistrates' court may punish any contempt committed before the court or against persons coming to or leaving the court by one months' imprisonment and a fine. The High Court may make an order on behalf of other inferior courts if necessary. There is an appeal from all orders or decisions punishing for contempt of court.[36]

Civil contempt of court consists in disobedience to an order of the court made in civil proceedings giving rise to a right of reparation to the injured party. The Contempt of Court Act 1981 confines strict liability to publications carrying a substantial risk of prejudicing justice and removes it from conduct. In respect of strict liability it allows defences of innocent distribution, fair and accurate reporting and discussion of matters of public interest.

Superior courts of record may commit for contempt and punish it by fine and up to two years imprisonment. County courts are treated as superior courts in this regard. Inferior courts of record may imprison for one month and impose a smaller fine.

3. THE LEGAL PROFESSION

The legal profession in England has a long and varied history. It is now divided into two main branches, solicitors and barristers, a division which has no equivalent in most other countries.

Solicitors

A person who has served a period of articles to a solicitor and who has passed the examinations prescribed by the Law Society (incorporated in 1831) may be admitted as a solicitor by having

---

[34] R. v. *Commissioner of Metropolitan Police, ex p. Blackburn* (No. 2) [1968] 2 Q.B. 150 (C.A.).

[35] *Balogh* v. *St. Albans Crown Court* [1975] Q.B. 73 (C.A.). In particular contempt should *not* be punished summarily when the jury might take a different view at the subsequent trial. R. v. *Griffin* (1988) *The Times*, March 1.

[36] Administration of Justice Act 1960, s.13. A litigants' right to a fair trial survives contempt unless his conduct is such as to render justice impossible. *Logicrose Ltd.* v. *Southend United Football Club* (1988) *The Times*, March 5.

his name entered on the rolls of solicitors. He thereby becomes an officer of the Supreme Court. In practice he takes his instructions directly from lay clients, gives advice, drafts documents, and consults barristers ("counsel") in difficult cases. The scope of his activities is wider than that of a barrister, though he is not allowed to appear as advocate in the superior courts.[37] The Acts regulating the organisation and remuneration of the solicitors' profession were consolidated by the Solicitors Act 1974. The Law Society has power, with the concurrence of the Lord Chancellor, the Lord Chief Justice and the Master of the Rolls, to make regulations about education and training for persons seeking to be admitted or to practise as solicitors. The Council of the Society is required to make rules, with the concurrence of the Master of the Rolls, for regulating the professional practice, conduct and discipline of solicitors.[38] A committee including the Lord Chancellor, the Lord Chief Justice and the Master of the Rolls may make rules regulating the remuneration of solicitors in non-contentious business. A solicitor may be liable to his client for professional negligence and he is insured against this by means of a "master policy" maintained by the Law Society. The Law Society also maintains a Compensation Fund to relieve clients who have suffered as a result of a solicitors failure to account for money held by him. Solicitors are now permitted to advertise the fields of law in which they practise. Since 1974 a Lay Observer has been appointed by the Lord Chancellor to report on the handling of complaints against solicitors. Many aspects of professional practice and etiquette have been queried of late. In particular it has been proposed that solicitors be permitted to form partnerships with members of other professions such as accountants and estate agents, against which it has been objected that such firms may give rise to acute conflicts of interest.

Formerly, the non-barrister members of the legal profession who were engaged in common law practice were called "attorneys," *i.e.*, representatives. Their admission was controlled by the judges, because the early stages of litigation were conducted in court, and attorneys came to be regarded as officers of the court. "Solicitors" in the fifteenth century were inferior officers practising in the Court of Chancery, but by the

---

[37] In *Abse* v. *Smith* [1986] Q.B. 536 it was held that the Court of Appeal and the High Court have a discretion to permit a solicitor to appear in open court, but this would only be exercised in exceptional circumstances. Solicitors may now appear in court in formal or unopposed proceedings; Practice Direction [1986] 1 W.L.R. 545. See n. 40.

[38] For the Solicitors Disciplinary Tribunal, see below, p. 115.

end of the sixteenth century their status was virtually equal to that of attorneys. In the seventeenth century an attorney attached to one court could act as solicitor for the same client in another court, and by the end of that century a solicitor after five years' practice could be admitted as an attorney. Attorneys continued to be primarily associated with the common law courts and to be regarded as somewhat superior to solicitors, who were primarily associated with the Chancery; but from the middle of the eighteenth century the two classes became assimilated, until the distinction between the two was abolished by the Judicature Act 1873.

The corresponding practitioners in the Ecclesiastical and Admiralty Courts were called "proctors." Solicitors may be appointed Recorders and after a qualifying period Circuit Judges.[39] The division of the legal profession between solicitors and barristers has been queried on the ground that a fused profession could provide a cheaper and more efficient service. Against that it has been contended that an independent Bar offers the clients of firms of solicitors of widely varying size and resources an equal opportunity of securing the services of effective advocates who can also provide an objective second opinion on their cases.[40]

Barristers

A person who has joined an Inn of the Court and has passed the examinations required by the Council of Legal Education may be called to the Bar by the Benchers of his Inn, and thereby become a barrister. In earlier times a member who was called by the Benchers to the Bar of his Inn was called an "utter (outer) barrister," because he was allowed to sit on the outside of the forms or bar for the judging of moots. The reception of an utter barrister by the judges of the Bar of the Court entitled him to practise in the courts. The other learners in the Inns were called "inner barristers," and later "students." Nowadays it seems that "the degree of utter barrister" conferred by the Benchers of an Inn on his call is commonly regarded as distinguishing the recipient from a Queen's Counsel who is called within the Bar of

---

[39] See below, Ch. 4.
[40] Megarry, *Lawyer and Litigant in England*. The Marre Committee, (1988) *The Times*, March 12, proposes that lay clients should be allowed to approach barristers directly, that barristers should be able to sue for fees, that audience in all courts should be open to some solicitors and that all judicial appointments be open to solicitors. The Bar rejects these proposals.

the Court. Bar students, "properly habited in students' gowns," were always allowed a place in court from which they could listen to the proceedings.

The Inns of Court now require a person intending to practise to serve twelve months' pupillage in the chambers of an established barrister, and not to accept a brief until he has been a pupil for six months. A barrister may appear as advocate before any court in England. His practice will also consist to a varying extent of drawing up legal documents and giving expert advice in his chambers. According to professional etiquette, which is judicially noticed, a barrister may take instructions only from solicitors and not directly from lay clients; and he is not entitled to sue for his fees, though he may refuse to take work unless he is paid in advance. Barristers practise individually and not in firms or partnerships. The Attorney-General and Solicitor-General for the time being are considered to be the heads of the Bar.

Barristers who practised in the common law courts were called "apprentices at law" in the Middle Ages, probably because they learnt their law from the serjeants. The origin of these barristers lies in the "narrators" or "counters" who were engaged by the attorneys[41] as experts in presenting a case to the court. Formerly there were also specialists, *e.g.*, equity conveyancers, special pleaders. The serjeants-at-law (*servientes ad legem*), who existed from the early fourteenth century until the Judicature Acts, were appointed by royal patent as a superior order of advocates. They wore a silk gown and a coif (a white silk cap fastened under the chin). They were members of Serjeants' Inn, had exclusive right of audience in the Court of Common Pleas, and came to be the sole source from which the common law judges were drawn. An "advocate" generically is one who argues cases in court; specifically, the name was applied to the doctors who practised before the Ecclesiastical and Admiralty Courts. In spite of the fusion of administration of common law and Equity by the Judicature Acts 1873–75, barristers—and to a lesser extent solicitors—tend to specialise in one branch or the other. Thus, of the barristers practising in London, the Equity or Chancery lawyers will generally be found in Lincoln's Inn and the common lawyers in the other Inns.

The four Inns of Court—Inner Temple, Middle Temple, Lincoln's Inn and Gray's Inn—are anomalous unincorporated bodies of medieval origin, owned and controlled by the Masters of the Bench ("Benchers") for the time being. A Senate of the

---

[41] Above.

Inns of Court was established by agreement in 1966, and in 1974 this became the Senate of the Inns of Court and the Bar. The Senate regulated admission to the Inns, the policy of legal education for Bar students and standards of professional conduct. The Senate also exercised disciplinary powers over practising barristers.[42] The Bar Council was concerned with maintaining the independence, and promoting the services, of the profession. The functions of the Senate and the Bar Council have now been united in the General Council of the Bar.

The Council of Legal Education organises syllabuses, tuition and examinations qualifying for call to the Bar.

Queen's Counsel

Queen's Counsel were appointed in the reign of Elizabeth I, among the earliest being Francis Bacon. At first they were not allowed to appear against the Crown without a licence, but from the eighteenth century they ceased to perform their original functions and remained a superior rank of barrister. Nowadays when a barrister has had considerable practical experience and thinks that he has attained some distinction at the Bar, he may apply to the Lord Chancellor for permission to "take silk." If permission is granted, letters patent are issued, he is sworn as a Queen's Counsel and is called within the Bar of the Supreme Court wearing a silk instead of a stuff gown.[43] In future he will undertake less routine work and will usually have the assistance of junior counsel in court. The old rule requiring the assistance of a junior was abolished in 1976 and a Queen's Counsel may now also draft documents and settle pleadings if he is not appearing with a junior.

Immunity of Advocate

It was confirmed by the House of Lords in *Rondel* v. *Worsley*[44] that barristers are immune, for reasons of public policy, from actions for negligence in respect of their professional work in conducting litigation. A majority of their Lordships also expressed the opinion *obiter* that this immunity should not extend to a barrister's non-litigious advisory work, but that it should extend to solicitors appearing as advocates in court.

---

[42] Below, p. 115.
[43] Robes are convenient but not essential; see, *per* Megarry J. in *St. Edmundsbury Diocesan Board* v. *Clark* [1973] Ch. 323.
[44] [1969] 1 A.C. 191. See also, *Saif Ali* v. *Mitchell* [1980] A.C. 198.

Judges

A distinguishing characteristic of the English judicial system is that there is no separate judicial profession as a branch of the public service, but the judges (other than lay magistrates) are selected from among the leading members of the Bar. This also accounts for the fact that the professional education of barristers and the organisation of the Bar are controlled by the profession itself, and are not on a statutory basis.

It is from the ranks of Queen's Counsel that judges of the Supreme Court are usually selected. There is no formal system of promotion in the judicial hierarchy, so that a barrister of the requisite number of years' standing may, though rarely, be appointed a Lord of Appeal in Ordinary without having been a puisne judge or a Lord Justice of Appeal. County court and Circuit judges have occasionally been made judges of the High Court and solicitors who have served a qualifying period as Recorders may be appointed Circuit Judges.

Crown Prosecution Service

Two new sub-divisions of the legal profession have recently appeared. The Prosecution of Offences Act 1985 brought into being the Crown Prosecution Service, comprising barristers and solicitors, which has taken over the prosecuting functions of the police and local authorities in Magistrates' Courts. Private prosecutions are still permitted but they may be taken over by the Service at any stage. The Director of Public Prosecutions is the head of the Service and by section 10 is empowered to issue a Code of Guidelines for the Service on the preferment of charges and representations to the Court as to mode of trial.

Licensed Conveyancers

Dissatisfaction with the conveyancing monopoly of solicitors resulted in pressure for the creation of a new category of persons qualified to practise in this field. The Administration of Justice Act 1985, Part I sets up a Council for Licensed Conveyancers, makes provision for their training and licensing, for a Code of Conduct and for disciplinary and other proceedings. Under section 32 provision is made for permitting certain "recognised" bodies corporate to provide conveyancing services.

Legal Executives

Solicitors were traditionally assisted by unadmitted staff known as "managing clerks." These are now known as legal executives and the Institute of Legal Executives provides their professional organisation and system of qualification.

4. TRIAL BY JURY

Origins

Trial by jury in its modern form is a means of ascertaining the facts in issue in a judicial proceeding according to the evidence adduced in court. Its history can be traced back to the use by Norman and Plantagenet Kings of the continental *inquisitio*, an inquiry into the conduct of local administration. It is only as a judicial institution that the jury may be said to be of English origin, and to have been borrowed for criminal trials by foreign countries.

Civil Jury

As a judicial institution in England we trace the history of the jury in civil cases back to legislation of Henry II providing for bodies of neighbours to be summoned to decide questions relating to the ownership or possession of land. In questions of ownership this procedure was the Grand Assize, which was introduced in real actions as an alternative to trial by battle, probably by a Council at Windsor about the year 1179. The cases of dispossession arose under the Petty or Possessory Assizes introduced from the year 1166 onwards.[45] At first, and for a long time, the twelve jurors answered questions of fact of their own knowledge, though not necessarily as eye-witnesses. By a gradual process, culminating perhaps by the end of the fifteenth century, the jury came to determine facts from the sworn evidence of witnesses produced by the parties.

Criminal Juries

In criminal cases we trace the history of the *petty* (*petit*) *jury* of twelve back to the thirteenth and early fourteenth centuries, when the courts were inducing prisoners to accept this mode of trial as a substitute for the ancient ordeals which disappeared after the Lateran Council in 1215 had forbidden the clergy to assist at them. The *Grand Jury* (now abolished) originated with

---

[45] These were speedy procedures for controlling wrongful dispossession.

the jury of presentment provided for by the Assize of Clarendon, 1166, and the Assize of Northampton, 1176, to prefer charges or indictments of serious crime, as a jury of accusation not of trial, its function being to decide whether the prosecution had made out a prima facie[45a] case against the accused.

Civil Jury at the Present Day

The use of the jury in civil cases has greatly declined in the past hundred years or more. The Common Law Procedure Act 1854, allowed the jury to be dispensed with if both parties consented, and after the Judicature Acts of 1873–75 the influence of Chancery practice exerted itself on the common law courts. Thus by 1933 a jury was used in only about half the civil actions in the King's Bench Division. In that year the Administration of Justice (Miscellaneous Provisions) Act provided that the court should have a discretion whether or not a jury should be summoned; except that a jury must be ordered on the application of either party in cases of defamation, malicious prosecution or false imprisonment, or on the application of a party against whom fraud is alleged, unless the court considers that the trial will involve a prolonged examination of documents or accounts, or a scientific or local investigation which cannot conveniently be made with a jury. Civil juries are now most commonly used in defamation cases, though the Faulks Committee on Defamation has recommended that these actions should be put on the same footing in regard to the discretion of the court as other actions in tort.[46]

Where the court has a discretion under the Act it must be exercised judicially, in the same way as any other discretion.[47] Actions for personal injuries, which include the results of motor accidents, constitute 40 per cent. of the cases in the Queen's Bench Division. The Court of Appeal has ruled[48] that these should be tried by the judge alone in the absence of special circumstances; and the Faulks Committee (above) has recommended that where a jury is used in defamation cases its function in the assessment of damages should be limited. Where a

---

[45a] "At first sight." A prima facie case is one which, taken by itself, without any representation from the defence, would justify a court or tribunal deciding in favour of the prosecution or plaintiff presenting the case.

[46] (1975) Cmnd. 5909.

[47] *Ward* v. *James* [1966] 1 Q.B. 273 (C.A.).

[48] *Ward* v. *James*, above.

judge sits without a jury, of course, he determines the facts as well as the law, and also assesses the damages. The number of jury trials in this Division is likely to be not much more than one per cent. in the future.

It has been the practice to accept a majority verdict with the consent of the parties. The Juries Act 1974,[49] now provides that the verdict of a jury in proceedings in the High Court or Crown Court need not be unanimous if ten out of eleven or twelve jurors, or nine out of ten jurors, agree on the verdict though a smaller majority may still be accepted by agreement in civil cases.

Trial by jury was not used in the Court of Chancery before the Chancery Amendment Act 1858, and the power to summon juries in the Chancery Division given by the Judicature Acts 1873–1925, has been practically neglected. A jury of eight may be applied for in a county court, but this also is very rare.[50]

Criminal Juries at the Present Day

The *Grand Jury* of twenty-three county gentlemen, which had for centuries considered the prima facie guilt of the accused by preferring or throwing out bills of indictment, was abolished (except for certain purposes in London and Middlesex) by the Administration of Justice (Miscellaneous Provisions) Act 1933, and altogether by the Criminal Justice Act 1948.

Criminal proceedings take place either on indictment or summarily before the magistrates. An indictment is a written or printed accusation of crime (whether arrestable or non-arrestable), usually against a person who has been committed for trial by examining justices, and signed by the proper officer of the court.[51] A trial on indictment is now by the Crown Court with a jury (Courts Act 1971).

A (petty) jury traditionally consists of twelve persons, but the Juries Act 1974,[52] provides that where in the course of a criminal trial any member of the jury dies or is discharged because of illness or otherwise, the trial may continue,

---

[49] Replacing the Courts Act 1971.
[50] A majority verdict of seven may be accepted (Juries Act 1974, replacing Courts Act 1971). For the Coroner's jury, see below.
[51] Formerly a bill of indictment was presented by a Grand Jury; above and below. If the indictment is defective the trial will be a nullity *R.* v. *Newland* [1988] 2 W.L.R. 382. *R.* v. *Morais* (1988) *The Times*, March 11.
[52] Re-enacting Criminal Justice Act 1965.

provided the number of jurors is not reduced below nine. This does not apply to a trial for any offence punishable with death, unless both the prosecution and the accused assent.[53]

"Ever since 1367," said Denning J., in *Brain* v. *Minister of Pensions*,[54] "the law has required that the decision of a jury should be unanimous. If they cannot agree, even if only one dissents, the case must be tried before another jury." The Juries Act 1974,[55] however, allows a majority verdict to be taken in criminal proceedings under the following conditions: (i) where there are not less than eleven jurors, ten of them agree on the verdict; or where there are ten jurors, nine of them agree on the verdict; (ii) a majority verdict of *Guilty* may not be accepted unless the foreman states in open court[56] the number of jurors who agree with the verdict; and (iii) a majority verdict may not be accepted unless the jury have had at least two hours for deliberation. Condition (ii) and the practice of the court ensure that it will not be known that a verdict of *Not guilty* is by majority. The judge must encourage the jury in the first instance to try to reach a unanimous decision. He may not accept a majority verdict after less than two hours' deliberation. If they are not agreed after two hours, he should send them back at least once to try to reach unanimity; and then (if necessary) should send them back at least once to see if they can reach the required majority.[57] If all these efforts fail, the jury will have to be discharged, and the case tried before another jury.

Minor offences, including a large number of violations of statutory regulations, are triable on information or complaint by Magistrates' Courts summarily, that is to say, without formal indictment or jury. There is also a third category of offences triable either on indictment or summarily.[58] At the present day the vast majority of indictable offences are in fact tried without a jury.[59]

---

[53] The requirement of assent in the case of murder was to be removed by the Criminal Justice Bill 1987.
[54] [1947] K.B. 625. A direction to avoid undue pressure on a jury to reach a verdict was formulated in *R.* v. *Watson* [1988] 1 All E.R. 897 (H.L.).
[55] Re-enacting Criminal Justice Act 1967.
[56] *R.* v. *Barry (Christopher)* [1975] 1 W.L.R. 1190 (C.A.).
[57] *Practice Direction (C.A.) (Crime: Majority Verdicts)* [1967] 1 W.L.R. 1198; [1967] 3 All E.R. 137; supplemented by *Practice Direction (Crime: Majority Verdict)* [1970] 1 W.L.R. 916; [1970] 2 All E.R. 215 (C.A.).
[58] Magistrates' Courts Act 1980; re-enacting Criminal Law Act 1977; see Chap. 3.
[59] Proposals to abandon jury trial in complex fraud cases have now been rejected: *The Times*, December 2, (1987). See Report of the Roskill Committee on Fraud Trials (H.M.S.O. 1986) and the Criminal Justice Act 1987 setting up the Serious Fraud Office.

Jury Service

The Juries Act 1974, a consolidating Act, incorporates many of the recommendations of the Morris Committee on Jury Service,[60] reforming the law which in some respects dated back to 1825. To qualify for jury service a person must be on the register of electors, aged from eighteen to seventy years, and have been ordinarily resident in the United Kingdom for at least five years. The Lord Chancellor is responsible for summoning jurors in the Crown Court, High Court and county courts, and he is to prepare lists ("panels") of persons summoned as jurors. The court may now permit a jury to separate at any time before they consider their verdict. A juror is entitled to an allowance: (a) for travelling and subsistence, and (b) for consequential financial loss or loss of earnings. If a person summoned fails to attend, he is liable to a fine. The judiciary, justices of the peace, barristers and solicitors (whether or not in practice), clergy and the mentally ill are ineligible for jury service. Persons sentenced to imprisonment for life or for a term of five years or to be detained during Her Majesty's pleasure or (within the last ten years) to imprisonment for three months are disqualified. Members of Parliament, the Forces, medical and other professions are excusable as of right, as will be persons between the ages of sixty-five and seventy. Composition of the jury could be controlled by challenges, peremptory (without giving reasons) or for cause, by the defence, or by the prosecution requesting a juror to "stand by," which effectively excludes him from serving. Police checks on the records of jurors, known as "jury-vetting" were permitted in some cases, subject to stringent guidelines set out in the report of *R. v. Mason*.[61] The Criminal Justice Bill 1988 aims to limit peremptory control by requiring cause to be shown by the defence and the Attorney-General has issued new guidelines restricting the prosecution's right to request a "stand by" to cases involving terrorism and national security. It also provides that pleas that the defendant has already been convicted (*autrefois convict*) or acquitted (*autrefois acquit*) be dealt with by the judge, not the jury.

5. LEGAL AID AND ADVICE

Legal Aid in Criminal Cases

Legal aid for persons of limited means in defending criminal charges was first provided by the Poor Prisoners' Defence Act

---

[60] 1965, Cmnd. 2627.
[61] [1980] 3 All E.R. 777.

1903, which applied only to trials on indictment. The Acts of 1930 and 1949 provided a more comprehensive scheme of legal aid in summary trials and preliminary examinations as well as trials on indictment and appeals.

Legal aid in criminal cases is now governed by the consolidating Legal Aid Act 1974. The costs are funded by the Home Office. Application is made to the appropriate court together with a statement of the applicant's means. A legal aid order must be made if his means appear to be inadequate and the interests of justice so require. Legal aid is seldom refused (except on financial grounds) where the charge is a serious one, and it must be granted on a charge of murder.

Legal aid includes advice by solicitor on the preparation of the defence, and usually consists of representation by solicitor and counsel, or by solicitor only in magistrates' courts. An assisted person may be required to make a reasonable contribution after his case has been dealt with, regard being had to his commitments and resources. Appeal against refusal may be made to legal aid committees.

The Legal Aid Act 1982 made provision for the setting up of a system of "duty solicitors" under which rotas of duty solicitors to attend at local criminal courts to advise unrepresented defendants have been set up.

Legal Aid in Civil Cases

The Legal Aid and Advice Acts 1949 and 1960, made provision for a service of legal aid and advice in civil cases, administered by the Law Society under the direction of the Lord Chancellor, to supersede the previous Poor Persons' procedure.

Legal aid in civil cases is also now governed by the Legal Aid Acts 1974 and 1982. Legal aid covers representation by solicitor and, where necessary, by counsel in the preparation of claims and the conduct of litigation, excluding defamation,[62] in courts generally, including domestic cases in magistrates' courts. It is not available in tribunals other than the Lands Tribunal nor in arbitration.[63] The Law Society, in consultation with the Bar Council and under the general guidance of the Lord Chancellor, acts through Area Committees. The cost is met out of the Legal Aid Fund. Solicitors and barristers are paid for their services out of the Fund, receiving a percentage of their usual fees.

---

[62] Legal aid has been stopped generally for the determination of undefended divorce cases, though not for ancillary disputes in chambers.

[63] But, see below "assistance by way of representation" under the Legal Aid Act 1979 which is available in tribunals.

A means test determines whether an applicant needs financial assistance. The Department of Health and Social Security assesses disposable income and disposable capital for this purpose. A person who is granted legal aid may be required to make a contribution towards his own costs. If he is unsuccessful in the action, his liability for his opponent's costs will be limited to the amount (if any) which it is reasonable in all the circumstances for him to pay.

An applicant whose financial position entitles him to legal aid must satisfy a General Committee that he has reasonable grounds for taking, defending or being a party to proceedings. Against a refusal to grant a certificate he may appeal to the Area Committee.

Legal Advice

The Legal Aid and Advice Act 1949, also provided for the setting up of legal advice centres where oral legal advice could be given by solicitors in non-litigious matters. A new legal advice and assistance scheme for both civil and criminal matters outside the courts was introduced by the Legal Advice and Assistance Act 1972. People of low income and limited capital, as defined in the Act and statutory regulations, are able to obtain the services of a solicitor to a limited amount with a minimum of formalities (the "green form scheme"). Further help can be obtained with the consent of a legal aid office. Assistance did not originally extend to taking any steps in legal proceedings, since these are covered by the legal aid scheme, except that a county court or magistrates' court might request a solicitor who is present to give, or consent to his giving, such assistance. The Legal Aid Act 1979 introduced a limited "assistance by way of representation" which extends to appearance before a wide range of tribunals.

No contribution is payable by a person whose disposable income does not exceed a certain amount, or is in receipt of supplementary benefit or family income supplement, and whose disposable capital does not exceed a certain amount. Otherwise, he may be required to make a contribution, within a certain maximum.[64] The Act of 1972 empowered the Law Society to establish local law centres, staffed by solicitors employed by the Law Society. This has not been done and the various law centres found in larger cities are all independent institutions. Citizens Advice Bureaux also give legal advice and

---

[64] The Lord Chancellor has power to make regulations by Statutory Instrument varying these amounts above the statutory minimum.

the extension of their activities in this area has been contemplated. The American "contingent fee" system under which a
lawyer undertakes a case for a share of damages or property
recovered is regarded as contrary to public policy and any such
agreement is void as champertous.[65]

The Legal Aid Bill 1988 will set up a new board with a majority
of non-lawyers, appointed by the Lord Chancellor, to manage
legal aid from 1989 instead of the Law Society. The Bill provides
for the board to "contract-out" work hitherto done by the legal
profession to non-lawyers, such as Citizens' Advice Bureaux.
The Board will assess applicants means, fix remuneration for
lawyers, and an applicant will choose legal representatives from
prescribed panels. In other respects the Bill consolidates the
Acts of 1974 and 1982, but also contains provisions to facilitate
"group" or "class" actions when many parties have suffered a
common calamity, as with drug side effects or transport
disasters. The Bill has been criticised as being merely a
framework for delegated legislation.

[65] See *Wallersteiner* v. *Moir* (No. 2) [1975] Q.B. 373.

CHAPTER 3

Magistrates' and Coroners' Courts

1. JUSTICES OF THE PEACE

History of Justices of the Peace

Origin

In the reign of Richard I (1195) the maintenance of order by the co-operative system of frankpledge was supplemented by royal commissions to knights of the shire to receive oaths for the preservation of the peace. Local knights and gentlemen were appointed occasionally by Henry III as *custodes pacis* to help the sheriff in enforcing the law by receiving prisoners and producing them to the royal justices of gaol delivery. Various statutes of Edward I[1] and Edward III confirmed and extended the practice of commissioning conservators, custodians or guardians of the peace. The commissions were put on a permanent basis in 1327, and in 1344 the *custodes pacis* were given judicial powers to hear and determine felonies and trespasses.

After the Black Death, Justices of Labourers were appointed to enforce the Statutes of Labourers, and soon their commission came to be merged with that of the guardians of the peace. We find these officially called Justices of the Peace in a statute of 34 Edw. III, which has now been given the short title of the Justices of the Peace Act 1361.[2] Each county had a separate commission.

---

[1] Statute of Winchester 1285.
[2] Amended by the Criminal Law Act 1967.

Justices of the Peace were originally paid a salary out of fines they imposed, but the salary became so small owing to the fall in the value of money that they early ceased to collect it.

The Former Quarter Sessions

It was enacted in 1363[3] that the Justices of the Peace for each county should meet at least four times a year. After the ancient county courts died out it was these general meetings of the justices that became for some centuries the chief organs of local government outside certain boroughs, but in the nineteenth century almost all their administrative functions were transferred to other bodies, leaving their judicial work as magistrates as their chief function. A court of County Quarter Sessions, according to the Justices of the Peace Act 1949, was to consist of two to nine of the county justices, presided over by a chairman. A paid legally qualified chairman became optional in 1938[4] and obligatory in 1962,[5] the result being some extension of the court's jurisdiction. The legally qualified chairman was in fact often a High Court or county court judge.

Some of the boroughs possessing separate commissions of the peace had their own Quarter Sessions which were required to meet at least once in every quarter.[6] In this event the court consisted of the Recorder with a jury. Recorders were practising barristers, appointed part-time for this purpose by the Queen on the recommendation of the Lord Chancellor, and paid a salary.

In addition to hearing appeals from magistrates' courts[7] exercising summary criminal jurisdiction, Quarter Sessions had an extensive original criminal jurisdiction covering all indictable offences except those very serious crimes triable only at Assizes. Trial was by jury, except in appeals from magistrates' courts.

These courts were abolished by the Courts Act 1971 and their jurisdiction transferred to the Crown Court. In certain cases magistrates must, and in others may, sit in the Crown Court as full members of the court.[8]

---

[3] 36 Edw. 3, c. 12.
[4] Administration of Justice (Miscellaneous Provisions) Act 1938.
[5] Criminal Justice Administration Act 1962.
[6] Municipal Corporations Act 1882.
[7] "Magistrate" is an alternative expression for "justice of the peace." See Justices of the Peace Act 1979, s.70, " 'Magistrate' . . . means a justice of the peace . . ." Magistrates Courts Act 1980, s.148 " 'magistrates' court' means any justice or justices of the peace acting under any enactment or by virtue of his or their commission or under the common law."
[8] See below, Chap. 4, p. 66.

Petty Sessions

Justices of the Peace over the years were given jurisdiction by a series of statutes over a large number of petty or minor offences, which they tried summarily, *i.e.* without a jury. The sittings of justices for this purpose came to be called Petty Sessions. The statute law governing the justices' summary jurisdiction, and as examining justices in respect of indictable offences, was the subject of amending and consolidating statutes from time to time, beginning with Jervis's Acts of 1848.[9]

Justices of the Peace or Magistrates at the Present Day

There is no legal qualification for a lay justice of the peace, but he must be resident within fifteen miles of the area for which he is commissioned. His jurisdiction is limited to the area for which he is commissioned. The commission areas outside London coincide with the counties (metropolitan or non-metropolitan) laid down by the Local Government Act 1972. In the appointment of magistrates the Lord Chancellor consults confidential advisory committees, which are set up principally on a county basis. Lay magistrates are now expected to attend courses of instruction organised by the local Magistrates' Courts Committees (also on a county basis) and paid for by a statutory grant to the Lord Chancellor.[10]

There is no limit to the number of lay magistrates that may be appointed. The present number is more than 25,000 in England and Wales. They are now entitled to allowances for travel and subsistence expenses for financial loss incurred in the performance of their functions.[11]

Lay magistrates are supplemented in London by legally qualified and salaried Metropolitan Stipendiary Magistrates, and in some of the larger provincial towns by Stipendiary Magistrates. They must be barristers or solicitors of not

[9] Indictable Offences Act and Summary Jurisdiction Act 1848. Jervis was Attorney-General at the time, and later a judge. Other landmarks were the Petty Sessions Act 1849, and the Summary Jurisdiction Act 1879.

[10] Many local branches of the Magistrates' Association organised voluntary training courses before they became obligatory.

[11] Justices of the Peace Act 1949 and 1968; Administration of Justice Act 1973. The Act of 1968 abolished most *ex-officio* justices. The Lord Mayor and Aldermen of the City of London are *ex-officio* justices by charters of the city, but the Administration of Justice Act 1973, allows the Lord Chancellor to exclude any of them from the exercise of his functions as a justice.

less than seven years' standing. The Lord Chancellor may authorise them to continue in office between the ages of seventy and seventy-two.[12]

Functions of Justices of the Peace

The chief functions of the magistrates are:—

(i) Summary criminal jurisdiction in (a) magistrates' courts and (b) juvenile courts.

(ii) Preliminary examination of persons accused of indictable offences.

(iii) The issue of summonses and warrants for arrest or search, and the granting of bail, which may be done "out of sessions," *i.e.*, not necessarily in a court house.

(iv) Domestic jurisdiction, *e.g.*, matrimonial orders; maintenance orders; adoption orders; and orders as to the custody of children.[13]

(v) Miscellaneous civil jurisdiction, including the recovery of local rates, and charges for electricity, gas and water.

(vi) Miscellaneous administrative functions, *e.g.*, licensing premises for the sale of intoxicating liquors, and for the provision of music, dancing and entertainment.[14]

The effect of (i) and (ii) is that almost every criminal charge comes before the magistrates in the first instance, and the vast majority are disposed of by the Magistrates' Courts. A majority of the cases dealt with by these courts are motoring offences.

Supplemental List

The Justices of the Peace Act 1949, provided that the Lord Chancellor should keep a "supplemental list" of Justices who had reached retiring age or were by infirmity or otherwise unfitted to exercise judicial functions. The Act of 1968 reduced the retiring age by stages from seventy-five to seventy. Justices on the supplemental list may not sit judicially or sign any information, complaint, summons or warrant; but they may authenticate signatures or declarations on oath, and the Justices

---

[12] Justices of the Peace Act 1979.

[13] Magistrates' Courts Act 1978, below, pp. 358–359.

[14] Licensing sessions of justices constitute a Magistrates' Court for the purpose of stating a case for the High Court: *Jeffrey* v. *Evans* [1964] 1 W.L.R. 505; [1964] 1 All E.R. 536 (D.C.); and the liquor-licensing functions of justices have long been held to be judicial for the purpose of review by certiorari: *R*. v. *Brighton Borough Justices, ex p. Jarvis* [1954] 1 W.L.R. 203; [1954] 1 All E.R. 197 (D.C.).

of the Peace Act 1979 (following the Courts Act 1971), allows them, if authorised by the Lord Chancellor, to act as judges of the Crown Court until the age of seventy-two years.[15]

2. MAGISTRATES' COURTS

Most of the enactments relating to the criminal jurisdiction, practice and procedure of Magistrates' Courts have been consolidated by the Magistrates' Courts Act 1980. "Magistrates' Court" for the purposes of the Act of 1980 means any justice or justices of the peace acting under any enactment or by virtue of his or their commission or under common law.[16] The expression "Magistrates' Courts" covers what were previously known as Courts of Summary Jurisdiction (or Petty Sessions), and Examining Justices.

Clerks to the Justices

Clerks are appointed to the various benches by the Magistrates' Courts Committees, subject to the approval of the Lord Chancellor.[17] From 1949 the principle has been that a clerk to the justices should be a barrister or solicitor of not less than five years' standing. They are usually solicitors. Clerks have been empowered since 1968 to do things that can be done by a single justice. They have been authorised, for example, to grant, though not to refuse, legal aid. It is the duty of the clerk[18] to advise the justices on questions of law, practice, procedure and evidence arising in connection with their functions, whether in or out of sessions.[19] Magistrates are not obliged to accept the advice of their clerk; they are responsible for their own adjudications and sentences.[20]

Prior to any proceeding commencing an accused may have been in police custody. The Police and Criminal Evidence Act 1984 imposes time-limits and requires that the detention be reviewed from time to time by a senior officer. A suspect may be detained for 24 hours without being charged and extensions may be granted up to a maximum of 96 hours. The magistrates may also have to consider the question of granting bail since the

---

[15] This is the retiring age for Circuit judges. Below, Chap. 4.
[16] s.148.
[17] Justices of the Peace Act 1979, s.25.
[18] The Clerk to the Justices may have assistants who act as court clerks where a number of Magistrates' Courts sit at the same time in a given area.
[19] Justices of the Peace Acts 1949, 1968; Justices Clerks Rules 1970.
[20] R. v. *East Kerrier Justices* [1952] 2 Q.B. 719; Practice Direction (Justices: Clerk to the Court) [1981] 1 W.L.R. 1163.

Bail Act 1976 effectively creates a strong presumption that this should normally be granted.[21]

Committal Proceedings

A person charged with an offence which is to be tried on *indictment*, whether he has been summoned, or arrested with or without a warrant, or is already in custody, is brought before one or more magistrates—called for this purpose "examining justices"—for a preliminary examination into the charge. Until recently the examining justices always heard the witnesses for the prosecution, and asked the accused—after cautioning him that he need not say anything, that he had nothing to hope or fear from any promise or threat, and that whatever he said would be taken down and might be used at his trial—whether he wished to make a statement or to call any witness. If they were then satisfied that prima facie case had been made out against the accused, they would commit him with or without bail for trial at the next assizes or quarter sessions: otherwise they discharged him.

The Criminal Justice Act 1967, however, provided that a Magistrates' Court inquiring into an offence as examining justices might commit the defendant for trial without considering the evidence if all the evidence, both of the prosecution and the defence, consisted of written statements tendered as evidence, exchanged between the parties beforehand and not objected to by either party; but this only applied if the defendant was represented by counsel or a solicitor, and if the defendant did not submit that on the evidence there was no case to answer. Previously examining justices were not obliged to sit in open court, but by the Act of 1967 they had to do so unless there is some statutory provision to the contrary or it appeared to them that the ends of justice would not be served by their sitting in open court. The same Act imposed restrictions on the publication or broadcasting of reports of committal proceedings, unless the defendant requested that the restrictions should not apply.[22]

---

[21] See below, Chap. 16.

[22] See now Magistrates Courts Act 1980, ss.4–8. If one or more of several defendants objects to the lifting of restrictions on publicity these are only to be lifted if justice requires it: s.8(2) and Criminal Justice (Amendment) Act 1981, s.1. The Criminal Justice Act 1987, s.11 makes similar provision for reporting restrictions on applications for dismissal and preparatory hearings in serious fraud cases. Justices have a general inherent jurisdiction to sit *in camera*, but should exercise it rarely. *R. v. Malvern JJ ex p. Evans* [1988] 2 W.L.R. 218.

In serious fraud cases the Criminal Justice Act 1987 now provides for the transfer of cases to the Crown Court and for a preparatory hearing before a judge instead of committal proceedings in order to simplify the issues.[23]

Criminal Jurisdiction

The criminal jurisdiction of Magistrates' Courts is exercisable by not less than two lay justices or a stipendiary magistrate. It consists mainly of the trial of summary offences, *i.e.*, offences triable without a jury. There are some hundreds of offences triable summarily by various statutes. Where an information is laid before one or more justices the accused may be summoned to appear before a Magistrates' Court, or (if the offence is indictable or punishable by imprisonment) a warrant may be issued for his arrest so that he may be brought to trial. A Magistrates' Court has power to hear a case in the absence of the accused, and originally under the Magistrates' Courts Act 1957, it may in certain circumstances accept a plea of "Guilty" by letter; but a person may not be sentenced in his absence to imprisonment or detention.[24] The judicial proceedings before the Magistrates' Courts are relatively informal and without a jury.

Criminal proceedings in Magistrates' Courts were re-shaped by Part III of the Criminal Law Act 1977. After 1952 there were five classes of offence as regards mode of trial. The Act of 1977 reduced this number to three classes: (1) offences triable only on indictment; (2) offences triable only summarily; and (3) offences triable either way. It also laid down a single procedure where a person (aged seventeen or over) is charged with an offence triable either way.

The 1977 Act added to the offences that, by other statutes, were triable only summarily, the use of threatening, insulting or abusive words or behaviour, assaulting a police constable, and motoring offences caused by unfitness through drink or drugs. The 1977 Act also added to the offences that by other statutes are triable either way, most of the indictable offences that could previously be tried summarily with the consent of the accused, and some offences that previously could be tried on indictment only, including reckless driving, bigamy and certain kinds of

---

[23] ss.4–10.
[24] See now, Magistrates Courts Act 1980, s.11(3), (4) and s.12. He should not be disqualified from driving until he has had an opportunity to state orally any reasons why he should not be disqualified.

burglary and forgery. One offence, namely, libel by a newspaper, became triable only on indictment. Most cases of criminal damage where the value did not exceed £200 were to be tried summarily.[25]

Procedure for Determining Mode of Trial of Offences Triable Either Way

The Magistrates' Court is required to begin by considering whether, having regard to the circumstances of the offence, its powers of punishment and any representations made by the prosecutor or the accused, an offence triable either way is more suitable for summary trial or for trial on indictment. Where the court considers the offence more suitable for summary trial, the accused is to be asked whether he consents to be tried summarily or wishes to be tried by a jury. If he consents to be tried summarily, the court is to proceed to summary trial. If he does not so consent, the court is to proceed as examining justices. Where the court considers the offence more suitable for trial on indictment, the court is to proceed as examining justices. Where the court has begun to try the information summarily and the offence is triable either way, it may at any time before the conclusion of the prosecution evidence change from summary trial to committal proceedings. Conversely, if the court has begun to inquire into the information as examining justices, it may (but only with the consent of the accused) change to summary trial.

Committal to Crown Court for Sentence

The maximum punishments that a Magistrates' Court may impose are strictly limited. The maximum term of imprisonment is six months for offences triable either way. For many minor offences no imprisonment may be imposed. The maximum fine that a Magistrates' Court may impose is restricted and for some offences is quite small. Where a person has been convicted of an offence triable either way, and the court is satisfied on the basis of information relevant to sentence (*e.g.*, character and previous convictions)[26] that its powers of punishment are inadequate, it may commit him to the Crown Court for sentence.

---

[25] See now Magistrates Courts Act 1980 ss.17–28 (now £400).

[26] Magistrates, like a jury, have no knowledge of previous convictions until the question of guilty or not guilty has been decided.

Appeals from Magistrates' Courts

A person who has been convicted by a Magistrates' Court for any offence has a right of appeal to the Crown Court[27] against conviction or sentence on a question of law or fact, except that if he pleaded "Guilty" or admitted the truth of the charge he can appeal only against the sentence.[28] The appeal is by way of rehearing with witnesses and without a jury. The Crown Court may confirm, reverse or vary the decision, and may increase or reduce the punishment within the limits allowed to a Magistrates' Court. On a point of law either party may then apply for the Crown Court to state a case for the opinion of the High Court. (See below)

Case Stated

Either the defendant or the prosecutor may require the magistrates to state a case for the opinion of the High Court (Divisional Court of the Queen's Bench Division), on the ground that a proceeding of a Magistrates' Court is wrong in law or is in excess of jurisdiction,[29] and the Divisional Court may affirm, amend or reverse the decision of the magistrates. The magistrates need not be represented by counsel unless misconduct is alleged against them. Appeal now lies to the House of Lords subject to certification by the High Court of a point of law of general public importance and leave of either the Divisional Court or the House of Lords.[30]

Juvenile Courts

No charge against a *child* (*i.e.*, a person under fourteen[31]) or *young person* (*i.e.*, a person of fourteen or upwards and under seventeen) may be heard by a court of summary jurisdiction other than a Juvenile Court, that is, a Magistrates' Court sitting for that purpose and consisting of local magistrates on a special panel. At least one member of the court must be a woman.

A Juvenile Court must sit in a different building or room from that in which courts for adults are held, or on different days.

---

[27] Appeal formerly lay to Quarter Sessions.

[28] The plea must be unequivocal to bar appeal. *R.* v. *Blandford JJ.* [1967] 1 Q.B. 82.

[29] Magistrates' Courts Act 1980, s.111. Only the facts not the evidence should be set out in the case stated *Laird* v. *Simms* (1988) *The Times*, March 7.

[30] Administration of Justice Act 1960.

[31] The minimum age of *criminal* responsibility was raised from eight to ten years by the Children and Young Persons Act 1963.

The only persons permitted to be present in court, besides the members and officers of the court and the parties, are solicitors, counsel, witnesses, newspaper reporters, and other persons specifically authorised to be present. No names or photographs may be published in a newspaper report or in sound or television broadcasts, unless directed by the court or the Home Secretary. The words "conviction" or "sentence" may not be used in relation to children or young persons.[32]

A Magistrates' Court may remit a juvenile for trial to a juvenile court if an adult with whom he is charged pleads guilty or is committed for trial to the Crown Court whereas the juvenile is to be tried summarily; and a Magistrates' Court may commit a juvenile for trial in the Crown Court for any indictable offence that arises out of the same circumstances as those that gave rise to an offence with which he is jointly charged with an adult.[33]

Proceedings in respect of *children under ten* are civil, and mainly result in care orders involving parents or guardians and supervision orders involving local authorities or probation officers. *Children aged ten to fourteen*, if the presumption that they are incapable of crime is rebutted, may be fined; or (if the offence is one for which an adult may be sentenced to imprisonment) the court may make an care order, or supervision order, or compensation order, or attendance centre order. *Young persons* (fourteen to seventeen) may be charged with any offence. Instead of a care order or supervision order they may be fined, or sentenced to an attendance centre or a detention centre or if over fifteen to youth custody. For murder and the most serious indictable offences, a child (not under ten) or young person must be committed to the Crown Court for trial. Parents may be ordered to pay a fine imposed on a child or young person unless this would be unreasonable.

3. CORONERS' COURTS

Origin

The Coroner's Court is perhaps the oldest existing English court. It exists at common law, but its functions are now regulated by statute.[34] Coroners, first mentioned in the reign of Richard I (1194), were appointed to look after the King's local

---

[32] Children and Young Persons Acts 1933–1963. The expressions to be used are "finding of guilt" and "order made upon finding of guilt."

[33] Magistrates' Courts Act 1980, s.29.

[34] Coroners Acts 1887–1980; Criminal Law Act 1977, s.56.

pecuniary interests as keepers of the pleas. Hence they were interested in fines and forfeitures. They acted as a check on the sheriffs and juries of presentment, and also came to inquire into such matters as wrecks, treasure trove and unexplained deaths. They once had a variety of functions in connection with local administration and criminal law, but all that remains is their duty to inquire into sudden and unexplained deaths and the suspected concealment of treasure trove, of which the former is by far the most important.

Appointment of Coroners

A coroner must be a barrister, solicitor or general medical practitioner of at least five years' standing. Although coroners are royal officers they have always been locally appointed. Formerly they were elected in the old county courts. Now they are appointed by local authorities.[35] The Lord Chief Justice and judges of the High Court are coroners *ex-officio*.

Inquests into Cause of Death

It is the duty of a coroner to hold an inquisition or inquest[36] where a person has died in his district and there is reasonable cause to suspect that he died a violent or unnatural death, or the death was sudden and the cause unknown, or the person died in prison or the death occurred in police custody or as a result of an injury inflicted by a police officer in purported execution of his duty. The person need not have died in this country.[37]

The purpose of a coroner's inquest where a person's death was caused by murder, manslaughter or infanticide, no longer includes the finding of any person guilty of such offence, and a coroner's inquest may not charge a person with any of those offences. A coroner may and in some cases must summon a jury of between seven and eleven persons, but the requirement to do so has been reduced in recent years.[38]

The coroner may exclude the public or particular persons from the court. There is no right of interested persons to be represented by a barrister or a solicitor. The coroner may, however, allow them or their representatives to put questions to the witnesses. He may accept the verdict of a majority of the

[35] Local Government Act 1972, s.220. This Act abolished franchise coroners except the Queen's Coroner or Coroner of the Queen's Household.
[36] *R.* v. *Haslewood* [1926] 2 K.B. 468. An inquest may, however, be held although the body has been destroyed or cannot be found.
[37] *R.* v. *West Yorkshire Coroner ex p. Smith* [1983] Q.B. 335 (Saudi Arabia).
[38] Criminal Law Act 1977, s.56.

jury, if the minority is not more than two. There is no appeal, but judicial review by the High Court is possible *e.g. R. v. Surrey Coroner ex p. Campbell* [1982] Q.B. 661.

If before the conclusion of an inquest the coroner is officially informed that some person has been charged with murder, manslaughter or infanticide, or with the offence of causing death by reckless driving, or with aiding, abetting or counselling the suicide of the deceased, or with some other offence connected with his death, then the coroner must (in the absence of reason to the contrary) adjourn the inquest. After the conclusion of the relevant criminal proceedings he may resume the inquest if he thinks there is sufficient cause to do so; but the finding of the resumed inquest must not be inconsistent with the outcome of those criminal proceedings.[39]

Treasure Trove

Blackstone says that "where any money or coin, gold, silver, plate, or bullion, is found hidden in the earth, or other private place, the owner thereof being unknown, ... the treasure belongs to the King: but if he that hid it be known, or afterwards found out, the owner and not the King is entitled to it."[40] It is the hiding, not the mere abandoning of it, that gives the Sovereign the right of ownership.[41] Formerly, all treasure trove belonged to the finder, but it was later thought expedient, especially for coinage purposes, to award to the Sovereign such treasure as was hidden.

Treasure trove is part of the royal revenue that is now surrendered to the Exchequer in return for the Civil List. The nature of the treasure and the circumstances of the finding are inquired into at a coroner's inquest. It is customary for the Treasury to recompense the owner of the land and the finder if it is declared treasure trove, as was the case with the collection of Roman silver plate found some years ago at Mildenhall and now deposited in the British Museum.

Treasure Trove is in effect a very unsatisfactory method of protecting archaeological remains and many reforms have been proposed.

---

[39] Criminal Law Act 1977, Sched. 10.
[40] I. Comm. 295–296.
[41] *Att.-Gen.* v. *Trustees of the British Museum* [1903] 2 Ch. 598; *Att.-Gen. (Duchy of Lancaster)* v. *Overton* [1981] Ch. 333 (there must be a substantial bullion content).

CHAPTER 4

The Crown Court

The Crown Court has since 1971 provided a system covering England and Wales for the trial of the more serious forms of crime known as indictable[1] offences. Trial is by judge and jury, the seniority of the judge varying with the gravity of the alleged offences. The more serious are tried by High Court judges and the less serious by circuit judges or recorders who may sit with magistrates. The Crown Court may also hear certain appeals from magistrates' courts but then it sits without a jury. It also has a licensing jurisdiction inherited from the courts it replaced. There may be committals for sentence from magistrates' courts when these courts feel they cannot impose a sufficiently severe sentence and these, too, are heard without a jury.

Background

Before the Courts Act 1971, came into force serious crimes were tried on indictment either at assizes[2] or quarter sessions. These courts, which had existed for many centuries, also had some civil jurisdiction. For assizes the country was divided into seven

---

[1] An indictment is a written accusation of crime at the suit of the Crown. "Indictable offences" are contrasted with "summary offences," tried in magistrates' courts without a jury. If the indictment is defective there can be no valid trial. *R. v. Newland* [1988] 2 W.L.R. 382.

[2] The word "assize" (sitting or session) was used indiscriminately in the Middle Ages for an Ordinance issued at a session of the King's Council, the form of proceedings instituted by such an Ordinance and the court in which such proceedings took place.

areas called circuits, and judges of the Queen's Bench Division and after 1944 the Probate, Divorce and Admiralty Division would visit towns in each circuit for fixed periods to administer criminal and civil justice. Any crime, however serious, could be tried at assizes, and their civil jurisdiction broadly corresponded to that of the Queen's Bench Division and the matrimonial jurisdiction of the Probate, Divorce and Admiralty Division. The Central Criminal Court from 1834 provided criminal assizes for the Greater London area. This court sat throughtout the year.

Quarter sessions, as their name indicated, used to meet every quarter. There were two types of quarter sessions, borough and county. The judge of a borough quarter sessions was the Recorder, who took this part-time judicial office in addition to practice at the Bar. The judges of county quarter sessions were all the magistrates for the area in question. Statute imposed limits on the number entitled to sit together and also encouraged and eventually enforced the appointment of legally qualified chairmen, who had to be barristers or solicitors of some standing.

Origins of the Crown Court

Judges of the royal courts had been sent on circuit since the reign of Henry II, their jurisdiction depending on the terms of their commission and these developed into the assize courts. The history of quarter sessions similarly went far back into the Middle Ages and has been outlined in connection with magistrates' courts.[3]

After 1945 it became apparent that an increase in crime was imposing strains on this old-established system of periodic courts. In particular the amount of crime in South Lancashire made it necessary to set up Crown Courts in Liverpool and Manchester in 1956. These acted as quarter sessions for their cities and criminal assizes both for their cities and for areas of the county, and were presided over by full-time judges with the title of Recorder. Civil assizes continued in these cities, and assize judges sat in the Crown Courts to hear very serious criminal cases. These courts provided a model for the present comprehensive Crown Court.

The Beeching Commission

A Royal Commission on Assizes and Quarter Sessions under the chairmanship of Lord Beeching[4] reported in 1969. The

---

[3] See Chap. 3, p. 51.
[4] Cmnd. 4153. Lord Beeching is well known for an earlier inquiry which resulted in a considerable curtailment of the railway system of this country.

Commission approved of the circulation of judges between London and the Provinces and between various parts of the country as this ensured a distribution of judicial talent and information.[5] Much else, however, was found to be in need of reform.

Defects of the Old System

The chief defect of the system was found to be its excessive rigidity. The Commission thought that the emphasis should be on the important towns which were centres for judicial work rather than on the precise location of boundaries of areas for courts.[6] Whilst accepting that different tiers of courts and judges should take cases of differing gravity, the Commission also thought that any demarcation between tiers should be less inflexible than it was.[7] Timetables for assizes were prepared long in advance of the judges going on circuit, and hence could not make allowance in the time assigned to each assize town for the amount of work to be done there. Criminal work took precedence over civil, and the criminal work frequently prevented civil cases being heard by the time the judge had to leave the town. The parties might then have to accept a long and uncertain delay.[8] Much time was spent in travelling when it was not possible for practitioners to communicate with the court.[9] Some of the administrative staff travelled with the court and the remainder was the responsibility of local authorities.[10]

In the case of quarter sessions the Beeching Commission found the principal defect was the large number of part-time judicial posts.[11] This made consistency in sentencing difficult to maintain. Again the fact that the recorders and chairmen often had to combine their judicial duties with their practices led to the holding of many courts throughout the country at the same time, with consequent strain upon the legal profession, the police and the prison service.[12] The Commission, whilst approving the use of part-time appointments to train those who might later be appointed to the Bench, thought that such appointments, carrying the title of Recorder, should be for fixed periods and should not be associated with particular localities.[13]

[5] para. 69.
[6] paras. 158–162.
[7] paras. 134–139.
[8] paras. 76–77.
[9] para. 79.
[10] para. 80.
[11] para. 87.
[12] paras. 87–88.
[13] paras. 234–240.

The Commission also considered the position of county court judges, and thought it unsatisfactory that these should be confined to civil work unless they also happened to hold an appointment such as chairman of county quarter sessions.[14]

Recommendations

The Commission recommended that a new bench of judges, to be known as circuit judges, should be created. This would include the then county court judges and certain other full-time judges of less than High Court standing. Members of the new bench would divide their time between acting as county court judges and trying criminal cases.[15] The chief recommendation of the Commission, however, was that assizes, quarter sessions and the Crown Courts of Liverpool and Manchester should be abolished, and be replaced by a single Crown Court with countrywide jurisdiction which would sit at a number of centres chosen on grounds of geographic convenience.[16]

This would deal with all indictable crime. It would also take over certain appellate and other functions of quarter sessions.

The timetables for civil High Court work in the provinces and criminal work were no longer to be interlocked.[17] Moreover judges were to sit at particular centres as long as there was work for them to do, and would not be obliged to leave in deference to a timetable prepared long in advance in ignorance of that work.[18] A unified courts service under the Lord Chancellor, instead of the various local authorities, was to provide administrative staff for the courts.[19] In each circuit two High Court judges were to be appointed as Presiding Judges to assist with some aspects of administration.[20]

Courts Act 1971

Effect has been given to almost all the recommendations of the Commission either by the Courts Act 1971, or through administrative action.

The Crown Court

Courts of assize and quarter sessions were abolished, and the

---

[14] paras. 107–108.
[15] paras. 174–176; 188–195; 240–253.
[16] paras. 173–174; 274–298.
[17] para. 184.
[18] para. 185.
[19] paras. 299–330.
[20] paras. 256–265.

Crown Court was brought into being as part of the Supreme Court[21] to try all indictable offences tried with judge and jury and exercise other functions of quarter sessions.[22] The judges are High Court judges, members of the new circuit bench, recorders of the new type and magistrates.[23] Offences are divided into four classes. Those in the first class are tried only by a High Court judge. Those in the second are normally tried by a High Court judge unless a particular case is released. Those in the third class may be tried by a High Court judge, circuit judge or recorder. Those in the fourth class may be tried by a High Court judge but are normally listed for trial by a circuit judge or recorder.[24]

Circuit Judges and Recorders

As the Beeching Commission contemplated, all former county court judges and certain other full-time judges have now become circuit judges.[25] Qualification for appointment as a circuit judge is ten years' standing at the Bar or three years' service as a "new" recorder. Retirement is at seventy-two with the possibility of extension to seventy-five. Barristers or solicitors of ten years' standing may be appointed as recorders and this means a solicitor may qualify for appointment as a circuit judge.[26] Recorders have the powers of circuit judges.[27]

Justices of the Peace had played a major part in county quarter sessions, but the Beeching Commission envisaged that they should serve in the Crown Court merely as assessors.[28] The Courts Act 1971, however, provides that in some cases justices must sit and in others they may sit always with a judge or recorder and always as full members of the court.[29] Justices must sit at the hearing of any appeal from a magistrates' court or committal for sentence. On an appeal or on a committal for sentence two to four justices must sit. On licensing appeals four justices must sit, two at least from the area in question. For

---

[21] Courts Act 1971, s.1.
[22] *Ibid.*, ss.3, 4, 6, 8 and 9.
[23] *Ibid.*, ss.4, 5 and 16–24.
[24] *Practice Direction* [1971] 1 W.L.R. 1535; [1978] 1 W.L.R. 926.
[25] Courts Act 1971, s.16 and Sched. 2.
[26] *Ibid.*, ss.16, 17 and 21.
[27] *Ibid.*, ss.21 and 23. New recorders are not specifically appointed for towns but s.54 provides that boroughs might make honorary appointments and advantage has been taken of this in some large towns such as Liverpool and Manchester to confer the title of Recorder of the town on a senior Circuit Judge.
[28] paras. 271–273.
[29] Courts Act 1971, s.5; See Practice Direction [1986] 1 W.L.R. 1041 (magistrates now to sit only for guilty pleas in trials on indictment).

appeals and committals from juvenile courts two justices must sit, both from the juvenile panel and the court must include a man and a woman. The Lord Chancellor may dispense with any requirement that they should sit, and any objection that the court is improperly constituted by reason of the presence or absence of magistrates must be taken at the time when the proceedings or the irregularity began. The statutory provisions and regulations allow for considerable flexibility in respect of the sitting of justices in the Crown Court.

It has also been provided that the High Court may sit anywhere in the country designated by the Lord Chancellor to take civil work.[30] Its timetable is no longer linked to the criminal timetable, though such sittings are often held in old assize court buildings.

The Lord Chancellor has divided towns which are court centres into three tiers. In the First Tier centres High Court judges sit to try both civil and criminal cases and circuit judges also sit, primarily to hear criminal cases although civil cases may be released to them or to recorders. In the Second Tier centres High Court and circuit judges try criminal cases, and in the more numerous Third Tier centres circuit judges try criminal cases.[31] In accordance with the recommendations of the Beeching Commission, the local Chancery Courts of Lancaster and Durham have been merged with the High Court, and the Vice-Chancellor of Lancaster is now a circuit judge.[32] The Central Criminal Court is now a sitting of the Crown Court though it retains its title. The Recorder and Common Serjeant of the City of London are now members of the Circuit bench, though they also retain their titles.[33] The Commission recommended that a number of historic local courts such as the Salford Hundred Court, the Liverpool Court of Passage and the Bristol Tolzey Court, which all had jurisdictions wider than that of the county court, should be abolished.[34] This has been done by the Courts Act 1971, but in London the Mayor's Court survives, though with its jurisdiction reduced to county court limits.[35]

Official Referees

The office and title of Official Referee was abolished, the existing holders becoming circuit judges; but rather quaintly their

---

[30] *Ibid.*, s.2.
[31] See I.R. Scott, *The Crown Court*, Appendix IV.
[32] Courts Act 1971, s.41 and Sched. 2. A High Court judge has now been appointed to this office.
[33] *Ibid.*, s.4(7) and Sched. 2.
[34] paras. 349–384.
[35] Courts Act 1971, ss.42 and 43.

separate work, concerned with cases involving prolonged examination of documents and accounts or scientific and local investigations, survives under the designation of "Official Referee's Business" and is taken by circuit judges.[36]

Circuit judges sit as county court judges. Recorders may also sit in these courts.[37]

A court service under the charge of the Lord Chancellor has been set up, and he is now also responsible for summoning juries.[38] The number of circuits has been reduced from seven to six and a Circuit Administrator, with headquarters and staff, has been appointed in each circuit. Presiding Judges have also been appointed to supervise aspects of administration.

The Criminal Justice Bill 1988 provides that summary offences may be included as additional counts when a more serious charge is tried on indictment and that when the defendant is convicted of an indictable offence and pleads guilty to associated summary offences the Crown Court may sentence him for those offences.

---

[36] *Ibid.*, s.25. Much of the work involves the construction and engineering industries.
[37] *Ibid.*, s.20.
[38] *Ibid.*, s.27 and ss.31–33. Now Juries Act 1974, s.2.

CHAPTER 5

County Courts

Origin

The County Courts Act 1846, established a system of local courts with a civil jurisdiction, and at the present day a vast number of actions, mostly for debts of small amount, are brought every year in these county courts. The position in 1846 was that the medieval local courts—the communal courts of the county and hundred,[1] the manorial and other feudal courts, and the borough courts—had fallen into decay, with the exception of manorial courts for copyhold conveyancing and some of the borough courts. The necessity of bringing actions into the royal courts at Westminster, even if the facts were tried at *nisi prius*,[2] often meant delay and expense out of all proportion to the value of the claim. Various attempts to remedy this state of affairs by providing local civil courts with cheap and speedy process had therefore been made in the eighteenth century.

---

[1] These were the ancient county court (Anglo-Saxon shire moot) presided over by the sheriff, in which the suitors (the freeholders of the county) applied the customary law; and the similar court of the hundred, a subdivision of the county, presided over by the sheriff or his bailiff.

[2] The civil side of Assizes. See above, Chap. 4. The Latin means "unless before" and derives from the commission which directed that a case should be heard at Westminster "unless before" a specified date the royal justices visited the county and took a verdict from a jury. In practice they always did.

Organisation

The law is contained mainly in the County Courts Act 1984, consolidating earlier statutes. The jurisdiction of the courts has been extended from time to time, but the general principles of the nineteenth-century legislation remain. There are about four hundred county court districts in England and Wales, in each of which county courts are held regularly. The districts are grouped into circuits, and at least one Circuit judge is appointed to each circuit. Circuit judges must be barristers of at least ten years' standing or Recorders of three years' standing.[3] They are appointed by the Crown on the recommendation of the Lord Chancellor.

Jurisdiction

The jurisdiction of a county court is limited to its district. The district is generally that in which the defendant resides or carries on business or where the cause of action arose. Jurisdiction is limited also by the value of the claim, unless both parties consent to the case being heard there instead of in the High Court.

Apart from the latter exception, a county court has jurisdiction in: (i) actions founded on contract or tort (except libel and slander, unless the defendant consents to the action being tried in a county court)[4] where the claim does not exceed £5,000[5]; (ii) actions for the recovery of land and questions of title to land, where the rateable value does not exceed £1,000; (iii) actions of an equitable nature such as administration of estates, execution of trusts, foreclosure and redemption of mortgages, and specific performance of contracts relating to land, where the value of the property, etc., concerned does not exceed £30,000; (iv) probate proceedings where the net value of the deceased's estate is less than £30,000. Some county courts also have a limited jurisdiction in Admiralty. In company insolvency they have jurisdiction

---

[3] Courts Act 1971, ss.16, 20 and 21. Administration of Justice Act 1977. See above, pp. 64–66 for the origin of these offices.

[4] The Committee on Defamation (1975) Cmnd. 5909 recommended that ordinary jurisdiction be given to the county court.

[5] The claim may be transferred to the High Court if an important question of law or fact is likely to arise; or if the Court considers that the county court limit will be exceeded or there is a counterclaim exceeding the limit. To ease congestion in the High Court, claims for less than £20,000 not involving difficult questions of law or fact, professional negligence, actions against the police, fraud or undue influence, fatal accidents or public interest are to be heard in the County Court. See Practice Statement (Listings) (1988) *The Times*, January 13.

concurrent with the High Court when the paid up capital of a company does not exceed £120,000 and the company's registered office is within the district[6] and in personal insolvency they have jurisdiction outside London.[7] Civil proceedings in county courts, within the limits of their jurisdiction, may be brought by the Crown[8] and against the Crown.[9]

The High Court may transfer to the county court an action which should have been commenced in the latter; and if an action which could have been tried in the county court is tried in the High Court the plaintiff, though successful, may lose all or part of the costs if he recovers less than certain specified amounts in different classes of action.

County courts have had jurisdiction in undefended matrimonial causes since 1967,[10] but they have no criminal jurisdiction.

Much of the time of the county courts is taken up with proceedings under social legislation such as Agricultural Holdings Acts, Rents Acts and the Consumer Credit Act 1974. Proceedings may also be brought in county courts to enforce the Sex Discrimination Act 1975, and the Race Relations Act 1976.

The proceedings are speedy and informal compared with those in the High Court.[11] The parties may be represented by barristers or solicitors. Very rarely a jury (of eight persons) is summoned.

In his manifold duties the judge has the assistance of the county court registrar who must be a solicitor of at least seven years' standing. In addition to his administrative functions, the registrar may deputise for the judge in undefended cases, defended actions involving not more than £500, and any other actions subject to any arrangements made by the judge. Appeal lies to the judge.

Recent legislation conferred an arbitral jurisdiction on county courts which is designed to make better provision for small claims. It is frequently administered by the registrar.[12] This was a response to complaints that the county court was failing to provide a satisfactory forum for such cases,[13] which also led to the setting up of arbitral tribunals to handle small consumer claims outside the ordinary court system.

[6] Insolvency Act 1986, s.117.
[7] *Ibid.*, s.373.
[8] Administration of Justice (Miscellaneous Provisions) Act 1933.
[9] Crown Proceedings Act 1947.
[10] Matrimonial Causes Act 1967.
[11] See below, p. 374 for procedure.
[12] Administration of Justice Act 1973, s.7.
[13] *Justice out of Reach* (1970), Consumer Council.

Appeals from County Courts

Since 1934 the right of appeal has lain direct to the Court of
Appeal; but the leave of the judge is now generally required if
the claim (or counterclaim if greater) is less than one half of the
county court limit for the case or if the appeal is from the judge
in his appellate capacity. Previously, under the Judicature Act
1873, appeal lay from county courts on a point of law to a
Divisional Court of the High Court, and thence to the Court of
Appeal. Appeals in insolvency matters go to a single judge of
the High Court and thereafter, with leave, to the Court of
Appeal, which is final.[14]

It has been proposed that all civil proceedings should
commence in the county court and only go to the High Court if
they involve questions of difficulty or importance. This proposal
is, however, highly controversial as is a proposal by the Law
Society for a merger of the County Court with the High Court.
This proposal is impliedly rejected in a recent report on the High
Court which does envisage raising the County Court limit of
£5,000 to £50,000.[15]

[14] Insolvency Act 1986, s.375.
[15] *Report of the Committee on the Deployment of the High Court Bench*, below, p. 82.

CHAPTER 6

The High Court of Justice

Creation of the Supreme Court of Judicature

In the year 1873 there was a multiplicity of superior courts in England, each with its own jurisdiction, procedure and staff, and its peculiar principles, terminology and practice.

At first instance there were three central courts administering different branches of the common law, and derived from the *Curia Regis*, from which they gradually separated during the thirteenth and fourteenth centuries. These were the *Court of Queen's Bench*[1] which issued prerogative writs against inferior courts and public officers, heard cases of trespass and other pleas of the Crown and certain other personal actions, and had an appellate civil and criminal jurisdiction by writ of error: the *Court of Common Pleas* (or Common Bench) which heard pleas between subject and subject in which the Sovereign's interests were not involved, particularly actions relating to land and debt: and the *Court of Exchequer*[2] which tried revenue cases and certain personal actions. The jurisdictions of the three common law courts in their later history overlapped to a great extent, largely owing to the use of procedural fictions by the Court of King's (Queen's) Bench through the Bill of Middlesex and Writ of

---

[1] Actions in this court were in early times said to be heard, as originally they were, *coram Rege.*; "before the King."

[2] Sometimes called the Exchequer of Pleas, to distinguish it from the Court of Exchequer Chamber.

Latitat with *ac etiam* clause,[3] by the Court of Common Pleas through the writ *quare clausum fregit* with *ac etiam* clause,[4] and by the Court of Exchequer through the writ of *quominus*.[5] There were also the *High Court of Chancery*, a fourteenth-century emanation of the King's Council, administering Equity: the *High Court of Admiralty*, also dating from the fourteenth century, administering Admiralty law: and the *Court for Divorce and Matrimonial Causes* and the *Court of Probate*, both created by statute in 1857 to take over matrimonial and testamentary causes from the Ecclesiastical Courts.

On appeal there were the *Court of Exchequer Chamber*, created in 1830 to supersede two existing courts of that name between the common law courts and the House of Lords: the *Court of Appeal in Chancery*, established in 1851, between the Court of Chancery and the House of Lords: and the *Judicial Committee of the Privy Council*, regularised by statute in 1833 to hear appeals from Colonial, Admiralty and Ecclesiastical Courts, but derived from the prerogative jurisdiction of the Privy Council.

In addition to these central courts there still remained a few courts which originated as franchise courts connected with *Palatinates*, such as the Court of Common Pleas at Lancaster, the Court of Pleas in Durham, and the Chancery Courts of Lancaster and Durham.

The greatest inconvenience of this state of affairs was the separation of the courts that administered common law and Equity. This had been only partially remedied by the Common Law Procedure Acts 1852–60, which gave to the common law courts a limited power to grant certain equitable remedies; and by the Chancery Amendment Acts 1852 and 1858, which gave to the Court of Chancery power to decide for itself questions of common law involved in cases before it, and certain powers of the common law courts such as the granting of damages and the taking of oral evidence. These statutes were passed on the recommendation of a series of Commissions inspired by the

---

[3] The Bill of Middlesex alleged a fictitious trespass by the defendant in Middlesex, this giving the court a general jurisdiction. The writ of *latitat* alleged that the defendant then "lay hid" in his locality outside Middlesex. In the seventeenth century statute restricted the effect of fictitious process and "ac etiam" (and also) introduced a statement of the true cause of action in order to evade this legislation.

[4] This was a fictitious allegation of trespass to land giving certain procedural advantages and *ac etiam* was added for the same reason as in Queen's Bench.

[5] This was a fictitious allegation that, because of the legal wrong alleged against the defendant, the plaintiff was "the less" able to satisfy his revenue obligations to the Crown, this giving the court a general jurisdiction.

work of Jeremy Bentham (1748–1832) and other individuals zealous for law reform.

The judicial system of England and Wales was entirely reorganised by the Supreme Court of Judicature Acts, passed in 1873 and 1875, which came into force together. The present system is contained in the consolidating Supreme Court Act 1981. The Acts of 1873–75 established a *Supreme Court of Judicature*, consisting of the *High Court of Justice* and the *Court of Appeal*. These courts are housed in the Strand, Westminster though the High Court also sits at a number of provincial centres. The *Crown Court* is also included in the Supreme Court by the Courts Act 1971.[6]

There are many district registries of the Supreme Court outside London where writs may be issued, and a number of district probate registries for non-contentious probate work.

1. THE HIGH COURT OF JUSTICE

Jurisdiction

The High Court of Justice incorporated the jurisdiction of the Courts of Queen's Bench (civil and criminal), Common Pleas, Exchequer (common law and revenue), Chancery, Admiralty, Divorce and Matrimonial Causes, Probate, Assize, Crown Cases Reserved, the Court of Common Pleas at Lancaster and the Court of Pleas in Durham. The jurisdiction of the London Court of Bankruptcy was added by the Bankruptcy Act 1883, and that of the Court for Crown Cases Reserved was taken away by the Criminal Appeal Act 1907.

The High Court became a court of first instance with practically unlimited jurisdiction.[7] It was also given appellate jurisdiction from the county courts established in 1846, most of which it lost to the Court of Appeal in 1934, and in cases stated from Quarter Sessions and Petty Sessions (now the Crown Court and Magistrates' Courts).

Each High Court judge was given the whole legal and equitable jurisdiction of the High Court, except in cases where two or more judges were required to sit together as a Divisional Court.

---

[6] Above, Chap. 4.

[7] Generally, if the defendant is in England or Wales, or the writ or notice of writ can be served on him abroad, and the property concerned (if land) is in England or Wales.

The High Court has jurisdiction to try civil proceedings by and against the Crown, within the limits allowed by the Crown Proceedings Act 1947.

The Divisions

The High Court was divided for convenience into Divisions, and provision was made whereby the Divisions could be altered from time to time by Order in Council; but the Divisions are not separate courts, and their existence does not affect the jurisdiction of each judge. The Divisions made in 1875 were: (i) the Chancery Division, (ii) the Queen's Bench Division, (iii) the Common Pleas Division, (iv) the Exchequer Division, and (v) the Probate, Divorce and Admiralty Division. By an Order in Council issued in 1880 the three common law Divisions were amalgamated into the Queen's Bench Division.

The Rule Committee of the Supreme Court and the Lord Chancellor have authority to assign certain causes and matters to a particular Division as may be convenient, and any particular jurisdiction of the High Court may now be assigned to two or more Divisions concurrently.[8] If a litigant brings his action in the wrong Division he will not lose the action altogether, as he would formerly have done if he sued in the wrong court, but he may be ordered to pay the costs of having the action transferred.

Composition of the High Court

The number of High Court judges has been gradually raised, until now there are more than eighty.[9] These puisne judges, as they are sometimes called, must be barristers of not less than ten years' standing. The Lord Chancellor allots them to the various Divisions. The other members of the court are the Lord Chief Justice, the President of the Family Division (formerly the Probate, Divorce and Admiralty Division) and the Vice-Chancellor.[10] It is also the duty of the Lords Justices of Appeal to sit in the High Court when requested by the Lord Chancellor to do so. The Courts Act 1971, makes provision for the Lord Chancellor to call upon Circuit judges or Recorders to sit as High Court judges, and for the appointment of Deputy High Court judges.

[8] Supreme Court Act 1981, s.61. Abolition of the Divisions is proposed, below, p. 82.

[9] The number may be increased by statutory Order in Council, after approval of the draft Order by resolution of each House. Now eighty-five (1987).

[10] The Lord Chancellor's functions as president of the Chancery Division are now handled by the Vice-Chancellor. See below, p. 77. See on this "The Vice-Chancellors" by The Vice-Chancellor (Sir Robert Megarry) (1982) 98 L.Q.R. 370.

(a) The Chancery Division

The Judicature Acts expressly assigned to the Chancery Division those matters which formerly had been within the exclusive jurisdiction of the Court of Chancery, in particular, the execution of trusts, the redemption and foreclosure of mortgages, the dissolution and accounts of partnerships, the administration of the estates of deceased persons, the rectification or cancellation of documents, the wardship of infants, and the specific performance of contracts for the sale or lease of land.[11]

The administration of Companies Acts[12] and Bankruptcy Acts,[13] including the bankruptcy jurisdiction for London, the Landlord and Tenant Acts and the hearing of applications under the property statutes of 1925 have subsequently been assigned to this Division. Since 1950 the Chancery Division has taken over from the Queen's Bench Division the revenue jurisdiction of the former Court of Exchequer. This now includes the hearing of income tax appeals from the Commissioners of Inland Revenue. Judges of the Chancery Division also sit as the Court of Protection to hear applications concerning the management of the property of mental patients,[14] and as the Patents Court under the Patents Act 1977.

The Administration of Justice Act 1970, transferred the jurisdiction in wardship, adoption and guardianship to the new *Family Division,* but transferred contentious probate work (probate in solemn form) to the Chancery Division.[15]

About twelve puisne judges are allotted to the Chancery Division. The Lord Chancellor is its president, but in practice he no longer sits at first instance. Of the other former judges of the Court of Chancery, the Master of the Rolls sits in the Court of Appeal and the former Vice-Chancellors have been abolished. These Vice-Chancellors corresponded to the present puisne judges. The title of Vice-Chancellor was revived in 1970 for a judge of the Division who is responsible to the Lord Chancellor for the organisation and management of the business of the Division.

---

[11] See now, Supreme Court Act 1981, s.61 and Sched. 1.
[12] "The Companies Court" is not a distinct tribunal but merely describes the High Court when exercising companies jurisdiction. *Fabric Sales* v. *Eratex* [1984] 1 W.L.R. 863.
[13] Now Insolvency Act 1986.
[14] Mental Health Act 1983.
[15] Probate is concerned with the authenticity and validity of wills and the appointment of personal representatives.

Masters of the Chancery Division. There are six Masters of the Chancery Division who are barristers or solicitors appointed by the Lord Chancellor. They are the successors of the former Chief Clerks and are to be distinguished from the former Masters in Chancery who were abolished in 1852.

Applications are made to the Masters in Chambers in the preliminary stages of litigation in the Chancery Division, and they make orders thereon in the name of the judge to whom they are assigned. Complicated accounts and inquiries are also referred to them. A party may adjourn the matter into court if he is not satisfied with the Master's ruling.

(b) The Queen's Bench Division

This Division is presided over by the Lord Chief Justice of England, the successor to the Chief Justices of the Queen's Bench.[16] The actual strength at the present day is about fifty puisne judges.

Two main classes of work are dealt with by the Queen's Bench Division:[17]

(i) It tries *civil actions* corresponding to those which used to be brought in the three common law courts, and which are not properly brought in county courts. It was the practice after 1895 to draw up a special list of commercial actions to be tried in the "Commercial Court." This was really one of the judges of the Queen's Bench Division who was experienced in commercial law, and who could dispense with some of the formalities of pleading and evidence.

The Administration of Justice Act 1970, created a new Commercial Court within this Division, and also made provision for judges of this Court to sit as arbitrators. Admiralty jurisdiction was also transferred from the former Probate, Divorce and Admiralty Division by this Act to the Queen's Bench Division and a new Admiralty Court was set up to administer it. For historical reasons Admiralty jurisdiction is now largely concerned with collisions at sea, salvage and claims for seamen's wages. Other transactions with a maritime element, such as carriage of goods by sea, are dealt with under the other jurisdiction of the Division.

(ii) The Queen's Bench Division exercises on the *"Crown Side"* the supervisory and criminal jurisdiction of the former court of

[16] The offices of Chief Justice of the Common Pleas and Chief Baron of the Exchequer were abolished in 1880.
[17] See now, Supreme Court Act 1981, s.61 and Sched. 1.

King's (Queen's) Bench. The supervisory jurisdiction includes the issue of the prerogative writ of habeas corpus and through the process of judicial review the orders (formerly prerogative writs) of certiorari, prohibition and mandamus.[18] The criminal business formerly included the taking of criminal assizes, but judges of the Division now sit both in the Crown Court and the Court of Appeal, Criminal Division.[19]

Before 1938 the Queen's Bench Division had a criminal jurisdiction at first instance concurrent with that of assizes and quarter sessions, though it was rarely exercised except by way of certiorari where a fair trial could not be expected locally and was further restricted in 1948.

The Courts Act 1971, now provides that all trials on indictment must be in the Crown Court. This abolished trial at Bar in the Queen's Bench Division. Proceedings by way of criminal information in the High Court were abolished by the Criminal Law Act 1967, and the Courts Act 1971, gives wide powers to the Crown Court to fix the place of trial if either party is dissatisfied. A Divisional Court of the Queen's Bench Division[20] hears appeals on points of law by way of case stated from Magistrates' Courts and from the Crown Court when the court has exercised appellate jurisdiction over Magistrates' Courts.

Two judges of the Queen's Bench Division may form an Election Court to determine a disputed Parliamentary election. Their decision is notified to the Speaker, and adopted by the House of Commons.[21]

Masters of the Queen's Bench Division. There are eleven Masters of the Supreme Court attached to the Queen's Bench Division who must be barristers or solicitors of ten years' standing. The Masters of the Queen's Bench Division supervise the Central Office of the Supreme Court in which official documents are issued and registered, the Master of the Crown Office (appointed by the Lord Chief Justice) being in charge of the Crown side. The Masters may exercise most of the functions of the judge in chambers and, with consent of the parties can try actions. They may also give summary judgment under Ord.14.[22]

---

[18] R.S.C. Ord. 53. See below, pp. 112–113.
[19] See above, pp. 64–66 for the abolition of assizes by the Courts Act 1971, and their replacement by the Crown Court.
[20] See below, p. 81.
[21] Representation of the People Act 1983.
[22] See below, Chap. 21, p. 369.

(c) The Family Division

This Division, formerly known as the Probate, Divorce and Admiralty Division, was re-named when the Administration of Justice Act 1970, came into operation in 1971. The Act also effected a considerable redistribution of business between the Divisions of the High Court. Admiralty work was transferred to a new Admiralty Court in the Queen's Bench Division, contentious probate work (probate in solemn form) was transferred to the Chancery Division, whilst adoption and wardship proceedings were transferred from the Chancery Division to the Family Division, which retained all the former matrimonial and family jurisdiction. Probate in common form, when there is no dispute as to the proof of a will and which is therefore largely administrative, remains under the supervision of the Family Division. The Division consists of a President and about sixteen puisne judges.

History. The Judicature Acts assigned to the Division the jurisdiction formerly exercised separately by the three Courts of Probate, Divorce and Matrimonial Causes, and Admiralty. At first sight its business seemed to comprise a heterogeneous assortment of matters, but history explained, if it did not excuse, the existence of this Division. The Admiralty law administered by the Court of Admiralty was based on an international body of maritime customs, formerly applied in local maritime courts and originally derived in large part from Roman civil law; while the law administered in the Court of Probate and the Court of Divorce and Matrimonial Causes[23] was based on the ecclesiastical law formerly administered in Ecclesiastical Courts, and originally derived in large part from Roman canon law. Although both systems had become anglicised, they were fundamentally Roman rather than English in substance and procedure, and until 1857 they were administered in special courts at Doctors' Commons by judges and practitioners who were "civilians," that is, learned in Roman law.

With the passage of time the Roman law background became of diminishing importance, and this brought to the fore both the incongruity of associating these very diverse subjects in the one Division and the fact that Admiralty work was linked to the commercial work of the Queen's Bench Division and Probate to the work of the Chancery Division. At the same time the

[23] *e.g.*, nullity of marriage and judicial separation. Divorce, in the sense of the dissolution of a valid marriage, was introduced by statute in 1857; previously it was only possible by private Act of Parliament. See below, Chap. 20.

matrimonial and family business of the Probate, Divorce and Admiralty Division, originally small, had grown to an extent out of all proportion to the other elements of the Division's jurisdiction. This explains why redistribution was felt to be necessary and the pattern which it followed.[24]

Divisional Courts

The judges of the common law courts used to sit together (*in banc*) to hear appeals from inferior courts and to deliver judgment in cases heard at *nisi prius*, whereas trials at first instance in the other courts had always been before a single judge. The Judicature Acts provided that the trial of actions at first instance in the High Court should generally be before a single judge, although certain cases should be tried by a Divisional Court. At the present day, statutes or rules of court require two or more judges of the High Court to sit together in certain cases as a Divisional Court.[25]

A Divisional Court of the Family Division hears appeals from Magistrates' Courts in such civil matters as separation and maintenance orders. The most important use of Divisional Courts, however, is in the Queen's Bench Division.

Divisional Courts of the Queen's Bench Division. Since appeals from county courts were diverted by statute in 1934 direct to the Court of Appeal, the work of Divisional Courts of the Queen's (King's) Bench Division has been mainly of a criminal or administrative nature. It includes the following:

(i) the issue of the writ of habeas corpus and the orders of certiorari, prohibition and mandamus[26];

(ii) the determination of questions of law on cases stated by the Crown Court, Magistrates' Courts,[27] or certain administrative tribunals[28];

(iii) appeals from certain inferior courts, *e.g.*, from the justices in the exercise of their civil jurisdiction under certain statutes; and

(iv) applications relating to parliamentary and local government election petitions.

---

[24] See now, Supreme Court Act 1981, s.61 and Sched. 1.

[25] Supreme Court Act 1981, s.66.

[26] For an account of these proceedings, see O. Hood Phillips, *Constitutional and Administrative Law* (7th ed.), pp. 682–689 *et seq.* See also, below, pp. 112–113.

[27] The High Court has power to reverse, amend or affirm the order of the Magistrates' Court or the Crown Court or to remit it to the magistrates' reconsideration or to make such order as it thinks fit.

[28] Tribunals and Inquiries Act 1971, s.13.

Official Referees

Before the Courts Act 1971, cases involving prolonged examination of documents or accounts might be referred to an Official Referee for trial, and the court might refer questions of fact to an Official Referee for inquiry and report. The Courts Act 1971, abolished the office of Official Referee, but provides that the work they had formerly done was to be known as "official referees' business" and to be carried out by nominated Circuit judges.

2. THE HIGH COURT IN THE PROVINCES

Before the Courts Act 1971, the civil side of assizes provided throughout the country periodic courts administering the civil jurisdiction of the Queen's Bench Division and the matrimonial jurisdiction of the Probate, Divorce and Admiralty Division. High Court Chancery jurisdiction was provided in their areas by the Palatine courts of Lancaster and Durham. It has been seen that the assize system was criticised by the Beeching Commission because of the inflexibility of its timetabling and the fact that the timetable for criminal work took precedence over that for civil business.[29] Following the recommendations of the Beeching Commission, the Courts Act 1971, abolished civil assizes, and provides that the High Court may sit at any place in England or Wales determined by the Lord Chancellor. Sittings are in fact held at certain "First tier" centres and the timetable is no longer linked to that for criminal work. The work continues to be largely that of the civil side of the Queen's Bench Division. The Palatine Chancery courts of Lancaster and Durham have been merged in the High Court, but the Vice-Chancellor of Lancaster sits not only in Manchester, Liverpool and Preston, but also in Leeds and Newcastle, administering a High Court Chancery jurisdiction.[30]

Reform

Lord Donaldson M.R. has said that the time has come to abolish the Divisions of the High Court,[31] as both judges and barristers are often familiar with the work of more than one Division and the Divisions result in maldistribution of work.

[29] See above, pp. 64–65.
[30] [1972] 1 W.L.R. 1; 1 All E.R. 103.
[31] *Barclay's Bank* v. *Bemister* (1987) *The Times*, December 15, supported by the *Report of the Committee on the Deployment of the High Court Bench* (1988) *The Times*, May 12.

CHAPTER 7

The Court of Appeal

Reference has been made at the beginning of the previous chapter to the creation by the Judicature Acts 1873–75, of the Supreme Court of Judicature, of which the Court of Appeal forms part. The composition and powers of this court now rest on the Supreme Court Act 1981, and the Criminal Appeal Acts 1966 and 1968. From its creation until the coming into force of the Criminal Appeal Act 1966, the Court of Appeal was a purely civil court, corresponding in composition and function to the present Civil Division; the 1966 Act brought into being the Criminal Division to replace the Court of Criminal Appeal set up by the Criminal Appeal Act 1907.

Composition of the court[1]

The Lord Chancellor (President), any ex-Lord Chancellor and any Lord of Appeal in Ordinary who consents to act, the Lord Chief Justice, the Master of the Rolls, the Vice-Chancellor and the President of the Family Division are *ex-officio* members of the Court of Appeal. The only one of these who sits regularly in the Civil Division of the Court of Appeal is the Master of the Rolls, who gave up sitting at first instance in the Chancery Division in 1881. He was for long a judge of the Court of Chancery, but originally he was the senior of those officials known as the Masters in Chancery, and had the duty of preserving the rolls of

[1] See Supreme Court Act 1981, ss.2, 3, 15–18 and 53–60.

the court.[2] The Lord Chief Justice presides in the Criminal Division.

The Master of the Rolls is assisted in the Court of Appeal, Civil Division, by the Lords Justices of Appeal, whose office was created by the Judicature Acts 1873–75, and who now number up to twenty-eight.[3] They must be barristers of not less than fifteen years' standing, unless they are transferred from the High Court. The Lord Chancellor may also require a High Court judge to assist in the Civil Division, and the Lord Chief Justice after consulting the Master of the Rolls may require the attendance of any judge of the High Court in the Criminal Division, this being regularly done.

Any number of courts of either Division may sit at the same time.

1. THE CIVIL DIVISION

Jurisdiction

The Judicature Acts 1873–1875, gave to the Court of Appeal the civil jurisdiction formerly exercised by the Court of Appeal in Chancery and the Lord Chancellor (appeals from the Court of Chancery and the Vice-Chancellors[4] and bankruptcy and lunacy appeals); the Court of Exchequer Chamber (appeals from the three common law courts); the Privy Council on appeal from the Court of Admiralty, except in Prize Cases; the Court of Appeal in Chancery of the County Palatine of Lancaster (appeals from the Chancery Court of Lancaster)[5]; and the Lord Warden of the Stannaries (appeals from the Stannary Courts).[6] Appeals from county courts were added in 1934,[7] from the Restrictive Practices Court in 1956,[8] and from the Employment Appeal Tribunal in 1975.[9] Appeals in civil proceedings by and against the Crown lie in a similar way to appeals in actions between subjects.[10] All this jurisdiction was given to the Civil Division of the Court of Appeal when the Criminal Division was created in 1966.

---

[2] The records of the superior courts were formerly deemed to be in the custody of the Master of the Rolls; but the Public Records Act 1958, gave to the Lord Chancellor general responsibility for court records, and made the Master of the Rolls chairman of the Lord Chancellor's Advisory Council on Public Records.

[3] Supreme Court Act 1981, s.10. Maximum Number of Judges Order 1987.

[4] For the office of Vice-Chancellor, see above, pp. 76–77.

[5] This court has now been merged with the High Court above, pp. 67 and 82.

[6] Below, p. 104.

[7] Administration of Justice (Appeals) Act 1934.

[8] Restrictive Trade Practices Act 1956.

[9] Employment Protection Act 1975.

[10] Crown Proceedings Act 1947.

Normally three judges of the Court of Appeal hear an appeal, unless the parties consent or the appeal is in an interlocutory matter,[11] when two sit. The Civil Division has no jurisdiction "in any criminal cause or matter."[12] These words have been construed as meaning a matter of which the direct outcome may be the person's trial and punishment for an illegal act by a court claiming jurisdiction.[13] The main work of this Division consists in hearing appeals—except in criminal matters —from the three Divisions of the High Court (including Divisional Courts), and county courts. In appeals from county courts the general rule is that, except by consent of the other party, no point of law may be argued that was not raised in the county court.

In two respects the Civil Division follows the former Court of Appeal in Chancery rather than the Court of Exchequer Chamber, for, except in applications for a new trial or to set aside the verdict of a jury, it rehears the case on its merits (with a note of the oral evidence) instead of confining its attention to errors apparent on the face of the record; and it has a permanent staff of special judges (the Lords Justices of Appeal) instead of being composed of puisne judges appointed *pro hac vice* to hear particular appeals.

The office of Registrar of Civil Appeals to handle the administrative work of the Division was created by the Supreme Court Act 1981.[14]

Right of Appeal to Court of Appeal

There is a general right of appeal to the Court of Appeal, Civil Division, from final orders of the High Court in civil matters, on a question of law or fact; and a general right of appeal from a Divisional Court in applications for habeas corpus or one of the prerogative orders, unless the order is sought in connection with a criminal cause or matter. The leave of the court below or of the Court of Appeal, Civil Division, is, however, usually necessary in appeals from interlocutory orders or judgments,

---

[11] Supreme Court Act 1981, s.54(2)(e) gives the Lord Chancellor power to direct that certain types of case be heard by a court of two judges and use has been made of this power since 1982, in particular for appeals from county courts. If a case is likely to be complex counsel should ask for a court of three. *Coldunell* v. *Gallon* [1986] Q.B. 1184. A single judge may deal with some procedural matters.

[12] Supreme Court Act 1981, s.18(1).

[13] *Amand* v. *Home Secretary and Minister of Defence of the Royal Netherlands Government* [1943] A.C. 147.

[14] s.89.

and in appeals from Divisional Courts in the exercise of their appellate jurisdiction.[14a]

The Civil Division may either order a new trial, *e.g.*, because the judge misdirected the jury, or reverse the decision of the court below. It is very reluctant to disturb findings of fact, especially if the case was tried with a jury.[15]

It will not alter an award of damages merely because it would itself have awarded a different sum but will intervene if the sum awarded is either so large or so small that it is clear the court below acted on some wrong principle.[16]

Certain appeals from county courts require leave.[17]

Appeals from the Court of Appeal, Civil Division

Appeal lies from the Civil Division to the House of Lords, with leave either of the Court of Appeal or of the House of Lords,[18] except where by special statutory provisions the decision of the Court of Appeal is final. Examples of these last are appeals from the High Court on insolvency appeals from a county court,[19] appeals from county courts in probate matters,[20] and appeals from an election court.[21]

The Judicature Act 1873, envisaged the new Court of Appeal as the final court of appeal for civil cases. Besides providing for the abolition of the House of Lords,[22] it made another provision which never came into force, namely, that the jurisdiction of the Privy Council might be transferred by Order in Council to the Court of Appeal.[23] It has been suggested for some time that there is no need for two courts of appeal above the High Court, and that if the House of Lords is to be retained, the Court of Appeal might well be abolished. One difficulty in making the English Court of Appeal the highest appellate court is that this would not be appropriate for appeals from Scotland, Northern Ireland or overseas territories; and on the other hand it might not be thought desirable that cases should go direct from the

---

[14a] When leave is required it may be obtained from a court or tribunal of the same standing as the original, not necessarily the original court itself. *Warren v. Kilroe* [1988] 1 All E.R. 638.

[15] Above, pp. 42–44 and below Chap. 21, pp. 372–373 on direct and inferential facts.

[16] *Ward* v. *James* [1966] 1 Q.B. 273.

[17] See above, Chap. 5, p. 72.

[18] Below, Chap. 8.

[19] Insolvency Act 1986, s.375.

[20] County Courts Act 1984.

[21] Representation of the People Act 1983.

[22] Below, p. 92.

[23] Below, pp. 98–99.

High Court and county courts to such an august tribunal as the House of Lords, though this is now allowed to a limited extent in the case of "leap-frog" appeals from the High Court.[24]

2. THE CRIMINAL DIVISION

History

At common law there was no appeal from a criminal conviction, although in rare cases a prisoner might succeed in the Court of King's (Queen's) Bench on a writ of error from assizes or quarter sessions on account of some error apparent on the record. It became usual for a judge to reserve difficult questions of law until he had consulted the other judges at Westminster. In 1848 the Court for the Crown Cases Reserved, consisting of common law judges, was established to decide questions of law reserved by the justices of assize, recorders or chairmen of quarter sessions, the sentence being respited until its decision was given. There was, however, no appeal on questions of fact, and no certainty that a difficult point of law would be reserved by the trial judge. There was always the royal prerogative of mercy exercisable by the Home Secretary, whereby a convicted person might be reprieved or pardoned for reasons extraneous to the trial, or on evidence which would not be admissible in a court of law. But that the position was unsatisfactory was shown by the case of Adolf Beck (1905), who was twice convicted and was sentenced to penal servitude through being mistakenly identified for another person. This brought matters to a head. The Court for Crown Cases Reserved was abolished, and a Court of Criminal Appeal was created by the Criminal Appeal Act 1907, consisting of the Lord Chief Justice and all the judges of the Queen's Bench Division of the High Court.[25]

The Court of Appeal, Criminal Division, was set up on the recommendation of the Donovan Committee which reported in 1965.[26] The principal criticisms of the Court of Criminal Appeal were that lack of permanent judicial staff led to discrepancies in rulings both on matters of law and on sentencing. The Committee rejected a full-time appeal court, a two-tier court and permanently selected puisne judges of the Queen's Bench

---

[24] Below, p. 95. Administration of Justice Act 1969. See Blom-Cooper and Drewry *Final Appeal*, Ch. XIX, pp. 396–413 for discussion.

[25] Criminal Appeal (Amendment) Act 1908.

[26] *Report of Interdepartmental Committee on the Court of Criminal Appeal*, Cmnd. 2755.

Division, but recommended an increase in the number of Lords Justices of Appeal and the setting up of the present Criminal Division. Queen's Bench Division judges would be summoned to sit in the new Division because their trial experience would be valuable to the Court and appeal work would be useful for them. Most of the recommendations of the Donovan Committee were accepted, and the Criminal Division of the Court of Appeal was created by the Criminal Appeal Act 1966. The law on this subject is now largely consolidated by the Criminal Appeal Act 1968.

At least three judges must sit to hear an appeal against a final order or judgment. The Criminal Division is usually composed of the Lord Chief Justice, a Lord Justice of Appeal and a judge of the Queen's Bench Division. There may also be another court composed of a Lord Justice and two judges of the Queen's Bench Division. One judgment only is pronounced, unless the presiding judge considers that the question is one of law on which it is convenient that separate judgments should be pronounced. The Criminal Division may sit during vacation if necessary.

Right of Appeal to the Court of Appeal

This matter is now governed by Part I of the Criminal Appeal Act 1968. A person convicted on indictment has a right of appeal against conviction on a question of law alone, or (with leave of the Court of Appeal or on a certificate of the trial judge) on a question of fact alone or a question of mixed law and fact (section 1).[27] The Court of Appeal must allow an appeal against conviction if they think (a) that the conviction should be set aside on the ground that in all the circumstances of the case it is unsafe or unsatisfactory; or (b) that the judgment of the trial court should be set aside on the ground of a wrong decision on any question of law; or (c) that there was a material irregularity in the course of the trial; provided that the court may, although they are of opinion that the point raised might be decided in

---

[27] Replacing the Criminal Appeal Act 1907, s.3, as amended by the Criminal Appeal Act 1966. There is no right to a second appeal, except when the first was a nullity or by its dismissal the appellant suffered an injustice: *R.* v. *Pinfold* [1988] 2 W.L.R. 635. Allowing a trial to proceed against an unrepresented defendant who wished to be represented and held a legal aid certificate was a material irregularity, *R.* v. *McAllister* (1988) *The Times*, February 25. Where the defendant was in effect charged with three different thefts on one count, the case having taken an unforeseen turn, and prosecuting counsel did not make submission on this or a final speech, the conviction was unsatisfactory and unsafe, *R.* v. *Bagshaw* (1988) *The Times*, January 13.

favour of the appellant, dismiss the appeal if they consider that no miscarriage of justice has actually occurred (section 2).[28] The court may substitute conviction of an alternative offence if it appears that the jury must have been satisfied of facts which proved the appellant guilty of that other offence (section 3). Where the Court of Appeal allows an appeal against conviction only on the basis of evidence which the court itself orders to be produced to it under section 23, that is, on the basis of fresh evidence not tendered at the trial and it appears that the interests of justice so require, they may order a retrial (section 7).[29] A person who has been convicted on indictment may, with leave of the Court of Appeal, appeal against sentence, not being a sentence fixed by law (sections 9, 11). A person who has been dealt with by the Crown Court (otherwise than on appeal from a Magistrates' Court) but not on indictment may also, with leave of the Court of Appeal, appeal against sentence subject to certain conditions (sections 10, 11). The Court of Appeal may quash the sentence and replace it with such other sentence as they think appropriate and as the court below had power to pass; but they may not deal with the appellant more severely than he was dealt with by the court below (section 11).[30] There is also an appeal against a verdict of not guilty by reason of insanity (sections 12, 13).[31]

The Court of Appeal may grant the appellant bail pending his appeal. The time during which an appellant is in custody pending his appeal is to be reckoned as part of his sentence, unless the Court of Appeal direct otherwise for reasons stated; but any time during which he is on bail is to be disregarded in computing his sentence.

A single judge may make certain orders such as giving leave to appeal or granting bail. On the other hand, a judge may not sit in the Criminal Division of the Court of Appeal on the hearing of any appeal against conviction or sentence from himself or any court of which he was a member.[32]

---

[28] Replacing with amendment s.4(1) of the 1907 Act, as amended by the 1966 Act and Criminal Law Act 1977, s.44. This is the well-known "proviso." The proviso cannot be used if the trial was a nullity because of a defective indictment *R.* v. *Newland* [1988] 2 W.L.R. 382. See also *Att.-Gen. Hong Kong* v. *Yip Kai Foon* [1988] 2 W.L.R. 326.

[29] Extended by Criminal Justice Bill 1988. If the original trial was a nullity a *venire de novo*, in effect a re-trial may be ordered, *R.* v. *Rose* [1982] A.C. 822.

[30] The Court of Criminal Appeal before 1966 had power to increase a sentence on appeal.

[31] Verdict introduced by the Criminal Procedure (Insanity) Act 1964, in place of the verdict of "guilty but insane" introduced in 1883.

[32] Criminal Appeal Act 1966.

Reference by the Home Secretary

Where a person has been convicted on indictment, or been tried on indictment and found not guilty by reason of insanity, the Home Secretary may at any time either refer the whole case to the Court of Appeal, and the case is then to be treated as an appeal to the Court by that person; or refer any point to the Court for their opinion. No application from the person concerned is necessary (Criminal Appeal Act 1968, s.17).[33]

Reference by the Attorney-General

A remarkable innovation was effected by the Criminal Justice Act 1972, s.36, which allows the Attorney-General to refer to the Court of Appeal, Criminal Division, a point of law following an acquittal on indictment, for the opinion of the court. The person acquitted is safeguarded since his acquittal is not to be affected, he may be represented if he wishes and he is not to be identified without his consent. When the Court of Appeal have given their opinion they may further refer the point to the House of Lords if they think the point ought to be considered by the House. This is a considerable inroad into the general rule that English courts will not give advisory opinions when there is no real issue between parties.[34]

The Criminal Justice Bill 1988 would enable the Attorney-General when he considers a sentence in the Crown Court is unduly lenient to refer the case with leave to the Court of Appeal, to increase it if they think it inadequate. A point of law may, with leave, be further referred to the House of Lords, if the Court of Appeal certifies it is of general public importance.

Appeals from the Court of Appeal, Criminal Division

Appeal lies, subject to certain conditions, from the Court of Appeal, Criminal Division, to the House of Lords.[35]

---

[33] Replacing Criminal Appeal Act 1907, s.19, which until the Administration of Justice Act 1960, was confined to the consideration of petitions for the exercise of the prerogative of mercy.

[34] See *e.g.*, *Sun Life of Canada* v. *Jervis* [1944] A.C. 111. *Ainsbury* v. *Millington* [1987] 1 W.L.R. 379n. But see below, p. 101 for special references to the Judicial Committee of the Privy Council.

[35] Below, Chap. 8.

CHAPTER 8

The House of Lords, the Judicial Committee and the European Court

1. THE HOUSE OF LORDS

Introduction

The word "court" (*curia*) was used in medieval times, as it still is, in several different senses. Its primary sense now in the language of lawyers is a body exercising judicial functions, and secondarily, the place where it sits. The expression "The High Court of Parliament" used, for example, in the Book of Common Prayer and in Coke's *Institutes*, implies that Parliament is a court. Putting aside the jurisdiction of each House over its own proceedings and the Committee of Privileges of the House of Lords, however, we may say that for legal purposes at the present day the High Court of Parliament means the House of Lords functioning judicially. The origin of the House of Lords is to be found in the feudal Great Council (*magnum concilium*) of Norman times, and may even be traced back to the Anglo-Saxon Witenagemot. The primary function of the King's Council in Parliament down to the fourteenth century was judicial.

The jurisdiction of the House of Lords is mainly appellate. It has no first instance jurisdiction in civil cases[1] or in

---

[1] *Skinner* v. *East India Co.* (1666) 6 St.Tr. 710.

91

criminal cases,[2] though until 1948 it had an ancient customary jurisdiction to try peers for treason and felony or misprision of either.

The procedure of impeachment, whereby the House of Lords has jurisdiction to try persons in high places who are indicted by the Commons for political misdemeanours or serious crimes, has become obsolete through the development of une convention of ministerial responsibility.[3]

Criticism of Double Appeals[4]

It will be seen that appeal in many cases lies first to the Court of Appeal and then to the House of Lords. There has been much criticism of this two-tier system of appeals. Duplication of appeals is thought to be inadvisable on several grounds; namely, that the present system is expensive, dilatory and irrational because the case of the party finally successful may have received the support of a minority of the judges (including the judge at first instance) who heard the case. One suggestion made is to constitute the Court of Appeal as the final appeal court, strengthened with the addition of the Law Lords; but in that event separate provision for appeals from Scotland and Northern Ireland would need to be made, as the Court of Appeal is an appeal court for England and Wales. Another suggestion is to merge the jurisdiction of the Court of Appeal with that of the House of Lords, perhaps enabling Lords Justices of Appeal to sit in the Appellate Committee of the House; but appeals to the House of Lords would have to be made less expensive and more speedy than now.[5]

Civil Appeals

England

It was affirmed by all the judges in the reign of Henry VII that writs of error from the King's Bench lay not to the Council but to

---

[2] *Cf. Floyd's Case* (1621) 2 St.Tr. 1153.

[3] The Select Committee on Parliamentary Privilege in 1967 recommended the abolition of this procedure: (1967) H.C. 34.

[4] See, *e.g.*, Gerald Gardiner and Andrew Martin, *Law Reform Now* (1963); Lord Radcliffe (1973) 36 M.L.R. 559; R. M. Jackson, *Machinery of Justice in England* (7th ed., 1977), pp. 100–104; L. Blom-Cooper, Q.C., and G. Drewry, *Final Appeal: A Study of the House of Lords in its Judicial Capacity* (1972), Chap. 19. See also, R. Stevens, *Law and Politics*; Paterson, *The Law Lords*.

[5] And for the House of Lords and the Judicial Committee of the Privy Council, see below, p. 99.

Parliament.[6] This meant the Council in Parliament, and would refer to the Lords but not to the Commons, who were not councillors. Anyway, the Commons had always been concerned primarily with the satisfaction of the grievances of those whom they represented, and they wanted to avoid the task of dealing with judicial matters. In common law cases, then, error lay to the House of Lords from the King's Bench and the Courts of Exchequer Chamber. It was finally decided in *Shirley* v. *Fagg*[7] that the House of Lords had jurisdiction to hear appeals from the Lord Chancellor and the Court of Chancery; and after 1851 appeal lay from the Court of Appeal in Chancery established in that year.

Few of the Lords had legal qualifications, and the House discouraged reports of its proceedings, so that the House of Lords was scarcely regarded as a regular and ordinary court of justice before the end of the eighteenth century. It has only attained its present pre-eminence as an expositor of legal principles since its reconstitution in 1876. Before that time, the most learned pronouncements often came either from the Exchequer Chamber or from the judges who were called upon to advise their Lordships. An attempt was made to reinforce the legal strength of the House of Lords, without increasing the number of hereditary peers, by the exercise of the prerogative in creating Baron Parke[8] a peer for life; but this device was frustrated by the decision that life peer would not be entitled at common law to sit and vote in the House of Lords.[9] A few years later, Parliament went so far as to provide for the abolition of the appellate jurisdiction of the House of Lords by the Judicature Act 1873. Before this provision came into force, however, a Conservative Government succeeded the Liberal Government and, partly for fear that the abolition of its appellate jurisdiction might be merely the prelude to the total abolition of the House of Lords, it decided to preserve this jurisdiction, and this was done by the Appellate Jurisdiction Act 1876. The House of Lords in its judicial capacity was indeed given a fresh and more vigorous lease of life in hearing appeals from the new Court of Appeal and by the introduction of Lords of Appeal in Ordinary. Probably by an oversight, it was not included

---

[6] Y.B. 1 Hen. 7, P., pl. 5.

[7] (1675) 6 St.Tr. 1122.

[8] He was not a peer, but one of the judges of the Court of Exchequer who were called "Barons."

[9] *Wensleydale Peerage Case* (1856) 5 H.L.C. 958.

in the "Supreme Court of Judicature," the name given by the Judicature Acts 1873–75, to the Court of Appeal and the High Court.[10]

Scotland

When the Union with Scotland was being negotiated, some discussion took place in the English House of Lords as to whether the union of the Parliaments of England and Scotland would result in civil appeals lying to the House of Lords of Great Britain in Scottish cases. Appeal did not apparently lie to the Scottish House of Lords, and there was a good deal of opposition in Scotland to the idea of the new British House of Lords exercising jurisdiction over the courts of that country. The matter was purposely omitted from the English and Scottish Acts of Union 1706, which ratified the treaty. Soon afterwards, in the case of the episcopalian *Greenshields* (1711),[11] the House of Lords assumed such jurisdiction without controversy, and since then it has regularly heard appeals from the Court of Session, the superior civil court of Scotland. The House takes judicial notice of Scots law.

Northern Ireland

Express provision was made in the Act of Union with Ireland, 1800, giving to the House of Lords of the United Kingdom an appellate jurisdiction in civil cases from Irish courts similar to that which it exercised over English courts. Since the Irish Free State (now the Republic of Ireland) ceased to form part of the United Kingdom in 1922, this jurisdiction is limited to hearing appeals from Northern Ireland.[12]

Right of Appeal in Civil Cases

Appeal to the House of Lords from the Court of Appeal, Civil Division, lies with the leave either of the Court of Appeal or of the House of Lords,[13] except in cases where by various statutes the decision of the Court of Appeal

---

[10] The Crown Court was included in the Supreme Court by the Courts Act 1971; above, p. 66.

[11] Robertson, 12; Dicey and Rait, *Thoughts on the Union between England and Scotland*, pp. 194–195.

[12] Government of Ireland Act 1920; Northern Ireland Act 1962.

[13] Administration of Justice (Appeals) Act 1934.

is declared to be final. Appeals are nearly always, although they need not be, on questions of law.

Appeal lies in civil proceedings by and against the Crown from courts in the United Kingdom in a similar manner as appeals in actions between subjects.[14]

The Administration of Justice Act 1969, in order to save costs, provides that appeals may in certain cases go direct from the High Court to the House of Lords. This is popularly known as "leap-frogging" the Court of Appeal, though "by-passing" would be more precise. A High Court judge, with the consent of both parties, may certify that a sufficient case for an appeal direct to the House of Lords has been made out to justify an application to the Appeal Committee of the House of Lords for leave to bring such appeal, if a point of law of general public importance is involved which either: (i) relates wholly or mainly to the construction of an enactment or statutory instrument, and was fully argued in the proceedings and fully considered in the judgment; or (ii) is a point of law concerning which the judge is bound by a previous decision of the Court of Appeal or the House of Lords.[15] Such applications to the Appeal Committee are to be determined without a hearing.

Criminal Appeals

There was no general right of appeal to the House of Lords in criminal cases before 1907, although in exceptional cases a writ of error might be brought. The Criminal Appeal Act 1907, made the House of Lords the final court of appeal in all cases cognisable by the Court of Criminal Appeal; but the certificate of the Attorney-General had first to be obtained that the decision of the Court of Criminal Appeal involved a point of law of exceptional public importance, and that it was desirable in the public interest that a further appeal should be brought.

The Administration of Justice Act 1960, s.1, abolished the requirement of the Attorney-General's certificate. It provided that either the defendant or the prosecutor might appeal to the House of Lords from a decision of the Court of Criminal Appeal or from a decision of a Divisional Court of the Queen's Bench Division in a criminal case, with the leave either of the court below or of the House of Lords; but such leave might not be granted unless the court below certified

---

[14] Crown Proceedings Act 1947.
[15] *Cf. I.R.C.* v. *Church Commissioners for England* [1975] 1 W.L.R. 251; certificate refused by Megarry J.

that a point of law of general public importance was involved and it appeared to that court or to the House of Lords that the point was one which ought to be considered by that House. The certificate was not required in appeals from a Divisional Court in *habeas corpus* cases.[16]

With regard to appeals to the House of Lords from the Court of Appeal, Criminal Division, this right of appeal is now contained in the Criminal Appeal Act, 1968. If the court below certifies that a point of law of general public importance is involved but refuses leave to appeal, application for leave to appeal may be made to the House of Lords; but if the court below refuses to certify no application may be made to the House of Lords.[17]

The Court of Appeal, or Divisional Court of the Queen's Bench Division, may grant an appellant bail pending his appeal. If the Crown appeals, the court may order the defendant's detention or grant him bail, but if he is released he is not liable to be again detained as the result of the decision of the House of Lords on the appeal. The time during which the person is admitted to bail is to be disregarded in computing his sentence.

Appeal also lies to the House of Lords under similar conditions from the Court of Criminal Appeal in Northern Ireland[18] and from the Courts-Martial Appeal Court.[19]

There is no appeal to the House of Lords in criminal cases from Scottish courts.

Reference of Point of Law

The Court of Appeal (Criminal Division), having given their opinion on a point of law, following an acquittal on indictment, referred to them by the Attorney-General,[20] may refer the point to the House of Lords if it appears to the court that the point ought to be considered by that House. For this purpose the House of Lords is to be composed as for appeals. Such reference does not affect the trial or any acquittal.[21]

---

[16] Administration of Justice Act 1960, s.15.

[17] *Gelberg* v. *Miller* [1961] 1 W.L.R. 459; [1961] 1 All E.R. 618 (H.L.). If the House of Lords does hear the appeal, it is not limited to considering the point of law certified by the court below: *Att.-Gen. for Northern Ireland* v. *Gallagher* [1963] A.C. 349 (H.L.).

[18] Criminal Appeal (Northern Ireland) Act 1968, Part. III. This was the first consolidation Act to include Acts of the Northern Ireland Parliament.

[19] Courts-Martial (Appeals) Act 1968, Part III. See below, Chap. 9.

[20] Above, p. 90, and see also for referred sentence.

[21] Criminal Justice Act 1972, s.36.

Composition of the Court

The Appellate Jurisdiction Act 1876, provided that there should be present at the hearing of an appeal at least three of the following Lords of Appeal: (i) the Lord Chancellor, (ii) the Lords of Appeal in Ordinary, and (iii) such Peers of Parliament as hold or have held "high judicial office" as defined in the Act.[22] Lords of Appeal in Ordinary, an office instituted by the Act, must either have held high judicial office for two years or be practising barristers of not less than fifteen years' standing. They have the dignity of Baron, and are entitled to sit and vote in the House of Lords for life.[23] Their number, at first two, has been gradually increased.[24] They are popularly known as "Law Lords."

It is the custom that one or two Law Lords should be Scotsmen, and that at least one of these should sit on an appeal from Scotland. Before 1922 there was also usually an Irish Law Lord, and there is occasionally one from Northern Ireland. In important cases the court often consists of five members. The Lord Chancellor in recent years has seldom been available to sit while Parliament is in session.

In the nineteenth century a constitutional *convention* grew up that lay peers should absent themselves when the House is sitting in its judicial capacity. This convention was established in *O'Connell* v. *R.*[25] when after some discussion lay peers withdrew without voting, but one or two minor breaches seem to have occurred since.

Procedure

Formerly the court sat in the House of Lords debating chamber when the House was not sitting for legislative business; but since the war a temporary arrangement has become permanent, whereby appeals are referred to an Appellate Committee consisting of Law Lords sitting in a committee room. In order to save time, since 1963 their Lordships' opinions in civil and criminal appeals are no longer as a general rule delivered orally in the House; but when the House meets for the delivery of opinions their Lordships confine themselves to stating that, for the reasons given in their opinions (copies of which are made available to counsel an hour beforehand), they would allow or

[22] See now Criminal Appeal Act 1968, s.35.
[23] Appellate Jurisdiction Act 1887.
[24] The number may be increased by Order in Council, after approval of the draft Order by resolution of each House: Administration of Justice Act 1968.
[25] (1844) 11 Cl. & Fin. 155, 421–426.

dismiss the appeal. This system is similar to that employed for many years by the Judicial Committee of the Privy Council. The question is then put from the Woolsack and the order made.[26]

The Appellate Jurisdiction Act 1876, allowed the court to sit when Parliament is prorogued and it may be authorised by the Crown to sit even after a dissolution of Parliament. The origin of the court is, however, preserved in the forms used. The appellant petitions for a review of the judgment, and asks for such relief "as to Her Majesty the Queen in Her High Court of Parliament may seem meet." Technically, the Lords give opinions in the form of speeches and not judgments, and an appeal is won or lost on a vote in the House.

The judges of the Queen's Bench Division may still be called upon to advise their Lordships on difficult questions of law, but they have been summoned for consultation very few times since Lords of Appeal were created in 1876. The last occasion in an English appeal was *Allen* v. *Flood* (1898),[27] one of the rare cases in which the House of Lords declined to follow the advice of the majority of the judges. The House had no authority to summon Chancery judges unless they were also peers.

2. THE JUDICIAL COMMITTEE OF THE PRIVY COUNCIL

Introduction

The Sovereign, as the fountain of justice, has a general residuary jurisdiction over all British subjects. Accordingly, petitions from the Channel Islands, the Isle of Man and the overseas possessions of the Crown, which were outside the jurisdiction of the courts of Westminster, were formerly sent to the Privy Council, which delegated the hearing of them to its Committee of Trade and Plantations.[28] The work of this committee greatly increased in the eighteenth century owing to the growth of the Empire, but the Privy Councillors, who were mostly laymen, were not competent to deal with it. The abolition in 1832 of the High Court of Delegates, which heard appeals from the Ecclesiastical and Admiralty Courts, led to the creation by the Judicial Committee Act 1933,[29] of a Judicial Committee of legal experts to hear Channel Islands, Isle of Man, Colonial, Indian, Ecclesiastical and Admiralty Appeals. The Judicature Act 1873, provided for the transfer of the appellate jurisdiction of the Privy Council

---

[26] *Practice Direction (H.L.) (Delivery of Opinions)* [1963] 1 W.L.R. 1382.
[27] [1898] A.C. 1.
[28] Swinfen (1974) 90 L.Q.R. 396.
[29] Further provisions were made by the Judicial Committee Act 1844.

to the Court of Appeal, but its jurisdiction was restored in 1876 before the provision took effect.

Composition

The Judicial Committee, created by the Judicial Committee Act 1833, whose constitution has been modified by the Appellate Jurisdiction Act 1876, and other Acts, is composed of the Lord Chancellor, the existing and former Lords President of the Council (who do not attend), Privy Councillors who hold or have held high judicial office as defined in the Act of 1833 (including retired English and Scottish judges), the Lords of Appeal in Ordinary, Lords Justices of the Court of Appeal (who seldom sit), former Lord Chancellors and Lords of Appeal, and such judges or former judges of the superior courts of certain Commonwealth countries as the Crown may appoint.[30] There is a quorum of three members, though five are usually present in important cases.

Procedure

The Judicial Committee sits in the Privy Council buildings at the corner of Whitehall and Downing Street. Its procedure is much like that of an ordinary appeal court, although it appears to be rather less formal as the judges do not wear wigs and robes. In theory, however, it is not a court but an advisory board. The opinion of the Board takes the form of "advice" tendered to Her Majesty,[31] which is by convention invariably accepted. The decision takes legal effect when an Order in Council is issued to implement it.[32] Formerly the Board was required to give unanimous advice and only one opinion was delivered, but since 1966 dissenting opinions may be delivered.[33]

Jurisdiction

Appeals in Prize Cases

Appeals in Prize cases come from the Queen's Bench Division, sitting as the Admiralty Court (Administration of Justice Act

---

[30] Judicial Committee Amendment Act 1895, as amended.
[31] Or to the Head of State of an independent Commonwealth country not owing allegiance to the Queen, *e.g.*, Malaysia.
[32] *British Coal Corporation* v. *The King* [1935] A.C. 500.
[33] Judicial Committee (Dissenting Opinions) Order in Council 1966. See, *e.g.*, *National and Grindlays Bank Ltd.* v. *Dharamshi Vallabhji* [1967] 1 A.C. 207; *Madzimbamuto* v. *Lardner-Burke* [1969] 1 A.C. 645.

1970). Prize cases are concerned with the ownership of ships and cargo and the validity of their capture by belligerent warships. In this capacity the Judicial Committee administers international law, subject to any Acts of Parliament that may be inconsistent therewith.[34] It has a similar jurisdiction relating to aircraft.[35]

Appeals in Ecclesiastical Cases

These now come before the Judicial Committee only from the Arches Court of Canterbury and the Chancery Court of York in causes of faculty,[36] not involving matter of doctrine, ritual or ceremonial.[37]

Appeals from Certain Domestic Tribunals

Statutes of the past twenty years have given a right of appeal to the Judicial Committee of the Privy Council from the tribunals of medical and allied professional bodies which have the power to strike a member off the register of practitioners.[38]

Appeals from Courts outside the United Kingdom[39]

This is the jurisdiction of the Privy Council to hear appeals from the overseas territories of the Crown, *viz.,* the Isle of Man, the Channel Islands, the dwindling number of British Colonies and other Dependencies,[40] and the few independent Commonwealth countries that have not abolished such appeals.[41]

Appeal is either by right of grant, *i.e.,* by British or local statute (in practice, smaller civil cases)[42] or by special leave of the Privy Council (in civil[43] or criminal[44] cases). The Crown has a prerogative right to determine the scope of the jurisdiction of the Judicial Committee.[45]

---

[34] *The Zamora* [1916] 2 A.C. 77.

[35] Prize Act 1939.

[36] *e.g.,* seeking permission to make certain alterations to church buildings and churchyards.

[37] Ecclesiastical Jurisdiction Measure 1963.

[38] *e.g.,* Medical Act 1983; Dentists Act 1984; Opticians Act 1958; Veterinary Surgeons Act 1966.

[39] Formerly also Protectorates, Protected States and Trust Territories: Foreign Jurisdiction Act 1890.

[40] *British Coal Corporation* v. *The King* [1935] A.C. 500.

[41] The Australian States have recently abolished appeals.

[42] *Meghji Lakhamski & Bros.* v. *Furniture Workshop* [1954] A.C. 80.

[43] *Prince* v. *Gagnon* (1882) 8 App.Cas. 103.

[44] *Re Dillet* (1887) 12 App.Cas. 459; *Arnold* v. *The King-Emperor* [1914] A.C. 644.

[45] *Australian Consolidated Press Ltd.* v. *Uren* [1969] 1 A.C. 590.

Because territories acquired by conquest or cession retain their own private law unless and until it is altered, appeals have come before the Judicial Committee involving points of Roman-Dutch law from Ceylon (now Sri-Lanka), old French law from Mauritius and St. Lucia, Norman customary law from Guernsey, old Spanish law from Trinidad, native African customs and the principles of Hindu and Islamic law.

It has been suggested that the miscellaneous jurisdiction of the Judicial Committee to hear appeals from English courts and tribunals should be merged with that of the House of Lords, leaving the Judicial Committee as a court of appeal from overseas courts.[46]

Special References

The Judicial Committee Act 1833, s.4, requires the Judicial Committee to advise on questions of law put to it by the Crown. Thus the Judicial Committee has been asked to advise on the meaning of certain resolutions of the Legislative Council of Southern Rhodesia.[47] It has had to advise on the elements of the international crime of piracy, following the acquittal of certain Chinese nationals by the Supreme Court of Hong Kong. As there was no appeal against an acquittal, the advice was needed to govern future cases.[48] More recently its advice has been sought concerning the disqualification of clergymen to sit in the House of Commons,[49] and concerning the meaning of an eighteenth-century statute on parliamentary privilege.[50]

The Judicial Committee may also make a declaration, on the application of any person under the House of Commons Disqualification Act 1975, that a person purporting to be a member of the House of Commons is disqualified by the Act. This is alternative to a proceeding in an Election Court.

3. THE COURT OF JUSTICE OF THE EUROPEAN COMMUNITIES

This Court sits at Luxembourg and has a wide jurisdiction over Community matters. It can hear complaints between Member

---

[46] Gerald Gardiner and Andrew Martin, *op. cit.* But see Blom-Cooper and Drewry *op. cit.*, who suggest that the title "Judicial Committee" be given to a new merged final appellate tribunal.
[47] *Re Southern Rhodesia* [1919] A.C. 211.
[48] *Re Piracy Jure Gentium* [1934] A.C. 586.
[49] *Re MacManaway* [1951] A.C. 161.
[50] *Re Parliamentary Privilege Act 1770* [1958] A.C. 331.

States and review the acts of the Council of Ministers and the Commission. Under Article 177 of the Treaty of Rome it can give preliminary rulings on the interpretation of the Treaty, the validity and interpretation of acts of institutions of the Communities and the constitutions of bodies established by the Council, if these so provide, when problems of this kind arise in litigation in the courts of Member States. All courts may refer,[51] and courts against whose judgments there is no "judicial remedy" must refer. The hearing in the Member State will be adjourned until the ruling of the European Court is available. The Court is composed of thirteen judges drawn from the Member States and a number of Advocates-General who assist the Court with reasoned submissions. The Advocates-General are independent officials and their submissions, which are often longer and fuller than the judgments proper, have been compared to judgments at first instance in this country. The whole court normally sits, though certain types of case may be heard by "Chambers" composed of three or five judges. Proceedings may be both written and oral, separate judgments are delivered and the Court does not regard itself as bound by its previous decisions.

---

[51] For guidelines on when to refer see *Bulmer* v. *Bollinger* [1974] Ch. 401 above, p. 21. See also, pp. 166–167. The Single European Act (see European Communities (Amendment) Act 1986) makes provision for a court of first instance to be associated with the present court.

CHAPTER 9

Miscellaneous Courts and Tribunals

The courts described in the preceding chapters are those in which English law, in the ordinary sense, is administered and whose precedents (in the case of the superior courts) declare and develop English Law. There are also certain miscellaneous courts and tribunals, some of which may be summarised here.

1. ANOMALOUS LOCAL COURTS

Some ancient courts with a local jurisdiction wider than that of county courts remained in existence until recently. The Royal Commission on Assizes and Quarter Sessions put forward recommendations[1] which resulted in the Courts Act 1971, making sweeping changes. The Chancery Courts of Lancaster and Durham were merged with the High Court. The Vice-Chancellor of Lancaster, though retaining his title, became a Circuit judge and, whilst continuing to sit in Liverpool, Manchester and Preston, may now also sit in Leeds and Newcastle.[2] The Mayor's and City of London Court retains its title but its jurisdiction has been reduced to that of an ordinary county court.[3] The Liverpool Court of Passage, the Salford

---

[1] Cmnd. 4153, paras. 349–384. The "Beeching Commission."
[2] Courts Act 1971, s.41 and Sched. 2. A High Court judge has now been appointed to this office.
[3] *Ibid.* s.42. Chancery role now enlarged (1988) *The Times*, May 27.

Hundred Court, the Tolzey and Pie Poudre Courts of Bristol and the Norwich Guildhall Court were all abolished.[4]

Actions by or against workers in the tin mines of Cornwall and Devon could at one time be heard only in the courts of the Stannaries.[5] The appellate jurisdiction of the Lord Warden of the Stannaries was transferred to the Court of Appeal by the Judicature Act 1873, and in 1896 the Stannaries Court was abolished, its jurisdiction being transferred to the county courts of Cornwall, which had concurrent jurisdiction with it since their creation in 1846.

2. COURTS OF SPECIAL JURISDICTION

Courts-Martial

These deal with certain serious offences committed by persons who, in addition to being subject to the ordinary law, are also subject to the discipline of the armed forces, *i.e.* military law, air force law or naval discipline. Courts-martial are staffed by officers of the services with the assistance of a judge advocate, who is a lawyer, on matters of law.[5a]

The Queen's Bench Division has supervisory jurisdiction over courts-martial, exercised by means of the prerogative writs and orders, provided some civil law right is involved.[6]

There was formerly no appeal from a court-martial, though a petition might be sent to the confirming authority. The Courts-Martial Appeal Court was set up in 1951, with final appeal to the House of Lords.[7] This consists of: (a) the judges of the Court of Appeal and Queen's Bench Division judges nominated by the Lord Chief Justice, (b) judges of the High Court of Justiciary[8] nominated by the Lord Justice-General, (c) judges of the Supreme Court of Northern Ireland nominated by the Lord Chief Justice of Northern Ireland, and (d) other persons of legal experience nominated by the Lord Chancellor. An uneven

---

[4] *Ibid.* s.43. The Local Government Act 1972, s.221, abolished other courts. The Administration of Justice Act 1977, s.23, removes the judicial powers of many others.

[5] *Stannum* = *tin*.

[5a] The Armed Forces Act 1976 set up Standing Civilian Courts for the trial abroad of offences by civilians subject to service law. Their jurisdiction broadly corresponds to that of magistrates' courts.

[6] *Grant* v. *Gould* (1792) 2 H.Bl. 69; *Re Mansergh* (1861) 1 B. & S. 400; *R.* v. *Wormwood Scrubs Prison Governor ex p. Boydell* [1948] 2 K.B. 193. For the prerogative writs and orders see below, pp. 113 and 320.

[7] See now Courts-Martial (Appeals) Act, 1968.

[8] The Scottish superior criminal court.

number of judges, not being less than three, must sit and the court may sit outside the United Kingdom.

A person convicted by a court-martial, if he wishes to appeal, must first petition the Defence Council to have the conviction quashed. If the petition is rejected he may then, with leave of the court, appeal to the Courts-Martial Appeal Court. The grounds on which an appeal must or may be granted are similar to those for appeals to the Criminal Division of the Court of Appeal,[9] except that there is no right to appeal against sentence and the power to order a retrial is more restricted. The appellant is not entitled without leave of the court to be present at the hearing. The court will generally adopt the procedure of the Criminal Division of the Court of Appeal and deliver only one judgment.[10]

Decisions of the court on important points of law are reported and constitute precedents.[11]

Appeal lies to the House of Lords at the instance either of the accused or the Defence Council, subject to conditions similar to those which apply to appeals from the Criminal Division of the Court of Appeal.[12]

Ecclesiastical Courts

These courts, which were reorganised by the Ecclesiastical Jurisdiction Measure 1963, administer English ecclesiastical law, now enforceable in the main only against the clergy of the Church of England. The most important ecclesiastical courts are the Arches Court of Canterbury and the Chancery Court of York, with appellate jurisdiction from the Consistory Courts of dioceses. There is also a court of Ecclesiastical Causes Reserved with original and appellate jurisdiction. This deals with matters of doctrine, ritual and ceremonial. There are Commissions of Convocation for the trial of archbishops and bishops, and the determinations of these last two courts may be reviewed by Commissions of Review.

Appeal from the Arches Court of Canterbury and the Chancery Court of York to the Judicial Committee of the Privy Council is now in matters of faculty only, not involving doctrine, ritual or ceremonial. The Queen's Bench Division can keep the ecclesiastical courts within their jurisdiction by means of the orders of mandamus and prohibition, but, as they

---

[9] Above, Chap. 7.
[10] *R.* v. *Houghton* [1952] 1 T.L.R. 1507.
[11] See *R.* v. *Davies* [1962] 1 W.L.R. 1111.
[12] Above, Chap. 8.

administer a different system of law, certiorari does not lie to have their proceedings brought before the High Court for review.[13]

The Restrictive Practices Court

This was set up by the Restrictive Trade Practices Act 1956, to examine restrictive trade agreements registered by the Registrar of Restrictive Trading Agreements (whose functions have now been taken over by the Director General of Fair Trading),[14] and declare void those found to be "contrary to the public interest." Legislation provides criteria for this determination.[15] The court also administered the Resale Prices Act 1964, and its jurisdiction was further extended by the Fair Trading Act 1973, to cover forms of trading thought by the Director General to be unfair to consumers.[16] The court consists of five judges and not more than ten lay members appointed by the Crown on the recommendation of the Lord Chancellor. Three of the judges are from the High Court and one each from the Court of Session and the Supreme Court of Northern Ireland. The quorum is three, of which one must be a judge who presides, except that a judge may sit alone if a case only involves issues of law. The presiding judge decides questions of law, questions of fact being determined by a majority. There is an appeal on questions of law only to the Court of Appeal, Civil Division, the Court of Session or the Court of Appeal in Northern Ireland.[17]

This court, like the Courts-Martial Appeal Court, differs from most of the other courts that have been described in being a court for the United Kingdom rather than England and Wales.

The Employment Appeal Tribunal

When the Industrial Relations Act 1971, was passed to provide a legal structure for industrial relations, a National Industrial Relations Court was set up to administer the new jurisdiction created by the Act. Like the Restrictive Practices Court its judicial staff included both judges and laymen. Both the Industrial Relations Act and the court were acutely controversial; the Act was repealed and the court abolished by the Trade

---

[13] *R.* v. *Edmundsbury and Ipswich Diocese* (Chancellor) [1948] 1 K.B. 195. For the prerogative writs and orders see below, pp. 112–113.

[14] Fair Trading Act 1973, s.94.

[15] See Restrictive Trade Practices Acts 1956, s.21 and 1976, s.10; Resale Prices Act 1976, s.14.

[16] Fair Trading Act 1973, ss.34–35.

[17] Restrictive Trade Practices Act 1956, and Restrictive Practices Court Act 1976.

Union and Labour Relations Act 1974.[18] With the introduction of a new statutory framework for many aspects of industrial relations in the Employment Protection Act 1975, a new tribunal, which in status, composition and in some of its jurisdiction resembles the National Industrial Relations Court, was brought into being to hear appeals on questions of law from Industrial Tribunals and the trade union Certification Officer. These appeals may arise on a wide range of matters such as redundancy, equal pay, sex discrimination, trade union certification and questions arising out of the Employment Protection Act itself. This new tribunal is the Employment Appeal Tribunal,[19] which is declared to be a superior court of record. It consists of judges from the Court of Appeal and High Court nominated by the Lord Chancellor, at least one judge from the Court of Session and appointed lay members qualified in virtue of knowledge or experience in industrial relations. As with the Restrictive Practices Court, there is an appeal to the Court of Appeal or Court of Session on questions of law. The procedure of the tribunal is cheap and informal and strict rules of evidence need not be observed. The Appeal Tribunal may sit in divisions anywhere in Great Britain. With the consent of the parties it may sit with one judge and one appointed lay member, but otherwise there must be a judge and two or four appointed lay members so chosen as to give equal representation to employers and workers.

Criminal Injuries Compensation Board

This was set up by administrative action in 1964 to administer a State-funded scheme of compensation for victims of crimes of violence. Compensation is assessed on the same basis as damages in tort and if damages are recovered compensation under the scheme will be reduced or excluded. The decisions of the Board were subject to judicial review but not to appeal. It is to be placed on a statutory basis, with appeal on law, by the Criminal Justice Bill 1988.

Arbitration

Arbitration is the adjudication of disputes otherwise than through the ordinary processes of the courts. Matters of

---

[18] s.1(3).
[19] See now Employment Protection (Consolidation) Act 1978, ss.135, 136 and Sched. 11.

criminal law and status cannot be referred to arbitration. Very frequently the arbitrator is not a member of the judicial staff of the ordinary courts and tribunals, but sometimes he may be. Thus the Administration of Justice Act 1970, provides that the judge of the Commercial Court may, with the consent of the Lord Chief Justice, sit as an arbitrator in commercial disputes.[20] Again, the High Court may refer a case to be heard by a Circuit judge as Official Referee's business if the parties consent or if the case involves accounts, prolonged investigation of documents or scientific or local investigations.[21] Both the judge and the registrar in county courts may act as arbitrators, and the jurisdiction was extended in 1973 in order to deal with small claims.[22] Very frequently the parties will have agreed to go to arbitration but, as in the case of the new county court arbitration, legislation may provide for arbitration in spite of objection from the parties.

Arbitration by agreement has many advantages and is widely used in commercial disputes. It can be cheap, informal and speedy. The hearing will be in private and at times fixed to suit the parties. Appeal may be very limited. Arbitrators may be appointed because of their special knowledge of the subject-matter, and they may use this in reaching their decision, which is known as an award.[23] It is often easier to enforce an arbitral award abroad than the judgment of a court.[24] Because of these advantages many commercial contracts provide for arbitration, the choice of arbitrator being frequently left to the officers of trade or professional associations who maintain panels of arbitrators. There may be a reference to two arbitrators, in which case they must appoint an umpire in the absence of some contrary provision. The umpire will make an award if the arbitrators differ.[25]

Arbitration by agreement has a long history and has been subject to close regulation. The present principal legislation is the Arbitration Act 1950, which applies when there has been a written agreement ("submission") to arbitrate.[26] The

---

[20] Administration of Justice Act 1970, s.4.
[21] Courts Act 1971, s.25.
[22] Administration of Justice Act 1973, s.7.
[23] *Mediterranean Export Co.* v. *Fortress Fabrics* [1948] 2 All E.R. 186.
[24] For these and their effect on the courts see Report of the Commercial Court Users Conference Cmnd. 1616 (1962) esp. paras. 23–31.
[25] Arbitration Act 1950, s.8.
[26] s.32. See also, Arbitration Acts 1975 and 1979.

ordinary rules of procedure and evidence apply[27] unless the parties, as they often do, agree to waive them. Arbitrators may apply to the High Court to *subpoena* witnesses (compel their attendance), may take evidence on oath and order discovery of documents and the administration of interrogatories.[28] If a party having agreed to arbitrate nevertheless takes ordinary proceedings in the courts, the court has a discretion to stay the action.[29] The parties may not, however, agree to dispense with rules of substantive law and instead allow the arbitrator to decide on grounds of fairness and abstract justice.[30]

An arbitrator's decision on a question of fact is ordinarily final, nor is there an unrestricted appeal to the courts on a question of law, though some commercial arbitration schemes provide for appeals to their own tribunals. The courts will, however, set aside an award if there has been misconduct on the part of the arbitrator.[31] Formerly the arbitrator, having determined the facts, could state a case for the opinion of the High Court on a point of law and could be compelled by the court, at the instance of the parties, to do so. Procedure by way of case stated was abolished by the Arbitration Act 1979 which provides for the determination by the High Court of a preliminary point of law and for an appeal on a point of law. The taking of the preliminary point of law is subject to the consent of the parties or of the arbitrator or umpire. The appeal is subject to the consent of all the parties or leave from the High Court, leave only to be granted if the High Court considers the point could substantially affect the parties. Further appeal is subject to the judge certifying that a point of law of general public importance is involved or there is some other special reason and to the leave of either the High Court or the Court of Appeal.[32] The Act makes complex provision for the validity of agreements between the parties excluding these recourses to the courts. An arbitrator may be compelled to give reasons for his award. The court may also remit an award for reconsideration if there is misconduct by the arbitrator

---

[27] *Re Enoch* [1910] 1 K.B. 327.
[28] Arbitration Act 1950, s.12, See also, below p. 370.
[29] *Ibid.* s.4.
[30] *Orion* v. *Belfort* [1962] 2 Lloyd's Rep. 257; *Overseas Union Insurance* v. *A.A. Mutual International Insurance* (1988) *The Times*, January 26.
[31] Arbitration Act 1950, s.23.
[32] See *Pioneer Shipping* v. *B.T.P. Tioxide, The Nema* [1982] A.C. 724 for guidelines.

not sufficiently serious to warrant setting it aside, or if fresh evidence comes to light.[33] Awards will be enforced in the same way as judgments of the courts.[34]

Arbitration also plays an important part in industrial relations. The Employment Protection Act 1975, set up an Advisory, Conciliation and Arbitration Service to handle trade disputes, and also a Central Arbitration Committee which may act as the tribunal.[35] This arbitration differs in a number of respects from ordinary arbitration by agreement.

3. ADMINISTRATIVE JURISDICTION

Many disputes at the present day are adjudicated upon and legal rights determined by persons or bodies falling outside what are traditionally called "the ordinary courts" and courts of special jurisdiction such as those mentioned in the previous section. Parliament has in recent years increasingly conferred on other kinds of tribunals the power of making decisions that may affect private rights, on the grounds of their expert knowledge, experience of the problems of administration, and relative cheapness, speed, flexibility and informality. For instance, in recent years a very wide jurisdiction covering many aspects of employment law has been given to industrial tribunals, with appeal to the Employment Appeal Tribunal.[36] These tribunals, which are outside the ordinary judicial system, are not for the most part staffed by lawyers, though a number of them have legally qualified chairmen. Their jurisdiction may be original or appellate. They vary so much in composition, method of appointment, functions and procedure, and in their relations to Ministers on the one hand and the ordinary courts on the other, that it is not possible to arrange them in a satisfactory classification.

Administrative Tribunals

The Tribunals and Inquiries Act 1958, implemented, with modifications, the recommendations of the Franks Committee on Administrative Tribunals and Enquiries, which reported in 1957.[37] The 1958 Act has now been repealed and

---

[33] Arbitration Act 1950, s.22.
[34] Arbitration Act 1950, s.26. See also below pp. 373–374.
[35] ss.1, 3 and 10. The Arbitration Act 1950, does not apply.
[36] See above, pp. 106–107.
[37] Cmnd. 218.

substantially re-enacted by the Tribunals and Inquiries Act 1971. Under these Acts there is a *Council on Tribunals* to keep under review the constitution and working of most of the more important tribunals, and from time to time to report on their constitution and working; and also to consider and report on such particular matters as may be referred to the Council with respect to any tribunals other than the ordinary courts of law. The Council on Tribunals consists of members appointed by the Lord Chancellor and the Secretary of State for Scotland. The Council reports to the Lord Chancellor and references to the Council are made by him. The Council is to make an annual report to the Lord Chancellor on its proceedings, and this is to be laid before Parliament.

The Tribunals and Inquiries Act provides that the chairmen of certain of the tribunals which are subject to the Council's review shall be selected by the appropriate Minister from a panel appointed by the Lord Chancellor. The Council may make general recommendations about the appointment of members of the specified tribunals or of panels, and the Minister must have regard to such recommendations. The removal, except by the Lord Chancellor, of members of most of the tribunals or panels requires the consent of the Lord Chancellor.

A Minister is to consult the Council before making procedural rules for the specified tribunals. The tribunals are required to give written or oral reasons for their decision, if requested by the persons concerned; and this statement of reasons is to form part of the record.[38]

A large number of tribunals are specified in the First Schedule to the Act as coming under the direct supervision of the Council on Tribunals and the above provisions in general apply to them. A recent and important addition is the Director General of Fair Trading under the Consumer Credit Act 1974. The Lord Chancellor may extend the Act to other tribunals by statutory instrument, subject to a negative resolution of either House.

Statutory Inquiries

Statutes confer on some Ministers the power—sometimes without appeal—to make decisions directly affecting the rights of individuals or of other public authorities. This power of adjudication may be either original or appellate. The final

---

[38] *Re Poyser and Mills' Arbitration* [1964] 2 Q.B. 467.

decision is one of policy, for which the Minister is conventionally responsible to Parliament; but if the enabling Act prescribes some specific procedure, *e.g.*, the holding of a public inquiry and the consideration of objections, such procedure must be complied with. Statutory inquiries are usually prescribed before land is compulsory acquired for such purposes as re-development or the building of housing estates, and also before planning schemes are confirmed.

The terms of reference of the Franks Committee included the holding of statutory inquiries and the hearing of appeals by or on behalf of Ministers, and in particular the procedure for the compulsory purchase of land. Many of its recommendations have been given effect to by Ministerial directions to local authorities and departmental regulations. The Tribunals and Inquiries Act includes the procedure of statutory inquiries held by or on behalf of a Minister among the matters for consideration and report by the Council on Tribunals. The Act also requires the Minister, if requested by persons concerned, to give reasons for a decision made by him after such an inquiry.

The Lord Chancellor may, after consulting the Council, make rules for regulating the procedure to be followed at statutory inquiries, including matters preparatory to and subsequent to such inquiries.

Judicial Control of Administrative Jurisdiction

There is no appeal from administrative tribunals to the ordinary courts unless it is granted by Act of Parliament.[39] It was for long a criticism of administrative jurisdiction that there was often no appeal to the courts. The Franks Committee was firmly of the opinion that all decisions of tribunals should be subject to review by the courts on points of law by certiorari or appeal and that generally appeal should not lie to a Minister. Appeals already lay to a Minister from local planning, housing, and road transport licensing authorities. Under various statutes appeal lay to the courts on a point of law from the Lands Tribunal, the Pensions Appeal Tribunal, the General and Special Commissioners of Income Tax and Agricultural Land Tribunals. Appeals from industrial tribunals lie on a point of law to the Employment Appeal Tribunal. The Tribunals and Inquiries Act provides for appeal or case stated on a point of law to the High Court from a number of other tribunals.

---

[39] *Racecourse Betting Control Board* v. *Secretary for Air* [1944] Ch. 114.

The supervisory jurisdiction of the High Court, exercisable through judicial review by a Divisional Court of the Queen's Bench Division by certiorari, prohibition and mandamus, is quite distinct from appeal and exists at common law.[40] The distinction is important for on an appeal the whole dispute can be re-heard on its merits, whereas review has been classified by Lord Diplock as going to illegality, irrationality and procedural impropriety.[41] The power of review by certiorari is designed to keep inferior courts— including administrative tribunals and Ministers exercising functions of a judicial nature—within their jurisdiction[42]; and to ensure than when acting in a judicial capacity they observe the principles of natural justice,[43] and that errors of law on the face of the record are corrected.[44] Prohibition is designed to prevent an inferior court or tribunal from exceeding its jurisdiction, and does not lie when once a final decision has been given.[45] Mandamus issues to inferior courts or tribunals or the holders of public offices, requiring them to exercise their jurisdiction or other functions.[46]

Certiorari and mandamus are not excluded by the provisions of statutes (passed before the Act of 1958) purporting to oust the jurisdiction of the courts, although there may be a special statutory time-limit during which application to the High Court must be made.[47] A declaration may also be granted, declaring the law on a disputed point.[48]

Judicial review, not private law procedure, must be used in public law issues.[49]

---

[40] *R.* v. *Electricity Commissioners* [1924] 1 K.B. 171. See R.S.C. Ord. 53 (1977); Supreme Court Act 1981, s.31. Above, p. 81.

[41] *Council of Civil Service Unions* v. *Minister for the Civil Service* [1985] A.C. 734.

[42] *R.* v. *Minister of Transport, ex p. Upminster Services* [1934] 1 K.B. 277.

[43] *Local Government Board* v. *Arlidge* [1915] A.C. 120.

[44] *R.* v. *Northumberland Compensation Appeal Tribunal, ex p. Shaw* [1952] 1 K.B. 338; *R.* v. *Knightsbridge Crown Court ex p. International Sporting Club (London) Ltd.* [1982] Q.B. 304.

[45] *R.* v. *Electricity Commissioners* [1929] 1 K.B. 171.

[46] *R.* v. *Graham-Campbell ex p. Herbert* [1935] 1 K.B. 594; *The King* v. *Housing Tribunal* [1920] 3 K.B. 334; *Board of Education* v. *Rice* [1911] A.C. 179; *The Queen* v. *Special Commissioners for Income Tax* (1888) 21 Q.B.D. 313.

[47] Tribunals and Inquiries Act 1958, s.11. See now Tribunals and Inquiries Act 1971, s.14 *Cf. Smith* v. *East Elloe R.D.C.* [1956] A.C. 736.

[48] See *R.* v. *Secretary of State for Transport ex p. Gwent C.C.* [1986] 1 W.L.R. 1055 (duties of inspector at inquiry).

[49] *O'Reilly* v. *Mackman* [1983] 2 A.C. 237.

The Parliamentary Commissioner

The office of Parliamentary Commissioner or "Ombudsman" was established by statute in 1967[50] to investigate and report on complaints of injustice suffered by reason of maladministration, *i.e.*, a government department's failure to observe proper standards of administration not amounting to illegality. An example would be the *Crichel Down* case (1954) where a landowner complained that the Ministry of Agriculture refused after the war to return to him land that had been requisitioned during the war and was no longer required by the Ministry for the purpose for which it had been requisitioned.

The Parliamentary Commissioner is appointed by the Crown, and he has the same security of tenure as a judge of the Supreme Court.[51] His functions overlap those of the Council on Tribunals, of which he has been made a member. Complaints are to be made by citizens through a member of Parliament. In most of the cases investigated as being within the Commissioner's terms of reference, the administration has in fact been exonerated. Among the relatively few complaints upheld the greater number have been cases of unjustifiable delay. Commissioners have also been appointed to undertake investigations in relation to local government[52] and the National Health Service.[53] A somewhat similar function in relation to solicitors is to be performed by "lay observers" appointed by the Lord Chancellor.[54]

4. DOMESTIC TRIBUNALS

Domestic Tribunals, whose jurisdiction is limited to certain professions or associations, are not part of the machinery of government, but some of them are on a statutory basis with a right to appeal to the courts. The supervisory jurisdiction of the High Court is exercised over them—even the voluntary ones—by means of remedies similar to those available against administrative tribunals.[55]

---

[50] Parliamentary Commissioner Act 1967.
[51] Above, p. 31.
[52] Local Government Act 1974, s.23.
[53] National Health Service Reorganisation Act 1973, s.31.
[54] Solicitors Act 1974, s.45.
[55] *Lee* v. *Showmen's Guild of Great Britain* [1952] 2 Q.B. 329; *Barnard* v. *National Dock Labour Board* [1953] 2 Q.B. 18. *Currie* v. *Barton* (1988) *The Times*, February 12 (tennis club.)

The Solicitors' Disciplinary Tribunal is appointed by the Master of the Rolls under the Solicitors Act, 1974.[56] It now includes both solicitors and lay members. Appeal by a solicitor struck off the rolls lies to the High Court, and thence to the Court of Appeal.

The General Council of the Bar (constituted in 1987 to succeed the Senate of the Inns of Court first set up in 1966), exercises by its disciplinary committee the disciplinary jurisdiction of the Benchers of the Inns of Court over barristers in respect of professional misconduct. Appeal by a barrister against an order disbarring him or suspending him from practice continues to be heard by the Judges as Visitors of the Inns.[57]

Various Acts have constituted Disciplinary Committees for medical and dental practitioners, opticians and professions supplementary to medicine, with appeal to the Judicial Committee of the Privy Council,[58] and there are similar bodies for pharmacists and architects, with appeal to the High Court.[59] An important group of domestic tribunals are those set up by trade unions; but there is no appeal from them to an outside body though they are subject to the supervisory jurisdiction of the High Court. University Disciplinary Committees are expected to observe the general principles of natural justice,[60] but the High Court does not sit as a court of appeal from University examiners.[61] A Prison Governor exercising disciplinary jurisdiction must also observe natural justice.[62]

---

[56] *Addis* v. *Crocker* [1961] 1 Q.B. 11.
[57] *Re S.* (*A Barrister*) [1970] 1 Q.B. 160.
[58] Medical Act 1983; Dentists Act 1984; Opticians Act 1958; Professions Supplementary to Medicine Act 1960; Veterinary Surgeons Act 1966.
[59] Pharmacy Act 1954; Architects (Registration) Acts 1931 and 1938.
[60] *R.* v. *Aston University Senate, ex p. Roffey* [1969] 2 Q.B. 538 (D.C.); *Ceylon University* v. *Fernando* [1960] 1 W.L.R. 223; [1960] 1 All E.R. 631 (P.C.). This also applies to a school pupil, *R.* v. *Governors of London Oratory School* (1988) *The Times*, February 17.
[61] *Thorne* v. *University of London* [1966] 2 Q.B. 237 (C.A.); *Sammy* v. *Birkbeck College, The Times*, May 20, 1965 (C.A.). On the jurisdiction of the Visitor and its exclusion of the courts on matters domestic to the institution see *Thomas* v. *University of Bradford* [1987] A.C. 795. This jurisdiction is restricted by the Education Reform Bill 1988.
[62] *Leech* v. *Parkhurst Prison Deputy Governor* [1988] 2 W.L.R. 290.

PART III

The Sources of English Law

CHAPTER 10

Legislation and Statutes

Meanings of "Source of Law"

The expression "source of law'" has several distinct meanings which are variously classified by different writers. In particular, some writers treat the terms "formal" and "legal" as synonymous.

First, the expression may mean that which gives the law its validity (*formal source*). What is taken to be the formal source of English law—the Sovereign, the State, the will of the people or otherwise—will depend on one's general theory of politics and law.

Secondly, it may refer to the direct means by which law is made or comes into existence (*legal sources*), which for English law are legislation, judicial precedent and custom. The courts must consciously look to these, and are bound to apply the rules which they create.

Thirdly, it may mean the written materials from which we obtain a knowledge of what the law is, or was at any given time (*literary sources*). With regard to English law, some of these literary sources are authoritative and are cited by litigants and relied on by judges, namely, statutes, law reports and books of authority. There are many others which are not authoritative, but which are unofficially employed either (a) indirectly for practical purposes, *e.g.*, other books, or (b) directly—especially by legal historians—for academic purposes, *e.g.*, medieval chronicles.

Lastly, it may refer to the factors that have influenced the development of the law, and to which the content of the law may be traced (*historical or material sources*), for example, mercantile customs, religious beliefs, ideas of reasonableness, natural justice, conscience, and public policy, borrowings from Roman civil and canon law, professional practice and juristic opinion. Some of these have been mentioned in connection with such topics as the law merchant, ecclesiastical law and equity. We must now add European Community law, *e.g.*, the European Communities Act 1972, s.9, which made a number of changes to English company law, whether there is a European element or not, in order to fulfil the First Directive of the EEC Council on Harmonisation of Company Law.

1. LEGISLATION

Legislation is the formulation of law by the appropriate organ or organs of the State, in such a manner that the actual words used are themselves part of the law: the words not only contain the law, but in a sense they constitute the law. Legislation includes the making of new law, and the alteration or repeal of existing law. It is the easiest and most common way of developing law in modern systems.

According to Maine, in his celebrated book *Ancient Law* (1861), legislation is historically the latest of the agencies by which progressive systems of law are brought into conformity with the needs of society. After the codification of customary law, exemplified by the XII Tables in Rome and the Laws of the Anglo-Saxon Kings, the agencies brought into play to prevent stagnation are fictions, or devices (mostly procedural) by which the substance of the law is changed while appearing to remain the same, and the extension of the law by judicial and juristic interpretation, then equity, then legislation. Any or all of these agencies may be in use at the same time, for a later does not necessarily displace an earlier; but, according to Maine, this is the invariable order in which they appear, or, at least, in which they exert their chief influence. Thus, a community which has known legislation as a method of general law-making does not revert to custom as a mode of developing its law.

Act of Parliament

Parliament has unlimited legal power to create, alter and repeal English law. Its legislative acts are expressed by means of the following formula:

"Be it enacted by the Queen's most Excellent Majesty,
by and with the advice and consent of the Lords
Spiritual and Temporal, and Commons, in this present
Parliament assembled, and by the authority of the same,
as follows...."[1]

The legislative supremacy or sovereignty of Parliament is
the product of political history. Parliament, which is called
by early writers "the King's Council in Parliament," came
into existence much later than the King's Council—its
predecessor and then its legislative rival—and later than the
common law courts which came to acknowledge its supremacy. Ordinances were sometimes issued which were
intended to have only temporary effect, and the courts had
to distinguish these from Acts intended to be permanent,
that is, to remain in force indefinitely. The terminology was
for a time unsettled, enactments being variously called
ordinances, assizes and provisions. Whether there was a
legal distinction in the fourteenth century between the terms
"statutes" and "ordinances," the former applying to parliamentary and the latter to royal legislation, is a matter of
controversy: perhaps the use of the two terms merely
expresses a love for synonyms. It cannot always have been
easy to know whether what was done was the Act of
Parliament, for the composition of early Parliaments was not
regular and it was not even certain whether the presence of
the Commons was necessary for legislation. Several important statutes of the Plantagenet period which are still in force
or were until recently, for example, *De Donis* (1285) and *Quia
Emptores* (1290), seem to have been enacted by the King and
Lords in the absence of the Commons.

It is doubtful whether, when the composition of Parliament had become settled, the courts treated all its Acts as
absolutely *binding* according to their terms: this may not have
come about until the end of the fifteenth century. Even after
statutes had attained their modern form in the reign of
Henry VIII there was still the competing legislative authority
of Orders in Council and royal proclamations.[2] Since
Parliament established its political ascendancy over the King
in the seventeenth century and the judges accepted the
Revolution settlement of 1688, the courts have considered
Acts of Parliament to be of supreme, if not unlimited,

[1] Or the special formula for Bills passed without the consent of the Lords
under the provisions of the Parliament Acts 1911 and 1949.
[2] *Cf. Case of Proclamations* (1610) 12 Co.Rep. 74.

legal authority.[3] Doubts were expressed even as late as Blackstone's *Commentaries*[4] whether an Act of Parliament would be valid if it was clearly repugnant to natural justice or the "law of nature"; but this is to be regarded as traditional rhetoric.[5]

Consolidation

Consolidation of statutes is the re-enactment in one statute of the provisions relating to some branch of law contained in a number of previous statutes. It may be "pure" consolidation; or consolidation under the Consolidation of Enactments (Procedure) Act 1949, which allows consolidation with "corrections and minor improvements" to be introduced by the Lord Chancellor for consideration by a Joint Committee of both Houses; or consolidation "with Law Commission amendments" under a parliamentary procedure adopted after the Law Commission Act 1965. Section 3 of this Act makes provision for the Law Commission to prepare draft Bills and for the Lord Chancellor to lay such draft Bills before Parliament, with a view to their being put before a Joint Committee of both Houses in expectation of speedy enactment.[6] Examples of the increasing number of consolidation Acts are the Magistrates' Courts Act 1980, the Solicitors Act 1974, and the Fatal Accidents Act 1976.

Consolidation should be distinguished from *codification*, which is the enactment in one statute of the whole body of law on a particular subject, including the case law. Notable nineteenth-century examples are the Bills of Exchange Act 1882, the Partnership Act 1890, and the Sale of Goods Act 1893.[7] A recent example is the Theft Act 1968, based on the report of the Criminal Law Revision Committee. Codification is one of the objects of the Law Commission, but so far it has not been able to do much preparatory work for this purpose.

Consolidation should also be distinguished from *statute law revision*, which is the reprinting of statute law with the repeal and omission of obsolete matter.[8]

---

[3] See, *e.g.*, dicta by Lord Denman C.J. in *Stockdale* v. *Hansard* (1839) 9 A. & E. 1; Lord Campbell in *Edinburgh and Dalkeith Ry.* v. *Wauchope* (1842) 8 Cl. & F. 710; Willes J. in *Lee* v. *Bude and Torrington Ry.* (1871) L.R. 6 C.P. 576; Lord Wright in *Liversidge* v. *Anderson* [1942] A.C. 206; and Lord Reid in *Pickin* v. *British Railways Board* [1974] A.C. 765 (H.L.); *Manuel* v. *Att.-Gen.* [1983] Ch. 77; 1 W.L.R. 1 (*pet* diss H.L.).

[4] 1765, Introd. s.2.

[5] *Cf.* earlier dicta by Coke C.J. in *Bonham's Case* (1609) 8 Co.Rep. 113b; Hobart C.J. in *Day* v. *Savadge* (1614) Hob. 85; and Holt C.J. in *City of London* v. *Wood* (1701) 12 Mod. 669.

[6] See, *per* Lord Simon of Glaisdale in *Farrell* v. *Alexander* [1976] A.C. 59 (H.L.).

[7] Replaced by the Sale of Goods Act 1979.

[8] See below, pp. 125–126.

Delegated Legislation

The activities of modern government are so varied, the facts with which it deals so complex and its problems so technical, that Parliament itself has not the time, inclination or capacity to initiate every detailed item of legislation. Parliament confers on the Queen in Council the power to legislate by *Orders in Council,* a method which is especially valuable in cases of emergency when regulations have to be issued promptly and Parliament may perhaps not be in session, *e.g.,* under the Emergency Powers Act 1920. Law-making powers are frequently delegated by Parliament to Ministers (*Ministerial Orders, Regulations, etc.*), *e.g.,* relating to transport, housing and the National Health Service.[9]

Local Authorities and Public Corporations have a delegated power to issue *By-laws* affecting the area of their functions. Rule Committees, consisting of judges and members of the legal profession, have a delegated power to make *Rules of Court,* notably for the Supreme Court (R.S.C.), the Crown Court and county courts.

Generally, we may say that the central and local government authorities are given power to make detailed provisions to enable them adequately to perform their executive and administrative functions; but this is only roughly true, for delegated legislation is sometimes wide in scope while Acts of Parliament often go into considerable detail.

The Ultra Vires Doctrine

The chief distinction for practical purposes between Acts of Parliament and delegated legislation is that, while the validity of the former cannot be called in question in a court of law, the latter is valid only within the limits of the power conferred. The doctrine of *ultra vires* means that if a case comes before the court in which an act infringing rights or causing loss to someone is sought to be justified as being authorised by delegated legislation, the court will refer to the Act of Parliament which is alleged to confer the power. The question for the court then will be whether the Act conferred the power, and if so, whether the terms of the Act have been complied with.[10]

---

[9] For *Statutory Instruments,* see below, p. 126.

[10] *e.g., Att.-Gen.* v. *Fulham Corporation* [1921] 1 Ch. 440; *Commissioners of Customs and Excise* v. *Cure and Deeley* [1962] 1 Q.B. 340; *R.* v. *Minister of Health, ex p. Yaffe* [1930] 2 K.B. 98; *R.* v. *Paddington Rent Tribunal ex p. Bell Properties Ltd.* [1949] 1 K.B. 666.

There are often several layers of delegated legislation. Thus the Emergency Powers (Defence) Acts 1939–40, conferred on the Government (technically, His Majesty in Council) the power to issue Defence Regulations by Order in Council. Under these Regulations more detailed directions might be issued by individual Ministers, and under these directions they might issue licences. Each piece of delegated legislation must be *intra vires* the rule above it in the hierarchy,[11] and so on up to the Act conferring the law-making power (the "enabling" or "parent" Act).[12]

By-laws, the force of which is limited to certain areas or premises, must not only be *intra vires* but also reasonable, or at least not unreasonable. The test of reasonableness, however, is benevolently construed by the courts in favour of local authorities, which are responsible elected government bodies.[13] It is doubtful whether the test of reasonableness would be benevolently construed in favour of the by-laws of public corporations, since they are neither elected nor directly responsible to Parliament. By-laws, although they are necessarily modifications of the law, must not be contrary to the general law, especially to Acts of Parliament.[14]

Codes of Practice, the earliest of which was the Highway Code, are an increasingly frequently found form of quasi-legislation. They are important in the law of employment, health and safety at work and in criminal procedure under the Police and Criminal Evidence Act 1984. Infringement of a Code is not itself usually illegal but may be relied on as evidence of illegality.

2. STATUTES

Publication

Contrary to continental practice, it has not been necessary since the fourteenth century for Parliament formally to promulgate its enactments, owing to the common law doctrine that everyone was presumed to know what Parliament had done as soon as it was done, as everyone is present by his representatives.[15] Blackstone at the end of the eighteenth century repeats this

---

[11] *Att.-Gen.* v. *Wilts United Dairies* (1922) 91 L.J.K.B. 897; 38 T.L.R. 781; *Liversidge* v. *Anderson* [1942] A.C. 206.

[12] *R.* v. *Halliday, ex p. Zadig* [1917] A.C. 260.

[13] *Kruse* v. *Johnson* [1898] 2 Q.B. 91.

[14] *Powell* v. *May* [1946] K.B. 330.

[15] *R.* v. *Bishop of Chichester* (1365) Y.B. 39 Edw. 3, Pasch, f. 7, *per* Thorpe C.J. For the commencement of statutes, see below, p. 135.

fiction. It was, however, the practice down to the reign of Henry VII to send copies of statutes to the sheriffs of the counties at the end of the session for proclamation by them. The first *printed* statute was in 1483. From that time printed copies were distributed by the King's Printer, but the distribution was defective. From the end of the eighteenth century printed Acts were required to be distributed throughout the country as soon as possible.

Those not engaged in historical research need generally only concern themselves with printed copies of the statutes. There is no "Statute Book." The *Statutes of the Realm*, comprising nine folio volumes published between 1810 and 1822 by Record Commissioners appointed on the recommendation of the House of Commons, contain texts and translations of the Acts of Parliament from the Statute of Merton 1235, down to the year 1713, excluding the Commonwealth period.[16]

Useful unofficial collections are the *Statutes at Large*, especially those made by Hawkins and Ruffhead in the eighteenth century and continued by later editors, which contain slightly abridged versions of statutes beginning with Magna Carta. They are not abridged so much as some earlier unofficial collections—hence the name.

The *Statutes Revised* in thirty two volumes are an authorised collection of statutes from 1235 to 1948 printed by the King's Printer, omitting statutes or sections that have been repealed.[17] That collection has been replaced by *Statutes in Force*, consisting of a series of booklets, one for each Act, contained in loose-leaf binders. This edition is to be kept up to date by annual cumulative supplements, with reprints of amended Acts where necessary. It is now one of the functions of the Law Commission to prepare comprehensive programmes of consolidation and statute law revision, and to undertake the preparation of draft Bills under such approved schemes.[18]

King's Printers have been appointed since the early sixteenth century, and King's Printer's copies are the chief printed source for statutes passed since 1713. The Controller of Her Majesty's Stationery Office has been Queen's Printer since 1882, and from 1884 the Stationery Office has printed and sold Acts of Parliament in the same way as other parliamentary papers. Each

---

[16] For enactments of the Commonwealth period, see Firth and Rait, *Acts and Ordinances of the Interregnum*, 3 vols.

[17] Supervised by the Statute Law Committee, above, p. 24.

[18] See above, pp. 24–25. *The Law Commission: Statute Law Revision: First Report* (1969) Cmnd. 4052, and Draft Statute Law (Repeals) Bill.

Act is available for sale to the public as soon as it is passed, and may be bought from a branch of H.M. Stationery Office or through booksellers.

The Stationery Office also publishes the statutes in annual volumes, *Public General Acts* for convenience being issued separately from *Local and Personal Acts*. The former volumes have, since 1924, included Measures of the Church of England Assembly.[19] Since 1940 a volume has contained the statutes passed in the calendar year, whereas previously a volume contained the statutes passed in a session, which often overlapped two calendar years.

The most convenient way of finding out whether a statute has been wholly or partly repealed or amended is to look it up in the *Chronological Table of the Statutes* published annually by the Stationery Office. This covers the period from 1235 to the end of the year preceding its publication. It comprises a list of all Acts printed in the *Statutes of the Realm* and all Public General Acts from 1714. The companion work is the *Index to the Statutes in Force* (2 volumes), arranged alphabetically under subject headings and also published annually by the Stationery Office.

The Incorporated Council of Law Reporting publish the statutes annually: they are taken from the Queen's Printer's copies. These (*Law Reports—Statutes*) provide the readiest means of access in most law libraries to Acts of Parliament from 1866 onwards. For the purposes of study or the preparation of cases *Halsbury's Statutes* is a convenient collection of the statutes in force, with annotations, supplemented by *Butterworths Annotated Legislation Service*. Other annotated copies are *Current Law Statutes Annotated* (annual volumes).

Subordinate Legislation

It must not be supposed that the statute law on a given subject is necessarily contained only in Acts of Parliament. In many matters reference will have to be made to the *Statutory Instruments* (from 1948), published singly and collected annually by the Stationery Office.[20] The annual volumes contain statutory Orders in Council and Departmental Regulations issued under authority delegated by Parliament, together with the more important prerogative Orders in Council relating to Colonies and other Dependencies.

---

[19] These Measures have been published in a revised form in a supplementary volume uniform with the 3rd ed. of the *Statutes Revised*.

[20] Or *Statutory Rules and Orders* before 1948.

The Statutory Instruments Act 1946,[21] makes general provision for the printing and publication of "statutory instruments" as defined in section 1. Generally, this term covers subordinate legislation by statutory Orders in Council and Ministerial orders, rules or regulations, where the parent Act provides that the law-making power shall be exercisable by Order in Council or by statutory instrument. As soon as possible after they are made, statutory instruments are to be printed by the Queen's Printer and made available for sale. They may be cited by the calendar year and number. The Stationery Office is required to publish lists showing the date on which every statutory instrument was first issued by that office, and a copy of such list purporting to bear the imprint of the Queen's Printer is to be received in evidence in any legal proceedings as a true copy.

The Statutory Rules and Orders and Statutory Instruments Revised, published by the Stationery Office, is a collection in twenty-five volumes of the Statutory Instruments to December 31, 1948 (including what were previously called Statutory Rules and Orders, and also for convenience the more important prerogative Orders in Council relating to Colonial Constitutions, etc.), still in force, showing what parts have been repealed or amended. It is analogous to the *Statutes Revised*.[22] It is kept up to date by the publication of annual volumes, and by the *Index to Government Orders*.[23] The *Table of Government Orders*[24] records the effect (amendments, revocation, etc.) of statutory instruments made since January 1, 1949, on any earlier statutory rules and orders or statutory instruments.

It may also be necessary to refer to copies of *local by-laws*, which are available for inspection at the offices of the local authority concerned. Copies may be bought for a small sum.[25]

Authenticity

Doubt may arise whether the text of a copy of an Act of Parliament is accurate, in which case it will be necessary to look at the original source,[26] for the Queen's Printer's copy is only

---

[21] Superseding the Rules Publication Act 1893.

[22] Above.

[23] Replacing the previous *Guide to Government Orders*.

[24] Replacing the previous *Statutory Instruments Effects*.

[25] Local Government Act 1972, s.236.

[26] The recital in the original that the measure was passed by the Sovereign and by the Lords and Commons would probably be held by the courts in an action between parties to be conclusive as to those facts, though they might perhaps be disputed by either House; *cf. The Prince's Case* (1606) 8 Co.Rep. la; *Heath* v. *Pryn* (1670) 1 Vent. 14.

prima facie evidence. It is legal historians who are most likely to be concerned with the authentic text of an early statute, but occasionally even a court has to consult original sources, as happened in 1917 with regard to the Treason Act 1351, in *R.* v. *Casement*.[27]

The most important original sources for Acts of Parliament since 1278, except for the Commonwealth period for which they have been destroyed, are various series of Statute Rolls and Parliament Rolls, consisting of enrolments in Chancery and proceedings in Parliament. We also have most of the original Acts since the reign of Henry VII. For the period before 1849 they are the rough drafts from which the Clerk of the Parliaments made up the enrolments, and by which the latter could be corrected in case of discrepancy.

Since 1849 the Queen's Printer has made two vellum prints anthenticated by the proper officers of each House, one of which is kept in the House of Lords and the other deposited in the Public Records Office. A third print is made of Church Assembly Measures.

Drafting and Language

In medieval times the judges and other royal officials who assisted the Council drafted legislation, but in the Tudor period this seems to have been done by committees of the Council. After the Restoration, judges and eminent lawyers were often employed to assist the House of Lords in drafting or revising Bills, for example, the Statute of Frauds 1677, introduced into the House of Lords by Lord Nottingham.[28] There was no regular practice even in the eighteenth century; Government Bills were drafted by the official staff and legal advisers of Ministers, but many Bills which would now be Government measures were prepared by private Members. Expert draftsmen were employed by the Treasury and the Home Office in the first half of the nineteenth century, but there was no regular system until 1869, when the office of Parliamentary Counsel to the Treasury was created.

The Parliamentary Counsel, with his staff of barristers and solicitors, is responsible for the preparation of nearly all Government Bills and not merely those emanating from the Treasury, though he has a special responsibility with regard to all legislative proposals which involve the expenditure of public

---

[27] [1917] 1 K.B. 98, 134.
[28] *Ash* v. *Abdy* (1678) 3 Swanst. 664.

money. Ministerial rules and orders, departmental regulations, etc., issued by the Treasury, are also drafted by Parliamentary Counsel; all others are drafted by the Departments concerned, usually in their legal branches.

Most of the earliest statutes are in Latin, though some—of which the Statutes of Westminster I 1275, Gloucester 1278, and Winchester 1285, are the most important—have come down to us in French. After the thirteenth century statutes tend to be in Norman French until the reign of Henry VII, since when all Acts of Parliament are in English. Thus, a well-known passage in the Treason Act 1351, which is still in force, says that a man will commit treason by levying war against the King, etc., *"Ou soit aherdant as enemys nostre Seignur le Roi en le Roialme donant a eux eid ou confort en son Roialme ou par aillours."*[29]

Down to the Tudor period the style of the draftsmen was good, but it deteriorated appreciably after that time. The drafting of the statutes probably reached its lowest depths at the beginning of the nineteenth century, but it has improved somewhat since about the time of the Reform Act of 1832.

Preparation of Legislation

The Renton Committee on the Preparation of Legislation[30] made a number of recommendations, including the following. A statute should be arranged to suit the convenience of its ultimate users, rather than the interests of legislators. The practice of publishing explanatory papers in advance of legislation should be extended, and the use of statements of purpose and principle should be encouraged. There is an urgent need to recruit and train more draftsmen. A new and more comprehensive Interpretation Act should be enacted.[31] The pace of consolidation should be accelerated. Computer-assisted typesetting would give greater speed and accuracy in the printing of public Bills.

Citation

In the thirteenth and early fourteenth centuries statutes were cited either by the name of the place where Council or Parliament met, *e.g.*, Merton (1235), Marlborough (1267), Westminster (1275, 1285), Gloucester (1278), Winchester (1285) and Northampton (1329); or, after the canonical manner, by the first

---

[29] *R.* v. *Casement*, above.
[30] (1975) Cmnd. 6053.
[31] The Interpretation Act 1978 was enacted.

words of the text, *e.g.*, *Quia Emptores* (1290)[32]; or according to the object of the enactment, *e.g.*, the Statute of Mortmain (1279, etc.) and the Statute of Labourers (1349, etc.).

From the end of the fourteenth century, when statutes (by this time all enacted at Westminster) became more frequent, until 1962 statutes were cited by *the date of the regnal year of the Parliamentary session* in which the statute was passed, the regnal year being reckoned from the Sovereign's accession.[33] Thus "14 Geo. 6" stands for the fourteenth year of the reign of George VI, and statutes passed in the Parliamentary *session* that fell in that *regnal* year (*e.g.*, Statute Law Revision Act 1950) are so cited, together with the "chapter" number (see below).

Formerly a "statute" included all the enactments passed in one session, owing to the ancient fiction that Parliament passed only one law in one session; and the individual enactments, equivalent to modern statutes rather than sections, were sometimes referred to as chapters. The Statute of Westminster II 1285,[34] contains a number of what are really separate Acts, including the important *De Donis* (c. 1), *In Consimili Casu* (c. 24) and *Nisi Prius* (c. 30). But for many centuries each Act (statute) passed in a given session was numbered as a *chapter* in the order in which it received the Royal Assent, and the divisions of each Act were numbered as sections and subsections.[35] Thus the Statute Law Revision Act 1950, was the sixth Act to receive the Royal Assent in the session 14 Geo. 6, and was therefore numbered 14 Geo. 6, c. 6.

This method of citation may have been convenient in early times when sessions were short and people were accustomed to dating public events by regnal years; but in modern times it became an inconvenient anachronism. A parliamentary session commonly falls into more than one regnal year; thus the Law of Property Act 1925, originally printed as 15 Geo. 5, c. 20, should be cited as 15 & 16 Geo. 5, c. 20, because the session in which it was passed, though it began in 15 Geo. 5, continued into 16 Geo. 5. Further, a session in modern times may be continued into the following reign, *e.g.*, the Ministers of the Crown Act 1937 is 1 Edw. 8 & 1 Geo. 6, c. 38. Hence the need for short titles (*infra*).

---

[32] The Statute of 1285, commonly called *De Donis Conditionalibus*, begins: "In primis, de tenementis quae multotiens dantur sub conditione. . . ."

[33] The Commonwealth period is disregarded, and the first Act of Charles II's reign is cited as "12 Car. 2, c. 1."
   Car. (*Carolus*) = Charles, and Jac. (*Jacobus*) = James.

[34] 13 Edw. 1.

[35] "Chapter" is abbreviated in writing to cap., ch. or c.

The Acts of Parliament Numbering and Citation Act 1962 (10 & 11 Eliz. 2, c. 34), however, now provides that the chapter numbers assigned to Acts of Parliament in and after the year 1963 shall refer to the calendar year and not the session in which the Acts were passed, and such Acts may be cited accordingly. The first was the Consolidated Fund Act 1963, which received the Royal Assent on February 28, 1963, and whose chapter number is 1963, c. 1.

The Interpretation Act 1889, s.35(2), provided that in Acts passed after that date, references to another Act shall be deemed to be references to: (a) the revised statutes, if the Act referred to is contained in that edition; (b) the Statutes of the Realm, if the Act referred to is before 1714 and is not contained in the Revised Statutes; and (c) in other cases, the Queen's Printer's copy. This is a matter of citation, and not a guarantee of authenticity or accuracy.[36]

Local Acts

These are distinguished by putting the chapter in small Roman numerals, *e.g.*, 24 & 25 Geo. 5, c. ix, and *Personal Acts* (if printed) by putting the chapter number in italicised Arabic figures (*e.g.*, c. 10).[37] *Church Assembly Measures* are cited by their number, *e.g.*, 19 & 20 Geo. 5, No. 3. The effect of the Acts of Parliament Numbering and Citation Act 1962, on these is shown, for example, by the Ecclesiastical Jurisdiction Measure, 1963, whose number is 1963, No. 1.

Statutory Instruments

These are cited: S.I. 1948, No. 1, etc. *Statutory Rules and Orders* were cited "S.R. & O.," followed by the date and number; thus the Defence (General) Regulations, 1939, were S.R. & O., 1939, No. 927.

Short Titles

It had become a convenient, though unofficial, practice to give nicknames to some of the more important Acts according to their subject-matter and date in the Christian era, for example,

---

[36] See now, Interpretation Act 1978, s.19.
[37] Local and Personal Acts come under the heading of Private Acts, the Bills for which are promoted by petition from outside Parliament and go through a distinct parliamentary procedure: see *Pickin* v. *British Railways Board* [1974] A.C. 765 (H.L.). They are no longer of much importance, except Local Acts promoted by large local authorities.

"The Statute of Uses 1535," and "the Statute of Frauds 1677."
This practice was confirmed, whether with or without the
chapter number, as an alternative to citation by regnal year and
chapter, by section 2(1) of the Short Titles Act 1896. This is itself
the short title for 59 & 60 Vict. c. 14. The Act also gave short titles
retrospectively to two thousand statutes passed before that
date, including the Treason Act 1351, the Act of Settlement 1700,
and the Union with Scotland Act 1707. In subsequent Acts there
is generally a section at the end which gives a short title; thus 15
& 16 Geo. 5, c. 20, s.209(1), provides that "This Act may be cited
as the Law of Property Act 1925." Some writers prefer to make
the best of both worlds by referring to "the Law of Property Act
1925 (c. 20)." The Statute Law Revision Act 1948, gave over a
hundred more short titles to Acts passed before 1860. An
interesting reversion to an old custom is contained in 22 & 23
Geo. 5, c. 4, s.12: "This Act may be cited as the Statute of
Westminster 1931."

Where there is no short title, or the short title is not given, the
date of an Act may be looked up in the *Chronological Table of the
Statutes*.[38]

Local and Private Acts, Church Assembly Measures, and
Statutory Instruments also commonly have short titles, though
the short titles of Statutory Instruments are sometimes rather
long.

---

[38] A complete table of regnal years of English sovereigns is given in Sweet &
Maxwell's *Guide to Law Reports, Statutes and Regnal Years* (4th ed., 1963). A
distinction obtained before 1763 between the civil or legal year and the
historical year.

CHAPTER 11

The Interpretation of Statutes

The Need for Interpretation

All matters that come before a court, whether they are human conduct or natural events or judicial decisions or statutes, must in a sense be interpreted so that their legal significance may be assessed. Interpretation or construction in a narrower sense is the ascertainment of the meaning of words formally used in statutes, wills and written contracts where more than one meaning is possible. Experience shows that, owing to the imperfections of language and draftsmen, different people will often interpret the same words in different ways. Guiding principles have accordingly been devised to aid the judge in construing the various kinds of documents. At the present day, more than half the reported cases in the High Court, and three-quarters of the reported cases on appeal to the House of Lords from England and Wales, involve some question of statutory interpretation. But statutes are not addressed only, or indeed primarily, to the courts. Employers and employees in trade and industry, officials, taxpayers, motorists, accountants and legal advisers, all need some knowledge of the statute law concerning them. There is an interaction between the manner of drafting and the rules of interpretation. We may notice that there is much in common between the principles for interpreting statutes, wills and written contracts,[1] though we are concerned

[1] *Curtis* v. *Stovin* (1889) 22 Q.B.D. 513, 517.

here only with statutes, and mainly with general Acts of Parliament.

Development of a Technique of Interpretation

The guides for the interpretation of legislation are mostly common law principles, dating from the sixteenth century. The civilian and canonist doctrine was that interpretation was within the province of the legislator. In the thirteenth and the first half of the fourteenth centuries this doctrine was often acted upon in England. Henry III and Edward I, in consultation with the Council, issued explanations of doubtful statutes, and these would be accepted as authoritative by the courts.[2] Sometimes the court itself would ask the Council what a statute meant.[3] Indeed, at a time when the judges were members of the Council they would often have first-hand knowledge of what a statute was intended to mean, so that Hengham C.J. could say to counsel: "Do not gloss the statute, for we know better than you; we made it."[4] In these early times, statutes were interpreted freely, as laying down a policy within the limits of which the court had considerable discretion.

From the middle of the fourteenth century the common law courts began to develop a technique for the objective interpretation of statutes. The reason for this change was the growth of Parliament as the law-making body, of which the judges were not members, in place of a small Council—including the judges—in close association with the King. At the same time the Court of Chancery was emerging as the body for exercising the discretion of the Council in exceptional cases. By the end of the sixteenth century an embarrassing complexity of rules of interpretation had been elaborated.

1. GENERAL PRINCIPLES FOR THE INTERPRETATION OF STATUTES

It is generally said[5] that the three main principles of interpretation, or methods of approach to the meaning of statutes, adopted by English courts are "literal interpretation,"[6] "the golden rule,"[7] and "the mischief rule."[8] As there is some doubt

---

[2] (1303), Y.B. 30 & 31 Edw. 1 (R.S.) 441, *per* Hengham C.J.
[3] (1366), Y.B. 40 Edw. 3, f. 34b, *per* Thorpe C.J.
[4] (1305), Y.B. 33 & 35 Edw. 1 (R.S.) 82.
[5] J. Willis "Statute Interpretation in a Nutshell" (1938) 16 Can. Bar Rev. 1.
[6] Below, p. 137.
[7] Below, p. 143.
[8] Below, p. 145.

how far these represent what the judges actually do—as distinct from what they say they do—and as the courts are not always consistent in the way they approach the problem of statutory interpretation,[9] it is perhaps wiser not to lay too much stress on one method at the expense of others.[10] The following paragraphs are, therefore, an attempt to summarise the important general principles of interpretation used by English courts at the present day, roughly in the order in which the various problems of interpretation arise in practice.

These principles refer chiefly to Public General Acts. Some different considerations apply to Local Acts and Private Acts. Similar principles apply generally to delegated legislation, subject to its being subordinate to the parent Act.

Commencement

The coming into operation of a statute does not depend on its publication. Formerly, an Act was deemed to come into operation on the first day of the session in which it was passed, owing to the ancient fiction that a session lasted one day.[11] The Acts of Parliament (Commencement) Act 1793, however, provided that an Act should come into operation on the date on which it receives the Royal Assent—which is always printed beneath the title—unless some other date is specified in the Act.[12] An Act passed, but not in operation at the date of a trial, is not to be applied even if it has come into operation at the time of any appeal.[13]

---

[9] "There is scarcely a rule of statutory interpretation, however orthodox, which is not qualified by large exceptions, some of which so nearly approach flat contradictions that the rule itself seems to totter on its base." Allen, *Law in the Making* (7th ed.) p. 518; "Not infrequently one rule points in one direction, another in a different direction": *Maunsell* v. *Ollins* [1975] A.C. 373, 382, *per* Lord Simon of Glaisdale.

[10] See Cross *Statutory Interpretation* 1st ed. p. 16 suggesting that there is now one rule of interpretation, a modernised literal rule. In the second edition the editors suggest at pp. 17–19 that since the review of statutory interpretation by the Law Commission in 1969 the courts have generally adopted a "purposive approach" which seeks to give effect to the general legislative purpose underlying a provision rather than to lay emphasis on strict literalism. Such an approach, which may involve a departure from the literal sense of the statutory language, owes more to the "golden" and "mischief" rules than to the literal rule.

[11] *Partridge* v. *Strange and Croker* (1553) 1 Plowd. 77.

[12] *R.* v. *Smith* [1910] 1 K.B. 17. See now, Interpretation Act 1978, s.4. It is now common practice to provide that an Act or parts of an Act are to be brought into operation by statutory instrument fixing a date of commencement.

[13] *Wilson* v. *Dagnall* [1972] 1 Q.B. 509 (C.A.).

Delegated legislation generally comes into operation when it is made, unless some other date is specified therein.[14] But the Statutory Instruments Act 1946, s.3, provides that where any person is charged with an offence under a statutory instrument as therein defined,[15] it shall be a defence to prove that the instrument had not been issued by the Stationery Office at the date of the alleged contravention, unless it is proved that at that date reasonable steps had been taken for the purpose of bringing the purport of the instrument to the notice of the public, or of persons likely to be affected by it, or of the person charged.[16] An entry of the date of issue of a statutory instrument in the Queen's Printer's list is conclusive evidence of the date on which such instrument was first issued by the Stationery Office.

Statutory Definitions

Sometimes Parliament itself prescribes the manner in which certain words or expressions used in Acts are to be interpreted. The *Interpretation Act 1889*, consolidated a number of such statutory provisions, and this has been re-enacted with amendment by the Interpretation Act 1978 *e.g.,* "unless the contrary intention appears, (a) words importing the masculine gender shall include the feminine; and words importing the feminine gender shall include the masculine; and (b) words in the singular shall include the plural, and words in the plural shall include the singular."[17] It also provides a number of new definitions, *e.g.,* "person" includes any body of persons corporate or unincorporate,[18] and "writing" includes printing, photography, and other modes of representing or reproducing words in a visible form.[19] These definitions may themselves be altered by Parliament, as in the Statute of Westminster 1931, s.11, which excluded from the expression "Colony," in any Act passed thereafter, a Dominion or any Province or State of a Dominion.

It is now common for an Act of Parliament to contain an *interpretation clause* defining some of the terms used in the Act and forming, as it were, its own dictionary. Thus the Dangerous Wild Animals Act 1976, s.7, provides that " 'veterinary surgeon'

---

[14] *Cf. Johnson* v. *Sargant* [1918] 1 K.B. 101.
[15] Above, p. 126.
[16] *Simmonds* v. *Newell* [1953] 1 W.L.R. 826, *sub nom. Defiant Cycle Co.* v. *Newell* [1953] 2 All E.R. 38; *R.* v. *Sheer Metalcraft* [1954] 1 Q.B. 586.
[17] s.6.
[18] s.5 and Sched. 1.
[19] s.20.

means a person who is for the time being registered in the register of veterinary surgeons," and that " 'damage' *includes* the death of, or injury to, any person."[20] The expression "includes" usually extends the ordinary meaning.

Statutory definitions only apply if the contrary intention does not appear in the context, whether this qualification is expressly stated or not.

Statutory instruments also frequently contain definition clauses.

Precedents of Interpretation

When the courts have interpreted an Act, or any section or word of it, that interpretation is a precedent in subsequent cases[21] relating to *that Act*, in accordance with the principles relating to judicial precedents described in the next chapter. This rule extends to precedents interpreting previous statutes replaced by a Consolidating Act, though when the words of a Consolidating Act are clear, it is not necessary to examine its legislative antecedents.[22] The commercial law codifying Acts such as the Sale of Goods Act 1893 and the Bills of Exchange Act 1882 expressly preserved the pre-existing case law on their subject matter, but in *Bank of England* v. *Vagliano*[23] Lord Herschell said the proper course was first to construe the language of the Act without reference to the prior case law and only to resort to that if the Act was ambiguous, or used terms which had previously acquired a technical meaning or if the Act did not cover a problem. It was not proper first to look at the older cases and then construe the Act to render it consistent with them.

Statutory definitions themselves may have to be judicially interpreted, *e.g.*, "trust for sale" in the Law of Property Act 1925, s.205(1).[24] Even the Interpretation Act 1889, had to be interpreted in 1947 by the House of Lords, who held that section 38(2) (effect of repeal) applies to Acts which have been repealed, but not to an Act or regulation which expires by effluxion of time.[25] Further, the interpretation put by the courts on a given word, expression or provision in one Act will be presumed, unless the contrary intention appears, to apply to the same

---

[20] Italics supplied.
[21] See *Hoe* v. *Dirs* [1941] 1 K.B. 34 (Goddard L.J.).
[22] *Farrell* v. *Alexander* [1976] A.C. 59 (H.L.).
[23] [1891] A.C. 107, 144. See also, *Bristol Tramways* v. *Fiat* [1910] 2 K.B. 381.
[24] *Re Leigh's Settled Estate (No. 1)* [1926] Ch. 852; *(No. 2)* [1927] 2 Ch. 13; *Re Parker's Settled Estate* [1928] Ch. 247; and *Re Norton* [1929] 1 Ch. 84.
[25] *Wicks* v. *Director of Public Prosecutions* [1947] A.C. 362. This is now covered by Interpretation Act 1978, s.16(2).

word, expression or provision in a later Act if the Acts are *in pari materia* or the context is similar.[26] Thus in *Barras* v. *Aberdeen Steam Trawling and Fishing Co.*[27] the House of Lords interpreted the word "wreck" in the Merchant Shipping Act 1925, in the light of the definition given by the Court of Appeal in *The Olympic*[28] to that word as used in the Act of 1894. This presumption may apply to a whole section.[29] On the other hand, it does not necessarily apply if the contexts are not similar,[30] and Salmon L.J. described this presumption as a guide that is not binding.[31]

In *R.* v. *Chard*[32] Lord Diplock was critical of *Barras* and said it was not authority for either (a) that the failure of Parliament when passing amending legislation to change words which had been interpreted by a lower court in a sense which the House of Lords regards as wrong could throw light on the intention of a later Parliament or (b) that the re-enactment of the very words of earlier legislation in a consolidating Act (where Parliamentary debate is not possible) could affect the interpretation of those words. Lords Roskill and Scarman agreed, but the latter, following Lord Macmillan in *Barras*, thought there was a presumption that in re-enacting Parliament had approved earlier interpretation of the re-enacted legislation and Lord Templeman agreed with this.

We must notice the limits of precedents of interpretation. Lord Evershed M.R. pointed out that the courts must construe Acts of Parliament and not previous judicial expositions of Acts of Parliament, because such expositions are made with reference to the particular facts of particular cases.[33] Lord Reid in *Goodrich* v. *Paisner*,[34] which concerned the question whether part of a house was "let as a separate dwelling" for the purposes of the Act,[35] said that when the Court of Appeal has laid down a test, "that test ought to be followed in all cases which do not present

---

[26] *R.* v. *Loxdale* (1758) 1 Burr. 445 (Poor Law Acts); *Att.-Gen.* v. *Prince Ernest Augustus of Hanover* [1957] A.C. 436 (H.L.) (Naturalisation Acts). See also *The Goring* [1988] 2 W.L.R. 460, 467, using the Civil Aviation Act 1949 and its subordinate legislation in aid of the decision that the Merchant Shipping Act 1894 did not apply to salvage in non-tidal waters. See also p. 471.

[27] [1933] A.C. 402.

[28] [1913] P. 92.

[29] *Sparrow* v. *Fairey Aviation Co. Ltd.* [1964] A.C. 1019 (H.L.).

[30] *London Corporation* v. *Cusack-Smith* [1955] A.C. 337, *per* Lord Reid.

[31] *R.* v. *Bow Road Justices, ex p. Adedigba* [1968] 2 Q.B. 572, 583.

[32] [1984] A.C. 279.

[33] *Wright* v. *Walford* [1955] 1 Q.B. 363.

[34] [1957] A.C. 65.

[35] Increase of Rent and Mortgage Interest (Restrictions) Act 1920.

substantial relevant differences. . . . That does not mean that the words used by the Court of Appeal are to be treated as if they were words in an Act of Parliament. In substantially different circumstances they are only a guide, and not a rule."

Literal Interpretation

The words of a statute must be interpreted according to their *literal* meaning, and sentences according to their *grammatical* meaning (*litera legis*). The courts are supposed to find out the intention of the legislature, but it is that intention as expressed in the words used. "The intention of Parliament," said Lord Thankerton in *Wicks* v. *Director of Public Prosecutions*,[36] "is not to be judged by what is in its mind, but by its expression of that mind in the statute itself." Where the words are clear and unambiguous and logically complete on the face of them, the meaning of the statute is the meaning of those words: they are, as it were, conclusive evidence of the legislature's intention. As Tindal C.J. said in the *Sussex Peerage Case*,[37] where the question before the Committee for Privileges was whether the Royal Marriages Act 1772, extended to marriages celebrated outside England:

> "The only rule for the construction of Acts of Parliament is, that they should be construed according to the intent of the Parliament which passed the Act. If the words of the statute are in themselves precise and unambiguous, then no more can be necessary than to expound those words in their natural and ordinary sense. The words themselves alone do, in such case, best declare the intention of the lawgiver."

There are numerous dicta to the same effect. Thus in *Black-Clawson International Ltd.* v. *Papierwerke etc. AG*[38] Lord Reid said: "We are seeking the meaning of the words which Parliament used. We are seeking not what Parliament meant but the true meaning of what they said." As Lord Simon of Glaisdale observed in the same case, draftsmen, civil servants, members of Parliament and judges are all fallible human beings; and also most words in the English language have a number of shades of meaning.

The Bankruptcy Act 1914, s.157(1), provided that any person who had been adjudged bankrupt should be guilty of a

---

[36] [1947] A.C. 362.
[37] (1844) 11 Cl. & Fin. 85, 143.
[38] [1975] A.C. 591 (H.L.).

misdemeanour if, having at the date of the receiving order "any debts contracted in the course and for the furtherance of [such] trade or business," he materially contributed to or increased his insolvency by gambling. In *R.* v. *Vaccari*[39] it was found that Vaccari, when adjudicated bankrupt, owed £7,000 to the Inland Revenue; he had lost £6,000 to bookmakers within the two preceding years, and he paid his gambling debts but not his income tax. It was held that the debt to the Inland Revenue was not a debt "contracted in the course and for the purposes of trade or business," but a statutory liability to pay over part of the profits of his business. He had not, therefore, committed the offence. The result might seem very strange, said Cassels J., but that was not a matter for the court but for Parliament. The court had to interpret the law as they found it. The Inland Revenue fared better in *I.R.C.* v. *Hinchy*,[40] where the House of Lords had to construe the Income Tax Act 1952, s.25(3), which provided that a person who failed to deliver a correct income tax return should forfeit "the sum of £20 and treble the tax which he ought to be charged under this Act." Reversing the Court of Appeal, there Lordships held that, in addition to the penalty of £20, a taxpayer who had declared only part of his Post Office interest was liable to pay treble the whole tax chargeable for the year and not merely treble the tax on the undeclared income.

In a statute dealing with matters affecting everybody generally, words are given their common and ordinary meaning; whereas in a statute referring to a particular trade or business, words will be construed as having the particular meaning that persons conversant with that trade or business know and understand. Thus "lop" in the Highways Act 1835, with reference to trees growing near the highway was construed in the popular sense of cutting off branches laterally and not extending to topping.[41] But there may be disagreement as to the ordinary meaning of words. In *London and North-Eastern Railway Co.* v. *Berriman*[42] the Court of Appeal unanimously held that "repairing" in certain statutory rules relating to the permanent way included oiling and cleaning signals near the permanent way; but the House of Lords held by three to two that repairing did not include oiling and cleaning. Standard dictionaries may be looked at for help, such as the *Oxford English Dictionary* and

[39] [1958] 1 W.L.R. 297.
[40] [1960] A.C. 748. *Cf.* Finance Act 1960, ss. 44 and 46, passed in consequence of this decision.
[41] *Unwin* v. *Hanson* [1891] 2 Q.B. 115. And see *Mersey Docks and Harbour Board* v. *Turner* [1893] A.C. 468 ("damage").
[42] [1946] A.C. 278.

even *Dr. Johnson's Dictionary*, for example, to elucidate the meaning of "rubbish",[43] but dictionaries are often not of much help: the meaning of expressions depends on the context of the statute, and it is the duty of the court to arrive at its own construction. Judicial *dicta* in previous cases are usually a safer guide.[44]

Words are taken to be used prima facie in the sense they bore at the time the statute was passed, *e.g.*, the Treason Act 1351.[45] In the case of old statutes the practice of those implementing them were used in aid of interpretation as *contemporanea expositio*[46] but this does not apply to modern legislation.[47] Delegated legislation made under an Act, especially when made under a power to modify the Act and when it is consistent with the Act, may be used as "a kind of Parliamentary *contemporanea expositio.*"[48] There is a presumption that every word counts, or against surplusage,[49] though this is less strong in the case of complex modern legislation such as revenue statutes.[50] There is also a presumption that the same word bears the same meaning throughout a statute.[51] It is not permissible to employ the fact that an amendment has been proposed to legislation to influence its interpretation.[52] The fact that the members of a multiple court differ as to the meaning of words does not mean that the judges in the majority must treat the words as unclear or ambiguous if they in fact regard them as unambiguous.[53]

---

[43] *McVittie* v. *Bolton Corporation* [1945] 1 K.B. 281. *Flack* v. *Baldry* [1988] 1 W.L.R. 393 (O.E.D. "discharge").

[44] *Midland Ry.* v. *Robinson* (1889) 15 App.Cas. 19, at p. 34, *per* Lord Macnaghten. See also, *Mandla* v. *Dowell Lee* [1983] 2 A.C. 548.

[45] *R.* v. *Casement* [1917] 1 K.B. 98: "adhering to the King's enemies," etc.; *Joyce* v. *Director of Public Prosecutions* [1946] A.C. 347: "if a man do levy war, etc." See also, *The Longford* (1889) 14 P.D. 34 ("action" in Admiralty Court). This is often stated as a rule of general application, but some writers suggest that it may be limited to statutes passed to deal with specific contemporary problems. See Cross, *Statutory Interpretation* (2nd ed.) p. 49 and authorities there cited.

[46] *Campbell College (Governors)* v. *Commissioners for Valuation* [1964] 1 W.L.R. 912 (100 years not enough).

[47] *L.C.C.* v. *Central Land Board* [1958] 1 W.L.R. 1269 (notes for civil servants). In a nicely balanced case it might sway the outcome, *Wicks* v. *Frith* [1982] 2 A.C. at 230. See also, *Notts. County Council* v. *Secretary of State for the Environment* [1980] A.C. 240 for use of a report to which the statute was to give effect.

[48] *Hanlon* v. *Law Society* [1981] A.C. 124.

[49] *Hill* v. *William Hill* [1949] A.C. 530.

[50] *Phillipson-Stow* v. *I.R.C.* [1961] A.C. 727.

[51] *R.* v. *Buttle* (1870) L.R. 1 C.C.R. 248 but see *Hadley* v. *Perks* (1866) L.R. 1 Q.B. 444. See Offences Against the Person Act 1861, s.57 where the word "marry" is used in two different meanings in the same section.

[52] *Willow Wren* v. *B.T.C.* [1956] 1 W.L.R. 1269.

[53] *Kirkness* v. *John Hudson* [1955] A.C. 696, 712.

Words to be taken in their Context

A word in itself has no absolute meaning: its meaning is relative
to the context. *"Noscitur a sociis"* is sometimes translated as "a
word is known by the company it keeps." The words within a
section must therefore be read in their context; and a statute
must be read as a whole, for one section may be explained or
modified by another. As Viscount Simonds said in *Att.-Gen.* v.
Prince Ernest Augustus of Hanover,[54] no one should profess to
understand any part of a statute or any other document before
he has read the whole of it. "Until he has done so he is not
entitled to say that it or any part of it is clear or unambiguous."
His Lordship said the context includes the preamble, the
existing state of the law, other statutes *in pari materia*, and the
mischief that was intended to be remedied. In that case the
House of Lords in 1957 decided that the clear provision in an Act
of 1705[55] naturalising lineal descendants of Princess Sophia
"born or hereafter to be born" applied to the respondent,
although the preamble referred to naturalisation "in Your
Majesty's life-time."[56] On the other hand it was found permissible in *Kruhlak* v. *Kruhlak*[57] for the court to hold that a married
woman living apart from her husband under a separation order
was a "single woman" for the purpose of the Bastardy Laws
Amendment Act 1872.

An important application of the context principle is the
ejusdem generis rule, a canon of construction whereby general
words used by way of summary, after the enumeration of
particulars forming a category, are taken to refer only to things
of the kind which fall within that category. Thus in *Brownsea
Haven Properties* v. *Poole Corporation*,[58] where a local authority
had power under an Act of 1847 to make orders for prescribing
traffic routes and for preventing obstruction of the streets "in all
times of public processions, rejoicings, or illuminations, and *in
any case* when the streets are thronged or liable to be
obstructed," the Court of Appeal held that the words "in any
case" must be confined to such occasions as public processions,
rejoicings and illuminations, and so did not give power to
prescribe one-way traffic for six months in ordinary conditions.
Similarly, in *Powell* v. *Kempton Park Racecourse Co.*,[59] an Act

[54] [1957] A.C. 436, 461, 463.
[55] 4 & 5 Anne, c. 16.
[56] Below, p. 152.
[57] [1958] 2 Q.B. 32. And see *R.* v. *MacDonagh* (1974) 59 Cr.App.R. 55 (C.A.), *per*
Lord Widgery C.J. on the meaning of "drive" while disqualified.
[58] [1958] Ch. 574.
[59] [1899] A.C. 143.

prohibited the keeping of a "house, office, room or other place" for betting with persons resorting thereto, and the House of Lords held that the words "or other place" did not apply to an uncovered enclosure adjacent to the racecourse[60]; and in *Evans* v. *Cross*[61] it was held that the word "device," following "signals, warning signposts, direction posts and signs," did not include a white line painted on the road. But there must be a category for the *ejusdem generis* rule to apply, and so it was held in *R.* v. *Payne*[62] that the wording of a statute which made it a felony to convey into a prison, with intent to facilitate the escape of any prisoner, any mask, dress or other disguise, or any letter, or any other article or thing, did include a crowbar.

A related guide to interpretation is expressed in the maxim, *expressio unius (est) exclusio alterius*. Thus, the requirement in the Statute of Frauds 1677, s.17, that contracts for the sale of "goods, wares and merchandise" for £10 or upwards should be in writing, was held not to apply to the sale of stocks and shares.[63] But this maxim is to be treated with caution, as the failure to make the *expressio* complete often arises from inadvertence.[64]

The "Golden Rule"

What is sometimes called the "Golden Rule" appears to be merely a modification of the rule of literal interpretation.[65] Blackstone said that one may look at the effects and consequences, and a little deviation is allowed if a literal interpretation produces no meaning or an absurb meaning.[66] "It is a very useful rule in the construction of a statute," said Parke B. in *Becke* v. *Smith*,[67]

"to adhere to the ordinary meaning of the words used, and to the grammatical construction, *unless that is at variance with*

---

[60] *Cf. Culley* v. *Harrison* [1956] 2 Q.B. 71 (Div.Ct.): park used for motor-cycle scramble on Sunday held to be a "place" within the meaning of the Sunday Observance Act 1780 ("any house, room or other place").

[61] [1938] 1 K.B. 694. See also, *Gregory* v. *Fearn* [1953] 1 W.L.R. 974.

[62] (1866) 35 L.J.M.C. 170 (C.C.R.).

[63] *Tempest* v. *Kilner* (1846) 3 C.B. 249. See also *The Goring* [1988] 2 W.L.R. 460, 465. Failure to mention salvage in non-tidal waters indicates Act did not apply to it.

[64] *Colquhoun* v. *Brooks* (1887) 19 Q.B.D. 400, *per* Wills J.

[65] See Cross *op cit.* p. 170, though the Law Commission regarded it as a weaker form of "the mischief rule." See below, p. 145. The approach underlying these two rules is now often spoken of as "purposive construction". *Nothman* v. *Barnet London Borough Council* [1978] 1 W.L.R. 220; *R.* v. *Barnet ex p. Shah* [1983] 2 A.C. 309.

[66] Bl.Comm.I. 59–62.

[67] (1836) 2 M. & W. 191, 195.

> *the intention of the legislature to be collected from the
> statute itself, or leads to any manifest absurdity or re-
> pugnance,* in which case the language may be varied
> or modified so as to avoid such inconvenience, but no
> further."[68]

The words "repugnance" and "inconvenience" here mean
a logical inconsistency, either between two parts of the
same statute or between the statute and some other legal
principle in the same branch of law, such inconsistency
resulting from pursuing the interpretation to its logical
conclusion.[69]

Clauson J. was able to hold in *Re Sigsworth*[70] that the son
of a woman whom he had murdered was not entitled to
succeed to her estate, although he was her sole issue and
the Administration of Estates Act 1925, s.46, provided that
the residuary estate of an intestate should be distributed
among "the issue." Harman J. in *Re Lockwood*[71] could not
believe that on an intestacy Parliament preferred first cousins
twice removed to nephews and nieces. The word "and" has
been taken to mean "or" so as to give a sensible meaning to
section 7 of the Official Secrets Act 1911[72]; and the words
"owner or master" have been read conjunctively so that both
owner and master could be prosecuted under the Oil in
Navigable Waters Act 1955.[73] In *Adler* v. *George*[74] it was held
that persons who obstructed H.M. forces *in* a prohibited
place were guilty under the Official Secrets Act 1920, of
obstructing H.M. forces "in the vicinity" of a prohibited
place; and in *Barnard* v. *Gorman*[75] the power to arrest an
"offender" given by the Customs Consolidation Act 1876,
s.186, was held to include a person reasonably suspected of
having committed an offence.

---

[68] See also by the same judge, as Lord Wensleydale, in *Grey* v. *Pearson*
(1857) 6 H.L.C. 61, 106; *per* Lord Blackburn in *River Wear Commissioners* v.
Adamson (1877) 2 App.Cas. 743, 764–765; and, *per* Lord Macnaghten in
Vacher v. *London Society of Compositors* [1913] A.C. 107, 117.

[69] As to whether the absurdity or inconsistency must arise within the statute
or as between the statute and external matters, see Cross (2nd ed.) *op cit.*,
pp. 91–93 citing *Richard Thomas and Baldwins* v. *Cummings* [1955] A.C. 321
as authority for taking account of external matters.

[70] [1935] Ch. 89. See now, Forfeiture Act 1982.

[71] [1958] Ch. 231.

[72] R. v. *Oakes* [1959] 2 Q.B. 350 (C.C.A.).

[73] R. v. *Federal Steam Navigation Co. Ltd.* [1974] 1 W.L.R. 505; [1974] 2 All
E.R. 97 (H.L. majority 3:2).

[74] [1964] 2 Q.B. 7.

[75] [1941] A.C. 378 (H.L.).

The "Mischief Rule" or the Rules in Heydon's Case

Tindal C.J. in the *Sussex Peerage Case*[76] said:

> "But if any doubt arises from the terms employed by the Legislature, it has always been held a safe means of collecting the intention, to call in aid the ground and cause of making the statute, and to have recourse to the preamble, which, according to Chief Justice Dyer[77] is 'a key to open the minds of the makers of the Act, and the mischiefs which they intended to redress.'"

The rule that one may look to the mischief[78] in order to discover the intention was already described by the Court of Exchequer in 1559 as an old one.[79] Blackstone said the most universal and effectual way when the words are dubious is to consider the reason and spirit of the statute, or the cause which moved the legislator to enact it.[80]

When the words are logically defective—because they are ambiguous (*i.e.*, capable of more than one meaning, it being doubtful which meaning the legislature intended), inconsistent with each other, or incomplete—the statute must be considered as a whole in order to find guidance from the general purpose of the legislature. There may be disagreement as to whether the words are ambiguous, *e.g.*, whether "has reasonable cause to believe" can have other than an objective meaning.[81] If the court considers that the *litera legis* is not clear, it must interpret according to the "purpose," "policy" or "spirit" of the statute (*ratio legis*).

In this task the court is guided by the rules laid down in 1584 in *Heydon's Case*.[82] As reported by Coke, the court is to consider:

> "(1) *what was the common law before the making of the Act; (2) what was the mischief and defect for which the common law did not provide; (3) what remedy the Parliament hath resolved and appointed to cure the disease of the commonwealth; (4) the true reason of the remedy. And then the*

[76] (1844) 11 Cl. & Fin. 85; above, p. 139.
[77] *Stowel* v. *Lord Zouch*, 1 Plowd. 369.
[78] "Mischief" was used in the fifteenth century to mean harm or evil, and the injury caused thereby; in the sixteenth century "mischief" in legal usage covered a condition in which a person suffers a wrong or is under some disability (*O.E.D.*).
[79] *Stradling* v. *Morgan*, Plowd. 199, 203–206.
[80] Bl.Comm.I. 59–62.
[81] *Liversidge* v. *Anderson* [1942] A.C. 206.
[82] 3 Co.Rep. 7a.

office of all the Judges is always to make such construction as shall *suppress the mischief and advance the remedy....*"

In Lord Halsbury's modern paraphrase, "we are to see what was the law before the Act was passed, and what was the mischief or defect for which the law had not provided, what remedy Parliament appointed, and the reason of the remedy."[83] Here the court may look, not only to the various intrinsic aids mentioned below, but also to previous statute law and case law dealing with the same matter. In *Sweet* v. *Parsley,*[84] where the question was the meaning of the expression "concerned in the management of premises used for the purpose of smoking cannabis" in the Dangerous Drugs Act 1965, the judgments of both Lord Pearce and Lord Wilberforce were based partly on the interpretation of a similar expression in the Dangerous Drugs Act 1920. Lord Wilberforce also referred to the Gaming Act 1845 ("management" in relation to gaming houses), and the Criminal Law Amendment Act 1885 ("the management of a brothel").

Thus, when an individual has been injured by the breach of a statutory duty, in determining whether he has a right of action for damages the court will consider such questions as: whether the statute was intended for the protection of all citizens or only of a certain class of persons in certain circumstances; and whether the statute provides a special penalty, and if so, whether other remedies are excluded.[85] A bicycle was held to be a "carriage" for the purposes of the Licensing Act 1872, which provided that a person who was drunk in charge of a carriage on the highway might be arrested without warrant.[86] Where a Road Traffic Act permitted a constable to arrest without warrant a person "committing an offence" under the Act, Lord Denning M.R. read the words as meaning *"apparently* committing an offence" so as to include the case where a constable reasonably thinks that an offence is being committed although his superiors later decide not to prosecute.[87]

---

[83] *Eastman Photographic Co.* v. *Comptroller of Patents* [1898] A.C. 571, at p. 573, Lord Diplock pointed out in *Black-Clawson International Ltd.* v. *Papierwerke etc. AG* [1975] A.C. 591 (H.L.) that at the time when *Heydon's Case* was decided, and for long afterwards, the mischief intended to be remedied was commonly set out in the preamble.
[84] [1970] A.C. 132 (H.L.).
[85] *Gorris* v. *Scott* (1874) L.R. 9 Ex. 125.
[86] *Corkery* v. *Carpenter* [1951] 1 K.B. 102 (D.C.).
[87] *Wiltshire* v. *Barrett* [1966] 1 Q.B. 312.

"Wife" has been held to include the wife of a polygamous the wife of a polygamous marriage for the purposes of the National Assistance Act 1948.[88]

But the rules in *Heydon's Case* (as modified to include an examination of the previous statute law, as well as the common law) are the limits to which the courts allow themselves to go. They will not read words into an Act of Parliament unless clear reason for it is found within the four corners of the Act itself.[89] So where an Act provided that an order for the protection of the earnings of a deserted married woman might be discharged by the magistrate who made it, this was held not to apply to his successor, even though the magistrate who made the order was dead.[90] (The *casus omissus*[91] was provided for later in the same year by an Act containing one section.) The policy of an Act, however, is quite often referred to as confirming a literal interpretation already reached, as by Scott L.J. in *National Union of General and Municipal Workers* v. *Gillian*.[92]

The Law Commission, whilst accepting that the mischief rule was more satisfactory than the literal, considered its description and statement archaic not only in language but as representing a different relationship between Parliament and the courts than prevails at the present day. It was also misleading in suggesting that legislation led to the negative task of suppressing evils and not to the positive promotion of betterment hence the Commission suggested a broader formula stating that a construction which would promote the general legislative purpose was to be preferred to one which did not.[93]

Restricted Use of Extrinsic Materials

While the courts, in the circumstances of the preceding paragraph, may consider the *legal* history of a statute, they do not permit themselves to inquire into its social, political or literary history, such as parliamentary debates, reports of commissions or advisory committees, or ministerial pronouncements on the Bill.

---

[88] *Imam Din* v. *National Assistance Board* [1967] 2 Q.B. 213 (D.C.).
[89] *Per* Lord Loreburn in *Vickers* v. *Evans* [1910] A.C. 444 and see, *per* Lord Diplock in *Jones* v. *Wrotham Park Settled Estates* [1980] A.C. 74.
[90] *Ex p. Sharpe* (1864) 5 B. & S. 322.
[91] See below, pp. 154–156.
[92] [1946] K.B. 81, 85–87.
[93] *The Law Commission: The Interpretation of Statutes*, pp. 19–20 and 49 n. 177.

The modern English rule was first stated in 1769 in *Millar* v. *Taylor*[94] by Willes J. In *Salkeld* v. *Johnson* (1848)[95] the report of the Real Property Commissioners was not admitted to elucidate legislation ostensibly based on their report. The rule was applied most strictly at the end of the nineteenth century. In *Hilder* v. *Dexter*[96] Lord Halsbury L.C. even declined to deliver judgment on the interpretation of a statute, on the ground that he had taken a prominent part in drafting it. This is a far cry from the attitude of Hengham C.J. in the fourteenth century,[97] and Lord Nottingham in the seventeenth.[98] Viscount Haldane L.C., an expert on trade union questions, in *Vacher* v. *London Society of Compositors*,[99] said:

> "In endeavouring to place the proper interpretation on the sections of the statute [Trade Disputes Act 1906] before this House sitting in its judicial capacity, I propose . . . to exclude consideration of everything excepting the state of the law as it was when the statute was passed. . . ."

The Merchant Shipping Act 1925, was passed (as the preamble showed) to give effect to an International Labour Convention, which was scheduled to the Act; nevertheless, the majority of the Court of Appeal and of the House of Lords in *Ellerman Lines* v. *Murray*[1] refused to look at the schedule or the preamble—and hence to the International Convention—to explain what they considered to be the clear words of the section. Lord Wright in *Assam Railways and Trading Co.* v. *Inland Revenue Commissioners*[2] declined to look at the Report of a Royal Commission on income tax issued in 1920 to show the purpose or object of Parliament in passing the Finance Act 1920. In *Black-Clawson International Ltd.* v. *Papierwerke etc. AG*,[3] Lords Reid, Wilberforce and Diplock thought the court was entitled to have regard to the statement contained in the report of the committee that prepared a draft Bill presented to Parliament before the passing of the Foreign

---

[94] 4 Burr. 2303.
[95] 2 Ex. 256.
[96] [1902] A.C. 474.
[97] Above, p. 134.
[98] Above, p. 128.
[99] [1913] A.C. 107, 113.
[1] [1931] A.C. 126. See below, pp. 151–152 (preamble, below, pp. 153–154 (schedule), and below, pp. 164–165 (International Law), but see now, *Buchanan* v. *Babco* [1978] A.C. 141, also involving a Convention, where it was said that perhaps *Ellerman Lines* v. *Murray* was wrong.
[2] [1935] A.C. 445, 457.
[3] [1975] A.C. 591 (H.L.). And see *Letang* v. *Cooper* [1965] 1 Q.B. 232, *per* Lord Denning M.R.; *R.* v. *Kemp* [1988] 2 W.L.R. 975.

Judgments (Reciprocal Enforcement) Act 1933, concerning the mischief aimed at and the state of the law as it was then understood to be; but that the court was not entitled to take into account the committee's recommendations or its comments on the draft Bill. The use of Hansard has been strongly condemned by the House of Lords.[4] The Law Commission suggested the preparation of Explanatory Material which would accompany a Bill on its way through Parliament and would be subject to amendment as the Bill was altered. This Material would be more detailed than the old Preambles and the Explanatory Memoranda which accompany Bills for guidance of members of both Houses and unlike the confidential Notes on Clauses for Ministers piloting legislation it would be generally accessible.[5] An objection to this has been that the Material would amount to a second Act of Parliament, itself requiring interpretation.[6]

Apparent exceptions are cases where extrinsic materials have been looked at to explain the state of the law or "mischief" existing when the Act was passed, rather than the intention of the legislature in the Act itself.[7] For example, in construing the Church Discipline Act 1840, the Court of Appeal in 1879 considered an opinion given extrajudicially by Lord Cairns L.C. to the House of Lords on the Public Worship Regulation Act 1874.[8] In the case of *Boy Andrew (Owners) Ltd.* v. *St. Rognvald (Owners) Ltd.*[9] Viscount Simon quoted the Report of the Law Revision Committee on the law relating to contributory negligence,[10] to explain the common law concerning the causation of accidents, not to expound the Law Reform (Contributory Negligence) Act 1945.[11]

The decision of the House of Lords in *Chandler* v. *D.P.P.*[12] that the "Committee of 100" were guilty under section 1 of the Official Secrets Act 1911, has been shown by reference to the reports of parliamentary debates to be contrary to statements

---

[4] *Davis* v. *Johnson* [1979] A.C. 264; *Hadmor* v. *Hamilton* [1983] 1 A.C. 191.
[5] *Law Commission: The Interpretation of Statutes*, pp. 38–43.
[6] See, for reservations, *The Preparation of Legislation* (1975) (Cmnd. 6053) (the report of the Renton Committee) pp. 139–148.
[7] *Per* Lord Wright in *Assam Railways and Trading Co.* v. *Inland Revenue Commissioners*, above, at pp. 457–459; *Hadmor* v. *Hamilton* [1983] 1 A.C. 191.
[8] *R.* v. *Bishop of Oxford* (1879) 4 Q.B.D. 525.
[9] [1948] A.C. 140.
[10] Cmd. 6032.
[11] Sometimes recent statutes have expressly enacted that specified preparatory material should be used in interpretation, *e.g.* Civil Jurisdiction and Judgments Act 1982, s.3.
[12] [1964] A.C. 763, below, p. 154. See D. Thompson, "Committee of 100 and Official Secrets Act 1971, s.1" [1963] *Public Law* 201.

made by Lord Chancellors and Attorneys-General in Parliament. The rule against looking at parliamentary debates, however, is strict, and there is little support for altering it. In *Beswick* v. *Beswick*[13] Lord Upjohn referred to the report of the Joint Committee of the two Houses on Consolidating Bills, not directly on the construction of section 56 of the Law of Property Act 1925 (a Consolidating Act), but to confirm the presumption that Consolidating Bills do not intend to change the law. The Law Commission have pointed out the difficulty of extracting relevant and helpful information from parliamentary proceedings, and of providing such information in convenient and accessible form for this purpose[14]; and Lord Simon of Glaisdale has suggested[15] that where a Minister in answer to a question expresses an opinion as to the operation of a Bill in particular circumstances, it should be made a constitutional convention that such contingency should ordinarily be covered by specific enactment.

In the case of statutes giving effect to international conventions the House of Lords have held that it is permissible to look at the preparatory materials (*Travaux préparatoires*) of the convention in consequence of this country's adherence to the Vienna Convention on the Law of Treaties 1969.[16] The materials must be publicly accessible and clearly point to a solution.[17]

Intrinsic Aids

If the enacting or operative words of an Act are not clear and unambiguous in themselves, there are several intrinsic aids to which the courts may look for guidance concerning the intention of Parliament.

Long Title

Since 1496, Acts of Parliament have been given titles—or "long titles" as they are usually called to distinguish them from the more modern short title. Formerly the long title was not considered to be part of the Act, but it could be looked at—if the operative part of the Act was not clear—for guidance concerning the intention of the legislature and the scope of the Act.[18] The

---

[13] [1968] A.C. 58, 105.
[14] *The Law Commission: The Interpretation of Statutes*, below, pp. 168–169.
[15] *Race Relations Board* v. *Dockers' Labour Club and Institute Ltd.* [1976] A.C. 285 (H.L.).
[16] See below, pp. 164–165, 167.
[17] *Fothergill* v. *Monarch Airlines* [1980] A.C. 251.
[18] *Johnson* v. *Upham* (1859) 2 E. & E. 250, 263.

modern position is thus stated by Lindley M.R. in *Fielding* v. *Morley Corporation*[19]:

> "I read the title advisedly, because now, and for some years past, the title of an Act of Parliament has been part of the Act. In old days it used not to be so, and in the old books we were told not so to regard it; but now the title is an important part of the Act, and is so treated in both Houses of Parliament."

The title of the Act referred to in that case, *viz.*, the Public Authorities Protection Act 1893, read: "An Act to generalise and amend certain statutory provisions for the protection of persons acting in the execution of statutory and other public duties."[20] The reason for the change in attitude of the courts is that the title was formerly the product merely of the draftsman, whereas now it is subject to amendment by both Houses at various stages of the Bill. The long title of the Debtors Act 1869, was looked at by Lord Dilhorne L.C. in *Fisher* v. *Raven*[21] for guidance on the meaning of obtaining credit by fraud in incurring "any debt or liability." The title will not be allowed to restrict the clear meaning of the operative part. Thus, in *Re Groos*[22] Gorell Barnes J. held that section 3 of the Wills Act 1861 ("Lord Kingsdown's Act"),[23] applied to the will of an alien, although the long title read: "An Act to amend the law with respect to wills of personal estate made by British subjects." On the other hand, it has been said that recourse to the long title need not be confined to cases of ambiguity.[24]

Preamble

In the Tudor and Stuart periods Acts of Parliament often had lengthy—and sometimes fanciful—preambles.[25] Examples are the Statute of Uses 1535, and the Statute of Frauds 1677. One preamble, that to the Statute of Charitable Uses 1601,[26] has had an extraordinary history; for, although the 1601 Act was repealed by the Mortmain and Charitable Uses Act 1888, its

---

[19] [1899] 1 Ch. 1, 3.

[20] This Act was repealed by the Law Reform (Limitation of Actions, etc.) Act 1954.

[21] [1964] A.C. 210.

[22] [1904] P. 269. This Act was repealed by the Wills Act 1963.

[23] Repealed by the Wills Act 1963.

[24] *Per* Lord Simon of Glaisdale in *Black-Clawson International Ltd.* v. *Papierwerke etc. AG* [1975] A.C. 591 (H.L.).

[25] See, *per* Lord Diplock, in the *Black-Clawson* case (above).

[26] 43 Eliz. 1, c. 4.

preamble was preserved by the 1888 Act until the repeal of the latter by the Charities Act 1960, and to this day no object is regarded by the Courts as "charitable" unless it comes within the spirit and intendment of the preamble to the Act of 1601.[27] Preambles, which correspond to recitals in deeds, have not been common in recent times, though some modern Acts have fairly full preambles, such as the Parliament Act 1911, the Statute of Westminster 1931, and the Matrimonial Causes Act 1947.

Blackstone regarded the preamble as one of the first things to look at in applying the mischief rule where the words are dubious,[28] but a preamble may be wider or narrower than the enacting words, and the modern practice is that it is only if the body of the Act is not clear and unambiguous that the preamble may be looked to for guidance.[29] Thus in *Attorney-General* v. *Prince Ernest Augustus of Hanover*[30] the House of Lords held that the words of an Act of 1705,[31] "all persons lineally descending from [Princess Sophia, Electress of Hanover] born or *hereafter to be born*" must be interpreted literally, so as to confer British nationality on the respondent, although the preamble recited that

> "to the end the said Princess ... and the issue of her body, and all persons lineally descending from her, may be encouraged to become acquainted with the laws and constitutions of this realm, it is just and highly reasonable that they, *in Your Majesty's lifetime* ... should be naturalised."

The enacting words were held to be clear and unambiguous and therefore to be applied although they apparently went farther than the preamble indicated.[32] Nevertheless, there are dicta by Viscount Simonds and Lord Somervell in this case that the preamble is part of the context of a statute.

Punctuation

There was usually no punctuation on the former Parliament Rolls,[33] though there is sometimes punctuation on the printed

---

[27] *Income Tax Commissioners* v. *Pemsel* [1891] A.C. 531, 543; *Williams' Trustees* v. *Inland Revenue Commissioners* [1947] A.C. 447. And see *Incorporated Council of Law Reporting* v. *Att.-Gen.* [1972] Ch. 73 (C.A.).

[28] Bl.Comm.I. 59–62.

[29] *Powell* v. *Kempton Park Racecourse Co.* [1899] A.C. 143, 157, *per* Lord Halsbury. See also, *The Norwhale* [1975] Q.B. 589. *The Goring* [1988] 2 W.L.R. 460, 466.

[30] [1957] A.C. 436, above, p. 142.

[31] 4 & 5 Anne, c. 16.

[32] The Act had been repealed by the British Nationality Act 1948, but without affecting the status of persons who were British subjects before that date.

[33] See *Barrow* v. *Wadkin* (1857) 24 Beav. 327; *R.* v. *Casement* [1917] 1 K.B. 98.

vellum copies deposited in the House of Lords since 1849. Modern Parliamentary draftsmen, unlike conveyancers, tend to use normal punctuation, and this appears in the Queen's Printer's copies. Punctuation was not formerly regarded as part of the Act.[34] "Even if punctuation in more modern Acts can be looked at (which is very doubtful)," said Lord Reid in *I.R.C.* v. *Hinchy*,[35] "I do not think that one can have any regard to punctuation in older Acts"; but more recently he said it might be more realistic to accept the Companies Act 1948, as printed as being the product of the whole legislative process.[36]

Headings

Some statutes have headings prefixed to sections or parts of the Act. They were first used in 1845. If the words of an Act are not clear and unambiguous, headings may be looked at for guidance as if they were preambles to the section or part.[37] Thus, the heading to section 10 of the Naturalisation Act 1870, read: "National status of married women and infant children," and Cohen J. held that the word "child" in that section meant a child under 21 years of age.[38] Headings were used by the majority of the House of Lords in *D.P.P.* v. *Schildkamp*[39] in the construction of the Companies Act 1948, s.332.

Schedules

Schedules were first used in 1765, and are employed for various purposes, such as transitional provisions, forms, lists and illustrations, being especially important in such statutes as Planning Acts and Finance Acts. They are part of the Act.[40] A

---

[34] *Duke of Devonshire* v. *O'Connor* (1890) 24 Q.B.D. 468, 478, *per* Lord Esher, M.R.
[35] [1960] A.C. 748.
[36] *D.P.P.* v. *Schildkamp* [1971] A.C. 1 (H.L.). See Cross *op. cit.* (2nd ed.) pp. 122–123, suggesting that on first reading a provision the judge may read all that is printed to see if there is ambiguity. If he finds ambiguity then in resolving it he is confined to recognised aids. See also, *Hanlon* v. *Law Society* [1981] A.C. 124, 198. These cases have in effect given judicial sanction to the proposal of the Law Commission that these matters could be used but that no more effect should be given to them than was appropriate in the circumstances.
[37] *Fletcher* v. *Birkenhead Corporation* [1907] 1 K.B. 205, 218, *per* Farwell L.J.; *cf. R.* v. *Surrey Assessment Committee* [1948] 1 K.B. 28, 32, *per* Lord Goddard C.J.; *Qualter, Hall & Co.* v. *Board of Trade* [1961] Ch. 121, 131.
[38] *Re Carlton* [1945] 1 Ch. 280. The decision was affirmed by the Court of Appeal without consideration of the use of headings. And see *Fisher* v. *Raven* [1964] A.C. 210 (H.L.). *Cf.* Marginal Notes, below.
[39] Above, n. 36.
[40] *Att.-Gen.* v. *Lamplough* (1878) 3 Ex.D. 214.

schedule cannot affect the interpretation of words in the body of an Act unless they are held to be ambiguous. This was the reason for the somewhat unsatisfactory decision of the House of Lords in *Ellerman Lines* v. *Murray*.[41]

Short Title[42]

Though enacted in the Act, this is merely a description, more or less accurate, and does not itself enact anything.[43] A judge sometimes quotes it rhetorically to give force to a decision already reached, in such expressions as: "This [the Infants Relief Act 1874] is an Infants *Relief* Act, not an Infants *Liability* Act."

Marginal (or Side) Notes

These are not discussed in Parliament: they are not part of a general Act, and may not normally be looked at. So in *Chandler* v. *D.P.P.*[44] the House of Lords held that section 1 of the Official Secrets Act 1911, covers sabotage as well as espionage, although the side note read "Penalties for spying." "Side notes," said Lord Reid, "are mere catchwords."[45] It was the opinion of Evershed M.R., however, that it is permissible to have regard to marginal notes in a modern statute if (though only if) the meaning of the section is ambiguous.[46]

Illustrations or examples have been little used in English legislation but have appeared in the Consumer Credit Act 1974. The Privy Council has held that illustrations appended to the Indian Codes could be used as an aid to interpretation.[47]

Filling in Gaps

The draftsman should, by inclusion or exclusion, expressly or implicitly provide for all the foreseeable consequences of the statute, that is to say, facts likely to occur and to raise the questions whether the case falls within the statute and, if so, what is the effect of the statute on it. This he sometimes fails to do, giving rise to one kind of "*casus omissus*," that is, where the

---

[41] See now, *Buchanan* v. *Babco*, above, p. 148 n. 1, where it was said that *Ellerman Lines* v. *Murray* was now doubtful.

[42] Above, pp. 131–132.

[43] *Re Boaler* [1915] 1 K.B. 21, but see Scrutton L.J. at pp. 40–41.

[44] [1964] A.C. 763. And see *Gosling* v. *Gosling* [1968] P. 1, *per* Sachs L.J.

[45] An expression used by Lord Hanworth M.R. in *Nixon* v. *Att.-Gen.* [1930] 1 Ch. 566. but see Lord Reid in *D.P.P.* v. *Schildkamp* [1971] A.C. 1 and Cross *op. cit.* above, n. 36.

[46] *Pride of Derby Angling Association, Ltd.* v. *British Celanese, Ltd.* [1953] Ch. 149.

[47] *Mohamed Syedol Ariffin* v. *Yeoh Ooi Gark* [1916] 2 A.C. 575.

matter is not dealt with by the statute, either directly or indirectly. The courts no longer allow themselves to extend the Act in order to fill the gap, as they did in the old doctrine of the "equity" of a statute mentioned by Blackstone. "We cannot legislate for a *casus omissus*," said Devlin L.J.[48] Thus the Restriction of Offensive Weapons Act 1959, made it an offence to sell, offer for sale, manufacture, etc., flickknives. It was held that this did not cover exhibiting flickknives in a shop window, which is merely an invitation to treat,[49] and another Act had to be passed to fill this gap.

It was necessary at common law for a plaintiff bringing an action of tort against a married woman to join the husband as defendant, but the Married Women's Property Act 1882, provided that a married woman might be sued alone in tort and her husband "need not be joined"; and it fell to be decided in *Edwards* v. *Porter*[50] whether a husband could still be sued jointly with his wife and so be made liable for her torts. A majority of the House of Lords (two former Lord Chancellors, Lord Birkenhead and Lord Cave, dissenting) held that the husband could be joined; the Act said he *need* not be joined, not that he *could* not be. (The law has since been altered by the Law Reform (Married Women and Tortfeasors) Act 1935). It is doubtful whether Parliament intended this result or indeed whether it expected that in future a plaintiff *would* join the husband as defendant. Indeed, it probably had no intention on the matter at all. The case in issue was not dealt with by Parliament, and a strict interpretation will not attribute to the legislature an intention which is neither explicit nor implicit.

The other kind of *casus omissus* arises where Parliament has given a general indication, but has not specifically included the particular case in issue. This may be because it could not be foreseen. The invention of radio and aircraft could not have been foreseen by Parliament a hundred years ago, and yet they may legitimately be brought within the principle of an Act passed at that time. Thus the Judicial Committee held in 1932 that wireless broadcasting was covered by the word "telegraphs" in the British North America Act 1867.[51] The decision in this kind of case is said to involve "ascertaining the intention of the Legislature," though many writers consider this to be a

---

[48] *Gladstone* v. *Bower* [1960] 2 Q.B. 384.
[49] *Fisher* v. *Bell* [1961] 1 Q.B. 394.
[50] [1925] A.C. 1, below, Chap. 20.
[51] *Re Radio Communications in Canada (Regulation and Control)* [1932] A.C. 304, 315. And see *Att.-Gen.* v. *Edison Telephone Co. of London Ltd.* (1881) 6 Q.B.D. 244.

fiction.[52] In *Hearts of Oak Assurance Co.* v. *Att.-Gen.*[53] the statute concerned provided for inspection of the affairs of an industrial assurance company. Was such inspection to be in public or in private? "The statute itself is silent on the subject," said Lord Macmillan, "and your Lordships have accordingly to undertake the responsibility of inferring what was the intention of Parliament in the matter from other provisions of the Act." In the result the House of Lords decided by a majority that the inspection should be in private.

In *Magor and St. Mellons R.D.C.* v. *Newport Corporation*,[54] where the question included the construction of a statutory order made by the Minister of Health, Denning L.J. (dissenting) in the Court of Appeal said: "We sit here to find out the intention of Parliament and of Ministers and carry it out, and we do this better by filling in the gaps and making sense of the enactment than by opening it up to destructive analysis." On which Lord Simonds in the House of Lords commented that "the general proposition that it is the duty of the court to find out the intention of Parliament—and not only of Parliament but of Ministers also—cannot by any means be supported," adding that "the power and duty of the court to travel outside them [the words of a statute] on a voyage of discovery are strictly limited. . . . If a gap is disclosed, the remedy lies in an amending Act."[55] It has been suggested[56] that the two views may be reconciled by saying that Lord Denning is right as regards *general* legislative intent (*e.g.*, legislation concerning houses "unfit for habitation"), and that Lord Simonds is right as regards *particular* legislative intent (*e.g.*, is a house "unfit for habitation" if the window of one of two bedrooms has a defective sash cord?)[57]

Repeal

Repeal of a statute may be either express, in which case it is commonly stated in a schedule, or implied.[58] At common law

---

[52] Cross calls "the intention of Parliament" an analogy or metaphor: *Statutory Interpretation* (2nd ed.) (1987) pp. 22–30 indicating the varying uses made of the concept.

[53] [1932] A.C. 392.

[54] [1950] 2 All E.R. 1226, 1236.

[55] [1952] A.C. 189, 191. And see *The Goring* [1988] 2 W.L.R. 460, 473, where the House of Lords refused to extend by analogy the Merchant Shipping Acts to salvage in non-tidal waters.

[56] *The Law Commission: The Interpretation of Statutes*, p. 32.

[57] See *Summers* v. *Salford Corporation* [1943] A.C. 283.

[58] *Vauxhall Estates Ltd.* v. *Liverpool Corporation* [1932] 1 K.B. 733; above, p. 159.

the effect of repealing a statute was "to obliterate it completely from the records of Parliament as if it had never been passed."[59] The modern law, however, is contained in sections 15 and 16 of the Interpretation Act 1978, which provide that, unless the contrary intention appears, repeal does not (a) revive any law not in force when the repeal takes effect (*e.g.*, the repeal of a repealing Act); or (b) affect existing rights and liabilities, or legal proceedings, civil or criminal.[60] Many early statutes have been repealed as "spent" in recent Statute Law (Repeals) Acts, especially since the establishment of the Law Commission. Thus the Act of 1969 repealed most of the Confirmation of Magna Carta (1297) and the Confirmation of the Charters (1297), and the whole of the Statute of Northampton, c. 8 (1328) and the Confirmation of Liberties, c. 1 (1340).

No Desuetude

There was in earlier times a theory, occasionally acted upon, that an Act need not be applied by the court if, after an appreciable period, it had never been enforced,[61] and this argument was urged—though unsuccessfully—as late as 1823 in *Stewart* v. *Lawton*.[62] But English law, unlike Roman and Scots law, has never admitted that an Act of Parliament may be repealed or cease to have effect by obsolescence. So in 1931 a common informer was held entitled to bring a penal action against the manager of a cinema under the Sunday Observance Act 1780, although it had long been neglected: *Orpen* v. *New Empire Ltd.*[63]

Presumptions

Although its legislative power is legally unlimited, Parliament is presumed not to intend to pass certain kinds of laws except by express words or—in some cases—necessary intendment. The latter expression means that the implication is so strong that the court cannot help drawing it. Among the most important presumptions, which have not already been incidentally discussed, are the following:

---

[59] *Kay* v. *Goodwin* (1830) 6 Bing. 576, *per* Tindal C.J.
[60] These apply to the expiry of a temporary enactment, unlike Interpretation Act 1889, s.38. If an Act is repealed in part, in interpreting the surviving part it is permissible to refer to the repealed part, *Att.-Gen.* v. *Lamplough* (1878) 3 Ex.D. 214.
[61] *e.g.*, R. v. *Bishop of Lincoln* (1345) Y.B. 19 Edw. III (R.S.), 170.
[62] 1 Bing. 374, 375.
[63] 48 T.L.R. 8. Common informer procedure was abolished by the Common Informers Act 1951, and the House of Commons Disqualification Act 1957.

An Act applies to the United Kingdom

The operation of an Act of Parliament is presumed to extend, and to extend only, to the United Kingdom, because Parliament is the Parliament of the United Kingdom. If it is desired to exclude any part of the United Kingdom, this must be done expressly. For example, the Latent Damage Act 1986, s.5(4), says: "This Act extends to England and Wales only." It is common for Parliament to legislate for Scotland only. References in Acts of Parliament to "England" between 1746 and 1967 included Wales.[64]

Conversely, if the Act is intended to apply to territories, or acts done, outside the United Kingdom, this must be expressly stated or obviously apparent from the purpose of the Act, *e.g.*, Colonial Laws Validity Act 1865; Offences against the Person Act 1861, s.57[65]; Internationally Protected Persons Act 1978, Protection of Trading Interests Act 1980.

The Crown is not bound by Act of Parliament

"It is, of course, a settled rule," said Denning L.J., reading the judgment of the Court of Appeal in *Tamlin* v. *Hannaford*,[66] "that the Crown is not bound by a statute unless there can be gathered from it an intention that the Crown should be bound." This principle was formerly regarded as one of the prerogatives of the Crown[67]; but it is now based on the presumed intention of Parliament. It extends to Crown servants in the course of their official duties,[68] Crown property,[69] and property occupied by the Crown for public purposes.[70] The matter was fully discussed by the House of Lords in *Bank voor Handel en Scheepvaart N.V.* v. *Administrator of Hungarian Property*,[71] where it was held that the income on investments held by the Custodian of Enemy Property in his official capacity was exempt from income tax. The presumption may be rebutted by express words,[72] or necessary implication.[73]

---

[64] Wales and Berwick Act 1746, s.3, amended by Welsh Language Act 1967, s.4.
[65] *R.* v. *Earl Russell* [1901] A.C. 446.
[66] [1950] 1 K.B. 18, 22.
[67] *Cf. Case of Ecclesiastical Persons* (1601) 5 Co.Rep. 14b; *Magdalen College Case*, below.
[68] *Cooper* v. *Hawkins* [1904] 2 K.B. 164; since the Road Traffic Act 1930, Crown vehicles have been bound by speed limits subject to certain exceptions.
[69] *Wirral Estates* v. *Shaw* [1932] 2 K.B. 247.
[70] *Smith* v. *Birmingham* (1857) 26 L.J.M.C. 105.
[71] [1954] A.C. 584.
[72] *e.g.*, Crown Proceedings Act 1947.
[73] *Re Wi Matua's Will* [1908] A.C. 448.

In the *Magdalen College* (Cambridge) *Case* (1615)[74] where the question was whether Queen Elizabeth I was bound by the Ecclesiastical Leases Act 1571, it was said that the Sovereign is bound, even though not named therein, by statutes for the public good, for the preservation of public rights, suppression of public wrong, relief and maintenance of the poor, advancement of learning, religion and justice, and the prevention of fraud, and by statutes tending to perform the will of a grantor, donor or founder. The Judicial Committee has held, however, that such inference could only be drawn if it was apparent, from the terms of the statute at the time of its enactment, that its beneficial purpose would be wholly frustrated if the Crown were not bound.[75]

Presumption against Implied Repeal

If a later Act is inconsistent with an earlier Act, the later Act impliedly repeals the earlier *pro tanto*.[76] But there is a presumption against an implied repeal, and therefore two apparently inconsistent Acts must be reconciled if logically possible.[77] In particular, a special Act is not impliedly repealed by a general Act, for *"generalia specialibus non derogant."*[78] Similarly, the sections of a statute must be reconciled with each other if possible, but "If there is any inconsistency between the provisions of [two sections of a statute] . . . , then by the ordinary rule of construction of a statute we must give effect to the later one."[79]

Presumption against Alteration of the Common Law

This canon of interpretation is probably at least as old as the time of Edward III. In 1314 Staunton J. said that a statute did not alter the common law unless it expressly purported to do so.[80] The rule was considered reasonable, for the common law was wider and more fundamental than statute. The basis of the law is still common law: statutes provide, as it were, *addenda* and *corrigenda*, although of ever-increasing importance. Thus, where

---

[74] *Warren* v. *Smith*, 11 Co.Rep. 66b.
[75] *Bombay Province* v. *Bombay Municipal Corporation* [1947] A.C. 58.
[76] *Vauxhall Estates, Ltd.* v. *Liverpool Corporation* [1932] 1 K.B. 733.
[77] *Ellen Street Estates* v. *Minister of Health* [1934] 1 K.B. 590.
[78] Per Lord Selborne L.C. in *Seward* v. *The Vera Cruz* (1884) 10 App.Cas. 59, 68.
[79] *Jobbins* v. *Middlesex County Council* [1948] 1 K.B. 392, per Croom Johnson J. *Castrique* v. *Page* (1853) 15 C.B. 458; *Wood* v. *Riley* (1867) L.R. 3 C.P. 26; *Re Gare* [1952] Ch. 80.
[80] *Bakewell* v. *Wandsworth*, Y.B. 6 & 7 Edw. 2 (Eyre of Kent, SS. viii), iii 78.

the Criminal Evidence Act 1898, allowed a spouse to be called as a witness for the prosecution or defence without the consent of the accused, the House of Lords held that this only made a wife a competent, and not a compellable, witness against her husband.[81]

However, comparatively few Acts of Parliament nowadays deal with the general principles of the common law, such as contract, tort, the private law of property and criminal law: most modern statutes are of an administrative or social nature, and many give effect to new policies that render the old presumption irrelevant. In so far as Parliament does deal with the common law it can, of course, change it; but an intention to change it will not be implied. Parliament is presumed to know the existing law and to fit new provisions into the old framework.

This presumption, together with that against the implied repeal of a statute,[82] amounts to a presumption against changes in the existing law.

(a) Presumption against the restriction of individual liberty. This is an application of the presumption against changes in general common law principles.[83] In particular, very clear words are necessary if the citizen is to be deprived of his right of access to the ordinary courts.[84] So where the Wheat Act 1932, empowered the Wheat Commission to make by-laws for the settlement of disputes by arbitration, the House of Lords held *ultra vires* a by-law excluding the provisions of the Arbitration Act 1889, which provide for reference to the courts in certain circumstances. "Both Roche J. and all the learned judges in the Court of Appeal," said Lord Macmillan,

> "agree in affirming the general principle that the subject cannot be deprived of his right to resort to the courts of law of his country except by express enactment, and they find in the statute no words expressly ousting the jurisdiction of the courts or expressly authorising the Wheat Commission to frame by-laws which shall have this effect."[85]

It is probably not correct to say that the courts construe statutes "benevolently" in favour of personal freedom: the

[81] *Leach* v. *R.* [1912] A.C. 305.
[82] Above.
[83] It is now reinforced by the presumption against infringement of international obligations as this country is a party to the European Convention on Human Rights. Even though it is not part of our law the courts will take account of it. See above, p. 23; below, p. 164 and *Ahmad* v. *I.L.E.A.* [1978] Q.B. 36.
[84] *Chester* v. *Bateson* [1920] 1 K.B. 829.
[85] *R. & W. Paul* v. *Wheat Commission* [1937] A.C. 139, 153–155.

balance is held even, and in time of war may be said to be shifted slightly in favour of the executive.[86]

(b) Presumption against deprivation of property. There is similarly a presumption against the abrogation of vested rights, such as the compulsory acquisition of property, at least without compensation.[87] As Lord Warrington of Clyffe said in *Colonial Sugar Refining Co. Ltd.* v. *Melbourne Harbour Trust Commissioners*,[88] "a statute should not be held to take away private rights of property without compensation unless the intention to do so is expressed in clear and unambiguous terms." Very clear words are necessary for the courts to hold that Parliament has delegated the power to impose any form of taxation, in view of the Bill of Rights.[89]

(c) Mens rea required for criminal liability. *Mens rea* (guilty mind) is necessary for criminal liability at common law, and usually by statute. There is a very strong presumption that a statute creating a criminal offence does not intend to attach liability without guilty intent. This principle was clearly reiterated by Lord Goddard C.J. in *Harding* v. *Price*[90] (motorist ignorant of accident, not liable for failing to report to police) when he said:

> "The general rule applicable to criminal cases is *actus non facit reum nisi mens sit rea*, and I venture to repeat what I said in *Brend* v. *Wood*[91]: 'It is of the utmost importance for the protection of the liberty of the subject that a court should always bear in mind that, unless a statute, either clearly or by necessary implication, rules out *mens rea* as a constituent part of a crime, the court should not find a man guilty of an offence against the criminal law unless he has a guilty mind'."

---

[86] See *R.* v. *Halliday, ex p. Zadig* [1917] A.C. 260; *Liversidge* v. *Anderson* [1942] A.C. 206.

[87] *Central Control Board (Liquor Traffic)* v. *Cannon Brewery Co., Ltd.* [1919] A.C. 744, 757, *per* Lord Atkinson; *Foster Wheeler* v. *Green & Son, Ltd.* [1946] Ch. 101, 108, *per* du Parcq L.J.

[88] [1927] A.C. 343, 359 (P.C.). Approved by Lord Evershed in *Hartnell* v. *Minister of Housing and Local Government* [1965] A.C. 1134 (H.L.). See also, *Westminster Bank Ltd.* v. *Beverley Borough Council* [1969] 1 Q.B. 499 (C.A.).

[89] *Att.-Gen.* v. *Wilts United Dairies* (1922) 91 L.J.K.B. 897; *cf.* Emergency Powers (Defence) Act 1939, s.2.

[90] [1948] 1 K.B. 695.

[91] (1946) 175 L.T. 306.

The same principle applies to offences against by-laws[92] and
statutory regulations.[93]

This presumption was greatly strengthened by the unanimous decision of the House of Lords in *Sweet* v. *Parsley*,[94]
allowing the appeal of a school teacher against conviction on a
charge of being concerned in the management of premises used
for the purpose of smoking cannabis under section 5(*b*) of the
Dangerous Drugs Act 1965. As Lord Diplock said, where no
special state of mind is expressed in the statute creating an
offence—such as "maliciously," "fraudulently" or "know-
ingly"—the words are "to be read as subject to the
implication that a necessary element in the offence is the
absence of a belief, held honestly and upon reasonable grounds,
in the existence of facts which, if true, would make the act
innocent." In order to make the accused liable in this case it
would have to be shown that she intended the premises to be
used for that purpose, or at least that she knew the purpose to
which the premises were being put by the tenants.

The presumption may be rebutted: indeed, in modern times a
number of minor statutory offences—many of them involving
little or no moral blame—have been held to involve strict
liability, especially where the statute imposes a prohibition.
Thus in *Hobbs* v. *Winchester Corporation*[95] it was held that a
person might be convicted under the Public Health Act 1875, if
unsound meat intended for human consumption was found on
his premises, even if he did not know the meat was unsound.[96]
Again, it has been held that a publican can be convicted under
the Licensing Acts if he sells liquor to a drunken person even
though he has no reason to think that the person is drunk;
similarly if his servant, acting in the course of his employment
but without the publican's knowledge, does so.[97] Ignorance of
the facts, however, may mitigate the sentence.

Penal statutes used to be construed strictly in favour of the
citizen. So Blackstone tells us that a statute of Edward VI, which
enacted that a person who was convicted of stealing "horses"

---

[92] *London Passenger Transport Board* v. *Sumner* (1936) 52 T.L.R. 13, non-payment
of tram fare.
[93] *James & Son* v. *Smee* [1955] 1 Q.B. 78; Motor Vehicles (Construction and Use)
Regulations 1969.
[94] [1970] A.C. 132, approving Stephen J. in *R.* v. *Tolson* (1889) 23 Q.B.D. 168
(bigamy).
[95] [1910] 2 K.B. 471.
[96] *Cf.* Food and Drugs Act 1938, and later legislation.
[97] *Cundy* v. *Lecocq* (1884) 13 Q.B.D. 207.

should not have benefit of clergy, was held not to apply to a person who stole one horse.[98] When in the second quarter of the nineteenth century transportation became obsolete owing to the unwillingness of the colonies to receive convicts, the number of capital offences was greatly reduced, since when penal statutes are no longer construed strictly. The meaning of a doubtful expression will be interpreted in favour of the citizen,[99] but difficulty of interpretation is not the same as doubt.[1]

Presumption against Retrospective Effect

This is not a question of when the statute comes into operation, but whether it affects acts done or rights acquired before that date.[2] The general principle is that legislation regulating conduct ought when introduced to deal with future acts and ought not to alter the character of past transactions done in reliance on the existing law. Accordingly, said Willes J. in *Phillips* v. *Eyre*,[3] "the court will not ascribe retrospective force to new laws affecting rights unless by express words or necessary implication it appears that such was the intention of the legislature." Thus in *R.* v. *Miah*[4] the House of Lords held that sections 24 and 26 of the Immigration Act 1971, creating the offences of being an illegal immigrant and being in possession of a false passport, did not embrace acts done before these provisions came into operation, which was fourteen months after the Act was passed.

Retrospective (or retroactive) legislation is possible, but uncommon. An example is the Public Service Vehicles (Travel Concessions) Act 1955, which retrospectively empowered local authorities to grant "established travel concessions" to qualified persons, so as to reverse the decision of the Court of Appeal in *Prescott* v. *Birmingham Corporation*.[5] Another is the War Damage Act 1965, the retrospective provision of which nullified the decision of the House of Lords in the *Burmah Oil Company* case.[6] Usually a retroactive Act is passed for the protection, not the

---

[98] The Act was amended a year later; 1 Bl.Comm. 88.
[99] *R.* v. *Chapman* [1931] 2 K.B. 606, *per* Lord Hewart C.J. *Windsor and Maidenhead Borough Council* v. *Secretary of State for the Environment, The Times*, January 6, 1988 (purpose overriding strict construction).
[1] *R.* v. *Wicks* [1946] 2 All E.R. 529, *per* Lord Goddard C.J.
[2] *Yew Bon Tew* v. *Kenderaan Bas Mara* [1983] 1 A.C. 553.
[3] (1870) L.R. 6 Q.B. 1.
[4] [1974] 1 W.L.R. 683; see *per* Lord Reid.
[5] [1955] Ch. 210.
[6] *Burmah Oil Company* v. *Lord Advocate* [1965] A.C. 75.

victimisation,[7] of individuals, *e.g.*, Indemnity Acts. Retrospective penal laws, however, would be a violation of international declarations of human rights; but there is no such protection for taxpayers, as was seen when the Finance Act 1974 (to which the Royal Assent was given in July 1974), amended the Finance Act 1973, by adding a percentage surcharge on surtax rates for 1972–73.

The presumption is against legislation retrospectively affecting substantive rights.[8] There was once said to be no such presumption in the case of statutes dealing with procedure, *e.g.*, Rights of Way Act 1932,[9] and Law Reform (Enforcement of Contracts) Act 1954,[10] but in *Yew Bon Tew* v. *Kenderaam Bas Mara*[11] the Privy Council said, in dealing with limitation of actions, that the true test was whether legislation if applied retrospectively, would affect existing rights and obligations. If so, the presumption operated.

The presumption does not apply to explanatory or declaratory Acts or those passed to correct errors in earlier legislation.[12]

Presumption against Infringement of International Law

Parliament cannot alter international law *qua* international law, but it can alter principles incorporated by recognition or adoption into English law *qua* English law, though it is presumed not to intend this. Thus, although there is no objection to England claiming less jurisdiction than international law permits,[13] there is a presumption against her claiming more.[14] Although it has been clearly stated judicially that the European Convention on Human Rights, to which this country is a party, is not part of English Law, nevertheless the courts have also said that they will "have regard" to it in arriving at decisions.[15]

This presumption has been applied by Diplock L.J. to specific treaty obligations, so that "if one of the meanings which can

---

[7] But see the Finance Act 1950, s.26.

[8] *Re A Debtor* [1936] 1 Ch. 237, 243, *per* Lord Wright M.R.

[9] *Fairey* v. *Southampton County Council* [1956] 2 Q.B. 439.

[10] *Craxfords* v. *Williams and Steer Manufacturing Co.* [1954] 1 W.L.R. 1130.

[11] Above, n. 2. See also *Arnold* v. *CEGB* [1987] 2 W.L.R. 245 (accrued time bar not removed retrospectively).

[12] *Att.-Gen.* v. *Pougett* (1816) 2 Price 381.

[13] *R.* v. *Keyn* (*The Franconia*) (1876) 2 Ex.D. 63; *cf.* Territorial Waters Jurisdiction Act 1878 (expressed to be declaratory).

[14] *Croft* v. *Dunphy* [1933] A.C. 156 (P.C.).

[15] See above, p. 23 and *Ahmad* v. *I.L.E.A.* [1978] Q.B. 36; *A.G.* v. *B.B.C.* [1981] A.C. 303; *R.* v. *Immigration Appeal Tribunal* [1987] Imm.A.R. 227.

reasonably be ascribed to the legislation is consonant with the treaty obligations and another or others are not, the meaning which is consonant is to be preferred."[16] As we have seen, if a treaty is referred to in the preamble or contained in a schedule to an Act, the court will look at the preamble or schedule,[17] but only if the words in the operative section are held to be unclear or ambiguous.[18] It has been said that in interpreting international conventions designed to provide transnational systems of law a liberal and purposive approach should be adopted, to promote as far as possible uniformity amongst the contracting States, but that there is no need to adopt foreign methods of interpretation or to use foreign case law as that may not be reported satisfactorily and may be inconsistent.[19]

The problems arising from the dubious existence and doubtful weight of many presumptions relating create great uncertainty, especially when they come into conflict with one another,[20] but the Law Commission declined to suggest that any formal hierarchy should be created to resolve this.[21] The general adoption of a more purposive approach to statutory interpretation has, however, reduced the significance of presumptions.[22]

2. CRITICISMS AND PROPOSALS FOR REFORM

Exaggerated Emphasis on Literal Interpretation

It was widely thought that English courts exaggerated both the possibility and the desirability of pursuing a literal interpretation as far as it will go. This practice ignored the fallibility of

---

[16] *Salomon* v. *Commissioners of Customs and Excise* [1967] 2 Q.B. 116, 143. This even though the treaty was not explicitly mentioned in the Act. And see *Post Office* v. *Estuary Radio Ltd.* [1968] 2 Q.B. 740.

[17] *Att.-Gen.* v. *Prince Ernest Augustus of Hanover* [1957] A.C. 436.

[18] *Ellerman Lines* v. *Murray* [1931] A.C. 126. Said to be now doubtful in *Buchanan* v. *Babco* [1978] A.C. 141.

[19] *Fothergill* v. *Monarch Airlines* [1980] A.C. 25; *Buchanan* v. *Babco* [1978] A.C. 141; *Stag Line* v. *Foscolo* [1932] A.C. 328; *Ulster-Swift* v. *Taunton* [1977] 1 W.L.R. 625. *Samuel Montagu & Co. Ltd.* v. *Swiss Air Transport Co. Ltd.* [1966] 2 Q.B. 306. In *Corocraft Ltd.* v. *Pan American Airways Inc.* [1969] 1 Q.B. 616 the Court of Appeal held that Parliament in the Carriage by Air Act 1932, intended to give effect to the French text of the Warsaw Convention rather than the (faulty) English translation. And see below, pp. 166, 167, 168. A judge may use his own knowledge of foreign languages, dictionaries, textbooks, articles, expert evidence or decided cases. The court may also use preparatory materials. See above, p. 150. *Fothergill* v. *Monarch Airlines*.

[20] See *L.N.E.R.* v. *Berriman* [1946] A.C. 278 (conflict between presumption that remedial legislation be construed liberally and penal strictly).

[21] *Law Commission: Interpretation of Statutes*, p. 22.

[22] Cross (2nd ed.), *op. cit.* p. 187.

draftsmen and the imperfections of language. Literal interpretation of modern Acts is often even more difficult than that of earlier Acts, since legislation is now drafted in wider terms than formerly because it requires to be understood by administrators and laymen as well as lawyers. The task of the courts in applying statute law is perhaps better described as "construction" rather than "interpretation," for it is a limited creative function capable of developing the law to a varying extent in different branches.[23] The Law Commission in its report (1969) on the interpretation of statutes,[24] criticised the use of the literal method mainly on the ground that, where the actual words are found to be unambiguous, the rule often inhibits judges from looking at the wider context, which might show that the words were reasonably capable of more than one meaning.[25]

The literal, golden, and mischief rules are acceptable if used as descriptions of various judicial approaches to the problems of statutory interpretation rather than as a justification of the court's decision. A synthesis of these methods was suggested by the Law Commission in stating that the function of the court is "to decide the meaning of the provision, taking into account, among other matters, the light which the actual words used, and the broader aspects of legislative policy arrived at by the golden and mischief rules, throw on that meaning." Although they thought the mischief rule was more satisfactory than a literal rule, *Heydon's Case* was somewhat antiquated in its emphasis on the suppression of the mischief rather than on the advancement of policy, in its language, and in its assumption that a statute is necessarily subsidiary to the common law.[26] Also, since that case was reported the courts had restricted their use of extrinsic materials, necessary to explain the context of the statute.

Membership of the European Community will doubtless influence the construction of statutes by English courts, if not draftsmen. Community Instruments are to be interpreted in accordance with decisions of the European Court of Justice, and the European legislative tradition is to express

---

[23] Lord Devlin, *Samples of Lawmaking* (1962).
[24] *The Law Commission: The Interpretation of Statutes*, 1969, H.C. 256, pp. 17–18.
[25] But see Lord Evershed in the preface to Maxwell, *Interpretation of Statutes* (12th ed.), p.v. "The length and detail of modern legislation has undoubtedly reinforced the claim of the literal rule as the only safe guide."
[26] *Op. cit.* pp. 19–20.

the law in general principles rather than to specify in detail the application of the law in particular circumstances.[27]

With regard to presumptions, it has been seen that some are doubtful and others imprecise. There is no acknowledged order of priority if presumptions conflict with one another. Special difficulties found by the Law Commission were the imputation of *mens rea*,[28] the question of civil liability arising from breach of statutory duty,[29] and statutes implementing treaties to which the United Kingdom is a party.

A Diplomatic Conference on the Law of Treaties (1968–69)[30] has since formulated principles for the interpretation of treaties. A treaty is to be interpreted in good faith in accordance with the ordinary meaning in its context and in the light of its object and purpose. The context includes the preamble and annexes. Recourse may be had to supplementary means of interpretation, including preparatory work, either in order to confirm the meaning resulting from the application of the general rules, or to determine the meaning when the application of the general rules leaves the meaning ambiguous or obscure or unreasonable.

Inconsistency of Application or Fusion of Canons

Although the judges usually talk about literal interpretation and the golden rule, examination of the reports over a number of years has been said to show that in fact they sometimes use one of the three methods (the third being the mischief rule) and sometimes another, and we cannot be sure which a court or judge will use in a given case. "A court invokes whichever of the rules produces a result that satisfies its sense of justice in the case before it," runs

[27] European Communities Act 1972, ss.2 and 3. See, *per* Lord Denning M.R. in *Bulmer (H.P.)* v. *Bollinger (J.) S.A.* [1974] Ch. 401 (C.A.); advocating a more relaxed and purposive approach to the interpretation of instruments not so technically drafted as English legislation. The Consumer Protection Act 1987, s.1(1) provides that Part I of the Act is to have effect to make provision to comply with the product liability Directive and is to be construed accordingly. However, the European Communities Act 1972 does not require a court to distort the meaning of British statutes to enforce against an individual a Directive which is not directly applicable to him. *Duke* v. *G.E.C. Reliance* [1988] 2 W.L.R. 359, 371.

[28] Above, pp. 161–163.

[29] Above, p. 146.

[30] (1969) Cmnd. 4140. See *Fothergill* v. *Monarch Airlines* [1980] A.C. 251. See above, pp. 150, 164–165.

one statement of this view.[31] "Although the literal rule is the one most frequently referred to in express terms," the same writer continues,

> "the courts treat all three as valid and refer to them as occasion demands, but, naturally enough, do not assign any reason for choosing one rather than another. Sometimes a court discusses all three approaches.[32] Sometimes it expressly rejects the 'mischief rule' in favour of the 'literal rule.'[33] Sometimes it prefers, although never expressly, the 'mischief rule' to the 'literal rule.'[34] Often the difference between majority and a dissenting minority is the difference between the adoption of the 'literal rule' and the adoption of the 'mischief rule.'[35] Most frequently of all the 'mischief rule' is used with and to back up the 'literal rule.' In short, the all-important practical question—which of the three approaches the court will adopt in my case—is a question which does not admit of an answer."

More recently it has been suggested that there is already a tendency towards a fusion or synthesis of canons of construction into a purposive approach to interpretation.[36]

Proposals for Reform

The Law Commission's proposals for reform emphasised the need to consider legislation in the light of its context, and to widen the limits of the contextual materials which the courts may and should consult.[37] They also emphasised the importance of the "general legislative purpose" (rather than the "mischief") underlying the statute.

For these purposes the Law Commission advocated, in the first place, the provision of specially prepared Explanatory

---

[31] Willis, "Statute Interpretation in a Nutshell" (1938) 16 *Canadian Bar Review* 1, 16. See also Odgers, *Construction of Deeds and Statutes* (5th ed.) pp. 449–451. Note the departure of the House of Lords in revenue cases from the literal approach in *I.R.C.* v. *Duke of Westminster* [1936] A.C. 1 to the purposive approach in *Ramsay* v. *I.R.C.* [1982] A.C. 300 and *Furniss* v. *Dawson* [1984] A.C. 474 now followed in regard to V.A.T. in *Commissioner for Customs and Excise* v. *Faith Construction* [1988] 1 All E.R. 919.

[32] *Vacher* v. *London Society of Compositors* [1913] A.C. 107.

[33] *Ellerman Lines* v. *Murray* [1931] A.C. 126.

[34] *Powell Lane Co.* v. *Putnam* [1931] 2 K.B. 305; *Duncan* v. *Aberdeen Council* [1936] 2 All E.R. 911.

[35] *Rowell* v. *Pratt* [1936] 2 K.B. 226.

[36] Cross, *op. cit.*, p. 18.

[37] *Law Commission: Interpretation of Statutes*, pp. 48–49.

Material, where suitable, as an aid in ascertaining the statutory context.[38]

The second and main proposal of the Law Commission was the enactment of a short statute indicating the materials to which the courts would be entitled to look in determining the proper context of a statutory provision, and to clarify two or three questions of special difficulty. New Zealand has for many years had an Interpretation Act[39] which states that "Every Act... shall be deemed remedial,... and shall accordingly receive such fair, large and liberal construction and interpretation as will best ensure the attainment of the object of the Act... according to its true intent, meaning and spirit." It has been described as a modern version of the mischief rule in statutory form, but it appears that the New Zealand courts have not paid much attention to it.[40] This may be because the Act, in directing the court to give a large and liberal construction, begs the question as the real intention of the legislature might call for either a broad or a narrow construction.[41] Canada has an Interpretation Act somewhat similar to the New Zealand Act, and Ghana an Interpretation Act indicating with some particularity the sources to which the courts may look in addition to any other accepted aids.

The Law Commission's Draft Clauses

The Appendix to the Law Commission's report set out four draft clauses for giving statutory effect to their recommendations.

Two attempts to secure the enactment of these clauses have, however, failed, though in cases such as *D.P.P.* v. *Schildcamp* [1971] A.C. 1 an approach has been made to give effect to them by judicial action.

---

[38] *Op. cit.*, pp. 38–43. See above, p. 149 for details.
[39] The (British) Interpretation Acts 1889 and 1978, above, p. 136, serve a different purpose.
[40] D. A. S. Ward, "A Criticism of the Interpretation of Statutes in the New Zealand Courts" (1963) *New Zealand Law Journal* 293.
[41] *Law Commission, op. cit.*, p. 20.

CHAPTER 12

Law Reports

Introduction

The art of law reporting developed gradually, and only reached maturity in the nineteenth century. It will appear from the previous chapter that full and accurate reports are necessary if the doctrine of binding precedents is to be applied. Conversely, the practice of relying on precedents and citing cases in court must become settled before the reporter can know what he is to report and how he is to report it. A modern law *report* gives the names of the parties,[1] the court and its composition, the date of the hearing, a headnote, the nature of the claim and proceedings, the essential facts, the names of counsel on each side and usually a summary of their arguments, and a full—often verbatim—report of the judgment ("opinion" or grounds of judgment, and actual decision). The names of the parties' solicitors and of the reporter are added. Cases should not be

---

[1] In civil proceedings, the plaintiff *v.* (= *versus*, "against" or "and") the defendant. The Queen (King) as a party is usually so called, *e.g.*, formerly in petitions of right.

In criminal proceedings on indictment, R. (= *Rex or Regina*) *v.* prisoner or defendant. In summary proceedings, the name of the prosecutor (often a police officer) *v.* defendant.

In the Court of Appeal, appellant *v.* respondent. From 1974 appeals to the House of Lords carry the same title as that which was used in the court of first instance. Thus the plaintiff is now shown first in the title whether he be appellant or respondent in the House of Lords: *Practice Direction (House of Lords: Case Title)* [1974] 1 W.L.R. 305.

cited in court if they are reported by persons who are not members of the Bar, since such reports might mislead rather than assist the court.[2]

The reporter's headnote is a summary, unauthoritative and not always reliable, of the principle or principles laid down in the case. Thus the headnote to the report of *Hadley* v. *Baxendale*[3] is misleading in its statement concerning the notification to the defendant of certain special facts which underlay the contract, and would affect the measure of damages.

The report of a case must be distinguished from the record of the court. The *record* is the official memorandum containing the names of the parties, the pleadings, the main facts, and the actual decision of the court on the respective rights of the parties to the action. The record establishes the right of the parties, and justifies acts done in execution of judgment.[4] It is not concerned with the general principles, but emphasises just those particulars which are of minor importance in a report. We have records of the royal courts from the end of the twelfth century. The earlier records are generally called Plea Rolls, being rolls of parchment which are now kept in the Public Record Office. The records until the time of George II are in Latin. Modern records are kept in the vaults of the courts for a time and are then transferred to the Public Record Office.

Three interesting facts may be noted here. In the first place, not by any means all cases—even in the superior courts at the present day—are reported. Whether a case is considered to be of sufficient general legal interest to be reported depends on the discretion of the reporter or editor. Secondly, in England, unlike most countries, judgment in the less difficult cases is often given orally and *ex tempore*, and is not necessarily taken down verbatim by the reporter even if it is reported. Thirdly, unlike the official court records, law reports have always been a product of private enterprise and, except for a period in James I's reign, the State has not contributed towards them. From early times the right has been established to cite in court any report vouched by a barrister who was present during the whole time when the judgment was given.[5]

---

[2] *Birtwistle* v. *Tweedale* [1954] 1 W.L.R. 190.

[3] (1854) 9 Exch. 341; see, *per* Asquith L.J. in *Victoria Laundry* v. *Newman Industries* [1949] 2 K.B. at p. 537.

[4] Below, p. 191.

[5] *e.g., Parkinson* v. *Parkinson* [1939] P. 346, 348, 351–352.

1. LAW REPORTS BEFORE 1865

The Year Books

Origin and Nature

These are anonymous reports, which were compiled annually and are cited by the regnal year and law term in which the plea was heard. The known manuscripts date from the early part of Edward I's reign (1272–1307), and some of the cases in the earliest appear to date from the 1270s. Their origin is unknown and has given rise to much speculation.

Legal historians suggest from internal evidence that the Year Books were made up from notes written in court, and probably compiled by students or junior members of the Bar. Perhaps they were intended to be used as prompt-books on procedural points by counsel engaged in litigation. The reports are cryptic and highly technical, often amounting to little more than hints on procedure and practice. The reporter traces the oral proceedings to joinder of issue, but he is not always interested in the final decision.

The Year Books continued to be compiled down to Henry VIII's reign, when they suddenly stop in the year 1535: we do not know why. Perhaps they came to an end because of the introduction of printing: the comparative cheapness and accessibility of printed Year Books may have led people to think that there were enough reports already.[6]

Use

The use of the Year Books in court declined after the sixteenth century, partly because their language was difficult and their subject-matter was becoming obsolete, and partly because much of the contents could be more conveniently found in various *Abridgments of the Year Books*, such as those of Fitzherbert (1516) and Brooke (1574).

The Year Books are an essential source for the study of the medieval common law: the Abridgments may be used as an index. They are also unique in England, and probably anywhere, as depicting the manners and speech of educated people of that period. For practical purposes it is seldom necessary to go back beyond Coke's Reports and Institutes, and perhaps the

---

[6] See Baker, *Introduction to English Legal History* (2nd ed.) pp. 152–155, who indicates that the change was not so sudden and radical as has been supposed.

Abridgments of Fitzherbert and Brooke. This is fortunate, for the modern reader who consults the Year Books is faced with the successive difficulties of transcription, translation, and understanding the old procedure.

Printed Editions

A number of Year Books were printed between the years 1482 and 1679, though these *Black Letter* editions, as they are called from their heavy Gothic type, contain many mistakes. Most leading libraries have the folio "Standard" edition of 1679, in eleven parts.

There are several modern editions of selected Year Books. These are the twenty volumes from Edward I and Edward III of the *Rolls Series*, edited between 1863 and 1911 under the supervision of the Master of the Rolls; the *Selden Society Series* from Edward II, brought out by a society named after the seventeenth-century parliamentarian and legal historian; and some published by the *Ames Foundation*, named after a distinguished American legal historian. These series contain the text and English translations, and are easily accessible in a good library.

Language

The language of the Year Books is best described as "Anglo-Norman," the language of the courts during this period. It began as good Norman French, but gradually became more English than French. By Henry VIII's reign pure English had long superseded Norman French in society, and English had for some time been spoken in the courts, though many technical terms were of Norman origin. The later Year Books, therefore, are really artificial translations from English into a hybrid of English, French and Latin.

Citation

The Year Books are cited by the regnal year and law term in which the action (plea) was heard, and the number of the plea. The terms were Michaelmas, Hilary, Easter (*Paschae*) and Trinity. Abbreviations are commonly used. Thus *Somer ton's Case*, which was argued three times in court in 1433, is reported in Y.B. 11 Hen. 6, Hil. pl. 10; Pasch. pl. 1; and Trin. pl. 26. Printed editions require such reference to edition and folio or page as is necessary to identify them, (R.S.) standing for Rolls Series and (S.S.) for Selden Society Series.

The Private or Named Reports

After the Year Books came a vast number of "private" or "named" reports, privately printed and separately published. Most of them are called by the name of the reporter, and are cited by abbreviations. Some were made for the reporter's own professional use, and were published later to prevent pirated editions being made from borrowed or stolen copies; others were published merely as an afterthought, or posthumously. They vary considerably in style, arrangement and reliability.[7] Some were compiled from full and accurate notes of a given judge's judgments.

These private reports cover the period from the cessation of the Year Books to the foundation of the Council of Law Reporting in 1865. The better ones show a great advance on the Year Books because they give the reasons for decisions, which the Year Books often did not. But most of them, especially Coke's, lack method. Some of the earlier ones are in "law-French," others in English. A sample of the former may be taken from Plowden, in the latter part of the sixteenth century, who says of Sir Humphrey Brown: "adonques esteant un des Justices ne argua pas per reason que il fut cy veiel que les senses fueront decay et son voice ne puit este oye del audience." Those published in the seventeenth century are often doubtful translations from Latin or French manuscripts. Perhaps the best-known example of the ridiculous depths to which law-French descended is contained in a note added to a seventeenth-century edition of Dyer's Reports. Chief Justice Richardson was taking the summer assizes at Salisbury in 1631: "fuit assault per prisoner la condemne pur felony que puis son condemnation ject un Brickbat a le dit Justice que narrowly mist, & pur ceo immediately fuit Indictment drawn per Noy envers le prisoner, & son dexter manus ampute & fix al Gibbet sur que luy mesme immediatement hange in presence de Court."[8]

Cases in Common Law Courts

The most valuable of the earlier reports are those of Plowden and Coke, to which we may add Dyer and Saunders. They all

---

[7] See Baker, *op. cit.*, pp. 155–158; Allen, *Law in the Making* (7th ed.) pp. 221 following.

[8] According to Thom's *Anecdotes and Traditions*: "The Chief Justice happened to be leaning low on his elbow when the stone was thrown, so it flew too high, and only took off his hat. Soon after, some friends congratulating him on his escape, he replied . . . 'If I had been an *upright* judge, I had been slain.' " See Baker (1984) 100 L.Q.R. 544.

cover decisions of the King's (Queen's) Bench, an indication of its predominant authority and prestige among the common law courts in the sixteenth and seventeenth centuries.

Plowden's Reports (or Commentaries) were the pioneer of a new kind of report. The change from oral to written pleadings enabled the point at issue to be defined more clearly: attention came to be concentrated more on the decision of the point than on the argument leading to the formulation of the issue. Plowden was perhaps the most learned lawyer of the sixteenth century, and it is said that he might have become Lord Chancellor if he had not been a Roman Catholic. His reports cover cases in the King's (Queen's) Bench from 1550 to 1580, and he says that they were corrected by the judges. They were published in 1571–84 at the request of all the judges, the first part in law-French.

Coke's Reports, often cited as "The Reports" (abbreviated as Rep., or Co.Rep.), cover cases in the Queen's (King's) Bench from 1572 to 1616. Parts 1–11 were published in Coke's lifetime between 1600 and 1615. Coke, who was Chief Justice first of the Common Pleas and then of the King's Bench, displays extraordinary erudition and industry. He cites a large number of cases, and insists upon the importance of searching the Year Books, though it seems that he sometimes took his Year Book law from the Abridgments. Many of his reports were written up some time after the notes were taken, with additional arguments and citations, so that a case is sometimes merely a peg on which to hang his exposition of the legal principles involved. The Reports are mostly in English, but in places he lapses into law-French. The whole concoction is garnished with Latin maxims, some of which Coke himself invented. Parts 12 (1655) and 13 (1658) were published posthumously, and have not the same authority as the other parts as they did not receive Coke's final revision: indeed, part of 13 has been considered spurious.

The Reports include many of the great constitutional cases of James I's reign, for example: *Monopolies* (1602) 11 Rep. 84b; *Calvin* (1608) 7 Rep. 1a; *Magdalen College* (1615) 11 Rep. 66b; *Saltpetre* (1606) 12 Rep. 12; *Prohibitions del Roy* (1607) 12 Rep. 63; and *Proclamations* (1610) 12 Rep. 74. If Coke covers a point, it is not usually necessary to go back any further: it is not possible now to check all his authorities; and, anyway, his prestige as a master of the common law is so great that the court is generally prepared to accept what Coke says.

Dyer's Reports cover cases in the King's (Queen's) Bench from 1513 to 1582. Sir James Dyer was Chief Justice of the Common Pleas.

Saunders was Chief Justice of the King's Bench. His reports, which were first published in 1686, cover cases in the King's Bench from 1666 to 1673. The later editions with notes by Williams are known as Williams' Saunders.

Chief Justice Holt's judgments are to be found in the reports of *Lord Raymond* (K.B. (Q.B.), 1694–1732).

Burrow's Reports are of great repute, and are said to mark the beginning of modern reporting. He gives a headnote and distinguishes clearly facts from arguments and arguments from decisions. His reports cover cases in the King's Bench from 1756 to 1772, including decisions of Lord Mansfield and Sir Michael Foster. Burrow was appointed Master of the Crown Office in 1773, and held the post until his death in 1782. Burrow's reports are not verbatim, as he did not write shorthand.

Lord Mansfield's work is also reported by *Cowper* (K.B., 1774–78) and *Douglas* (K.B., 1778–85).

Durnford and East's Term Reports (K.B., 1785–1800) represent the first regular publication of reports within a short time after the decisions. They were issued in parts at the end of each term, and hence came to be known as "The Term Reports."

Foster's Crown Cases, which were published in 1762, are of the highest authority in questions of treason and homicide. They form part of a treatise on criminal law which is discussed in Chapter 15 below. Constitutional and legal historians find a great deal of valuable material in the series of *State Trials*,[9] sometimes called "Cobbett and Howell's State Trials" or "Howell's State Trials," Cobbett being the publisher and Howell senior and junior the editors. They cover important cases in public law, from 1163 to 1820. The materials were collected from many sources, and the reports are therefore of varying authority. A new series edited by Macdonell covers the period 1820–58.

The Court of Common Pleas was rather later than the King's Bench in influencing the development of our case law. The best reports of its decisions, known as the *Common Bench Reports*, come right at the end of its career. They cover the period 1845–65, and were reported by Manning, Granger and Scott. Good early reports are those of *Orlando Bridgman* (1660–67). *Henry*

---

[9] (5th ed.) 1809–1826.

Blackstone (1788–96) was more successful as a reporter than his famous uncle, *William Blackstone* (K.B., 1746–80).

The Court of Exchequer was hardly regarded as a superior court before the end of the eighteenth century. The best reports of its decisions came in the nineteenth century, and include those of *Meeson and Welsby* (1836–47) and the *Exchequer Reports* (1847–56) of Welsby, Hurlstone and Gordon.

Regular House of Lords reports begin with the authorised reports of *Dow* (1812–18).

Cases heard on circuit were not reported before the end of the eighteenth century. Then we have reports of *nisi prius* cases from *Peake* (1790–1812) to *Foster and Finlason* (1856–67).

Cases in Courts outside the Common Law

The best of the early Equity reports are *Cases in Chancery* (1660–98). We have little first-hand evidence of the judicial work of such great Chancellors as Sir Thomas More and Sir Francis Bacon. Lord Nottingham's decisions have been later collected in Volume 3 of *Swanston's* reports and in two volumes of the *Selden Society* series.[10] The history of Equity before the Restoration is to be found in official records rather than reports. The first really good Equity reports are those of *Peere Williams*, which report cases in the Court of Chancery from 1695 to 1736. Among those who reported Lord Hardwicke's decisions are *Atkyns* (1736–55), *Ambler* (1737–84) and *Vesey Senior* (1747–56). Many of the cases heard during the Chancellorship of Lord Eldon are reported by *Vesey Junior* (1789–1817). The Vice-Chancellor's Court later found a reporter in *Hare* (1841–53) and the Master of the Rolls in *Beavan* (1838–66).

Admiralty and Ecclesiastical precedents virtually date from the time of Lord Stowell (brother of Lord Eldon), who was judge of the Court of Admiralty during the Napoleonic Wars, and also Chancellor of the Diocese of London and Judge of the Consistory Court. *Christopher Robinson*, who succeeded Lord Stowell in these offices, reported Admiralty and Prize Cases from 1798 to 1808. *Haggard* followed with reports of Admiralty (1822–38), Consistory (1789–1821) and Ecclesiastical (1827–33) cases.

Regular reports of Privy Council cases, such as those of *Knapp* (1829–36) and *Moore* (1836–73), date from about the time of the statutory reorganisation of the Judicial Committee.

[10] *Lord Nottingham's Chancery Cases*, S.S., Vols. 73 & 79 (ed. D.E.C. Yale). And see *Lord Nottingham's "Manual of Chancery Practice"* and *"Prolegomena of Chancery and Equity"* (ed. D.E.C. Yale, 1965).

"Authorised Reports"

During a period which lasted from about 1782 until about 1830, there were so-called "authorised" or "regular" reports for the various courts. Commercial firms paid reporters to whom the judges granted licences and the privilege of exclusive citation. The monopoly came to an end when the judges allowed citation from other reports.

The Authority of the Private Reports

It has been intimated that the private reports enjoy varying degrees of authority in the courts and legal profession. At one end of the scale we have reports of such high authority as Coke, Plowden, Dyer, Saunders and Burrow. At the other end we have very unreliable reports, such as those of *Barnardiston* (K.B. 1726–34), *Espinasse* (Nisi Prius, 1793–1807), *Siderfin* (K.B., 1657–70), and volumes 4, 8 and 11 of *Modern Reports* (K.B., 1669–1732). Lord Lyndhurst explained some of Barnardiston's lapses by suggesting that the reporter used to fall asleep in court, and wags sitting behind scribbed nonsense into his notebook. Espinasse is said to have heard only half of what went on in court, and to have reported the other half. However, a bad reporter is sometimes our only authority for an important case.

Citation

The private or named reports are cited by the name of the reporter or of the reports, with the number of the volume and page. The names when written are usually abbreviated. "A. & E." stands for the Reports of Adolphus and Ellis, which reported cases in the Court of King's (Queen's) Bench from 1834 to 1840. The date is not part of the reference, but may be added for convenience. Thus the case of *Wilkinson* v. *Byers*, decided in 1834, is reported in 1 A. & E. 106, or (1834) 1 A. & E. 106. *Reynell* v. *Sprye* (1852) is reported in 1 D.M. & G. 660, the reports of De Gex, Macnaghten and Gordon covering cases in the Court of Appeal in Chancery from 1851 to 1857. The "House of Lords Cases" are reports made by Clark of cases in the House of Lords from 1847 to 1866, and *Scott* v. *Avery* (1855) will be found reported in 5 H.L.C. 811.

When referring to a case merely for the purpose of drawing attention to a particular statement, it is convenient—especially if the report is long—to cite the page at which that statement will be found, as well as the page at which the report of the case begins. Thus Lord Eldon's statement in *Davis* v. *Duke of*

Marlborough concerning precedent in Equity[11] may be cited: "2 Swans. 108, at p. 163," or "2 Swans. 108, 163."

There is more than one customary abbreviation for some of these reports. A knowledge of these abbreviations is acquired gradually as a by-product of the use of the reports. The main consideration is that they should identify and be distinctive. There are a number of alphabetical reference lists, including the *Table of the English Reports*, published with the Chart mentioned below. The most complete and accurate is that contained in Sweet and Maxwell's *Guide to Law Reports and Statutes*.[12]

Reprints

Many of the cases reported between 1535 (when the Year Books came to an end) and 1865 (when the Reports of the Council of Law Reporting began) have for convenience been collected and republished.

The English Reports (E.R.) consist of 176 large and closely printed volumes of reprints of cases reported between 1220 and 1866, collected together according to the courts in which the cases were heard. They are arranged as follows:—

Vols. 1–11	House of Lords	1694–1866
Vols. 12–20	Privy Council	1809–1872
Vols. 21–47	Chancery	1557–1866
Vols. 48–55	Rolls Court	1829–1866
Vols. 56–71	Vice-Chancellors	1815–1865
Vols. 72–122	King's (or Queen's) Bench	1379–1865
Vols. 123–144	Common Pleas	1486–1865
Vols. 145–160	Exchequer	1220–1865
Vols. 161–167	Ecclesiastical, Admiralty and Probate	1752–1865
Vols. 168–169	Crown Cases	1746–1865
Vols. 170–176	*Nisi Prius*	1688–1867

There is an Index Chart showing where each volume of the old reports is reprinted in the English Reports.

The English Reports, which will be found in any law library, are often the quickest and most convenient means of access to the private reports for students and text-writers. They are annotated with reference to later cases. A few misprints will be encountered.

---

[11] Below, p. 216.
[12] (4th ed.) 1963.

The Revised Reports (R.R.) consist of 152 volumes of cases reported between 1785 and 1866. The various reports are collated, and obsolete matter is omitted.

Convenient modern works of reference are the *English and Empire Digest* of English, Scottish, Irish, Indian and Dominion reports from early times; and (since 1947) *Current Law*, the monthly issues of which include notes of recent cases, these notes being consolidated in annual year books.

2. SELECTED LIST OF PRIVATE REPORTS

(Cited by name or abbreviated name or initials, number of volume and page).

Reports	Courts	Period	Abbreviation
Adolphus & Ellis	K.B.(Q.B.)	1834–1840	A. & E.
Ambler	Ch.	1737–1784	Amb.
Atkyns	Ch.	1736–1755	Atk.
Barnewall & Adolphus	K.B.	1830–1834	B. & Ad.
Barnewall & Alderson	K.B.	1817–1822	B. & A.
Barnewall & Cresswell	K.B.	1822–1830	B.& C.
Beavan	Rolls Court (Ch.)	1838–1866	Beav.
Best & Smith	Q.B.	1861–1870	B. & S.[13]
Bingham	C.P.	1822–1834	Bing.
New Cases	C.P.	1834–1840	Bing.N.C.
Blackstone, Henry	C.P.	1788–1796	H.Bl.
Bligh	H.L.	1819–1821	Bli.
New Series	H.L.	1827–1837	Bli.(N.S.)
Bridgman, Orlando	C.P.	1660–1667	O.Bridg.
Brown's Parliamentary Cases	H.L.	1702–1801	Bro.P.C.
Burrow	K.B.	1756–1772	Burr.
Carrington & Payne	*Nisi Prius*	1823–1841	C. & P.
Cary	Ch.	1557–1604	
Cases in Chancery (Chancery Cases)	Ch.	1660–1697	Ch.Cas.
Clark & Finnelly	H.L.	1831–1846	Cl. & F.
Cobbett & Howell, *see* State Trials.			
Coke's Reports	Q.B.(K.B.)	1572–1616	Rep., or Co.Rep.
Common Bench (Manning, Granger & Scott)	C.P.	1845–1856	C.B.
New Series	C.P.	1856–1865	C.B.(N.S.)

[13] Vols. 8–10 are after 1865.

Reports	Courts	Period	Abbreviation
Cowper	K.B.	1774–1778	Cowp.
Croke	Q.B.	1582–1603	Cro.Eliz.
	K.B.	1603–1625	Cro.Jac.
	K.B.	1625–1641	Cro.Car.
Crompton & Meeson . .	Ex.	1832–1834	Cr.& M.
Curteis	Eccles.	1834–1844	Curt.
De Gex, Macnaghten & Gordon	Ch.	1851–1857	De G.M. & G.
Douglas	K.B.	1778–1785	Doug.
Dow	H.L.	1812–1818	
Durnford & East . .	K.B.	1785–1800	T.R.[14]
Dyer	K.B.(Q.B.)	1513–1582	Dy.
East	K.B.	1801–1812	Ea.
Ellis & Blackburn . .	Q.B.	1852–1858	E. & B.
Equity Cases Abridged .	Ch.	1667–1744	Eq.Cas.Abr.
Exchequer (Welsby, Hurl- stone & Gordon) . .	Ex.	1847–1856	Ex.
Foster & Finlason . .	*Nisi Prius*	1856–1867	F. & F.
Haggard	Adm.	1822–1838	Hag.Adm.
	Consistory	1789–1821	Hag.Con.
	Eccles.	1827–1833	Hag. Ecc.
Hare . . .	Vice-Chancel- lor's Court (Ch.)	1841–1853	Ha.
Hobart	K.B.	1603–1625	Hob.
House of Lords Cases (Clark)	H.L.	1847–1866	H.L.C.
Howell, *see* State Trials.			
Jurist Reports . .	All	1837–1854	Jur.
New Series . .	All	1855–1866	Jur.(N.S.)
Keble	K.B.	1661–1679	Keb.
Knapp	P.C.	1829–1836	Kn.
Lane	Ex.	1605–1611	La.
Lofft	K.B.	1772–1774	
Maule & Selwyn .	K.B.	1813–1817	M. & S.
Meeson & Welsby . .	Ex.	1836–1847	M. & W.
Merivale	Ch.	1815–1817	Mer.
Moore (Privy Council) .	P.C.	1836–1862	Moo.P.C.
New Series . .	P.C.	1862–1873	Moo.P.C.(N.S.)
Peake	*Nisi Prius*	1790–1812	Pea.
Peere Williams . .	Ch.	1695–1736	P.Wms.
Plowden	K.B.(Q.B.)	1550–1580	Plowd[15]
Queen's Bench (Adolphus & Ellis, New Series) .	Q.B.	1841–1852	Q.B.
Raymond, Lord . . .	K.B.(Q.B.)	1694–1732	Ld.Ray.

[14] See above, p. 176.
[15] See above, p. 175.

Reports		Courts	Period	Abbreviation
Robinson, Christopher	.	Adm. & Prize	1798–1808	Ch.Rob.
Rolle	.	K.B.	1614–1625	
Salkeld . . .	.	K.B.(Q.B.)	1689–1712	Salk.
Saunders (ed. Williams)	.	K.B.	1666–1673	Wms. Saund.
Shower . . .	.	K.B.	1678–1695	Show.
State trials (Cobbett &				
Howell) . . .	.	Various	1163–1820	St.Tr.
New Series				
(Macdonell)	. .	Various	1820–1858	St.Tr.(N.S.)
Swabey & Tristram	. .	Eccles.	1858–1865	Sw. & Tr.
Swanston . . .	.	Ch.	1818–1819	Swans.
Taunton . . .	.	C.P.	1807–1819	Taunt.
Term Reports, *see*				
Durnford & East.				
Tothill . . .	.	Ch.	1559–1646	Tot.
Vaughan . . .	.	C.P.	1665–1674	Vaugh.
Vesey Jnr. . . .	.	Ch.	1789–1817	Ves.
Vesey Snr. . .	.	Ch.	1747–1756	Ves.Sen.
Williams' Saunders, *see*				
Saunders.				

3. LAW REPORTS SINCE 1865

"The Law Reports"

The reports described in the preceding section often came out long after the cases were decided, they overlapped considerably, and, being sold for private profit, were often very expensive. To remedy this state of affairs, certain members of the Bar—inspired by W. T. S. Daniel Q.C.—set up a Council consisting of representatives of the four Inns of Court and the Law Society, together with the Attorney-General and Solicitor-General *ex officio*, to prepare and publish in a convenient form, at a moderate price under gratuitous professional control, reports of judicial decisions of the superior and appellate Courts of England. Its reports, known as "The Law Reports," began in 1865, and the council was incorporated in 1870 as the Incorporated Council of Law Reporting for England and Wales.

The object of this venture—which marks the beginning of an epoch in the history of English law reporting—was co-operation, not competition. The Law Reports absorbed the existing series of "authorised" reports, except that Beavan and Best & Smith continued for a short time. The Council did not interfere with "unauthorised" reports, but established a consolidated set of quasi-official reports over which the legal profession, through its representatives, had control.[16] The Council employs paid reporters, who must (of course) be barristers.

The Law Reports are not strictly "official," nor are they exclusive, but they are revised by the judges,[17] and the courts require that a case which is reported in the Law Reports should normally be cited from that series.[18] "Revision" should be a correction of the report of what was said, not a change of mind on the part of the judge.[19] The Law Reports are more accurate than other reports,[20] and they often report the arguments of counsel more fully.

Citation of the Law Reports

The *first series* of the Law Reports of the Incorporated Council, from their inception in 1865 to the reorganisation of the superior courts by the Judicature Acts in 1875, are cited according to the court in which the case was heard, the serial number of the volume since 1865, and the page, with the prefix "L.R." The abbreviations for the various courts are: A. & E. (Admiralty and Ecclesiastical Cases); C.C.R. (Crown Cases Reserved); C.P.; Ch.; H.L.; Eq.; Ex.; P.C.; P. & D.; Q.B.; Sc. & Div. (Scotch and Divorce Appeals). Thus *Matthews* v. *Baxter*, decided in the Court of Exchequer in 1873, is reported in L.R. 8 Ex. 132.

In the *second series*, from 1875–1890, the prefix "L.R." was dropped, and the reference is to the serial number of the volume since 1875, the series, according to whether the case was heard on appeal or in one of the Divisions of the High Court, and the

---

[16] See *Incorporated Council of Law Reporting* v. *Att.-Gen.* [1972] Ch. 73 (C.A.); above, p. 152.

[17] *R.* v. *Cockburn* [1968] 1 W.L.R. 281; [1968] 1 All E.R. 466, refers to a misleading passage in the report of *R.* v. *Williams* [1953] 2 W.L.R. 937, at p. 942, which had been corrected by Lord Goddard C.J. before it appeared in the *Law Reports* at [1953] 1 Q.B. 660.

[18] *Westminster Bank Executor and Trustee Co. (Channel Islands) Ltd.* v. *National Bank of Greece S.A. (Practice Note)* [1970] 1 W.L.R. 1400 (H.L.).

[19] *R.* v. *Kluczynski (Practice Note)* [1973] 1 W.L.R. 1230 (C.A.): trial judge not entitled to revise the certified shorthand transcript of his direction to the jury. *Cf.* the statement of Lord Goddard C.J. in *Edwards* v. *Jones* about precedents in a Divisional Court as reported in [1947] K.B. 659, at p. 664, and as reported in [1947] 1 All E.R. 830, at p. 833: the omission of the words "merely" and "also" from the former appears to alter the meaning. Lord Denning M.R. is said to have inserted a passage in the draft report of his judgment in *Ghani* v. *Jones* [1970] 1 Q.B. 693 (C.A.); see R. M. Jackson [1970] C.L.J. 1–4.

[20] For a divergence see *Kwei Tek Chao* v. *British Traders* [1954] 2 Q.B. 459; [1954] 1 All E.R. 779; note by Clifford Parker in 18 M.L.R. 496. In case of such divergence the Law Reports version is to be preferred; *Fairman* v. *Perpetual Building Society* [1923] A.C. 74, at 78–79, *per* Lord Buckmaster.

page. The abbreviated references are: App.Cas.; Ch.D.; C.P.D.; Ex.D.; P.D.; Q.B.D. After the alteration of the Divisions of the High Court in 1880, C.P.D. and Ex.D. drop out. Thus *Kearley* v. *Thomson*, decided in the Queen's Bench Division in 1890, is reported in 24 Q.B.D. 742.

It is often convenient, especially in textbooks, to give the date of cases reported in the first two series of the Law Reports, though the date is not strictly part of the reference. This is done by putting the year in which judgment was given into round brackets, thus: *Kearley* v. *Thomson* (1890) 24 Q.B.D. 742.

The *third series* of the Law Reports, which is that now current, began in 1891. The date of the report is part of the reference and is put into square brackets, displacing the serial number of the volume from 1875; and "D" for Division is left out as unnecessary. The volumes of the Law Reports for 1988 in their abbreviated form are: [1988] A.C. for Appeal Cases in the House of Lords and in the Judicial Committee of the Privy Council; [1988] Ch. for cases in the Chancery Division and appeals in the Court of Appeal from that Division; [1988] Q.B. for cases in the Queen's Bench Division, appeals in the Court of Appeal (Civil Division) from that Division, and appeals in the Court of Appeal (Criminal Division); [1988] Fam. for cases in the Family Division and appeals in the Court of Appeal from that Division. Reports of cases in Probate, Divorce and Admiralty Division and appeals in the Court of Appeal from that Division were cited as *e.g.*, [1969] P. There may have to be more than one of these volumes in a year, *e.g.*, [1988] 1 Q.B., [1988] 2 Q.B., etc. As it is not known at the beginning of the year whether a second volume will be required, the monthly parts may be issued as *e.g.*, [1988] 1 Ch., but if it is found that one volume is sufficient, it will be bound and cited as [1988] Ch.

In the Law Reports after 1890 the date is an integral part of the reference. And so the reference to *Joyce* v. *Director of Public Prosecutions*, which was reported in the Law Reports in 1946, is [1946] A.C. 347, although the case was decided by the House of Lords in 1945. A similar practice is followed with other series of reports in which the date [placed in square brackets] is an integral part of the reference, *e.g.*, *Weekly Law Reports* and *All England Law Reports*.

Weekly Notes

The Incorporated Council of Law Reporting also published from 1866 to 1952 *Weekly Notes*, which contained summary reports of recent decisions of the superior courts. Not all of these cases were considered of sufficient permanent importance to be included in the Law Reports. The series is cited thus: *Thorn* v. *Dickens* [1906] W.N. 54. Citation from *Weekly Notes* came to be allowed where there was no fuller report.[21]

The Weekly Law Reports

From January 1, 1953, the Incorporated Council of Law Reporting have published the *Weekly Law Reports*, which are intended to cover every decision likely to appear in any general series of reports. Every report is in full, except for the omission of argument. Each issue is in two parts. Part II includes only cases which are later to appear in the Law Reports, namely, those of major importance. Part I includes all other cases, namely, cases which are likely to go on appeal, and cases of lesser importance which are not intended to be included in the Law Reports.

Part I is contained in Volume 1, and Part II in Volumes 2 and 3. Citation is as follows: *Prescott* v. *Birmingham Corporation* [1954] 3 W.L.R. 990. The publication of the Weekly Law Reports (W.L.R.) takes the place of Weekly Notes but does not affect the Law Reports.

Other General Series

Several other series of law reports, issued on a commercial basis, continued or commenced publication after 1865, and some of these are still current. The series which cover all the superior English courts largely overlap the Law Reports of the Incorporated Council.

The All England Law Reports

These began in 1936 with the object of producing reports sooner than the other series. Some sacrifices are made for speed but they have been very useful, as they have often been the first full report of a case to reach the profession; they are briefly annotated; and they have reported many cases that have not found their way into the other series. The All England Law Reports are cited by the date in square brackets, the abbreviation "All E.R.," and the page. There are now usually three volumes in each year. Thus the decision of the Divisional Court in *R.* v. *Bottrill, Ex p. Kuechenmeister* is reported in [1946] 1 All E.R. 635, and that of the Court of Appeal in [1946] 2 All E.R. 434.

---

[21] *Re Hooper* [1932] 1 Ch. 38, *per* Maugham J.; *cf. Re Loveridge* [1902] 2 Ch. 859, 865, *per* Buckley J.

The All England Law Reports from 1948 incorporate *The Law Times Reports*. The old series of the latter covers the period 1843–59, and the new series covers the period 1859–1947. The Law Times Reports are cited by the serial number of the volume (in the new series, two each year from 1859), the abbreviation "L.T." and the page. Thus *Anderson* v. *Gorrie*, decided by the Court of Appeal in 1895, is reported in 71 L.T. 382. The date may for covenience be added, thus: (1895) 71 L.T. 382. *The All England Law Reports Reprint* began as a reprint of about 4,000 selected "living cases" from the Law Times Reports, publication proceeding backwards from 1935. The sources of the *Reprint* have been extended back beyond the starting date of the *Law Times Reports*, and run from 1558 to 1935.

From 1950 the All England Law Reports also incorporate the *Law Journal Reports*. The first series of the Law Journal Reports covers the period 1822–30. The second series covers the period 1831–1946, and is cited by the volume number from 1831, the initials "L.J.," the abbreviation "Ch.," etc., and page. They were at various times divided into a number of sets for different courts, the later ones being P.C. for Privy Council cases and appeals in the House of Lords from Scotland and Northern Ireland; Ch.; K.B. (Q.B.); and P.; the last three sets including appeals to the Court of Appeal and the House of Lords from the respective Divisions of the High Court. Thus *Bowles* v. *Bank of England*, decided in the Chancery Division in 1912, is reported in 82 L.J.Ch. 124. The date is not part of the reference but may for convenience be added in round brackets thus: (1912) 82 L.J.Ch 124.[22] The last series, from 1947 to 1949, is cited [1947] L.J.R. 1, etc.

The Times Law Reports

These began in 1884 with the object of filling in some of the gaps left by existing series of reports but ceased publication at the end of 1952, as it was considered that on the initiation of the Weekly Law Reports[23] they had fulfilled their purpose. In their last years of publication they were probably the promptest series of reports. Up to 1950 they are cited by the number of the volume since 1884, the initials "T.L.R." and page. Thus *Heddon* v. *Evans*, decided in the King's Bench Division in 1919, is reported in 35 T.L.R. 642. The date may for convenience be added, thus: (1919) 35 T.L.R. 642. In 1951 the manner of reference was modernised thus: *Paris* v. *Stepney Borough Council* [1951] 1 T.L.R. 25.

---

[22] The date printed at the top of the page and on the spine of the bound volume is "1913."

[23] Above, p. 185.

The Times

The Times newspaper continues to report summarily a few cases of more than professional interest, and these may be cited in court if no other authenticated report is available.[24] Citation is by the date of the issue, *e.g.*, R. v. *Casserley*, *The Times*, May 28, 1938.

The Solicitors' Journal

The Solicitors' Journal established in 1857, contains summary reports which are cited by the series number of the volume, the abbreviation "S.J." and page. Thus R. v. *Newland*, decided in 1953, is reported in 97 S.J. 782. In 1858 the Solicitors' Journal united with the *Weekly Reporter* (W.R.), which was founded in 1853, and absorbed it in 1906.

The Justice of the Peace

The Justice of the Peace established in 1837, issues reports in the Justice of the Peace and Local Government Review. Its report of *Cooper* v. *Hawkins*, decided in 1904, is similarly cited: 68 J.P. 25.

Special Reports

There are also a number of special reports, covering specific courts or kinds of cases. Official series include *Tax Cases*, published by the Inland Revenue (cited as Tax Cas. or T.C.); *Reports of Patent, Design and Trade Mark Cases*, published by the Patent Office (cited *e.g.*, 62 R.P.C. 151); and *Immigration Appeal Reports* (Imm.A.R.) published by H.M. Stationery Office. The Incorporated Council of Law Reporting publish *Industrial Cases Reports* (I.C.R.).

Private ventures include the *Criminal Appeal Reports* (C.A.R., or Cr.App.Rep., from 1908); *Lloyd's List Reports* (cited *e.g.*, 69 Ll.L.Rep. 147 and, since 1951, [1952] Lloyd's Rep. 485); *Knight's Local Government Reports* (cited *e.g.*, 40 L.G.R. 216); *Knight's Industrial Reports* (K.I.R.), or (K.I.L.R.), *Cox's Criminal Cases* (cited as Cox C.C. or C.C.C.) continued from 1844 to 1941, when they were incorporated in the Times Law Reports; the *Common Market Law Reports* (C.M.L.R.), the *Industrial Relations Law Reports* (I.R.L.R.) and the *Road Traffic Reports* (R.T.R.). The Law Journal newspaper published *County Courts Reports* (L.J.N.C.C.R.) from 1934 to 1947, and *The Times* published

[24] *King* v. *King* [1943] P. 91. Other newspapers have followed this, including *The Guardian*, *The Daily Telegraph*, *The Independent* and the *Financial Times*.

Commercial Cases (Com.Cas.) from 1895 to 1941. Other recent series include Butterworth's Company Law Cases (B.C.L.C.), Building Law Reports (Build.L.R.), Fleet Street Reports (F.S.R.), Financial Times Law Reports (F.T.L.R.), Family Law Reports (F.L.R.), Industrial Tribunal Reports (I.T.R.), and Housing Law Reports (H.L.R.).

Incorporated Council reporters contribute *summaries* of cases to several journals, including the *Criminal Law Review* (Crim.L.R.) and the *Solicitors' Journal* (S.J.): sometimes these are virtually the only available report of a particular case.[25]

Suggested Reforms in Law Reporting

A Committee to advise on the state of law reporting, reported in 1940.[26] A number of suggestions for reform were made — notably by Professor A. L. Goodhart in his minority report — but not accepted by the committee.

    (a) The committee advised against granting a monopoly of law reporting to the Incorporated Council, because the proposal ignores "the fundamental fact that the law of England is what it is, not because it has been so reported, but because it has been so decided."

    (b) The committee also advised against licensing law reporters. "The decisions of the court," they said, "must be open for publication, discussion and criticism. It is not consistent with this principle that a licence to report should be given to one man and withheld from another."

    (c) Professor Goodhart's proposals had much to commend them. He suggested that an official shorthand writer should take a note of every judgment, that he should send a transcript of it to the judge who delivered it, that it should be the duty of the judge to correct it, and that a copy of the corrected report should be filed in the records of the court. Any reporter or any other member of the public could then obtain a copy for a small fee. The objections of the majority were that: (i) a charge would be imposed on the public funds; (ii) an additional burden would be placed on the judges; and (iii) almost every decision of

---

[25] *e.g.*, R. v. *Colyer* [1974] Crim.L.R. 243 (Ipswich Crown Court); below, p. 204. R. v. *Jordan* [1976] Crim.L.R. 438 (D.C.): no jurisdiction to question validity of Act of Parliament.

[26] *Report of the Law Reporting Committee*, 1940 (Lord Chancellor's Department), H.M. Stationery Office.

any possible importance to the body of English law is already reported.

The majority contented themselves with the following suggestions: (i) The general rule of exclusive citation of a report in the "Law Reports" should be enforced, though this did not mean that if a case is not reported in the "Law Reports" it was not to be cited from other reports. (ii) Speed in publication is a consideration, though not a major consideration compared with accuracy. (iii) The "Law Reports" might take a more generous view of what is reportable. (iv) The attention of the judges be called to the rule, that a barrister who vouches a report must have been in court when judgment was delivered. The publication of the Weekly Law Reports has gone some way to meet points (ii) and (iii).

Since 1951 transcripts of all civil cases in the Court of Appeal have been filed, formerly in the Bar Library in the Law Courts but since 1978 in the Supreme Court Library.[27] The "Lexis" computer system made unreported decisions more freely available and in *Roberts Petroleum* v. *Kenny*[28] Lord Diplock said such cases were not to be cited in the House of Lords without leave, only to be granted if counsel undertook that the case contained some principle of *law binding* on the Court of Appeal and not otherwise available.[29] Some transcripts were noted in *Current Law*. Citation is by the names of the parties, date and filing numbers. Different arrangements apply in the Criminal Division.

Law Reports in other Jurisdictions

There is a growing tendency for academic and practising lawyers in this country to cite cases, not only from other parts of the United Kingdom, but also from the older Commonwealth countries. The following selection of abbreviated citations, with their explanations, may therefore be found useful.

Scotland. "S.C.": *Session Cases*, reporting cases in the Court of Session from 1906. (There are also five earlier series.) "S.L.T.": *Scots Law Times*, reporting cases in the Court of Session from 1893.

---

[27] Practice Note [1978] 1 W.L.R. 600.
[28] [1983] 2 A.C. 192.
[29] Munday (1983) L.S.Gaz. 1337; Bennion, *ibid.* 1635 and Harrison, *ibid.* (1984) 257.

Ireland. "I.R.": *Irish Reports*, reporting cases in all Irish courts from 1894. (There are also five earlier series.) "Ir.L.T." or "I.L.T.R.": *Irish Law Times*, reporting cases in all Irish courts from 1867.

Northern Ireland. "N.I.": *Northern Ireland Law Reports*, reporting cases in all Northern Ireland courts from 1925.

Canada. "D.L.R.": *Dominion Law Reports*, reporting cases in all Canadian courts from 1912. "W.W.R." Western Weekly Reports, reporting cases in the Western Provinces.

Australia. "C.L.R.": *Commonwealth Law Reports*, reporting cases in all Australian courts from 1903. "A.L.J.": *Australian Law Journal*, reporting cases in all Australian courts from 1927. From 1958 the citation is "32 A.L.J.R.", etc. Reports are also issued for the State courts *e.g.*, "N.S.W.L.R." for New South Wales, "V.R." for Victoria.

New Zealand. "N.Z.L.R.": *New Zealand Law Reports*, reporting cases in all New Zealand courts from 1883.

CHAPTER 13

Judicial Precedent

Introduction

When a judge decides a case he issues an order giving effect to his decision which is entered on the record of the court. This is a judicial decision or judgment in the strict sense, and is binding only on the parties to the case (*res judicata*). But the judgment will have been based on some legal principle (*ratio decidendi*) which should be applicable to all cases of a similar kind, and it is inevitable that judges should to a greater or less degree follow the former decisions of themselves and their colleagues and predecessors.

In most continental countries the consultation of previous decisions instead of thinking out the problem anew was formerly discouraged: it is usually unnecessary, and in some countries forbidden, to state the reason for a decision. As a corollary, far more attention is paid on the continent than in England to the opinion of jurists, the continental practice recalling the important part played in the development of Roman law by the responses of the jurists. In recent times, however, there has been a tendency on the continent to attach greater authority than before to previous decisions, so that when a number of consistent decisions have been given in a series of similar cases they establish a rule of law. It becomes the practice of the courts (*la jurisprudence*), and may be described as a kind of new customary law. Striking examples of this judicial development of the law in France, aided by the writings of jurists (*la doctrine*), are the system of *droit administratif* and the principles of civil liability.

The peculiarity of the English doctrine of judicial precedent is that, if the necessary conditions are present—notably, if the courts concerned stand in a certain relation to one another— previous decisions are not merely of persuasive authority but are *binding* on subsequent cases of a similar kind, and are binding *individually* and not merely as part of a series establishing judicial practice. A lower court is bound by the decision of a higher court, and is not entitled to disregard it on the ground that it was given *per incuriam*.[1] Conversely, a higher court can *reverse* a decision of a lower court on appeal in the same case, and can *overrule* the principle laid down by a lower court in a different case.[2]

The nature of *res judicata*, and its distinction from *ratio decidendi*, were well brought out in *Re Waring, Westminster Bank* v. *Burton-Butler*.[3] The testator had left annuities to H and L "free of income tax." In 1942 the Court of Appeal had held, on an appeal to which H (but not L) was a party, that in the circumstances income tax must be deducted, and leave to appeal to the House of Lords was refused[4]; but in 1946, in a similar case between different parties,[5] the House of Lords overruled the decision of the Court of Appeal in the *Awdry* case. H and L now applied to the Chancery Division to determine whether in view of the decision of the House of Lords in the *Berkeley* case, their annuities should not be paid in full. Jenkins J. held, "anomalous as the result may appear to be," that H's claim was *res judicata* as he was bound by the decision of the Court of Appeal in the *Awdry* case; but that L was not affected by that case (to which he was not a party), and so the *ratio decidendi* of the House of Lords decision in the *Berkeley* case applied to his claim.

The English doctrine of binding precedents in its developed form is, as we shall see, comparatively modern. It grew up in the common law courts and was extended by analogy to courts administering Equity and Admiralty law, and it has come to be applied—though not quite so strictly—in Scotland and South Africa, whose legal systems are largely based on Roman law. In the United States the Federal and State Supreme Courts do not consider themselves bound by their own decisions, and the other courts have tended to be more critical of precedents during the last fifty years, so that their modern practice seems to lie somewhere between English and continental practice.

---

[1] See *Broome* v. *Cassell & Co. Ltd.* [1972] A.C. 1027 (H.L.); below, p. 197.
[2] See *Metropolitan Police District Receiver* v. *Croydon Corporation* [1957] 2 Q.B. 154.
[3] [1948] Ch. 221 (Jenkins J.).
[4] *Re Waring, Westminster Bank* v. *Awdry* [1942] Ch. 426.
[5] *Berkeley* v. *Berkeley* [1946] A.C. 555.

The Modern English Doctrine of Judicial Precedents

When it is said that a judicial decision is a binding "precedent" it is meant that the legal principle on which the decision was based, or the reason for the decision, is binding on similar cases. What is binding is the *ratio decidendi*, the nature and determination of which are discussed below.[6]

Where the question for decision is one of fact and not law, the reasons given for a previous decision on other facts—even though the decision was made by a judge and not a jury—are of no authority in a latter case. Thus in *Qualcast (Wolverhampton)* v. *Haynes*,[7] where an experienced moulder had burnt his foot by accidentally pouring molten metal over it and brought an action against his employers for negligence in not providing a safe system of work, the House of Lords held that on the facts of the case the employers, who to the plaintiff's knowledge had provided protective spats, were not negligent, and that the trial judge was not bound by other cases cited to him on different facts which indicated that the employers would be negligent in not urging the plaintiff to wear the spats.

1. THE HIERARCHY OF COURTS AND PRECEDENTS

It will be seen from Part I of this book that the system of courts is a hierarchy, that is to say, the various courts are related to one another as higher and lower. A lower court is bound by the decisions (precedents) of a higher court. Thus Magistrates' Courts are bound by decisions of the High Court (usually in a Divisional Court) and courts above it; county courts are bound by decisions of the Court of Appeal and the House of Lords, and presumably by decisions of the High Court; a High Court judge is bound by the decisions of the Court of Appeal and the House of Lords; and the Court of Appeal is bound by the decisions of the House of Lords.

A separate question is whether, and to what extent, a given court is bound by its own previous decisions.

---

[6] Below, section 5.
[7] [1959] A.C. 743. Also, a decision as to the meaning of specific words used in one contract would not be binding as to the meaning of the same words in another contract. *Ashville Investments Ltd.* v. *Elmer Contractors Ltd.* (1987) *Daily Telegraph*, June 8, *per* May L.J., though courts may for clarity and certainty choose to follow such earlier decisions.

The House of Lords

Until 1966, the House of Lords held itself bound by its own previous decisions. The question was raised in *London Tramways Co.* v. *London County Council* (1898)[8] where a tramway company's appeal to the House of Lords was a petition to the House for the reconsideration of its previous decisions, but the Earl of Halsbury L.C. said:

> "a decision of this House once given upon a point of law is conclusive upon this House afterwards, and ... it is impossible to raise that question again as if it were *res integra*, and could be re-argued, and so the House be asked to reverse its own decision." He admitted that a bad decision might cause hardship in some cases, but "*interest reipublicae* that there should be *finis litium* at some time."

It is not easy to say exactly when this strict rule came to be established, but various dicta were cited, including one by Lord Campbell in 1852, based on the constitutional ground that the House of Lords would otherwise be usurping the functions of the legislature.[9] There was an apparent exception to the rule if the previous decision of the House of Lords was *per incuriam*, because their Lordships omitted to notice an Act of Parliament or acted on an Act which was afterwards found to have been repealed. That would not be a binding precedent, said Lord Halsbury, but would be regarded as a mistake of fact. A decision of the House of Lords might perhaps also be treated as *per incuriam* if another relevant decision of the House of Lords was overlooked.

This rule came under growing criticism from the 1930's, and by 1962 Lord Reid was saying in *Midland Silicones Ltd.* v. *Scruttons Ltd.*[10] that the rule laid down in the *London Tramways* case was too rigid and did not in fact create certainty, adding "I am bound by the rule until it is altered."

Practice Statement, 1966[11]

Before judgments were given in the House of Lords on July 26, 1966, Lord Gardiner L.C. made a statement on behalf of himself and the Lords of Appeal in Ordinary who were present together with Viscount Dilhorne (a former Lord Chancellor), Lord

---

[8] [1898] A.C. 375. See Cross, *Precedent in English Law* (3rd ed.), p. 107, n. 4.
[9] *Bright* v. *Hutton*, 3 H.L.C. 341.
[10] [1962] A.C. 446, referring to *Elder, Dempster & Co.* v. *Paterson* [1924] A.C. 522; *cf. Dunlop Pneumatic Tyre Co.* v. *Selfridge & Co.* [1915] A.C. 847.
[11] [1966] 1 W.L.R. 1234; [1966] 3 All E.R. 77.

Denning M.R. and Lord Parker C.J. The Practice Statement read:

"Their Lordships regard the use of precedent as an indispensable foundation upon which to decide what is the law and its application to individual cases. It provides at least some degree of certainty upon which individuals can rely in the conduct of their affairs as well as a basis for orderly development of legal rules. Their Lordships nevertheless recognise that too rigid adherence to precedent may lead to injustice in a particular case and also unduly restrict the proper development of the law. They propose, therefore, to modify their present practice and, while treating former decisions of this House as normally binding, to depart from a previous decision when it appears right to do so. In this connection they will bear in mind the danger of disturbing retrospectively the basis on which contracts, settlements of property and fiscal arrangements have been entered into and also the especial need for certainty as to the criminal law. This announcement is not intended to affect the use of precedent elsewhere than in this House."

In a Press Notice[12] issued by the House of Lords it was emphasised that the statement was one of great importance, although it should not be supposed that there would frequently be cases in which the House would think it right not to follow their own precedent. They might think it right to depart from precedent if they considered that the earlier decision had been influenced by conditions which no longer prevailed, and that in modern conditions the law ought to be different. The relaxation of the rule would enable the House to pay greater attention to judicial decisions reached in the superior courts of the Commonwealth. The change would also bring the practice of the House more into line with the superior courts of many other countries. The Law Commissions would not be precluded from considering the question of precedent in relation to other courts.

The Practice Statement of 1966 was generally welcomed by the legal profession and by academic lawyers, although some surprise was felt at the method adopted by the House of Lords for announcing what was after all a fundamental change in the English legal system. It was an exercise of the "inherent jurisdiction" of the court to declare its practice.[13] The view had

---

[12] See *Public Law* (1966), p. 348.
[13] Lord Simon of Glaisdale has called the new practice a constitutional convention: *R. v. Knuller (Publishing, Printing and Promotions) Ltd.* [1973] A.C. 435.

been held in the *London Tramways* case that only legislation could reverse the decision of the highest court. The change could not logically have been made in the course of a judicial decision on appeal, because the later decision would have been of no greater authority than the earlier one. The analogy to the practice of other countries is not entirely apt, because they nearly all have a written Constitution from which to start and to which to return, and their legal systems tend to be more codified than ours.

If parties intend to invite the House of Lords to depart from one of its own decisions, special attention must be drawn to this in "the case," and the intention must also be restated as one of the reasons.[14] Four out of seven Law Lords in *Jones* v. *Secretary of State for Social Services*[15] said that the Practice Statement should only rarely be invoked in cases of the construction of statutes and other documents; while Lord Wilberforce said that in questions of the construction of an Act of Parliament it is not proper to reconsider a decision of the House of Lords, even though it may be unacceptable. In *R.* v. *Knuller*[16] the House of Lords applied *Shaw* v. *D.P.P.*[17] as to the existence of the offence of conspiracy to corrupt public morals, on the ground that either it was rightly decided or, if wrongly decided, it must stand until altered by Parliament.

The House of Lords first referred to its new power to overrule its own decisions in *Conway* v. *Rimmer*,[18] where their Lordships unanimously overruled *Duncan* v. *Cammell, Laird & Co.*[19] in so far as that case decided that an English court would not inspect documents in a civil case in respect of which it was satisfied that the Crown was justified in claiming privilege. In *Herrington* v. *British Railways Board*[20] the House of Lords held that the decision in *Addie & Sons* v. *Dumbreck*,[21] on the liability of an occupier to a child trespasser, was out of date in changed physical and social conditions, and should be overruled or modified. Change in foreign exchange conditions, particularly the instability of sterling, led their Lordships in *Miliangos* v. *George Frank (Textiles) Ltd.*[22] to decide that a money judgment could be expressed in

---

[14] *Practice Statement (House of Lords: Preparation of Case)* [1971] 1 W.L.R. 534. "The Case" here means a written presentation of the party's contentions.
[15] [1972] A.C. 944 (H.L.).
[16] *R.* v. *Knuller (Publishing, Printing and Promotions) Ltd.* [1973] A.C. 435.
[17] [1962] A.C. 220.
[18] [1968] A.C. 910.
[19] [1942] A.C. 624.
[20] [1972] A.C. 877.
[21] [1929] A.C. 358.
[22] [1976] A.C. 443.

foreign currency, thus overruling *Re United Railways of Havana and Regla Warehouses Ltd.*[23]

The Statement will be used to avoid making subtle distinctions,[24] to advance commercial convenience[25] and avoid great injustice.[26] It seems that the House may be readier to overrule a recent decision which has not been relied on for long than one longer established.[27] Despite the express caution about criminal law in the Statement it has been employed in criminal cases.[28] It may well have affected the general attitude of the House since it has indicated that some of its persuasive pronouncements may no longer hold good[29] but the House of Lords has refused to use the Statement where there is no clear injustice[30] or the rule is long established[31] or there is special need for certainty as in commercial law.[32] A decision of the House of Lords could be in effect overruled by the European Court which does not itself follow a strict rule of precedent.

The Court of Appeal (Civil Division)

Decisions of the House of Lords are to be loyally observed by the Court of Appeal as well as by judges of lower courts. The Lord Chancellor and six Law Lords held in *Broome* v. *Cassell & Co. Ltd.*,[33] that the decision of the House in *Rookes* v. *Barnard*[34] correctly formulated the principles concerning the award of exemplary damages, and the Court of Appeal[35] was not entitled to disregard that decision on the ground that it was given *per incuriam*. The Court of Appeal is not, however, bound to follow the House of Lords when there is no discernible *ratio decidendi* in the speeches.[36]

---

[23] [1961] A.C. 1007.
[24] See Cross, *Precedent in English Law* (3rd ed.), pp. 134–135 and *The Johanna Oldendorff* [1974] A.C. 479.
[25] *Ibid.*
[26] *Miliangos* v. *Frank* [1976] A.C. 443.
[27] Cross, *op. cit.*, *R.* v. *Shivpuri* [1987] A.C. 1 at 11–12 and 23; *R.* v. *Secretary of State Ex p. Khavaya* [1984] A.C. 74.
[28] *R.* v. *Shivpuri.*
[29] *National Carriers* v. *Panalpina* [1981] A.C. 675.
[30] *Fitzleet* v. *Cherry* [1977] 1 W.L.R. 1345.
[31] *Hesperides Hotel* v. *Muftizade* [1979] A.C. 508.
[32] *Paal Wilson* v. *Hannah Blumenthal* [1983] 1 A.C. 854.
[33] [1972] A.C. 1027 (H.L.); see, *per* Lord Hailsham of St. Marylebone L.C.
[34] [1964] A.C. 1129; below, Chap. 18.
[35] See *Broome* v. *Cassell & Co.* [1971] 2 Q.B. 354.
[36] *Harper* v. *N.C.B.* [1974] Q.B. 614.

The Court of Appeal in 1944 set at rest previous doubts by holding that it was bound by its own previous decisions, as well as by those of former courts of co-ordinate jurisdiction. This was settled by a full Court of Appeal (whose authority, however, was held to be no greater than that of the ordinary court of three Lords Justices) composed of the Master of the Rolls and five Lords Justices in *Young* v. *Bristol Aeroplane Co.*[37] It had already been laid down by Jessel M.R. that the Court of Appeal was bound by decisions of the Court of Exchequer Chamber[38] and of the Court of Appeal in Chancery.[39]

To the rule that the Court of Appeal was bound by its own previous decisions, Lord Greene in *Young* v. *Bristol Aeroplane Co.* (above) laid down three exceptions. First, the court must decide which of two conflicting decisions or lines of decisions of its own it will follow, and it did in *Fisher* v. *Ruislip-Northwood Urban District Council,*[40] where the earlier cases had been considered in the later cases. It is doubtful whether when this choice has once been made, the court can reopen the matter in subsequent cases.[41] There are conflicting decisions as to whether, if the court has held that there is no conflict between two of its previous decisions, it can later hold that there is a conflict between them.[42] Secondly, the court must refuse to follow a decision of its own which, in its opinion, is inconsistent with a decision of the House of Lords. Some difficulty has been caused by this exception, which must apparently be limited to the position where the House of Lords decision is later than the previous Court of Appeal decision in question; for where the House of Lords decision was the earlier, the Court of Appeal cannot regard itself as having misunderstood that decision,[43] if

---

[37] [1944] K.B. 718. It is immaterial for the present purposes that the decision in this case was reversed by the House of Lords on the substantive point involved.

[38] *Ex p. Drake* (1877) 5 Ch.D. 866, 871.

[39] *Ex p. M'George* (1883) 20 Ch.D. 697, 700.

[40] [1945] K.B. 584.

[41] See Cross, *Precedent in English Law* (3rd ed.), pp. 136–137, citing Goodhart 9 C.L.J. 339 and Gooderson 10 C.L.J. 432. See also, Cross, *op. cit.*, pp. 131–133, applauding the greater readiness of courts to find conflicts, and p. 201.

[42] *Hogan* v. *Bentinck Colliery* [1948] 1 All E.R. 129 (no); *Ross-Smith* v. *Ross-Smith* [1961] P. 39 (yes). Cross, *op. cit.*, p. 138 regards *Hogan* as more in accord with *Young's Case. Tiverton Estates Ltd.* v. *Wearwell Ltd.* [1975] Ch. 146.

[43] *Williams* v. *Glasbrook* [1947] 2 All E.R. 884; *contra Fitzsimmons* v. *Ford Motor Co.* [1946] 1 All E.R. 429. In *Miliangos* v. *Frank* [1976] A.C. 443 Lord Simon favoured the first view, Lord Cross the second. See also *Verrall* v. *Great Yarmouth* [1981] Q.B. 202 favouring the second.

it was cited to it in the earlier case. If it was not, the earlier Court of Appeal case will not be binding as being *per incuriam*. Thirdly, the court is not bound to follow a decision of its own which it is satisfied was given *per incuriam, e.g.*, in ignorance of a relevant statute, or rule having the force of a statute, or (earlier) decision of the House of Lords.[44] A fourth exception has also appeared, namely, that the Court of Appeal is not bound by an interlocutory order made by two Lords Justices sitting as the Court of Appeal (*Boys* v. *Chaplin*)[45].

Further exceptions are that the Court of Appeal may choose to follow decisions of the Judicial Committee in preference to its own decisions,[46] that the Court of Appeal is not bound by its own previous decisions on matters of public international law[47] and that it may not be bound by the decision of an equally divided court.[48]

The Court of Appeal did not hold itself bound by decisions of the Court of Criminal Appeal, their jurisdiction being mutually exclusive.[49]

In *Tiverton Estates Ltd.* v. *Wearwell Ltd.*[50] the court held that *Law* v. *Jones*,[51] concerning the nature of the memorandum required by section 40 of the Law of Property Act 1925, was inconsistent with earlier decisions of equal authority and must be overruled or not followed.

---

[44] *Lancaster Motor Co.* v. *Bremith Ltd.* [1941] 1 K.B. 675 (Rule of the Supreme Court). *Cf. Royal Crown Derby Porcelain Co.* v. *Russell* [1949] 2 K.B. 417. And see, *per* Lord Evershed M.R. in *Morelle Ltd.* v. *Wakeling* [1955] 2 Q.B. 379. Failure to cite an E.E.C. Directive is not enough, *Duke* v. *Reliance Systems Ltd.* [1987] 2 W.L.R. 1225. The overlooked matters *must* have led to a different conclusion, *per* Donaldson M.R. at p. 1228 and see 103 L.Q.R. 500.

[45] [1968] 2 Q.B. 1. Affirmed [1971] A.C. 356 (H.L.) But see *Amanuel* v. *Alexandros* [1986] Q.B. 464, 469 holding that in *ex parte* rulings, where one party is not represented, the High Court is bound.

[46] *Doughty* v. *Turner* [1964] 2 Q.B. 510 preferring *The Wagon Mound* to *Re Polemis*; *Worcester Works* v. *Cooden Engineering* [1972] 1 Q.B. 210.

[47] *Trendtex* v. *Bank of Nigeria* [1977] Q.B. 529.

[48] *The Vera Cruz* (1880) 9 P.D. 96; *Galloway* v. *Galloway* [1954] P. 312, though in *Hart* v. *Riversdale Mill* [1928] 1 K.B. 176 it was said that the Court of Appeal was bound by the decision for the respondent in an equally divided Court of Exchequer Chamber, a court of co-ordinate authority.

[49] *Cf. Hardie and Lane* v. *Chilton* [1928] 2 K.B. 306 (C.A.); *R.* v. *Denyer* [1926] 2 K.B. 258 (C.C.A.); *Thorne* v. *Motor Trade Association* [1937] A.C. 797 (H.L.) on the legality of a threat to put a member of a trade association on its "stop list."

[50] [1975] Ch. 146.

[51] [1974] Ch. 112 (C.A.).

The self-limitation of the Court of Appeal was long disapproved of by Lord Denning M.R.[52]; but his Lordship gave way reluctantly in *Miliangos* v. *Frank*.[53] On the other hand Russell L.J. in *Gallie* v. *Lee*[54] and Scarman L.J. in the *Tiverton Estates* case (above) supported the rule on the ground of consistency and certainty of the law. In *Davis* v. *Johnson*[55] two further exceptions to Young's Case were proposed—that a previous decision did not bind when it was clearly wrong and conflicted with the intent of Parliament in recent legislation to remedy injustice and where an earlier Court of Appeal decision would deprive victims of violence of protection. The House of Lords rejected the first as too wide, the second as too narrow and Lord Diplock, with whom the other members of the House agreed, said it should "reaffirm expressly, unequivocally and unanimously" that the rule in *Young's Case* still bound the Court of Appeal. Hence any substantial change is unlikely in the foreseeable future. In one recent case, however, the Court of Appeal disapproved of guidelines for the exercise of judicial discretion propounded in an earlier Court of Appeal case and in effect but not in form overruled the earlier case by indicating that any exercise of jurisdiction in accordance with the earlier case would be treated as wrong.[56]

Inferior courts may not refuse to follow the Civil Division when its decision appears to be *per incuriam* but may choose between conflicting decisions.[57]

The Court of Appeal (Criminal Division)

The former Court of Criminal Appeal regarded itself as generally bound by its own previous decisions, and by those of its predecessor the Court for Crown Cases Reserved,[58] though not by decisions of the Court of Appeal (whose jurisdiction was formerly civil only). However, in *R.* v. *Norman*,[59] a case concerning habitual criminals, the Court of Criminal Appeal (composed in this case of thirteen judges) overruled by a

---

[52] See *e.g. Gallie* v. *Lee* [1969] 2 Ch. 17 (mistake as to document signed), and *Eastwood (W. & J.B.)* v. *Herrod* [1968] 2 Q.B. 923, 934 (whether chicken broiler houses were "agricultural premises" for rating purposes).

[53] [1975] Q.B. 487.

[54] Above.

[55] [1979] A.C. 264.

[56] *Turton* v. *Turton* [1987] 3 W.L.R. 622, disapproving *Hall* v. *Hall* (1982) 3 F.L.R. 379 and (1987) 103 L.Q.R. 500.

[57] *Cassell & Co.* v. *Broome* [1972] A.C. 1027; *Baker* v. *R.* [1975] A.C. 774.

[58] *R.* v. *Cade* [1914] 2 K.B. 209.

[59] [1924] 2 K.B. 315.

majority the decision given by the court in *R.* v. *Stanley*,[60] and in *R.* v. *Taylor*,[61] a case on bigamy , a full Court of Criminal Appeal of seven judges overruled the case of *R.* v. *Treanor (or McAvoy)*.[62]

It was stated in *R.* v. *Gould*[63] (*mens rea* required for bigamy) that the Court of Appeal in its criminal jurisdiction, inherited from the Court of Criminal Appeal, does not apply the doctrine of *stare decisis* as rigidly as in its civil jurisdiction. If it is of opinion, after due consideration, that the law has been misapplied or misunderstood in an earlier decision either of itself or of the Court of Criminal Appeal, it is entitled to depart from the view as to the law therein expressed, even though the case could not be brought within any of the exceptions in *Young* v. *Bristol Aeroplane Co.* Widgery L.J. in *R.* v. *Newsome*[64] said that a court of five might depart from an earlier view expressed by a court of three concerning the exercise of discretion with regard to suspended sentences. A choice between previous inconsistent decisions of the court has been expressed in a Practice Statement.[65] In the most recent restatement in *R.* v. *Spencer*[66] May L.J. said he thought that the rules as to precedent were the same in the Civil and Criminal Divisions of the Court of Appeal with the exception that in favour of the accused the Criminal Division could depart from one of its previous decisions when it thought it was wrong, even though it did not fall within one of the exceptions to *Young*. This meant that the Criminal Division could depart from a previous decision when to do so favoured the prosecution if it fell within one of those exceptions. Some earlier dicta[67] suggested that the Division could only depart from its previous decisions in favour of the accused. If it seems paradoxical that in criminal law, where the House of Lords said in their Practice Statement that certainty was specially desirable,

---

[60] [1920] 2 K.B. 235.
[61] [1950] 2 K.B. 368.
[62] [1939] 1 All E.R. 330.
[63] [1968] 2 Q.B. 65; declining to follow *R.* v. *Wheat* [1921] 2 K.B. 119 (C.C.A.).
[64] [1970] 2 Q.B. 711. And see *R.* v. *Charles* [1976] 1 W.L.R. 248, 257–258, *per* Bridge L.J.
[65] *Practice Direction (Crime: Inconsistent Decisions)* [1976] 1 W.L.R. 799 (C.A.), preferring *R.* v. *Turner* [1970] 2 Q.B. 321 to *R.* v. *Cain, The Times*, Feb. 23, 1976 (counsel advising change of plea after conversation with judge).
[66] [1985] Q.B. 771.
[67] *R.* v. *Merriman* [1973] A.C. 584; *R.* v. *Jenkins* [1983] 1 All E.R. 1000 at 1005.

there should be a more relaxed rule of precedent, this is explained by May L.J. as a protection for the liberty of the subject. Also, it seems the Division is not bound by one of its previous decisions argued on one side only.[68]

Divisional Courts

These are bound in civil cases by decisions of the Court of Appeal.[69] Divisional Courts were bound by decisions of the Court for Crown Cases Reserved[70] and they apparently came to regard themselves as bound in criminal cases by legal principles laid down by the Court of Criminal Appeal.[71]

Formerly, Divisional Courts did not hold themselves bound by previous decisions of a Divisional Court unless an appeal lay from it to the Court of Appeal, as was the case before 1934 in matters arising in a county court.[72] More recent practice, under the influence of the Court of Appeal, has been for a Divisional Court to regard itself in civil cases as bound by previous Divisional Court decisions, *Huddersfield* (*Police Authority*) v. *Watson*,[73] per Lord Goddard C.J., following *Young* and its exceptions. A full court of five judges has no greater powers than a court of two or three.[74] But if there are conflicting Divisional Court decisions, the court may choose which it will follow[75]; and the court may overrule one of its earlier decisions if important authorities were not there cited.[76]

A Criminal Divisional Court is subject to the more flexible rule which applies in the Court of Appeal (Criminal Division) (*Gould*) and in exercising its supervisory

---

[68] Cross, *op. cit.* p. 148 citing *R.* v. *Ettridge* [1909] 2 K.B. 27, but the rule for the Civil Division is the opposite. See Lord Denning in *Miliangos* v. *Frank* [1975] 1 Q.B. at 503.

[69] *Read* v. *Joannon* (1890) 25 Q.B.D. 300, 302–303, per Lord Coleridge C.J.; *Scott* v. *Director of Public Prosecutions* [1914] 2 K.B. 868, 879, per Atkin J. Even *ex parte* decisions, *Amanuel* v. *Alexandros* [1986] Q.B. 464 (only argued on one side) but not in any case if the Court of Appeal has assumed a proposition to be correct without addressing its mind to it. *Barrs* v. *Bethell* [1982] Ch. 294. Warner J. said this was of general application. See *sub silentio* precedent, below, p. 208.

[70] *Hawke* v. *Mackenzie* [1902] 2 K.B. 225, 231, per Lord Alverstone C.J.

[71] See *Russell* v. *Smith* [1958] 1 Q.B. 27.

[72] Above, p. 72.

[73] [1947] K.B. 842, 846.

[74] *Younghusband* v. *Luftig* [1949] 2 K.B. 354, 361, per Lord Goddard C.J.

[75] *Broughton* v. *Whittaker* [1944] K.B. 269, 274–275, per Lawrence J.

[76] *Nicholas* v. *Penny* [1950] 2 K.B. 466, 472.

jurisdiction it is in the same position as a single High Court judge and hence again is not bound by its previous decisions.[77]

A Divisional Court is not bound by the decision of a High Court judge sitting alone, although it cannot overrule him. In *Bretherton* v. *United Kingdom Totalisator Co. Ltd.*,[78] where the question was whether a football pool was a competition in which prizes were offered within the meaning of the Betting and Lotteries Act 1934, Lord Goddard C.J., delivering the judgment of a Divisional Court, declined to follow the decision of Eve J. in *Elderton* v. *United Kingdom Totalisator Co. Ltd.*,[79] and indeed purported to "overrule" it.

A Judge of the High Court

A judge of the High Court sitting alone is not bound by decisions of another High Court judge sitting at first instance; but he will treat such decisions as of strong persuasive authority, and will depart from them only after considerable hesitation and with a clear statement of the reason for so doing.[80] If a court declines to follow the decision of a court of coordinate authority, the latter decision is said to be "disapproved" or "not followed."[81] A number of decisions on the same point by different High Court judges may be made at about the same time, and there is a time lag before they are reported. Hence the conflicting cases on whether failure to wear a seat belt constitutes contributory negligence, before the decision of the Court of Appeal in *Froom* v. *Butcher*.[82]

A High Court judge has held that when in a conflict the earlier case was fully considered in the later, the latter should be

---

[77] R. v. *Greater Manchester Coroner Ex p. Tal* [1985] Q.B. 67; see also, *Hornigold* v. *Chief Constable of Lancs.* (1985) Crim.L.R. 792; *The Times*, July 11. R. v. *Greater Manchester Coroner* also questioned *Huddersfield Police* v. *Watson* both on the ground that earlier cases had held that Divisional Courts were not bound by their own decisions and because the finality of the Divisional Court, an express ground for the decision in *Huddersfield Police*, had gone with the Administration of Justice Act 1960.

[78] [1945] K.B. 555, 559.

[79] [1935] Ch. 373.

[80] *Green* v. *Berliner* [1936] 2 K.B. 477, 493–494, *per* du Parcq J.; *Re Hillas-Drake* [1944] Ch. 235, 241, *per* Simonds J. *Cf. Re Wheeler* [1928] W.N. 225, 226, *per* Tomlin J.; *Marquess of Zetland* v. *Driver* [1937] Ch. 651, 660–661, *per* Bennett J. (property rights or conveyancing practice).

[81] See *e.g. De Reneville* v. *De Reneville* [1947] P. 168, *per* Jones J. *Cf.* "overruled" and "reversed," above, p. 192.

[82] [1976] Q.B. 286 (contributory negligence if failure to wear seat belt caused injury).

followed unless it appears that the later decision was for example, *per incuriam.*[83]

Although a judge of the Queen's Bench Division will follow the decision of a Divisional Court of that Division,[84] the decision of a Queen's Bench Divisional Court will not bind a judge of the Chancery Division. Thus, a month after judgment was delivered by a Divisional Court in *Bretherton* v. *United Kingdom Totalisator Co. Ltd.,*[85] Uthwatt J., sitting in the Chancery Division, said that in view of the conflict between that decision and that of Eve J. in *Elderton* v. *United Kingdom Totalisator Co. Ltd.,*[86] he was free to express his own view.[87]

The Crown Court

A High Court judge sitting in the Crown Court presumably has the same status in the judicial hierarchy as if he were sitting at first instance in the High Court. On the other hand a Circuit judge or Recorder in the Crown Court should probably regard himself as bound by decisions of the High Court.[88]

County Courts

These are, of course, bound by decisions of the Court of Appeal, as they were by decisions of Divisional Courts to which appeal lay before 1934. A county court judge would apparently also regard himself as bound by the principles laid down by a single High Court judge.[89]

The Judicial Committee of the Privy Council

This does not hold itself bound in all circumstances by its previous decisions,[90] though it will hesitate long before disturbing

---

[83] *Colchester Estates* v. *Carlton Industries* [1984] 2 All E.R. 601. This was based on *Huddersfield Police* v. *Watson,* itself undermined in *R.* v. *Greater Manchester Coroner Ex p. Tal.* Above, n. 77.

[84] *Village Main Reef Gold Mining Co. Ltd.* v. *Stearns* (1900) 5 Com.Cas. 246, *per* Kennedy J.

[85] [1945] K.B. 555, above.

[86] [1935] Ch. 373, above, p. 203.

[87] *Elderton* v. *United Kingdom Totalisator Co. Ltd.* (1945) 61 T.L.R. 529 *Contra Ettenfield* v. *Ettenfield* [1939] P. 377; *Re Seaford* [1967] P. 325. revd. [1968] P. 53. *Chandris Isbrandtsen-Moller* [1951] 1 K.B. at 243 *dubitante.*

[88] *Cf. R.* v. *Colyer* [1974] Crim.L.R. 243 (Ipswich Crown Court), (not bound by Divisional Court).

[89] But see Cross, *op. cit.,* p. 122 citing Salmond, *Jurisprudence* (12th ed.), p. 163(w) for the suggestion that the County Court is not bound by a single High Court judge.

[90] They are not strictly decisions; see above, p. 99.

them,[91] and it seems that the Judicial Committee will not in practice review its previous decisions unless some point not previously considered arises.[92] In *Mercantile Bank of India Ltd.* v. *Central Bank of India, Ltd.*,[93] it reversed a previous decision of its own on mercantile law, and in *Nkambule (Gideon)* v. *R.*,[94] it refused to follow a previous decision in a criminal case; but "on constitutional questions," said Viscount Simon, "it must be seldom indeed that the Board would depart from a previous decision which it may be assumed will have been acted on both by government and subjects."[95]

The Judicial Committee in the application of the common law to overseas territories does not now regard itself as always bound by decisions of the House of Lords. One reason is that the common law in force in overseas territories is not necessarily the same as the law that prevails in England at the present day. Thus in *Australian Consolidated Press Ltd.* v. *Uren*[96] the Judicial Committee upheld the High Court of Australia in declining to follow the judicial law-making of the House of Lords in *Rookes* v. *Barnard*[97] with regard to punitive or exemplary damages.[98] In *Tai Hing* v. *Liu Chong*,[99] it was, however, said that where the applicable law is English the Privy Council will follow the House of Lords since the Privy Council is not entitled to apply the 1966 Practice Statement, but where because of statute or custom or other reasons the Privy Council is required to decide whether or not English law is applicable then it may depart from a House of Lords decision.

Decisions of the Judicial Committee are binding on courts from which appeals to the Privy Council lie. This means that decisions on appeal from English Ecclesiastical and Prize Courts are binding on those courts respectively, and appeals from the courts of a given overseas territory (whether independent,[1] or a

---

[91] *Re Transferred Civil Servants (Ireland) Compensation* [1929] A.C. 242, 247–248, *per* Marquess of Reading.
[92] *Fatuma Binti Mohammed Bin Salim Bakhshuwen* v. *Mohammed Bin Salim Bakhshuwen* [1952] A.C. 1.
[93] [1938] A.C. 287.
[94] [1950] A.C. 379.
[95] *Att.-Gen. for Ontario* v. *Canada Temperance Federation* [1946] A.C. 193, 206.
[96] [1969] 1 A.C. 590.
[97] [1964] A.C. 1129, *per* Lord Devlin.
[98] *Cf. Grant* v. *Australian Knitting Mills, Ltd.* [1936] A.C. 85 (P.C.), applying the principle of *Donoghue* v. *Stevenson* [1932] A.C. 562, to Australia. But a decision of the House on legislation common to England and the Commonwealth country may be treated as binding *de Lasala* v. *de Lasala* [1980] A.C. 546.
[99] [1986] A.C. 80.
[1] Independent members of the Commonwealth can abolish appeals from their courts to the Privy Council, and many have done so in whole or in part. See *Att.-Gen. for Ontario* v. *Att.-Gen. for Canada* [1947] A.C. 127.

colony or other dependency) are binding on the courts of that territory. The Board said in the *Bakhshuwen* case[2] that decisions of the Privy Council on Islamic law in appeals from India bound the Court of Appeal for Eastern Africa, and there are dicta to the effect that the Board's decisions are binding throughout the Privy Council's overseas jurisdiction[3]; but the statement should probably be restricted to cases where the relevant parts of the legal systems concerned are the same.

Privy Council decisions do not bind English courts (except Ecclesiastical and Prize); but for English courts below the House of Lords[4] they are of strong persuasive authority in those branches of English law that are common to England and other parts of the Commonwealth.[5] Privy Council decisions were not followed by Kennedy J. in *Dulieu* v. *White*,[6] by Diplock J. in *Port Line* v. *Ben Line Steamers*[7] or by the Court of Appeal in *Esso Petroleum Co. Ltd.* v. *Mardon*.[8] On the other hand, in *Doughty* v. *Turner Manufacturing Co. Ltd.*,[9] the Court of Appeal followed the Privy Council decision in *The Wagon Mound* (*No.* 1)[10] on the principle of liability for damage caused by negligence, and treated their own previous decision in *Re Polemis*[11] as being "no longer law." In doing this the Court of Appeal had the general approval of the legal profession, and could confidently rely on being upheld by the House of Lords.

The European Court of Justice[12]

The European Communities Act 1972, s.3(1), provides that for the purposes of any legal proceedings any question as to the meaning or effect of any of the Treaties, or as to the validity, meaning or effect of any Community instrument,

---

[2] *Fatuma Binti Mohammed Bin Salim Bakhshuwen* v. *Mohammed Bin Salim Bakhshuwen* [1952] A.C. 1.

[3] *e.g., Robins* v. *National Trust Co.* [1927] A.C. 515.

[4] *Cf. Duncan* v. *Cammell, Laird & Co.* [1942] A.C. 624, 641, *per* Viscount Simon L.C.

[5] *e.g., Vita Food Products, Inc.* v. *Unus Shipping Co.* [1939] A.C. 277, on the proper law of a contract.

[6] [1901] 2 K.B. 669, 677.

[7] [1958] 2 Q.B. 146.

[8] [1976] Q.B. 801; see *per* Ormrod L.J.

[9] [1964] 1 Q.B. 518.

[10] *Overseas Tankship (U.K.) Ltd.* v. *Morts Dock & Engineering Co. Ltd.* [1961] A.C. 388.

[11] *Re Polemis and Furness, Withy & Co. Ltd.* [1921] 3 K.B. 560.

[12] Distinguish the European Court of Human Rights set up under the European Convention of Human Rights. See above, p. 23.

shall be treated as a question of law,[13] and (if not referred to the European Court[14]) shall be determined in accordance with the principles laid down by, and any relevant decision of, the European Court. The European Court of Justice is therefore the highest authority on the interpretation of the Community Treaties, and the validity and interpretation of Community instruments, in so far as they affect cases arising in English courts. It is not bound by its previous decisions.

The Employment Appeal Tribunal is bound by the House of Lords in the Court of Appeal but not by the High Court.[15] Tribunals generally do not bind themselves[16] nor in strictness create binding precedent though their established course of practice will usually be followed. They are bound by decisions made in supervisory jurisdiction of the High Court but not necessarily by its special statutory jurisdiction.[17]

2. BINDING AND PERSUASIVE PRECEDENTS

The word "precedent" is ambiguous; unless there is a qualifying epithet the meaning depends on the context. Every decision of one of the superior courts, which has not been reversed on appeal or overruled, is in a sense a precedent; but the word is almost invariably used by lawyers for those which are either binding or persuasive, and in most legal contexts "precedent" means a precedent which is binding on the court concerned.

Binding Precedents

Where a precedent is *binding*, the court must follow it even though it disapproves of it.[18]

The Court itself, however, even a court of first instance, must decide for itself whether the earlier decision cited—even of the House of Lords—covers the case before it. The legal principle in issue must be the same, and the facts must be similar in material respects. The application of the doctrine of binding precedents is therefore not by any means mechanical. An apparent precedent may be evaded by *distinguishing* the facts, which are

---

[13] The general rule is that a question of foreign law arising in an English court is treated as a question of fact to be proved by expert witnesses.
[14] See above, pp. 20–23, 101–102.
[15] *Breach* v. *Epsylon Industries* [1976] I.C.R. 316.
[16] *Merchandise Transport* v. *B.T.C.* [1962] 2 Q.B. 173.
[17] *Chief Supplementary Benefit Officer* v. *Leary* [1985] 1 All E.R. 1061.
[18] See, *per* Lord Devlin in *Jones* v. *D.P.P.* [1962] A.C. at 711.

never identical in any two cases. Thus the decision in *Bridges* v. *Hawkesworth*[19] that the finder rather than the occupier became entitled to notes found on the floor of a shop, which met with much criticism, was distinguished in *South Staffordshire Water Co.* v. *Sharman*[20] on the ground that it applied where an object was found in a part of premises to which the public had access, and it was distinguished in *City of London Corporation* v. *Appleyard*[21] on the ground that the wall-safe in which money was found in the latter case was part of the premises, so that its contents went to the person in possession of the premises. Where a court assumes a proposition to be correct without addressing its mind to the point, this is known as *sub silentio* precedent and is not binding either on itself or on inferior courts.[22]

Persuasive Precedents

Persuasive authority is given, in the absence of binding precedents, to:

(a) Decisions of English courts which, owing to the relation between the courts as explained in the previous section, are not binding on the court concerned. The persuasive authority of Privy Council decisions on English courts, for example, has been mentioned. Propositions stated in a higher English court, especially the House of Lords, in a case which can be distinguished but is analogous, also have persuasive authority in lower courts.[23]

(b) *Obiter dicta* of English judges. This literally means "things said by the way," that is, statements of legal principle which were not necessary to the decision of the case that was being tried, *e.g.*, things said by way of explanation, illustration or analogy. They are not part of the *ratio decidendi*; and the judge may not have fully considered them,[24] or taken account of their possible consequences. The decision in *Bradlaugh* v. *Gossett*[25] was that the courts are excluded by Parliamentary privilege from questioning the conduct of

[19] (1851) 21 L.J.Q.B. 75. See now, on finding, *Parker* v. *B.A.B.* [1982] Q.B. 1004.
[20] [1896] 2 Q.B. 44.
[21] [1963] 1 W.L.R. 982.
[22] *Barrs* v. *Bethell* [1982] Ch. 294; *Baker* v. *R.* [1975] A.C. 774 at 788; *R.* v. *Warner* (*Ward*) (1661) 1 Keb. 66. See Salmond, *Jurisprudence* (12th ed.), p. 154.
[23] *Re House Property and Investment Co.* [1954] Ch. 576, *per* Roxburgh J.
[24] See, *per* Bramwell B. in *Andrews* v. *Styrap* (1872) 26 L.T. 704 "The matter does not appear to me now as it appears to have appeared to me then."
[25] (1884) 12 Q.B.D. 271.

proceedings inside the House; the dicta of Stephen
J. to the effect that the matter might be different if a
felony or breach of the peace occurred in the
House, and that the court would have jurisdiction if
the Commons by resolution purported to alter the
law with regard to things done outside Parliament,
were *obiter*. Lord Sterndale in one case distinguished
between dicta which are "almost casual expressions
of opinion" on a point extraneous to the case, and
those which, although not necessary for the decision of the case, are "deliberate expressions of
opinion given after consideration upon a point
clearly brought and argued before the court": the
latter have "much greater weight" than the
former.[26]

The expression, *obiter dictum*, also covers any part
of the purported *ratio decidendi* (as explained
below)[27] which was wider than necessary for that
particular decision, for a court only has jurisdiction
to decide the case before it. An oft-quoted dictum of
Atkin L.J. concerning the writs of prohibition and
certiorari in *R.* v. *Electricity Commissioners*,[28] was
held to be too wide by Wrottesley and Evershed
L.JJ. in *R.* v. *St. Edmundsbury and Ipswich Diocese
(Chancellor)*.[29] The Court of Appeal in *Royster* v.
Cavey[30] regarded itself as virtually bound by considered dicta of the House of Lords in *Adams* v.
Naylor,[31] and the law was later altered by the
Crown Proceedings Act 1947, s.2. According to
Ungoed-Thomas J. "a battery of howitzers off the
target is more impressive than a pop-gun on it";[32]
but Lord Wright once wrote[33] that "The lawyer
must beware of what Lord Sumner once called the
'will-o'-the-wisp' of the *obiter dictum*. How much bad
law would have been avoided if *obiter dicta*, often
unconsidered, of even eminent judges had been
forgotten and disregarded...."

---

[26] *Slack* v. *Leeds Industrial Co-operative Society* [1923] 1 Ch. 431, 451.
[27] Below, pp. 219–223.
[28] [1924] 1 K.B. 171, 204.
[29] [1948] 1 K.B. 195, 215, 222.
[30] [1947] K.B. 204.
[31] [1946] A.C. 543.
[32] *Re Grosvenor Hotel (No. 2)* [1965] Ch. 1210, 1223.
[33] Lord Wright, *Legal Essays and Addresses*, p. 396.

(c) Decisions of Irish, Scottish, Commonwealth and United States courts.[34] *Conway* v. *Rimmer*[35] is a House of Lords case in which Scottish, Australian and American cases were cited. The Court of Appeal in *Westward Television Ltd.* v. *Hart*,[36] where a revenue statute was applicable to England and Scotland, said that a decision of the Court of Session in another case should be followed, since there was no compelling reason for differing from it.

Directions at *nisi prius* or to a criminal jury are not usually regarded as precedents, though they may be cited as persuasive authorities.[37] Some of the older ones have been repeatedly accepted and confirmed, and are the only authority we have for some points of criminal law, *e.g.*, Alderson B.'s direction to the jury at Bedford Assizes concerning the duty of private citizens to assist police constables in the preservation of the peace.[38] A charge to a grand jury was not given after hearing legal argument, and would not usually be regarded as a judicial authority, though they are sometimes quoted, for example, the charge of Tindal C.J. to the Bristol grand jury concerning the duty of magistrates in suppressing riots.[39]

The judgments of inferior courts, *e.g.*, county courts, the former quarter sessions and magistrates' courts, are not regarded as precedents. The large number of cases (mostly questions of fact) tried by these courts, and the circumstances in which they are heard, make it undesirable that they should be reported, though county court cases were reported for a few years. Whether the Crown Court (though part of the Supreme Court) is to be regarded as a superior or inferior court probably depends on whether a High Court judge is presiding.

In the absence of direct authority, persuasive authority is also accorded to Roman law, especially the *Digest* of Justinian.[40] Well-known cases where Roman law has been followed as

---

[34] See, *e.g.*, *Dulieu* v. *White* [1901] 2 K.B. 669, at pp. 677, 678; *McLean* v. *Clydesdale Banking Co.* (1883) 9 App.Cas. 95, 105, *per* Lord Blackburn; *Eshugbayi Eleko* v. *Officer Administering the Government of Nigeria* [1928] A.C. 459; *Donoghue* v. *Stevenson* [1932] A.C. 562; *Haynes* v. *Harwood* [1935] 1 K.B. 146; *De Reneville* v. *De Reneville* [1948] P. 100; *Broom* v. *Morgan* [1953] 1 Q.B. 597; *R.* v. *Gould* [1968] 2 Q.B. 65; *Pettitt* v. *Pettitt* [1970] A.C. 777.

[35] [1968] A.C. 910.

[36] [1969] 1 Ch. 201.

[37] *Forster* v. *Baker* [1910] 2 K.B. 636, 638, *per* Bray J.

[38] *R.* v. *Brown* (1841) Car. & M. 314.

[39] *R.* v. *Pinney* (1832) 5 C. & P. 254, 258.

[40] See, *per* Tindal C.J. in *Acton* v. *Blundell* (1843) 12 M. & W. 324, 353.

offering a reasonable solution have been *Coggs* v. *Bernard*,[41] *per* Holt C.J. (bailment); *Moses* v. *Macferlan*.[42] *per* Lord Mansfield (quasi-contract); *Taylor* v. *Caldwell*,[43] *per* Blackburn J. (frustration of contract); and *Dalton* v. *Angus*,[44] *per* Lord Blackburn (easements). The *Digest* was also cited in *Re Knapton*,[45] and the Roman law rule as to the ownership of the progeny of animals was followed in *Tucker* v. *Farm and General Investment Trust*.[46] In *Kearry* v. *Pattinson*[47] Slesser L.J. referred to a passage in Justinian's *Institutes* that had been quoted by Bracton and Blackstone.

The Weight of Persuasive Precedents

Persuasive authority is a matter of degree. Among the factors to be taken into account in assessing the weight to be attached to persuasive precedents are: (i) the rank of the court; (ii) the prestige of the judge; (iii) whether it was a considered judgment, which is usually indicated in the report by the words *curia advisari vult* (*Cur. adv. vult,* or C.A.V.)[48]; (iv) the date of the decision, which should generally be neither too old nor too recent; (v) whether there were any dissenting judgments; (vi) whether there were different *rationes* for the same decision; (vii) whether it was a direction to a jury, in which case the law would not usually have been fully argued; (viii) whether the action was opposed, or the point argued by counsel; and (ix) the reliability of the reporter, in the case of the former private or named reports.[49]

3. DEVELOPMENT OF THE DOCTRINE OF BINDING PRECEDENTS

Four factors may be observed in the development of the doctrine of binding precedents at common law. The two chief factors were the declaratory theory of the judicial function, and the principles of judicial consistency and legal certainty. Auxiliary factors were the reorganisation of the judicial system in 1873–76,

---

[41] (1703) 2 Ld.Raym. 909.
[42] (1760) 2 Burr. 1005.
[43] (1863) 3 B. & S. 826.
[44] (1881) 6 App.Cas. 740.
[45] [1941] Ch. 428.
[46] [1966] 2 Q.B. 421 (C.A.).
[47] [1939] 1 K.B. 471.
[48] This point is emphasised by Lord Russell of Killowen in *Behind the Appellate Curtain* (Holdsworth Club, University of Birmingham, 1969).
[49] See Allen, *Law in the Making* (7th ed.), p. 221 *et seq.* on these.

and the foundation of the Incorporated Council of Law Reporting in 1865. The last three factors, together with the analogy of the common law, also affected the growth of the doctrine in Equity.

The Declaratory Theory of the Common Law

The old theory was that the common law consisted of the general customs of the realm, and that all the judges had to do was to discover these general customs and apply them; but in fact, as will be seen in Chapter 14, the Royal Courts exercised a creative influence in the development of the common law to an extent which is difficult to define. Judicial decisions in truth are partly declaratory and partly original. The theory that judicial decisions were merely declarations of existing law—conclusive evidence of what already exists—is stated by Blackstone.[50] Judges, he says,

> "are the depositories of the laws; the living oracles, who must decide in all cases of doubt, and who are bound by an oath to decide according to the law of the land.... And indeed these judicial decisions are the principal and most authoritative evidence that can be given of the existence of such a custom as shall form part of the common law."

This theory, imperfect though it be, has exerted a profound influence on the development of the doctrine of binding precedents at common law.

The origin of the declaratory theory of the judicial function may perhaps be found in the fact that William I ordained that Anglo-Saxon private law should in general be preserved: hence the authority of the decisions of the royal justices after the Conquest as evidence of the existing law. The personal authority of the royal judges was strengthened by the concentration of the judicial system at Westminster, and later by these royal justices going out on circuit into all parts of the country, and by the fact that they have always been few in number and generally of greater ability than the Bar.

The declaratory theory did not apply to Equity, for the Court of Chancery worked on the principle of conscience and not on the ascertainment of custom. The earlier Chancery precedents were avowedly original. "The rules of Courts of Equity are not, like the rules of the Common Law, supposed to have been established from time immemorial," said Jessel M.R. in

[50] Bl. Comm. I. 69.

Re Hallett's Estate.[51] "It is perfectly well known that they have been established from time to time—altered, improved, and refined from time to time.... Take such things as these: the separate use of a married woman, the restraint on alienation, the modern rule against perpetuities, and the rules of equitable waste. We can name the Chancellors who first invented them, and state the date when they were first introduced into Equity jurisprudence." He goes on to say that, "if we want to know what the rules of Equity are, we must look, of course, rather to the more modern than the more ancient cases."

The Principles of Judicial Consistency and Legal Certainty

At Common Law

The principle of judicial consistency may be traced back at least as far as the reign of Edward I, when the reports known as the Year Books begin. But judicial consistency is not the same as the binding force of precedent; it is merely one of the factors in its development. The judges did their best to keep the law consistent with itself; but this did not mean that they were bound to model it on previous decided cases.

Cases are rarely cited in medieval reports and textbooks. No judicial decisions are cited in Britton. Glanvil and Fleta only cite one decision each. Littleton cites eleven. Bracton's treatise *De Legibus Angliae* (*c.* 1250) contains 500 references to decided cases. But this citation was exceptional, and was far from being representative of the judicial method of the time. Moreover, Bracton cites cases to confirm his statements of the law rather than deduce principles from the cases. In the thirteenth and fourteenth centuries counsel and judges occasionally referred to previous decisions which they could recall from memory, often without the names of the parties; but the purpose was to establish the rulings and the practice of the court in particular cases rather than general principles or reasons for the decision. Until nearly the end of the fifteenth century such reports or notes of cases as there were existed only in manuscript, and often conflicting manuscripts; more often practitioners looked at the plea rolls and register of writs.

The citation of cases became more frequent from the sixteenth century onwards, owing to the introduction of printing and the improvement in the law reports; but for some time cases were

[51] (1879) 13 Ch.D. 696, 710.

still cited rather by way of example or analogy than as precedent or authority. Coke was a great citer of cases, and interesting remarks on the use of precedents are contained in the prefaces to some of the great reporters, such as Plowden. There was a continued improvement in law reporting in the seventeenth and eighteenth centuries, and we reach the position that while judges may make new law where the field is clear, they cannot change existing law. Some doubt, however, was felt as to whether a decision must be followed if the result would be unjust, unreasonable or "inconvenient." Special authority attached to decisions of the Court of the Exchequer Chamber, which were already regarded as binding in the seventeenth century.[52] Decisions of the House of Lords were not much regarded before the nineteenth century owing to the presence of lay lords and the absence of adequate reports before those of Dow (1812–18).

It is difficult to say precisely when the doctrine of precedent became settled substantially in its modern form. The estimates of legal historians vary between the latter half of the eighteenth and the middle of the nineteenth century. Blackstone, writing in the former period, says: "For it is an established rule to abide by former precedents, where the same points come again in litigation; as well as to keep the scale of justice even and steady, and not liable to waver with every new judge's opinion; as also because the law in that case being solemnly declared and determined, what before was uncertain, and perhaps indifferent, is now become a permanent rule, which it is not in the breast of any subsequent judge to alter or vary from, according to his private sentiments: he being sworn to determine, not according to his own private judgment, but according to the known laws and customs of the land."[53] On the other hand Lord Mansfield C.J. at about the same time was insisting that the unenacted law consists of principles and that the function of precedents is to illustrate principles.[54] These two aspects of the doctrine are fused in an opinion by Parke J. to the House of Lords in 1833: "Our common-law system consists in the applying to new combinations of circumstances *those rules of law which we derive from legal principles and judicial precedents*; and for the sake of attaining uniformity, consistency and certainty, we must apply those rules, where they are not plainly unreasonable and inconvenient, to all cases which arise; and we are not at

---

[52] 2 Co.Inst, 618; *Godden* v. *Hales* (1686) 11 St.Tr. 1165, 1254, *per* Herbert C.J.
[53] 1 Comm. 69.
[54] *Jones* v. *Randall* (1774) 1 Cowp. 37, 39.

liberty to reject them, and to abandon all analogy to them, in those to which they have not yet been judicially applied, because we think that the rules are not as convenient and reasonable as we ourselves could have devised."[55]

In Equity

The principles of judicial consistency and legal certainty began to operate in the Court of Chancery in the seventeenth century. The practice of relying on precedents, which was uncertain in the time of Lord Nottingham (L.C. 1673–82), became established under Lord Hardwicke (L.C. 1737–56). But even the earliest Chancery reports show us Chancellors, from Bacon onwards, consulting precedents. There are constant references in the seventeenth century to "the course of the Court of Chancery," and when reports are lacking Chancellors would consult the Registrar's books. It was common in the first half of the eighteenth century, before reports were regular, to adjourn the hearing so that the Chancellor might be "attended with precedents," for example, Lord Parker (later Macclesfield) in *Farrington* v. *Knightly.*[56]

In the eighteenth century a series of precedents was regarded as binding. We have a clear statement of Lord Hardwicke's attitude in a manuscript note of 1728 that "a number or course of precedents will and ought to bind in subsequent decisions, but it is not one or two judgments that will settle the law so as to bind down a Court of Justice in future judgments."[57] Two precedents were merely persuasive.[58] The Chancery in the eighteenth and nineteenth centuries tended especially to rely on precedent—even one "ancient" precedent—in matters affecting titles and conveyancing practice.

During Lord Eldon's long Chancellorships (1801–27) the practice became more settled. "The doctrines of this Court," he said in *Gee* v. *Pritchard,*[59]

> "ought to be as well settled, and made as uniform almost [*sic*] as those of the common law, laying down fixed principles, but taking care that they are to be applied according to the circumstances of each case. I cannot agree that the doctrines of this Court are to be changed with every succeeding judge. Nothing would inflict on me greater

---

[55] *Mirehouse* v. *Rennell* (1833) 1 Cl. & F. 527, 546.
[56] (1719) 1 P.Wms. 544.
[57] Cited Winder, "Precedent in Equity" (1941) 57 L.Q.R. 245, 252.
[58] *Evelyn* v. *Evelyn* (1753) Amb. 191–193, *per* Lord Hardwicke.
[59] (1818) 2 Swanst. 402, 414.

pain, in quitting this place, than the recollection that I had done anything to justify the reproach that the equity of this Court varies like the Chancellor's foot."[60]

Lord Eldon went even further when, after commenting on Lord Thurlow's following of precedent in the matter of expectant heirs, he said: "It is not the duty of a Judge in equity to vary rules, or to say that rules are not to be considered as fully settled here as in a court of law."[61]

Many statements on precedent in Equity were made by Sir George Jessel, who was Master of the Rolls at the time of the Judicature Acts 1873–75. Both the number and the age of the decisions were material. A decision less than (say) ten years old would be looked at critically. Reviewing four decisions—by two Chief Barons, a Vice-Chancellor, and a Master of the Rolls— Jessel M.R. in *Re Bethlem Hospital*[62] said: "Looking, then, at the number of these decisions, and at their dates . . . I am precluded from considering whether, apart from decision, I should be of the same opinion. I simply follow the decisions."[63]

Since the reorganisation of the courts by the Judicature Acts, if not before, a Chancery judge has been bound by one decision of a superior court. "It is the duty of a Judge of a Court of first instance," said Jessel M.R. in 1874, "to follow the decision of a superior Court";[64] and "No number of decisions by inferior Courts can overrule a decision of a superior Court."[65]

The reorganisation of Judicial System 1873–76

This has been dealt with in Part I. For present purposes the most important results were the abolition of competing jurisdictions in the superior courts of first instance and at the appellate level, and the establishment of a legally qualified House of Lords at the apex of the judicial system.

The Foundation of the Incorporated Council of Law Reporting 1865

This is dealt with in the previous chapter. The Law Reports of the Incorporated Council are not strictly official, nor is

---

[60] The reference is to Selden, *Table Talk*, title "Equity." See Pollock, *Table Talk of John Selden* (S.S.), p. 43.
[61] *Davis* v. *Duke of Marlborough* (1819) 2 Swanst. 108, 163.
[62] (1875) L.R. 19 Eq. 457, 461.
[63] See also, *Re Hallett's Estate*, above, pp. 212–213.
[64] *Meux* v. *Jacob* (1875) 44 L.J.Ch. 481, 483.
[65] *Re Hutchinson and Tenant* (1878) 8 Ch.D. 540, 543.

their citation in court exclusive; but they have maintained a consistently high level of reporting, which has also had an influence on the other current series.

4. CRITICISM OF THE DOCTRINE

Our system of case-law based on the doctrine of binding judicial precedents is sometimes contrasted with the legal system of a country like France, which is largely based on codes and in which precedents have no binding force.

The advantages of the English system are said to be:

(i) *Certainty*. Persons and their legal advisers can have confidence in the future action of the courts. "It is better," in the words of Lord Eldon L.C., "the law should be certain than that every Judge should speculate upon improvements in it."[66]

(ii) *Possibility of growth*. New statements of principle are made to meet new circumstances. Succeeding generations leave their mark on the law, and the effect of their work is not confined to the particular disputes which they decided.

(iii) *Wealth of detail,* as compared with even a long code.

(iv) *The practical character of case-law*. It is the product of problems which have actually arisen in fact, and is based on experience rather than logic. Some writers add:

(v) *Flexibility*.

The disadvantages of our system, on this line of argument, will be seen largely to cancel out the advantages. They include:

(i) *Rigidity*, the exact opposite of advantage (v). The binding force of individual precedents, even if they are wrongly decided, makes for rigidity. The discretion of the courts is fettered, and they quite frequently have to give decisions of which they strongly disapprove. Since the Practice Statement of the House of Lords in 1966,[67] however, this problem is not so serious.

(ii) *Danger of illogical distinctions*. Over-subtle distinctions are sometimes drawn to avoid applying a rule which causes hardship: this leads to technicality.

(iii) *Bulk and complexity*. There is a superabundance of detail. The bulk of law reports—several thousand volumes—makes it difficult to learn and apply the law. A precedent may be overlooked, only to be discovered in a later case. This disadvantage may be compared with advantage (iii) above ("wealth of detail").

---

[66] *Sheldon* v. *Goodrich* (1803) 8 Ves.Jr. 481, 497.
[67] Above, pp. 194–197.

One cure for these defects in case-law is the periodical codification of branches of the law, such as took place in the Bills of Exchange Act 1882, and the Sale of Goods Act 1893. This process is likely to be greatly accentuated by the programme of the Law Commission.[68]

The comparison between the doctrine of binding precedent and codification is not satisfactory, however, because if we codify we must still decide whether precedents of interpretation are to be binding. The comparison should be rather between the English doctrine of binding individual precedents and the continental practice (based on codes) of allowing persuasive authority to a line of consistent decisions. The adoption of the latter practice would avoid fixing a bad rule—perhaps the interpretation of a statute—by means of one binding precedent.

Prospective Overruling

When a court in case *A* overrules a previous case *B*, the effect is that the new principle laid down applies not only to subsequent cases arising out of events that took place after case *A* was decided, but also to the parties to case *A* itself and to subsequent cases arising out of events that took place before case *A* was decided. Retrospective (retroactive) overruling results from the theory propounded by Blackstone[69] that judges do not make law, but rather find it: the overruled case was not bad law, it was not law at all. This is thought to work injustice in some cases, since the parties may be supposed to have relied on what was regarded as the law at that time.

The practice of "prospective overruling," whereby the new decision is to apply to future transactions only, has therefore been adopted in some jurisdictions in exceptional cases where justice "compels" or clearly demands it.[70] Its adoption was advocated by Lord Simon of Glaisdale in *Jones* v. *Secretary of State for Social Services*,[71] though he thought legislation would be necessary. He questioned whether it would extend to the interpretation of statutes, and whether it would apply to the House of Lords only. Lord Diplock in the same case said he thought the question should be considered. Prospective overruling, however, might create as many problems as it would solve.

---

[68] Above, p. 23.

[69] Bl.Comm.I. 69–70.

[70] Notably in the United States Supreme Court, *e.g. Linkletter* v. *Walker*, 381 U.S. 618 (1965); also in the Indian Supreme Court and some American States.

[71] [1972] A.C. 944 (H.L.). And see Lord Diplock, *The Courts as Legislators* (Holdsworth Club, University of Birmingham, 1965), p. 17.

It involves the injustice of treating persons differently. If it is not applied to the instant case it discourages people from litigating. Above all there is the difficulty of determining which cases are suitable for its application.[72]

5. THE RATIO DECIDENDI

We have hitherto spoken of "decisions" as if they were binding or persuasive in subsequent cases. It must now be noted that the only part of a judicial decision which is binding in subsequent cases is the *ratio decidendi*—the reason for the decision, or the principle of law on which the decision was based.

A judgment usually consists of (i) a statement of the facts, with an express or implied indication of which facts are considered to be material; and (ii) an account of the process of reasoning, varying greatly in length, but including one or more of ingredients (a) a review of the precedents, (b) illustrations, arguments from analogy, etc., (c) statements of general legal principle; and it always includes (iii) the actual judgment, decree or order, *e.g.*, "Judgment for the plaintiff, £500 damages." Part (iii), the order, decision or judgment in the narrow sense, is, as we have seen, binding only on the parties to the case.[73] In order to find the *ratio decidendi*, on the other hand, we must look at the whole judgment in the wide sense, including part (ii), which American lawyers often call the judge's "opinion.' It may also be necessary to look at the pleadings and counsel's argument in order to identify the issue between the parties, and perhaps also to ascertain the material facts.

It is not so difficult to formulate a definition or description of the meaning of *ratio decidendi* which most lawyers would approve. The expressions "reason for the decision" and "principle of law on which the decision was based" given above are little more than translations of the Latin term. A more extended description suggested by Sir Rupert Cross runs: "The *ratio decidendi* of a case is any rule of law expressly or impliedly treated by the judge as a necessary step in reaching his conclusion, having regard to the line of reasoning adopted by him, or a necessary part of his direction to the jury."[74] Directions to a jury would nowadays usually be in criminal

---

[72] Cross, *Precedent in English Law* (3rd ed.) pp. 229–233; Freeman 26 C.L.P. 166; Nichol 39 M.L.R. 542; Devlin 39 M.L.R. 11. A major objection is that the process involves the judiciary in too creative a legislative function. Lord Mackay of Clashfern L.C. *The Times*, December 3, 1987.

[73] Above, p. 191.

[74] Rupert Cross, *Precedent in English Law* (3rd ed., 1977), p. 76.

trials. There is controversy on the question whether a *ratio decidendi* is "subjective" or "objective." It is often said that the *ratio* of a given case is what the judge thought it was; but for the purpose of applying judicial precedents the *ratio* of an earlier decision has to be found or determined by the courts in later cases, so that the *ratio*, in one sense at least, is what the later courts say it is. In other words, it is a construction by the later courts.[75]

It is much more difficult to describe the way in which judges find or determine the *ratio decidendi* of previous decisions. Professor Goodhart has made a well-known attempt to describe this process with regard to a single precedent.[76] If, says Goodhart, the judge in the previous case gave a clear statement of the reason for his decision, or laid down a legal principle, this purported *ratio* will usually be found to be the true *ratio*. Put the other way round, in most cases if the reversal of a proposition would not affect the decision of the case, that proposition is *obiter*.[77] But there may be no such statement of reason or principle, or the reason given may be illogical or based on a faulty analysis of previous cases or on a doubtful reading of legal history. An example of the last is the decision of the House of Lords in *Admiralty Commissioners* v. *S.S. Amerika*,[78] which is criticised by Holdsworth on that ground.[79] The statement of principle is quite often wider than the facts of the case warrant and to that extent *obiter dictum*[80]; but occasionally it is narrower than the facts of the case require, as in the statement of Willes J. giving the judgment of the Court of Exchequer Chamber in *Barwick* v. *English Joint Stock Bank*,[81] that where a servant commits fraud in the course of his employment the master is liable if the fraud was for the master's benefit.[82]

Further, a judge may give more than one *ratio* for his decision, *e.g.*, Astbury J., in the general strike case[83]; for a judge is entitled to decide on two *rationes*, and is not bound to choose one and to

---

[75] *Ibid.* pp. 77–78.
[76] A. L. Goodhart, "On Determining the Ratio Decidendi of a Case," *Essays in Jurisprudence and the Common Law*, Chap. 1, reprinted from (1930) 40 *Yale Law Journal*, 161; "The Ratio Decidendi of a Case" (1959) 22 M.L.R. 117.
[77] Wambaugh, *The Study of Cases*, p. 17; but this test does not apply where a decision is based on more than one ground.
[78] [1917] A.C. 38.
[79] *History of English Law*, Vol. III, App. VIII.
[80] *e.g.*, *R.* v. *Electricity Commissioners*, above, p. 209.
[81] (1867) L.R. 2 Ex. 259, at p. 265.
[82] *Cf. Lloyd* v. *Grace, Smith & Co.* [1912] A.C. 716.
[83] *National Sailors' and Firemen's Union* v. *Reed* [1926] Ch. 536.

relegate the other to the rank of *obiter dictum*[84] As Lord Simonds said in *Jacobs* v. *London County Council*,[85]

> "there is ... no justification for regarding as *obiter dictum* a reason given by a judge for his decision, because he has given another reason also. If it were a proper test to ask whether the decision would have been the same apart from the proposition alleged to be *obiter*, then a case which *ex facie* decided two things would decide nothing."

It is more common for several judges of a composite court, such as the House of Lords or the Court of Appeal in civil appeals, to state different reasons or to make different statements of principle in giving judgment for the same party, as in the cases on the tort of conspiracy before the law was settled by the House of Lords in *Crofter Harris Tweed Co.* v. *Veitch*.[86] In such cases the *ratio* will be that concurred in by the majority. It is sometimes suggested that the law could be made less uncertain, and the system more rational, if only one majority opinion were allowed in the House of Lords in civil cases, as used to be normal in criminal cases.[87] Dissenting opinions would still be allowed as they suggest distinctions or possible lines of law reform. Lord Reid, however, was among those who think that the true *ratio* of a decision generally appears more clearly from a comparison of two or more statements in different words which are intended to supplement each other.[88] One gets the highest common factor of the views of the majority.

Where there is no majority for any one *ratio*, there is nothing to bind a later court. In *Harper* v. *National Coal Board*[89] the Court of Appeal held that there was no discernible *ratio decidendi* common to the majority of three in the House of Lords in *Smith* v. *Central Asbestos Co. Ltd.*[90] (extension of time for application for leave to appeal under Limitation Act 1963, as amended), so the court adopted the reasoning of the Court of Appeal[91] and dicta of two of the Law Lords in the *Smith* case. If one judge in an appellate court is silent about a statement made by one of his

---

[84] *Per* Lord Bramwell, *Membery* v. *Great Western Ry.* (1889) 14 App.Cas. 179, 187.
[85] [1950] A.C. 361, 369.
[86] [1942] A.C. 435.
[87] The House of Lords since *Shaw* v. *D.P.P.* [1962] A.C. 220 allow more than one judgment in criminal appeals. The practice of delivering only one leading speech has become usual in civil cases.
[88] *Saunders (formerly Gallie)* v. *Anglia Building Society* [1971] A.C. 1004 (H.L.).
[89] [1974] Q.B. 614.
[90] [1973] A.C. 518.
[91] [1972] 1 Q.B. 244.

brethren, that should not be taken to mean consent; and if he says "I agree" that means he agrees to the order proposed, not necessarily with all the other's reasoning.[92]

The true *ratio decidendi* of a single precedent, Professor Goodhart concludes, is the product of the material facts (as found by the judge) and the actual decision. It is for the judge making the decision to determine what facts are material, and he will invariably exclude some of the actual facts. The problem is the same, though more complex, in the case of the decision of a composite court. The *ratio* must be derived from the majority judgments. The *ratio decidendi* then is the actual judgment in relation to the material facts, that is, the facts which the deciding judge—or the judges giving the majority decision—considered to be material.

The main criticisms made of Goodhart's description of how the *ratio* is determined are, first, that courts pay more attention than Goodhart suggests to statements of law made by judges in the course of their judgments, and in fact judges often take greater care over their statements of legal principle than they do over selecting the material facts; and, secondly, that in most branches of law, of which negligence is an example, a precedent is not (or should not be) considered in isolation but in relation to a series of precedents.[93]

The determination of the *ratio* is found to be more an art than a science. No coherent theory of the method seems to have been worked out by the court themselves or to be relied on in practice. The practice appears to be a combination of all these methods, namely, taking the reason given by the judge, adopting the statement of principle made by the judge, or relating the actual decision to the material facts. The *ratio decidendi* as a judicial construction has been described as the result of technique, skill, experience and plain wisdom; and the consequence of the application of judicial precedent is creative law-making within the limits given by authoritative legal materials, for the facts in different cases are never quite the same.[94]

It should be remembered that in hearing a case a judge will bear in mind not only the rules of precedent and evidence but also the "policy" aspects of the judgment he delivers. "Policy" is a word long used by common lawyers to denote the broader extra-legal merits of a case indicating a particular solution to the

---

[92] Lord Russell of Killowen, *op. cit.* n. 48.
[93] See Cross, *Precedent in English Law* (3rd ed.), pp. 66–76, esp. pp. 73–75.
[94] Julius Stone, *The Province and Function of Law*, Chap. 7.

dispute.[95] What these issues will be will depend very much on the particular case being heard and the relevant substantive law. Thus, in claims in tort for pure economic loss negligently caused the reluctance of the courts to grant remedies has been dictated by the policy consideration that it is difficult to set clear limits to liability and therefore to entertain claims might "open the floodgates" to excessively wide liability with catastrophic effect on insurance in particular and trade and industry generally.[96] The determination of the existence of a duty of care in tort involves a wide range of policy factors,[97] but to a greater or less extent this is true of most adjudication. At one time judges were very reluctant to canvass policy issues in their judgments. They were the "inarticulate major premise", but of later years this is less entirely true, though the old reticence has by no means disappeared.

---

[95] See Bell, *Policy Arguments in Judicial Decisions.*
[96] See below, Chap. 18, p. 313.
[97] See Macdonald J. in *Nova Mink* v. *T.C.A.* [1951] 2 D.L.R. 241; Fleming, *Torts* (6th ed.), pp. 131–132; Symmons (1971) 34 M.L.R. 394, 528.

CHAPTER 14

Custom

Introduction

Law has its origin in customary rules. The early Codes such as the XII Tables of Rome and the "Laws" of the Anglo-Saxon Kings are not really exceptions to this, for they were mainly collections of customs brought up to date. Custom is usage recognised by law. "Usage" in the wide sense is a generally observed course of conduct, which arises spontaneously out of habit, imitation or merely taking the line of least resistance, rather in the way that sheep-tracks are formed. If certain conditions are fulfilled, the law recognises and enforces usage as custom when it has come to be regarded as obligatory by the persons to whom it applies.

English lawyers commonly divide custom into (a) legal and (b) conventional. Legal custom is that which, if certain conditions (*e.g.*, antiquity, certainty and reasonableness) are satisfied, has the force of law. It may be either (1) general, or (2) particular (or local). Conventional customs, or "usages" in the narrow sense, confer legal rights and impose legal obligations on individuals by reason only of being impliedly incorporated in a contract (*conventio*). As this is an application of the general law of contract, conventional customs are not a source of law in the same sense as the two kinds of legal custom: they are what we have called historical sources, while general and local customs are legal sources; but it is necessary to say something about conventional customs in this chapter, as they have been a factor in the development of that part of English law which has grown out of the custom of merchants. There are, further, mercantile customs, which for convenience are treated separately as their position is anomalous. They begin by being conventional and sometimes local, but tend to become general and legal.

Conventional Customs

Conventional (*i.e.* contractual) customs, or "usages" in the narrow sense, are a source of rights and duties by reason of being impliedly incorporated into contracts. Being terms of a contract, they only bind the parties. Where the court has to determine what unexpressed terms (if any) the parties to a contract intended, or must be presumed to have intended to imply, evidence of usage may be brought to explain or supplement—though not to contradict—the express terms. In this task the court is helped by considering the practice of persons of that class, for example, persons in a particular trade,[1] sellers and buyers in a particular market, or landlords and tenants in a particular district.[2]

In order to establish a conventional custom the plaintiff must show that it is reasonable, certain, not contrary to the general law (for the parties cannot be taken to imply what they would not be entitled to express), and universally accepted by the particular trade or profession, place or market.[3] But such a custom need not be ancient. In *Noble* v. *Kennoway*,[4] where a usage of the fishing trade off the Newfoundland coast was held to be impliedly incorporated into a contract of marine insurance, Lord Mansfield said: "Every underwriter is presumed to be acquainted with the practice of the trade he insures.... It is no matter if the usage has only been for a year.... The point is not analogous to a question concerning a common-law custom." Thus there is a recent tendency to make commercial agents liable to third parties with whom they deal.

When such usages are established, they are presumed to be incorporated into contracts between such persons or between persons in such districts, but they may be excluded expressly or by necessary implication.[5] In *Smith* v. *Wilson*,[6] where the lessee of a rabbit warren covenanted to leave 10,000 rabbits in the warren at the end of his term, oral evidence was admitted that

---

[1] *Produce Brokers Co. Ltd.* v. *Olympia Oil and Cake Co. Ltd.* [1916] 1 A.C. 314.
[2] *Hutton* v. *Warren* (1836) 1 M. & W. 466, 475–476, per Parke B.
[3] *Oricon Waren-Handelsgesellschaft M.B.H.* v. *Intergraan N.V.* [1967] 2 Lloyd's Rep. 82.
[4] (1780) 2 Doug. 510, 513.
[5] *Affréteurs Réunis Société Anonyme (Les)* v. *Walford* [1919] A.C. 801.
[6] (1832) 3 B. & Ad. 728.

by local custom 1,000 meant 1,200.[7] Hence we have the "baker's dozen" and the curious arithmetical devices of printers and others for allowing discount.

Local Custom and Prescription

Local custom differs from prescription in that while prescription is a source of rights by way of long use to particular persons or the owners of particular estates and is presumed to lie in grant,[8] local custom is a source of law for a certain locality and is not presumed to lie in grant. Nevertheless, many of the rules discussed below in connection with custom apply to both. "Prescription and custom are brothers," said Coke C.J. in *Rowles* v. *Mason*[9] "and ought to have the same age, and reason ought to be the father and congruence the mother, and use the nurse, and time out of memory to fortify them both."

1. MERCANTILE CUSTOMS

There were in the Middle Ages many customs of mercantile towns and fairs, with local variations, administered for the most part in the Borough Courts. They partook more of the nature of conventional than local customs, and by a process of borrowing and assimilation they became the general custom of merchants (*Lex Mercatoria*). From the seventeenth century onwards the common law courts incorporated the law merchant—notably, customs relating to bills of exchange and marine insurance—into the common law,[10] so that it affected anyone who took part in such transactions. This they did, first, by not requiring special proof of such customs in each case, and then by not requiring the parties to be merchants.[11] The negotiability of bills of exchange was thus added to the common law in the seventeenth century.[12] This affected third parties, and so became part of the common law. The process, which owed much to the judicial activity of Lord Mansfield in the latter part of the eighteenth century, was illogical: first, because a general custom should be

---

[7] The Anglo-Saxon "long hundred" = six score.
[8] See Chap. 17, pp. 285–286.
[9] (1612) 2 Brownl. 192.
[10] See Co.Litt. 182a.
[11] *Woodward* v. *Rowe* (1666) 2 Keb. 132; *cf. Barnaby* v. *Rigalt* (1633) Cro.Car. 301–302.
[12] A "negotiable instrument" *e.g.* a banknote or cheque, is a security for money which is transferable by delivery so as to confer a good title on a holder for value and in good faith, even though he obtained it from one who had not a good title: *London Joint Stock Bank* v. *Simmons* [1892] A.C. 201.

ancient, whereas some of these customs were quite new; and secondly, because negotiability was contrary to the common law, which did not permit the assignment of choses in action. Lord Mansfield, however, distinguished assignment from negotiability, which gives instruments the character of currency: *Peacock* v. *Rhodes*.[13] From Lord Mansfield's time mercantile customs could be pleaded and proved as matters, not of law but of fact,[14] and use was made of special juries of city merchants for this purpose. The courts continued to control the recognition of mercantile customs through the test of reasonableness.

It was disputed in the nineteenth century whether modern mercantile customs could still be incorporated into the common law. The issue was fought on the question whether the custom of merchants could attach the quality of negotiability to bonds and debentures payable to bearer. The Court of Queen's Bench, in a judgment delivered by so great a master of the common law as Blackburn J., held that it could not: a legal custom, he said, must be of immemorial antiquity, and therefore an admittedly recent mercantile custom could only be conventional, and conventional custom could not affect third parties by making the instrument negotiable.[15] Two years later, however, in *Goodwin* v. *Robarts*,[16] a strong Court of Exchequer Chamber (Cockburn C.J., Mellor, Lush, Brett and Lindley JJ.) decided that it could.

"It is true," said Cockburn C.J., in *Goodwin* v. *Robarts*,[17] "that the law merchant is sometimes spoken of as a fixed body of law, forming part of the common law, and as it were coeval with it. But as a matter of legal history, this view is altogether incorrect. The law merchant thus spoken of with reference to bills of exchange and other negotiable securities, though forming part of the general body of the *lex mercatoria*, is of comparatively recent origin. It is neither more nor less than the usages of merchants and traders in the different departments of trade, ratified by the decisions of courts of law, which, upon such usages being proved before them, have adopted them as settled law with a view to the interests of trade and the public convenience, the court proceeding herein on the well-known principle of law that, with reference to transactions in the different departments of trade, courts of law, in giving effect to the

---

[13] (1781) 2 Doug. 633.
[14] *Edie* v. *East India Co.* (1761) 2 Burr. 1216, at p. 1228.
[15] *Crouch* v. *Crédit Foncier of England* (1873) L.R. 8 Q.B. 374, 386–397.
[16] (1875) L.R. 10 Ex. 337.
[17] *Ibid.* at pp. 346–353.

contracts and dealing of the parties, will assume that the latter have dealt with one another on the footing of any custom or usage prevailing generally in the particular department. By this process, what before was usage only, unsanctioned by legal decision, has become engrafted upon, and incorporated into, the common law, and may thus be said to form part of it."

He then went on to show that bills of exchange were of comparatively modern origin, having been first used in Florence and Venice in the twelfth and thirteenth centuries, and their use gradually came to England by way of France. They were used in England before the seventeenth century, although, said Cockburn C.J., this was denied by Gerard de Malynes in his *"Lex Mercatoria"* (1622). The first English case on a bill of exchange was a decision of the Court of Exchequer Chamber in *Martin* v. *Boure*.[18] Holt C.J., contrary to the wishes of the merchants and the opinion of the legal profession, set his face strongly against the negotiability of promissory notes,[19] but this was settled by statute in 1704.[20] Bankers' notes were treated as currency by Lord Mansfield in *Miller* v. *Race*.[21] Cockburn C.J. continued:

> "Usage, adopted by the Courts, having been thus the origin of the whole of the so-called law merchant as to negotiable securities, what is there to prevent our acting upon the principle acted upon by our predecessors, and follow in the precedents they have left to us? Why is it to be said that a new usage which has sprung up under altered circumstances, is to be less admissible than the usages of past times?"

There can be no doubt that the decision in *Goodwin* v. *Robarts*, however illogical it may be, holds the field. It was followed soon afterwards by a Divisional Court in *Rumball* v. *Metropolitan Bank*,[22] and by Kennedy J. in *Bechuanaland Exploration Co.* v. *London Trading Bank Ltd.*[23] Then Bigham J. in *Edelstein* v. *Schuler & Co.*,[24] another case of debentures payable to bearer, said: "I go, perhaps, further than Kennedy J. intended to go, for I think that it is no longer necessary to tender evidence in support of

---

[18] (1603) Cro.Jac. 6.
[19] *Cf. Buller* v. *Crips* (1703) 6 Mod. 29.
[20] 3 & 4 Ann. c. 9.
[21] (1758) 1 Burr. 452.
[22] (1877) 2 Q.B.D. 194.
[23] [1898] 2 Q.B. 658.
[24] [1902] 2 K.B. 144, 155–156.

the fact that such bonds are negotiable, and that the Courts of law ought to take judicial notice of it."

It was laid down in *Edie* v. *East India Co.*[25] that a rule of the common law derived from the custom of merchants cannot be changed by a later mercantile custom. There are modern dicta apparently inconsistent with this principle,[26] but they should probably be taken to mean that the judicial recognition of particular mercantile customs as part of the general law does not exclude the possibility of their being modified by new conventional customs[27] incorporated as implied terms into contracts.

Some groups of mercantile custom, after being received into the common law, have become historical sources of statute law by being codified in such statutes as the Bills of Exchange Act 1882, the Sale of Goods Act 1893,[28] and the Marine Insurance Act 1906.

2. GENERAL CUSTOMS

As we saw in Chapter 1, the foundation of English law is the unwritten "common law." There are, for example, no statutory definitions of murder, assault, libel, false imprisonment, negligence, or the consideration required for contracts not under seal. The traditional doctrine is that the common law of England consists of general "customs of the realm," but it was not propounded by Glanvill (*c.* 1190) nor probably intended without qualification by Bracton (*c.* 1250). "Though the laws of England are unwritten," says Glanvill in the preface to his treatise,

> "it seems not improper to give them the name of laws, since law is nothing else than the will of the head of the State which has the force of law[29]; such for instance are those laws which are recognised as established, when doubtful points are resolved in Council, by the advice of the great men with the sanction of the King's authority."

It is true that Bracton in the preface to book 1 of his treatise says: "In England the unwritten law is that which usage has

---

[25] (1761) 2 Burr. 1216.
[26] *Anglo-African Shipping* v. *Mortner* [1962] 1 Lloyd's Rep. 610; *Teheran-Europe* v. *Belton* [1968] 2 Q.B. 53 and 545. Difficulties as to the appropriate documents for sea container traffic result from the verdict as to the custom of merchants in regard to bills of lading in *Lickbarrow* v. *Mason* (1794) 5 T.R. 683. See *Scrutton on Charterparties* (19th ed.) p. 383.
[27] Above, p. 225.
[28] Now replaced by the Sale of Goods Act 1979.
[29] Echoing Justinian, *Inst.* 1, 2, 6; *Sed et quod Principi placuit legis habet vigorem*; *Digest*, 1, 4, 1, pr. (Ulpian).

approved;" but he goes on to say that the name of laws may properly be given to the laws of England, although they be unwritten, because "that has the force of law which has been rightfully laid down and approved on the previous authority of the King or other ruler, acting with the advice and consent of the chief men and the general approval of the community." The theory that the common law had its origin in popular custom was, however, established by the end of the fourteenth century. In 1350 we find counsel saying that "common usage is common law,"[30] and in 1400 the court says that "common custom of the realm is common law."[31] The theory is consistently held down to the time of Blackstone, who speaks in his *Commentaries* (1765) of "the first ground and chief corner stone of the laws of England, which is general immemorial custom, or common law, from time to time declared in the decisions of the courts of justice,"[32] although by that time the tradition was somewhat artificial.

To a great extent it is true of earlier times that the common law consisted of general immemorial customs; but not entirely. Some part of the law applied by the royal courts, which in the Middle Ages was attributed to general customs of the realm, included legislative provisions whose statutory origin had been forgotten; and it was also supplemented by principles which early judges had derived from Roman civil and canon law, feudal notions, and ideas of natural reason. It can even be said that in the medieval period, down to and including the reign of Edward I, custom was actually a method of introducing changes into the law; informal law-making was done by the issue of new writs and the adoption of new court practices. Yet a great part of the task of the King's judges was to weld the variety of local customs into a consistent whole. Custom, largely local, was still active in the Middle Ages, just as constitutional conventions are in modern times. No doubt there was considerable scope here for creative activity on the part of the judges. Moreover, emphasis was placed on procedure rather than substantive rights, so that no inconsiderable part of the common law consisted of the practice of the royal courts. In public law, custom—largely feudal in origin—gave us the royal prerogative and parliamentary privilege. Manorial customs developed copyhold tenure, which was of great importance in the land law until 1926.

---

[30] Y.B. 30 Edw. III, ff. 25, 26.
[31] Y.B. 2 Hen. IV, f. 18, Pasch. pl. 5.
[32] 1 Comm. 73, and see 63–69.

It is almost certain that general customs are no longer a creative source of English law, as they have all become embodied in the system of case-law or else been displaced by legislation. There may, however, be some constitutional customs which have not had occasion to be recognised by the courts, but which would (or would probably) be so recognised if the question came before them, and which are neither common law (in the sense of case-law) nor constitutional conventions, for example, such non-statutory rules as prescribe the forms according to which acts of the Crown are to be performed. If the existence of a general custom, not hitherto adjudicated upon, were to be alleged, the courts would probably apply tests similar to those which they apply to local customs (below). These tests, save for the illogical case of mercantile customs,[33] would include the rule of immemorial antiquity.

3. LOCAL CUSTOMS

Particular customs are distinguished from general customs by restriction of locality or class of persons (such as parishioners or fishermen) or both. In effect it seems that particular customs must be local, for a custom which applies to a class of persons throughout the realm, such as inn-keepers, when judicially recognised becomes part of the "common law,"[34] whereas Coke says that a "custom" must coincide with some recognised jurisdiction, such as a county, borough, parish or manor.[35] A custom for all the inhabitants of a parish to indulge in lawful games, sports or pastimes on certain land in the parish is good[36]; but it does not extend to all persons for the time being within the parish, such as strangers casually there.[37] Again, there cannot be a customary right for all the Queen's subjects to witness horse-races on Newmarket Heath.[38]

Among county customs was the custom of gavelkind, whereby until the Administration of Estates Act 1925, freeholds in Kent descended on an intestacy to all the sons or all the brothers equally.[39] This was probably a local survival of

---

[33] Above, p. 226.
[34] *Gifford* v. *Lord Yarborough* (1828) 5 Bing. 163, at p. 164, *per* Best C.J.
[35] Co.Litt. 33b. 110b; *Bourke* v. *Davis* (1890) 44 Ch.D. 110.
[36] See *New Windsor Corpn.* v. *Mellor* [1975] Ch. 380 (C.A.): right of inhabitants to indulge in lawful sports and pastimes on Bachelors' Acre enjoyed for over 300 years before 1875.
[37] *Fitch* v. *Rawling* (1795) 2 Hy.Bl. 393.
[38] *Coventry* v. *Wills* (1863) 12 W.R. 127.
[39] Co.Litt. 140a.

Anglo-Saxon custom, primogeniture having been introduced by the Normans.[40] The customs of cities and boroughs were of considerable importance in the Middle Ages. Even villages had their customs. In Selby in the fourteenth century a husband was not liable for the debts incurred by his wife in separate trading; and until quite recently there was a custom in Portland to convey certain lands by declaration in the parish church, the congregation acting as witnesses.

Local customs are not nearly so important at the present day owing to the effects of legislation. They are largely to be found in rights of way and common. Another custom not infrequently found is the right of the fishermen of a parish to dry their nets on private land within the parish. In *Iveagh (Earl)* v. *Martin*[41] the defendant claimed that as a "man of Bosham" he had a customary right as against the lord of the manor to free mooring on the quay in connection with his business as a boat repairer, but it was held that the custom applied to fishing boats and did not extend to the right claimed by the defendant.

"The rules relating to particular customs," says Blackstone,[42] "regard either the *proof* of their existence; their *legality* when proved; or their usual method of *allowance*."

Customs must be pleaded, and it is necessary to prove both the existence of the custom and that the thing in dispute is within the custom alleged.

A local custom is always an exception to the general law, but it must not be contrary to a statute or to a fundamental principle of the common law. This is not a question of proving the existence of a custom, but of whether the custom if proved will be allowed by the courts. Thus in *Noble* v. *Durell*[43] a local custom that every pound of butter sold in a certain market should weigh eighteen ozs. was held bad, for a statute of Charles II had enacted that a pound avoirdupois should be sixteen ozs. everywhere. It automatically ceased to be custom on the passing of the statute. Customs in derogation of the common law are construed strictly.

In order that an alleged local custom may be recognised by the courts as a binding legal custom, it must fulfil certain tests which the courts themselves have laid down (*Case of Tanistry*).[44] There is no general agreement about the way in which these tests

---

[40] Co.Litt. 110b. And see *Johnson* v. *Clark* [1908] 1 Ch. 303.
[41] [1961] 1 Q.B. 232.
[42] 1 Comn. 75.
[43] (1789) 3 T.R. 271.
[44] (1608) Davis Ir.R. 28 (Brehon law of succession in Ireland).

should be classified: the following arrangement follows Blackstone.[45]

Antiquity

The custom must have existed from time immemorial or from time whereof "the memory of man runneth not to the contrary." The doctrine of immemorial antiquity came to be used by the common law courts in the sixteenth century to restrict the growth of custom, and the commencing date was settled as the first year of the reign of Richard I (1189). This was the date of limitation fixed by the Statute of Westminster I 1275,[46] for bringing writs of right to recover freeholds, and the statute of *Quo Warranto* 1290, provided that the user of a franchise since 1189 was a good answer to a writ of *quo warranto*. By a vagary of legal history, then, the convenient date chosen in the thirteenth century for starting a limitation period of about one hundred years was later taken, for the purpose of establishing local customs, as fixing the beginning of legal memory.

In practice, however, it is sufficient if the person alleging the existence of a custom brings evidence that it has existed for a substantial period, such as the time of actual human memory, unless the party denying its existence can show that it did not exist or could not have existed at some particular time since 1189. In *Mercer* v. *Denne*,[47] where the custom of the fishermen of a parish to dry their nets on private land was held good, even though they dried their nets in a modern manner, Vaughan Williams L.J. said:

> "The fact is that reason recoils from the proposition that legal memory goes back to an arbitrary date at the beginning of the reign of Richard I, A.D. 1189, and, if one finds proof of uninterrupted modern usage, there is a natural inclination to presume the previous existence of the custom right back to 1189, even though the facts may be such as to force upon reason the conclusion that the modern usage could not in fact have been adopted for more than a few generations. Judges, therefore, presume everything possible which would give a custom a legal origin, and find in favour of a manifestly modern custom as being an extension which

[45] 1 Comm. 76–78.
[46] 3 Edw. 1, c. 39.
[47] [1905] 2 Ch. 538, 577.

falls within the reason of so much of the modern usage as may well have existed throughout legal memory."

No custom can take away the force of an Act of Parliament, since the statute itself is proof of a time when such a custom did not exist.[48] In *Simpson* v. *Wells*,[49] where a person who was charged with obstructing a public footway by setting up a refreshment stall pleaded that he did so by virtue of a custom existing at a "statute sessions," *i.e.*, a fair held for hiring servants, his defence failed because it was shown that such sessions were first introduced by a statute passed in the fourteenth century, so that the custom could not have existed before then. Otherwise, the defendant would only need to show (as he did) that the custom had in fact been exercised for as long as people acquainted with the matter could remember. It is not necessary for the person alleging the custom to show how it could have started.[50]

Continuance

The custom must have been in existence continuously, that is to say, the right to exercise it must not have been interrupted. A distinction is drawn between interruption of the right, and of the mere possession of the thing over which it is asserted.[51] So in *Wyld* v. *Silver*[52] it was held that a customary right could not be lost by disuse or waiver, only by Act of Parliament; and where the inhabitants were entitled to hold an annual fair or wake on certain land, an injunction was granted to prevent the defendant from building on the land although the fair had not been held in living memory.

Peaceable Enjoyment

The custom must have been peaceable, and acquiesced in; not subject to contention and dispute.[53] It must not have been exercised by means of force or violence, for its origin lies in common consent; nor secretly, for the law is public; nor by revocable licence, for that would depend on the will of individuals.[54]

---

[48] Co.Litt. 113a.
[49] (1872) 7 Q.B. 214.
[50] *Wolstanton, Ltd. and Duchy of Lancaster* v. *Newcastle-under-Lyme Corporation* [1940] A.C. 860.
[51] Co.Litt. 114.
[52] [1963] 1 Q.B. 169. See also *New Windsor Corpn.* v. *Mellor* [1975] Ch. 380 (C.A.): customary right not lost although not used since 1875.
[53] Co.Litt. 114.
[54] *Mills* v. *Corporation of Colchester* (1867) L.R. 2 C.P. 476.

Reasonableness

A custom must be reasonable, or rather, not unreasonable—a distinction that affects the burden of proof.[55] This is a question of law.[56] Thus, customary rights over land must be limited in some way so that their exercise will not exhaust or destroy the value of the land. It has been held that a custom for the lord of a manor to get and carry away minerals under a tenant's copyhold land without making compensation for subsidence and damage to buildings was unreasonable.[57]

The party disputing the existence of an alleged custom may show that it would be unreasonable at the time of origin, and presumably therefore never existed. Thus in *Bryant* v. *Foot*,[58] where a rector claimed that a fee of thirteen shillings was payable by custom on the celebration of every marriage in the parish and proved that the fee had been customary for forty-eight years, arguing that this raised a presumption of immemorial antiquity, it was held that a fee of thirteen shillings in 1189 would have been grossly unreasonable according to the value of money in the Middle Ages.[59]

Certainty

A custom must be certain in nature and scope, for there is no law which is uncertain.[60]

Recognition as Obligatory

Customs, though established by consent, must be (when established) recognised by those affected as being obligatory and not optional. A custom, says Blackstone, that all the inhabitants of a district should be rated towards the maintenance of a bridge, would be good; but a custom that every man was to contribute thereto at his own pleasure, would be "idle and absurd, and indeed no custom at all." Inhabitants of the County Palatine of Durham had for the whole of living memory taken sea-washed coal from the foreshore, but the Court of Appeal held in *Beckett* (*Alfred F.*) v. *Lyons*[61] that the only

---

[55] Litt. s.212; 1 Bl.Comm. 77.
[56] Co.Litt. 62a.
[57] *Wolstanton, Ltd. and Duchy of Lancaster* v. *Newcastle-under-Lyme Corporation* [1940] A.C. 860.
[58] (1868) L.R. 3 Q.B. 497.
[59] *Cf. Lawrence* v. *Hitch* (1868) L.R. 3 Q.B. 521, where the court refused to apply the same reasoning to a toll of one shilling per cart-load of vegetables.
[60] *Case of Tanistry* (1608) Davis Ir.R. 28.
[61] [1967] Ch. 449; *cf. Goodman* v. *Saltash Corporation* (1882) 7 App.Cas. 633.

established public rights of using the foreshore are fishing and navigation and rights ancillary to these. Beachcombing, walking and bathing may be tolerated by the Crown, but they are not rights.

Consistency

It is obvious that customs must be consistent with one another. If two parties set up contradictory "customs," either one is not a custom or neither is a custom; they cannot both be customs.[62]

---

[62] *Alfred's Case* (1610) 9 Co.Rep. 57b.

CHAPTER 15

Books of Authority

1. THE USE OF TEXTBOOKS IN COURT

General Rules

The general rule applied by English courts is that textbooks (by which we mean books other than statutes and law reports), however eminent their authors, are not treated as authorities. As Lord Goddard C.J. said in *Bastin* v. *Davies*,[1] the court "would never hesitate to disagree with a statement in a textbook, however authoritative or however long it had stood, if it thought right to do so." Textbooks are, of course, looked at by judges and practitioners, but this is for the purpose of seeking information and ideas for argument, and for finding references to statutes and reported cases. Statements contained in textbooks must not as a general rule be quoted and relied on in court on the authority of their authors: arguments founded on them, as distinct from arguments based on statute or precedent, stand or fall by their intrinsic merits. Counsel may, however, adopt the statements of text-writers as part of their argument, and judges sometimes accept them as correct statements of the law.[2] Despite the former reluctance of judges to cite anything

---

[1] [1950] 2 K.B. 579.
[2] See *per* Crossman J. in *Re O'Keefe* (1940) 109 L.J.Ch. 86,88. Textbooks and articles have been cited to their authors who have become judges. See *Cordell* v. *Second Clanfield* [1969] 2 Ch. 9 (Megarry J.); *Armstrong* v. *Strain* [1951] 1 T.L.R. 856 (Devlin J.).

that is not between hard covers,[3] this practice has extended to
the quotation of articles in legal periodicals.[4] It may well be, as a
learned French observer has suggested,[5] that judges allow
themselves more latitude in quoting textbooks than is permitted
to counsel. The comparatively small direct influence of jurists on
legal development in England is a corollary of the pre-eminent
authority which attaches to judicial decisions. It has been well
said that "our judges are our jurists." But the fact that an author
was, or became, a judge does not lend judicial authority to his
literary utterances.[6]

It was formerly a rule, occasionally broken, that living authors
might not be cited by name in argument. In *Ion's Case*,[7] counsel
said: "It is no doubt a rule that a writer on law is not to be
considered an authority in his lifetime. The only exception to the
rule, perhaps, is the case of Justice Story." To which Coleridge J.
replied: "Story is dead." And the following passage occurs in
the report of the hearing in the Court of Appeal of *Greenlands,
Ltd.* v. *Wilmshurst*[8]:

> "Counsel (Sir Edward Clarke) proceeded to refer to Mr.
> Blake Odgers's work on libel. Lord Justice Vaughan
> Williams: 'No doubt Mr. Odgers's book is a most
> admirable work, which we all use, but I think we ought in
> this Court still to maintain the old idea that counsel are not
> entitled to quote living authors as authorities for a proposi-
> tion they are putting forward, but they may adopt the
> author's statements as part of their argument.' *Sir Edward
> Clarke* said that he was only citing Mr. Odgers's proposition
> as part of his argument."

Lord Wright was expressing the older notion when in *Nicholls*
v. *Ely Beet Sugar Factory Ltd.*,[9] he described a treatise of the
nonagenarian Sir Frederick Pollock as "fortunately not a work of
authority;" but the modern attitude is that death in itself no
longer affects the authority of a writer. Probably no author,
while still living, so often had his writings adopted by the courts
as correct statements of the law as Pollock, with his works on

---

[3] A remark attributed to the distinguished American Judge Cardozo.
[4] See, *e.g.*, *Haynes* v. *Harwood* [1953] 1 K.B. 146; *Thomas* v. *University of Bradford* [1987] A.C. 795.
[5] R. David, *Introduction à l'étude du droit privé de l'Angleterre* (1948), pp. 168–169.
[6] *Cf. Johnes* v. *Johnes* (1814) 3 Dow 1, 15, *per* Lord Eldon.
[7] (1851) 2 Den.C.C. 475, 488.
[8] (1913) 29 T.L.R. 685, 687.
[9] [1936] Ch. 343, 349. The point was missed by more than one reporter who wrote "unfortunately": see 154 L.T. 533; 105 L.J.Ch. 282.

Tort, Contract and Partnership. McCardie J., for example, in *Performing Right Society, Ltd.* v. *Mitchell, Ltd.*,[10] adopted the definition of "independent contractor" from Pollock's *Torts*. The description of nuisance in Winfield's *Textbook of the Law of Tort* was accepted in his lifetime by Scott L.J. in *Read* v. *Lyons & Co.*,[11] and by Lord Goddard C.J. in *Howard* v. *Walker*.[12] The reason for the former rule was given by Lord Reid when he wrote: "In the House of Lords at least we turn a blind eye to the old rule that an academic writer is not an authority until he is dead, because then he can no longer change his mind."[13]

Books of Authority

Authority (in the absence of statute and binding precedent) should probably be regarded as a matter of degree by lawyers as it is by historians; but between later authors and some of the earlier writers there is a difference of authority so great as virtually to amount to a difference in kind. Some of the earlier textbooks are treated by the courts as authoritative statements of the law of their time, and of present law if it is not shown to have been changed, which may be quoted and relied on in court on the authority of their authors. It would, therefore, not be improper to say that the courts regard certain Abridgments and Treatises as authoritative in a special sense. They are, in Blackstone's words, of "intrinsic authority," "the authoritative writings of the venerable sages of the law."[14] The statements of such writers are presumed to be evidence of judicial decisions that have been lost; they are therefore accepted if consonant with reason. This is chiefly to be explained by the difficulty of ascertaining the law of former times, and of course only applies in the absence of statutes and reported decisions on the point. Whether a textbook will be treated as authoritative depends on the reputation of the author and the time when it was written, and is determined by professional tradition and practice.

Besides the reporters, says Blackstone,

> "there are also other authors, to whom great venera-
> tion and respect is paid by the students of the common
> law. Such are Glanvill and Bracton, Britton[15] and Fleta,

[10] [1924] 1 K.B. 762, 767–768.
[11] [1945] K.B. 216, 236.
[12] [1947] K.B. 860; [1947] 2 All E.R. 197.
[13] "The Judge as Law Maker" (1972) 12 J.S.P.T.L. 22. See also, Megarry, *Miscellany at Law*, pp. 326–329 for a justification of the old rule.
[14] 1 Comm. 72, 73.
[15] Britton, Fleta and (to some extent) Hengham were epitomes of Bracton.

Hengham and Littleton, Statham, Brooke, Fitzherbert, and Staundforde,[16] and some others of antient date; *whose treatises are cited as authority*, and are evidence that cases have formerly happened, in which such and such points were determined, which are now become settled and first principles.[17] One of the last of these methodical writers in point of time, whose works are of any *intrinsic authority* in the courts of justice, and do not entirely depend on the strength of their quotations from older authors, is the same learned judge we have just mentioned [in connection with reports], Sir Edward Coke; who hath written four volumes of institutes. . . . "[18]

In some cases almost the whole array of these books of authority has been drawn into the forensic struggle. When the law relating to trial by battle was being debated as a live issue in *Ashford* v. *Thornton*,[19] counsel cited Glanvill, Bracton, Fleta, Britton, Staunford's *Pleas of the Crown*, Fitzherbert's *Abridgment*, Coke's *Institutes*, Hawkins' *Pleas of the Crown*, and Blackstone. More recently Lord Denning in *Warner* v. *Sampson*[20] referred to Glanvill, the Year Books, Fitzherbert's *Abridgment*, Coke upon Littleton, and Blackstone; and Lord Gardiner L.C. in *Button* v. *D.P.P.*[21] referred to Fitzherbert, Lambard, Coke, Hale, Hawkins and Blackstone.

It is sometimes difficult to tell from the reports what kind or degree of authority a judge is attaching to particular writers. For instance, Lord Jowitt L.C., in *Joyce* v. *Director of Public Prosecutions*,[22] referred indiscriminately to Bracton, Foster's *Crown Cases*, Hawkins' *Pleas of the Crown*, East's Pleas of the Crown, Chitty's *Prerogatives of the Crown*, Oppenheim's *International Law* (edited by Professor Lauterpacht), and a paragraph in the second edition of Halsbury's *Laws of England* written by Sir William Holdsworth—recently deceased—"whose authority on such a matter is unequalled." Lord Porter added to this list Hale's *Pleas of the Crown* and an article in *The Law Quarterly Review* by Sir William Malkin, late legal adviser to the Foreign

[16] Staunford, *Plees del Coron* (1557).
[17] I Comm. 72–73. The italics are the author's.
[18] *Ibid.* The italics are the author's.
[19] (1818) 1 B. & Ald. 405.
[20] [1959] 1 Q.B. 297.
[21] [1966] A.C. 591, 623 *et seq.*; below p. 255. Lord Gardiner cited Fitzherbert's *New Book of Justices of the Peace* (1538) and *Office and Authority of Justices of the Peace* (1584), and also *Termes de la Ley*, Dalton's *Country Justice*, Cowell's *Law Dictionary*, Nelson's *Justice of the Peace* and Burn's *Justice of the Peace*.
[22] [1946] A.C. 347.

Office. In an appeal from Northern Ireland[23] on the question of duress as a defence to a charge of aiding and abetting murder, Lord Simon of Glaisdale in his dissenting judgment exclaimed; "Poor Hale, poor Blackstone; wretched Russell and Kenny; poor, poor Lord Denman."

The most important books of authority are discussed in more detail in section 2 of this chapter. It will be noticed that they are all books on the common law. Scarcely any books on other branches of law have found their way into this category. The *Doctor and Student*, published by Christopher St. Germain in 1523–30, was formerly regarded as of great authority on the principles of Equity, and the maxim "Equity follows the law" may be traced back to one of the arguments contained in it.[24] On the canon law in England there is William of Lyndwood's *Provinciale* (1430), a commentary on the provincial constitutions of the Archbishops of Canterbury; and on the medieval law merchant, Gerard de Malynes' *Lex Mercatoria* (1622).

Books Not of Authority

The critical way in which the other class of textbook is treated by the courts may be illustrated by another passage from Lord Porter's judgment in *Joyce* v. *Director of Public Prosecutions*[25]: "The Attorney-General supported this contention by a reference to Archbold's *Criminal Practice* (31st ed.) (1943), p. 330.... The true principle is, I think, set out in *Phipson on Evidence*, 8th ed., p. 34, and *Best on Evidence*, 12th ed., p. 252." In *Shenton* v. *Tyler*[26] Green M.R. referred to books on the law of evidence by Best, Cockle, Gilbert, Greenleaf, Peake, Phipson, Starkie, Stephen, Taylor, Wigmore and Wills, but came to the conclusion that they were wrong in saying that statements made between husband and wife during marriage were privileged at common law. In *Button* v. *D.P.P.*[27] Lord Gardiner L.C. said that *Archbold* and *Russell on Crime* were wrong in stating that an affray must be committed in a public place. This erroneous view had persisted for 150 years and was due to a misunderstanding of Blackstone, who may have misunderstood Hawkins.

A well-known example of judicial approval of the statement of a recent author is Lord Dunedin's adoption in

---

[23] *D.P.P. for Northern Ireland* v. *Lynch* [1975] A.C. 653 (H.L.).
[24] Bk. I, Chap. 26; Bk. II, Introd.
[25] [1946] A.C. 347.
[26] [1939] Ch. 620.
[27] [1966] A.C. 591 (H.L.).

Att.-Gen. v. *De Keyser's Royal Hotel, Ltd.*[28] of the definition of the royal prerogative given in Dicey's *Law of the Constitution*.

The opinions of Law Officers of the Crown have always been treated as of great persuasive authority. On questions relating to the royal prerogative and the colonies, for example, Forsyth's *Cases and Opinions* (1868) has often been brought into use.

The branches of English law in which modern textbooks have been most often referred to in court are Conflict of Laws, Conveyancing, Tort, and Criminal Law.

A large proportion of cases in Conflict of Laws, where they are not merely questions of fact, contain a reference to Dicey's *Conflict of Laws*.[29] In the latter part of the nineteenth century the same was true of Story's *Conflict of Laws*, which is itself full of references to earlier jurists, notably those of the seventeenth-century Dutch school. The reason for this is the late development of English private international law, the consequent paucity of decided cases, and the dearth of statutes. In later years Cheshire's *Private International Law* has frequently been cited.

"For the exposition of our very complicated real property law," said Byrne J., in *Re Hollis' Hospital and Hague's Contract*[30] (a case on the rule against perpetuities), "it is proper in the absence of judicial authority to resort to textbooks which have been recognised by the courts as representing the views and practice of conveyancers of repute." The reason for the extraordinary influence of the practice of conveyancers on the development of our land law is the great difficulty of the subject and the fact that a thorough mastery of it has only been gained by a few conveyancers in each generation. Sir Orlando Bridgman (*c.* 1606–74; L.K. 1667–72) was described by counsel in *Goodtitle* v. *Funucan*[31] as "the father of conveyancers." His *Precedents of Conveyances* was published in 1682, and initiated the modern strict settlement of land. As early as 1697 we find reliance placed on "the common received opinion of Westminster Hall and of all conveyancers,"[32] and Lord Eldon's statement in 1821 that the practice of conveyancers amounted to "a very considerable authority"[33] represents the opinion of the nineteenth century. The rejection by courts of first instance of schemes for the management of trust property, said

---

[28] [1920] A.C. 508, 526.
[29] Now Dicey and Morris.
[30] [1899] 2 Ch. 540, 551.
[31] (1781) 2 Doug.K.B. 565, 568.
[32] *Countess of Radnor* v. *Vandebendy*, Shower P.C. at p. 70.
[33] *Smith* v. *Doe*, 2 Brod. & Bing. 473, 599.

Denning L.J. in the Court of Appeal in *Re Downshire Settled Estates*,[34] "has taken Lincoln's Inn by surprise, so much so that many proposed schemes have been held up pending our decision. The practice of the profession in these cases is the best evidence of what the law is; indeed, it makes law."

In *Re Hollis' Hospital and Hague's Contract*[35] Byrne J. referred to Butler's notes to Coke upon Littleton; Sheppard's *Touchstone*, and a note thereon by Preston; Viner's *Abridgment*; *Sanders on Uses and Trusts*; *Lewis on Perpetuity*; Gray's *Law of Perpetuity*; and *Fry on Specific Performance*. He also discussed at length, and disagreed with, "the comparatively recent although most valuable book of the late Mr. Challis." In *Re Ashforth*,[36] Farwell J. referred to *Challis on Real Property*, *Williams on Real Property*, *Gray on Perpetuities*, *Jarman on Wills* and Stephen's *Commentaries*. The Court of Appeal in *Re Ellenborough Park*[37] adopted the formulation of the characteristics of a valid easement from Cheshire's *Modern Real Property*.

The practice of conveyancers has also been an historical source of parts of our statute law as contained in various Conveyancing and Settled Land Acts.

Tort is the branch of the common law which has developed most in modern times, especially since the abolition of the forms of action. Pollock's *Torts* and *Beven on Negligence* were probably the most frequently quoted in court on the subject in the earlier part of this century.[38] More recently the textbooks of Salmond and Winfield have been often quoted, as have Kenny's *Outlines of Criminal Law* and Cheshire and Fifoot's *Law of Contract*. Examples of these and other citations are now so numerous that there is no need to give specific examples. It is sufficient to mention that in *Nissan* v. *Att.-Gen.*,[39] concerning the liability of the Crown to compensate for damage done by British forces to the property of a British subject in Cyprus, reference was made to *Chalmers' Opinions of Eminent Lawyers* (1814), *Stephen's History of the Criminal Law* (1883), *Halsbury's Laws of England*, *Chitty's Prerogatives of the Crown*, *Winfield on Tort*, *Salmond on Torts*, *Wade and Phillips's Constitutional Law*, *Dicey's Conflict of Laws* and *Lord McNair's Law of Treaties* and *International Law Opinions*.

---

[34] [1953] Ch. 218.
[35] n. 30 (above), at p. 548.
[36] [1905] 1 Ch. 535, 546.
[37] [1956] Ch. 131.
[38] *e.g.*, *Admiralty Commissioners* v. *S.S. Amerika* [1917] A.C. 38; *Edwards* v. *Porter* [1923] 2 K.B. 538; *Phillips* v. *Britannia Hygienic Laundry Co.* [1923] 1 K.B. 539.
[39] [1970] A.C. 179 (H.L.).

In *R. v. Secretary of State for the Home Department ex p. Northumbria Police Authority*[39a] reference was made to *Glanvill, Chitty's Prerogatives of the Crown, Blackstone's Commentaries, Dicey's Law of the Constitution, Holdsworth's History of English Law* and *Hood Phillips and Jackson Constitutional Law* in deciding that the Home Secretary could supply riot equipment to a Chief Constable.

In Criminal Law also the courts often refer to textbooks such as *Archbold: Pleading, Evidence and Practice in Criminal Cases*, Smith and Hogan, *Criminal Law* and Glanville Williams, *Criminal Law*. Recent instances are *R. v. Sharp* on duress,[40] *R. v. King* on obtaining by deception,[41] *R. v. Cook*[42] on evidence and *R. v. Howe* on duress.[43]

The difference between academic and practitioners' textbooks was strikingly brought out in a review by Sir Alfred Denning (now Lord Denning) of an edition of Winfield's *Tort*. The reason why such books as *Winfield, Salmond* and *Pollock* are so useful in the courts, he wrote,[44] is that they are not digests of cases but repositories of principles.

> "They are written by men who have studied the law as a science with more detachment than is possible to men engaged in busy practice. The influence of the academic lawyers is greater now than it has ever been and is greater than they themselves realise. Their influence is largely through their writings. The notion that their works are not of authority except after the author's death has long been exploded. Indeed, the more recent the work, the more persuasive it is.... The vast tomes written and edited by practitioners for practitioners fulfil a different purpose. They are valuable as works of reference. They are cited not for principles but for detailed rules on special subjects."

As has been mentioned above,[45] there is an increasing tendency for the courts to refer to articles in learned legal periodicals in the same way as textbooks. Thus, the House of Lords has referred to articles in the *Law Quarterly Review* and *New Law Journal*[46] and the Court of Appeal made use of articles

[39a] [1987] 2 W.L.R. 590.
[40] [1987] Q.B. 853.
[41] [1987] Q.B. 547.
[42] [1987] Q.B. 417.
[43] [1987] A.C. 417.
[44] (1947) 63 *Law Quarterly Review*, p. 516.
[45] pp. 238 and 240.
[46] *Thomas v. University of Bradford* [1987] A.C. 795.

by Professor A.L. Goodhart in the *Cambridge Law Journal*[47] and the *Law Quarterly Review*,[48] and the Court of Criminal Appeal approved an article contributed by Dr. Stallybrass to the latter journal.[49] On the other hand, Professor E.C.S. Wade's definition of "act of state" in the *British Year Book of International Law*[50] was criticised in *Nissan* v. *Att.-Gen.* (above); and although Geoffrey Lane J. in one case[51] relied on the *Donovan Report on Trade Unions*[52] on the question of intention that agreements should be binding contracts, his Lordship did not think that articles in the *Modern Law Review* would have come to the notice of the executives of either the employers or the union.

2. SOME BOOKS OF AUTHORITY

Abridgments of the Year Books

Four Abridgments of the Year Books were compiled about the end of the Year Book period.[53] They were written in law-French. The best are those of *Fitzherbert* (editions 1516–86) and *Brooke* (editions 1574–86). The former abridges 14,000 and the latter over 20,000 cases arranged alphabetically under the headings of the various forms of action. They are not mere epitomes of the Year Books, for they sift and digest the cases, though they do not attempt a scientific arrangement. Brooke sometimes cites sources outside the Year Books. They were intended for practitioners and do not discuss general principles.

The other two, the Abridgment attributed to Statham (1495?) and the *Abridgment of the Book of Assizes* (c. 1510), have been comparatively little used, as they were soon superseded by the superior works of Fitzherbert and Brooke. We know little of Statham (whose name should apparently be spelt Stathum), nor are we certain that he wrote the *Abridgment* that goes by his name. The author of the *Abridgment of the Book of Assizes* is unknown. It is sometimes called the *Liber Assisarum*, but it should not be confused with another book of that name, Part V of the standard edition of the Year Books, from which about a quarter of the cases abridged by it are taken.

---

[47] *Haynes* v. *Harwood* [1935] 1 K.B. 146.
[48] *Gold* v. *Essex County Council* [1942] 2 K.B. 293.
[49] *R.* v. *Newland* [1954] 1 Q.B. 158.
[50] (1934) *British Year Book of International Law*, Vol. XV, p. 103, quoted in *Halsbury*.
[51] *Ford Motor Co. Ltd.* v. *Amalgamated Union of Engineering and Foundry Workers* [1969] 2 Q.B. 303.
[52] Cmnd. 3623, *Report of Royal Commission on Trade Unions, 1965–68.*
[53] There were probably a number of manuscript Abridgments before Statham, but they were not printed.

The Abridgments may be treated either as secondary authorities for the Year Books, to which they are our only index, or as primary authorities, for they include some Year Book cases reports of which are not known to be extant. They are to be distinguished from the later Abridgments or digests of English law, such as Viner's *Abridgment* (1741–53) and Comyns' *Digest of the Laws of England* (1762), which include statute law as well as case-law, are more systematic in arrangement, and do not necessarily try to cover the whole of the law.

Treatises, Institutes and Commentaries

There are, as we have seen, a few great textbooks of English law which are treated by the courts as authoritative. They are remarkable among English law books written before the nineteenth century as being attempts to expound the principles of English law, in whole or in part, scientifically and coherently.

Glanvill

A *Tractatus de Legibus et Consuetudinibus Angliae* was written in Latin in the time of Henry II. The probable date is 1187–1189. The Treatise was formerly attributed to Ranulf Glanvill (Glanvil, or de Glanville), chief justiciar to Henry II but it was probably written by Hubert Walter, who later became justiciar and chancellor. A modified version of the Treatise was officially introduced into Scotland in the early thirteenth century under the name of its opening words, *Regiam Majestatem*.[54] Glanvill is the first *scientific* treatise on English law. The critical edition of Woodbine (1932) is now replaced by the edition with translation of G.D.G. Hall.[55]

Glanvill would not often be cited in court at the present day, but it is much used by legal historians as an authority on the land law and criminal law of the twelfth century. It was used extensively by Bracton. After sharing with Bracton a temporary eclipse in the fifteenth century, "it has been cited and commented upon, and extolled by Lord Coke, Sir Matthew Hale, Sir Henry Spelman, Selden [and] Blackstone."[56] It was, as we have seen, cited in the case of *Ashford* v. *Thornton*,[57] and it was referred to in *Nissan* v. *Att.-Gen.*[58]

---

[54] Acts of Parliament of Scotland, Vol. I.
[55] Glanvill, *Tractatus* (Treatise), ed. with transl. by G.D.G. Hall (Nelson, in association with the Selden Society, 1965).
[56] Kent, *Commentaries*, I, 499.
[57] (1818) 1 B. & Ald. 405.
[58] [1970] A.C. 179, through Coke's report of *Calvin's Case* (1608) 7 Co.Rep. 1a. As also *R.* v. *Secretary of State for the Home Dept. Ex p. Northumbria Police Authority* [1987] 2 W.L.R. 590, 612.

Bracton

Henry de Bracton, a Devon man, probably born in Bratton
Fleming, was a judge of the Court of King's Bench and of Assize
in the reign of Henry III. His treatise *De Legibus et Consuetudinibus Angliae* was written in Latin about the year 1250.[59] It consists
of a general introduction, and a series of separate commentaries
on the various forms of action. Although left incomplete this
"crown and flower of English medieval jurisprudence"[60] is the
largest and most important treatise written on English law
before Coke's *Institutes*, and forms our main textual source of
medieval common law. The Treatise was first printed in 1569,
and a second edition was published in 1640. The critical edition
of Woodbine (1915–1942) forms the basis of the edition with
translation and notes by Professor S.E. Thorne.[61]

Coke in writing his *Institutes* made much use of Bracton's
treatise and Hale ranked it as of equal authority to the records of
the courts.[62] As we have seen, it was included by Blackstone
among the works of authority. It is cited in court less
infrequently than Glanvill, and its value to students of medieval
English law, particularly land law, is immense.

Bracton suffered some loss of prestige in the fifteenth and
early sixteenth centuries, as the enmity with France due to the
Hundred Years War led to a dislike of the foreign (Roman)
elements in his work. The quarrel with the Pope had a similar
effect. Plowden, reporting the judgment of Lord Chief Baron
Saunders in *Stowel* v. *Lord Zouch*,[63] says: "And to this purpose
he cited Bracton, not as an author in the law; for he said that
Bracton and Glanvill were not authors in our law, but, he said,
he cited him as an ornament to discourse where he agrees with
the law." Catline, Chief Justice of the Queen's Bench, made a
similar remark.[64] Shower, reporting his own argument in *R*. v.
Berchet more than a century later,[65] quotes these remarks, and
also says "in Fitzherbert's *Grand Abridgment* tit. 'Gard.' 71, it is
held by all the Court that Bracton, Glanvil and Fleta were never

[59] See Baker, *Introduction to English Legal History* (2nd ed.) p. 161 suggesting
1220–1240; *Biographical Dictionary of the Common Law* pp. 69–71. It seems
Bracton revised an earlier treatise.
[60] Pollock and Maitland, *History of English Law*, Vol. 1, p. 206.
[61] *Bracton de Legibus et Consuetudinibus Angliae*, ed. George E. Woodbine, transl.
with notes by Samuel E. Thorne (Harvard University, in association with the
Selden Society; vols. 1 and 2, 1967; vols. 3 and 4, 1972).
[62] *History of the Common Law*, p. 189.
[63] (1569) 1 Plowd. 353, 357.
[64] *Ibid*., pp. 358–359.
[65] (1689) 1 Show.K.B. 106, 121.

taken for authors in our law." But the use made of Bracton by Coke in the early seventeenth century, not only in the land law[66] but especially in constitutional cases,[67] restored his authority; and it was finally established through the adoption by Holt C.J. of Bracton's Roman law analogies in the law of bailment in *Coggs* v. *Bernard*.[68] There Holt C.J. said: "This Bracton I have cited is, I confess, an old author; but in this his doctrine is agreeable to reason, and to what the law is in other countries;"[69] and again: "I cite this author, though I confess he is an old one, because his opinion is reasonable, and very much to my present purpose, and there is no authority in the law to the contrary."[70] In the early nineteenth century, in *Ashford* v. *Thornton*,[71] Abbott J., discussing the exceptions to the right of the appellee to wager of battle in an appeal of felony, says: "Now as to this the rule is to be found in Bracton;" and a learned author, who became a distinguished judge, wrote in 1885 that Bracton is "generally accepted as binding, if no contrary decisions or customs can be produced."[72]

Littleton

Sir Thomas Littleton[73] was appointed a judge of the Common Pleas in 1466. Some time before his death in 1481 he wrote his *Tenures*, an account of the land law of his time, based on the various estates in land which a tenant could hold and the various incidents and conditions on which he might hold them. Its materials were derived mainly from the Year Books. It was written in law-French, and has been printed both in the original and in translation many times since 1481. It is probably the earliest *printed* treatise on English law. Citation is usually "Litt. s.1," or "Litt. §1," etc. Intended as a book for students, it instantly became the main authority for the principles of English land law, though used after 1628 chiefly with Coke's commentary (below).

In the preface to his commentary, Coke describes Littleton's book with some exaggeration as "the ornament of the common

---

[66] *e.g.*, Co.Litt. 56a.
[67] *e.g.*, *Prohibitions del Roy* (1607) 12 Co.Rep. 63.
[68] (1703) 2 Ld.Raym. 909.
[69] 1 Smith L.C., 13th ed., 175, 182–183.
[70] *Ibid.*, p. 184.
[71] (1818) 1 B. & Ald. 405, 459.
[72] Scrutton, *The Influence of the Roman Law on the Law of England*, p. 150.
[73] Variously spelt, Lyttelton, etc. He took the name of his mother's family, of Frankley, Worcestershire, his father coming from the less aristocratic family of Westcote. He is buried in Worcester Cathedral.

law, and the most perfect and absolute work that ever was written in any human science". It is, as we have seen, one of the list of books described by Blackstone as authoritative. His practical value in later times has, of course, been considerably diminished, first by the development of Equity and then by legislative reforms.

Fitzherbert

Sir Anthony Fitzherbert is mentioned above in connection with the Abridgments of the Year Books. His *Natura Brevium*, written in law-French and published in 1534 or 1537, is a commentary on the register of writs. It is commonly called the *"New Natura Brevium"* to distinguish it from the fourteenth century *Natura Brevium*, which is sometimes more distinctively called the *"Old Natura Brevium."* Coke described Fitzherbert's work as "of greatest authority and excellency." The Court of Exchequer Chamber cited it repeatedly in *Slade's Case*.[74] It was highly recommended by Hale, who edited one of the many English editions. Blackstone includes it in his list of authoritative books. It is usually cited as "F.N.B."

Coke

Sir Edward Coke[75] (1552–1633) is well known as one of the great figures in law and politics in the time of James I and Charles I. He was a man of immense erudition and of exhaustive learning in the common law, though it has been calculated that his law library—consisting of the statutes, 15 volumes of reports, three or four Abridgments and 15 treatises—could have been contained in a wheelbarrow. His own *Reports* have been mentioned in a previous chapter.

Coke was elected Speaker of the House of Commons towards the end of Elizabeth I's reign, and was appointed Attorney-General in 1594. In 1606 he was appointed Chief Justice of the Common Pleas, and in 1613 Chief Justice of the King's Bench. After his retirement from public affairs he devoted the rest of his life to the completion of his *Institutes of the Laws of England*. It was the first attempt since Bracton to provide a complete exposition of English law. The *Institutes* are written in English and are divided into four parts.

The First Institute is the Commentary upon Littleton. It is a copious and learned commentary on Littleton's *Tenures* and the

---

[74] (1603) 4 Co.Rep. 92b.
[75] The better pronunciation is *Cook*.

land law of Coke's own time. It is commonly called "Coke upon Littleton," and abbreviated in writing as "Co.Litt." or sometimes as "1 Inst."[76] The most useful editions, unless one is dealing with the earlier periods, are those of Hargrave and Butler, beginning with that of 1787, which incorporate an analysis of Littleton's *Tenures* together with notes by Sir Matthew Hale (below) and by Lord Nottingham, who filled the office of Lord Chancellor with great distinction from 1673 to 1682. This work, as we have seen, is the medium through which Littleton is chiefly used, though Coke lends the weight of his own great authority besides bringing the law 150 years nearer to our own time.

The Second Institute is an "Exposition of many ancient, and other Statutes." Here Coke the politician sometimes gets the better of Coke the legal historian. It is in his disquisitions on Magna Carta and other constitutional documents that he is least reliable, for he initiated or perpetuated many errors which it was left to subsequent historians to rectify.

The Third Institute deals with the common law and statute-law relating to "High Treason, and other Pleas of the Crown, and Criminal Cases." No doubt Coke's judicial experience first in the Court of Common Pleas and then in the Court of King's Bench dictated the order in which he completed the preparation of the work.

The Fourth Institute deals with "the Jurisdiction of Courts," beginning with the High Court of Parliament. It does less than justice to the claims of the Chancery and Admiralty.

Parts II, III and IV were published posthumously by order of the House of Commons. There are a number of seventeenth, eighteenth and early nineteenth century editions. They are cited "2 Inst.," etc.

Coke's *Institutes* have probably been more frequently cited in court than any other textbook. So soon after Coke's death as 1677, Twisden J. said that a single opinion of the *Institutes* was as good an authority as Fitzherbert's *Natura Brevium* or the *Doctor and Student*.[77] Sometimes there is no authority for what Coke says other than the fact that he says it; but, in the words used by Best C.J. in 1824, " we should get rid of a good deal of what is considered law in Westminster Hall,[78]

---

[76] *Inst.* in a work on Roman law means Justinian's *Institutes*, but in a work on English laws means Coke's *Institutes*.

[77] *Astry* v. *Ballard* (1677) 2 Mod. 193.

[78] The Common Law Courts formerly sat in Westminster Hall, adjoining the Houses of Parliament.

if what Lord Coke[79] says without authority is not law. He was one of the most eminent lawyers that ever presided as a judge in any court of justice, and what is said by such a person is good evidence of what the law is, particularly when it is in conformity with justice and common sense."[80] Darling J., citing this passage with approval in *R.* v. *Casement*,[81] says that Coke "has been recognised as a great authority in these Courts for centuries." Coke was cited by Lord Gardiner L.C. in *Button* v. *D.P.P.*[82] on the definition of affray and by the Court of Appeal in *Reid* v. *Commissioner of Police of the Metropolis*[83] on the definition of "market overt."

The practitioner will not often need to refer to the *Institutes* for existing law, as since Coke's time there has been a great deal of legislation, to say nothing of the development of Equity (which Coke scarcely mentions) and mercantile law. But if he finds it necessary to go so far back for his authority he will very seldom have to delve further. If, on the other hand, it is a question of what the law on a particular point was in the early seventeenth century, he will find the *Institutes* indispensable.

Hale and *Hawkins*

Sir Matthew Hale's *History of the Pleas of the Crown* was published posthumously in 1736 by order of the House of Commons given in 1680, the delay being partly due to the need for careful editing of the manuscript. Hale (1609–76) was first a judge of the Common Pleas, then Chief Baron of the Exchequer, and then Chief Justice of the King's Bench. He was a very great lawyer and judge, whose methodical analysis of the civil law provided Blackstone with a model arrangement for his *Commentaries*. Hale's was the first history of the criminal law, and is especially authoritative on criminal procedure.

William Hawkins, Serjeant-at-Law (1673–1746), published his *Pleas of the Crown*, a comprehensive treatise on criminal law, in 1716. It was the first work to give a complete survey of the substantive criminal law and of criminal procedure. It is clear, learned and reliable. Several other editions were published in the eighteenth century.

---

[79] Some eminent judges, *e.g.*, Sir Edward Coke C.J., Sir John Holt C.J., and Sir Matthew Hale C.J., have acquired the courtesy title of "Lord Coke," etc., in the legal profession, although they were never peers.
[80] *Garland* v. *Jekyll* (1824) 2 Bing. 273, 296–297.
[81] [1917] 1 K.B. 98, 141–142.
[82] [1966] A.C. 591 (H.L.).
[83] [1973] Q.B. 551 (C.A.).

In *Butt* v. *Conant*,[84] Dallas C.J. said:

> "Now if the authority of Lord Hale, and that of Mr. Serjeant
> Hawkins, are to be treated lightly, we may be without any
> authority whatever. ... These are books which are in the
> hand and head of every lawyer, and constantly referred to
> on every occasion of this sort."

Darling J., in *R.* v. *Casement*,[85] refers to Coke, Hawkins and Hale
as "all great names in the law, and persons whose opinions
have long been followed in many questions of extreme difficulty
which have puzzled lawyers for many generations." The Court
of Criminal Appeal in that case was relying, "confessedly
relying, upon the authority of Sir Matthew Hale and of Serjeant
Hawkins ... and also upon the opinion expressed by Lord
Coke." Sir James Fitzjames Stephen, a distinguished criminal
judge of the last century, described Hale's book as being "of the
highest authority."[86] Both Hale and Hawkins were cited in
Button v. *D.P.P.*[87]

Foster

Sir Michael Foster (1689–1763) was a judge of the King's Bench.
He published in 1762 a "Report of Some Proceedings on the
Commission for the Trial of the Rebels in the Year 1746, and of
other Crown Cases: to which are added Discourses upon a Few
Branches of the Crown Law." The Report covers the trial of
participants in the 1745 rebellion, and is usually known as
"Foster's *Crown Cases*": the Discourses are commonly called
"Foster's *Crown Law*." They may be found bound together as
"Foster's *Crown Cases*."

Blackstone described Foster as "a very great master of the
Crown law." The book is frequently cited in court at the present
day, and is of great authority within its rather narrow scope.
The decision in *Joyce* v. *Director of Public Prosecutions*[88] was based
almost entirely on an extra-judicial resolution of the judges
given in 1707, and contained in lost manuscripts, which was
quoted and approved by Foster and Hawkins. Lord Jowitt
L.C., discussing the question whether treason could in any

---

[84] (1820) 1 Br. & B. 548, 570.
[85] [1917] 1 K.B. 98, 139.
[86] *History of Criminal Law*, II, 211.
[87] [1966] A.C. 591 (H.L.). Hawkins was recently cited in *R.* v. *Marji* [1987] 1
W.L.R. 1388 on cheating the revenue and Hale in *R.* v. *Howe* [1987] A.C. 417
on duress.
[88] [1946] A.C. 347.

circumstances be committed by an alien abroad, said: "I refer first to authority. It is said in Foster's *Crown Cases*. . . ." Of the untraced manuscripts, Lord Jowitt said: "It is, indeed, impossible to suppose that Sir Michael Foster could have incorporated such a statement except upon the surest grounds, and it is to be noted that he accepts equally the fact of the judges' resolution and the validity of its content." Similarly, in the Court of Criminal Appeal in that case, Lord Caldecote C.J. said: "The law as stated and accepted by Foster and others has stood unchallenged . . . for nearly 250 years, and we cannot now hold that we are not bound by it."

Blackstone

Sir William Blackstone (1723–80) spent a rather unsuccessful period at the Bar before being asked in 1753 to deliver a series of lectures on English law at his old University of Oxford. The lectures were so well received that in 1758 he was elected the first Vinerian Professor of English law at that University, and he continued to lecture there until 1766. Up to that time the study of law at the two English universities had been confined to Roman civil law and (before the Reformation) canon law, and the only institutions which taught English law were the Inns of Court, so that Blackstone was the first holder of the first university chair of English law in the world. He subsequently became a Member of Parliament and Solicitor-General, and in 1770 a judge of the Common Pleas. Blackstone's *Commentaries on the Laws of England* were based on those lectures, and were first published in 1765–69. They are in four Books, with a theoretical introduction. Many English and Irish editions were published up to the middle of the nineteenth century, but it is advisable to refer to one of the earlier editions in which the author's text is distinguishable from the notes of other editors. The last edition which Blackstone himself brought out was the eighth edition in 1778.

The Introduction discusses the nature of law in general and English law in particular. Book I, entitled "The Rights of Persons," deals with constitutional law, family law and corporations. Book II, entitled "The Rights of Things," deals with the law of real and personal property, including succession. Book III, entitled "Private Wrongs," deals with civil courts, torts and civil procedure. Book IV, entitled "Public Wrongs," deals with criminal law and criminal procedure. A modern lawyer will notice, apart from the curious classification of the law, the unduly subordinate place taken by Equity and contract.

Otherwise the *Commentaries* are generally a reliable guide to English law as it was in the eighteenth century. They are frequently referred to in the English courts at the present day when there is no relevant statute or judicial precedent, and they are treated with even greater respect in the United States, the basis of whose legal system is the common law of Blackstone's time. The excellent style in which they are written is commended even by laymen. They have been translated into French, German, Italian and Russian.

Lord Mansfield cited Blackstone's *Commentaries* with approval a few years after their first publication.[89] In *R. v. Millis*[90] Lord Campbell said:

> "I do not find the subject again discussed until the publication of Blackstone's *Commentaries*; where, if anywhere, we may look to find the principles of our jurisprudence. If he has fallen into some minute mistakes in matter of detail, I believe upon a great question like this, as to the constitution of marriage, there is no authority to be more relied upon."

More recently, in *Thomas* v. *Sawkins*,[91] where the question was the right of the police to enter private premises in which a public meeting was being held, we find Lord Hewart C.J. and Avory J. giving the *Commentaries* virtually the same weight as decided cases. In the same year Humphreys J. said:

> "Blackstone says in terms that a magistrate may properly bind over a person in any case where it is apprehended that it is likely he will commit a breach of the peace or that he will do something against the law. That in my judgment is the law, and it is too late, in 1935, to attempt to show that Blackstone was wrong."[92]

A later tribute from the Bench is a statement by Wrottesley L.J. in *R. v. Edmundsbury and Ipswich Diocese (Chancellor)*[93]:

> "It is unthinkable that Blackstone would have described the writ of prohibition as being the remedy open to a person wronged [by the decision of an Ecclesiastical Court] if, in fact, there was another such remedy, namely, the writ of *certiorari*."

[89] *R. v. Wilkes* (1768) 4 Burr. 2527, 2567.
[90] (1844) 10 Cl. & Fin. 534, 767–768.
[91] [1935] 2 K.B. 249.
[92] *R. v. Sandbach* [1935] 2 K.B. 192, 197.
[93] [1948] 1 K.B. 195, 211.

Blackstone was also cited in *Rondel* v. *Worsley*[94] (a question of the liability of a barrister to be sued for negligence) on the reason why a barrister cannot sue for his fees, and in *R.* v. *Howe*[95] on the defence of duress in crime.

On the other hand, it should be remembered that Blackstone was making a general survey of the principles of English law for the purposes of instruction. "Blackstone's *Commentaries* form, to use the language of the Earl of Birkenhead in his short *Life of Blackstone* (p. 203), 'an elementary text book for students and must be judged as such'."[96] On the finer details of criminal law, for example, we are less likely to receive help from him than from Hale, Hawkins or Foster. Thus it was found in *Button* v. *D.P.P.*[97] that Blackstone was misleading, if not mistaken, on one of the elements of the crime of affray. On a question of the sale of goods in market overt, Lord Denning M.R. said in *Reid* v. *Commissioner of Police of the Metropolis*[98]: "I think one should follow the words of Sir Edward Coke rather than those of Sir William Blackstone."

Although, as has been said,[99] the fact that a text-writer was or became a judge does not of itself enhance the authority of his extra-judicial writings, it is interesting to notice that of all "authoritative" text-writers whom we have mentioned nearly all, namely, Glanvill, Bracton, Littleton, Fitzherbert, Brooke, Coke, Hale, Foster and Blackstone, were judges. And so we may give another meaning to the statement with which we began this chapter: "Our judges are our jurists."

[94] [1969] 1 A.C. 191 (H.L.), *per* Lord Pearson at pp. 287–288.
[95] [1987] A.C. 417.
[96] *Per* Lord Caldecote C.J. in *R.* v. *Joyce* (1945) 173 L.T. 377, 382.
[97] [1966] A.C. 591 (H.L.).
[98] [1973] Q.B. 551 (C.A.). The passage in Coke's *Institutes* was based on his report of the *Market Overt Case* (1596) 5 Co.Rep. 83b.
[99] Below, p. 238.

PART IV

Main Branches of English Law

CHAPTER 16

Criminal Law

1. WHAT IS A CRIME?

In early law no clear distinction was drawn between criminal offences and civil wrongs. The judicial proceedings consequent upon them were similar, and the result was a mixture of retribution and compensation. Both are wrongs done by persons in society. Both directly or indirectly harm society and may harm particular individuals. Nevertheless, the distinction between criminal offences and civil wrongs is now an accepted feature of our law, even if it is not always easy to see why certain kinds of conduct are treated as criminal and certain others are not, and even if it is sometimes difficult to distinguish between criminal and civil wrongs according to the nature of the act done.

"There appears to be no unquestioned definition of what constitutes or ought to constitute a crime," says the Wolfenden Report:[1] "To define it as 'an act which is punished by the State'" does not answer the question: What acts ought to be punished by the State?" It is not the function of law, the Report suggests, to intervene in the private lives of citizens, or to seek to enforce any particular pattern of behaviour, further than is necessary for such purposes as the preservation of public order and decency. Certain forms of behaviour, *e.g.*, adultery, are regarded by

[1] *Report of the Committee on Homosexual Offences and Prostitution* (1957), Cmnd. 247, §§13–16; *cf.* Sexual Offences Act 1967.

259

many as sinful or morally wrong, but the criminal law does not attempt to cover all such actions. Thus the criminal law of any period may be said to reflect the government policy of that period, influenced to a considerable extent—though not exclusively—by what is conceived to be "public opinion," and bearing through inertia the marks of previous generations.

The controversy on this subject ranges from the view that law is inseparably linked with morality, criminal law being the enforcement by the State of the minimum standards of morality accepted generally in a given community,[2] to the utilitarian or sociological attitude that would discard the concept of "responsibility," and would regard *mens rea* (guilty mind) as relevant, not to the commission of an offence, but to the choice of such treatment of the offender as is most likely to discourage future offences.[3]

If we had a Criminal Code a crime would be an offence specified in that Code, and although this definition would not be very satisfying to the intellect it would serve for practical purposes. As English law has no Criminal Code[4] it is difficult to establish a test for distinguishing between criminal and civil wrongs in English law. The difficulty may be better appreciated when it is remembered that historically the law of *wrongs* evolved before such conceptions as crime and tort, criminal and civil proceedings, punishment and compensation, were clearly formed.

Some prefer to take the distinction between civil and criminal *proceedings*, but this does not answer the question at all. Criminal proceedings ("prosecutions") may, and save in the case of certain less serious offences must, be taken in the name of the Queen, they have certain peculiarities of procedure and evidence, and they are outside the jurisdiction of certain courts. It would be simple, though evasive, to say that criminal proceedings are those taken in Criminal Courts, and civil proceedings those taken in Civil Courts; but this test will not work. County courts have no criminal jurisdiction,[5] but most other courts have both civil and criminal jurisdiction.

We cannot make the distinction turn on whether the proceedings are *initiated* by the State or the individual, for at common

---

[2] Patrick (Lord) Devlin, *The Enforcement of Morals* (1965).

[3] Barbara (Baroness) Wootton, *Crime and the Criminal Law* (Hamlyn Lectures, 1963). See further, H.L.A. Hart, *Law, Liberty and Morality* (1963); Eugene Rostow, "The Enforcement of Morals" (1960) C.L.J. 174.

[4] The Law Commission has now prepared a draft Criminal Code which is currently under consideration.

[5] The Court of Appeal had no criminal jurisdiction before 1966.

law criminal proceedings could be initiated by private persons, whether or not they were specially aggrieved, subject to the risk of an action for malicious prosecution if the accused were acquitted. The general rule now is that prosecutions may be initiated by any person (private individual or corporation, Government department or local authority, police officer, etc.) unless restricted by statute. Certain prosecutions may be instituted only by or with the consent of the Attorney-General (*e.g.* Official Secrets Acts) or the Director of Public Prosecutions, or by order of a judge; and in the case of some offences (*e.g.* common assault) a private informant must be the person aggrieved. Except for "shoplifting" and common assault private prosecutions are relatively few, because of the cost involved even if the prosecution is successful.

The test most commonly suggested for the distinguishing characteristic of crimes is that of the *purpose* for which the proceedings are taken, the object of criminal proceedings being punishment of the guilty, and the object of civil proceedings compensation for the injured. The purpose of taking proceedings in respect of a civil wrong is indeed usually to obtain compensation, which is designed to restore the injured party to his former position in so far as money can do this. In exceptional cases, however, exemplary or punitive damages may be awarded, which not only compensate the injured party for his actual loss but also satisfy his wounded pride and desire for vengeance, and act as a deterrent to other wrongdoers.[6] This method of distinguishing between criminal and civil proceedings was also complicated at one time by the anomalous "penal actions," whereby under various statutes common informers might bring civil proceedings to recover penalties; but this type of proceeding was abolished by the Common Informers Act 1951, and the House of Commons Disqualification Act 1957. The jurisdiction of the Court of Appeal before 1966 under the Judicature Acts excluded any "criminal cause or matter," and for this purpose the general test applied by the courts was whether the proceedings might result in punishment.[7] However, the purpose and result of criminal proceedings may be said always to be "punishment"[8] only if a wide meaning is given to that word, so as to make it include anything other than

---

[6] Such cases will be very few after the decision of the House of Lords in *Rookes* v. *Barnard* [1964] A.C. 1129, *per* Lord Devlin, below, Chap. 18.

[7] *Amand* v. *Home Secretary and Minister of Defence (Netherlands)* [1943] A.C. 147 (H.L.).

[8] *Cf. per* Lord Atkin in *Proprietary Articles Trade Association* v. *Att.-Gen. for Canada* [1931] A.C. 310, 324.

mere compensation or restitution of property,[9] for some treatment alternative to punishment may be provided. Criminal proceedings at the present day do not result only in imprisonment or fine: in appropriate cases they may result in such other treatment as youth custody, community service or supervision by a probation officer.

The distinction suggested by Kenny as being more accurate for English law, though it is technical and of less general interest, was that the State controls the *termination* of criminal proceedings. "Crimes are wrongs whose sanction is punitive, and is in no way remissible by any private person, but is remissible by the Crown alone, if remissible at all."[10] The Attorney-General may enter a *nolle prosequi* to an indictment; and the Home Secretary may advise the Crown to pardon a convicted criminal after sentence has been given, except for the offence of sending a prisoner out of England to evade the writ of habeas corpus[11]: but a private person cannot, without the consent of the court, withdraw a criminal charge initiated by him after proceedings have commenced. Conversely the Crown may not interrupt the course of civil proceedings, but the parties themselves may agree to settle the action at any time. In so far as crime is defined as that which the Crown has power to pardon, however, the argument is circular, for the only answer to the question "what may the Crown pardon?" is "crime."

The difficulty, or impossibility, of defining a crime in terms of *conduct* alone—which might at first sight seem the obvious method—lies in the fact that the same act may be both a crime and a tort, *e.g.*, assault and theft. Indeed this is quite common, for as a general rule a crime, such as criminal negligence, that causes damage to a private person is also a tort.[12] If a person kills a rook and a pigeon with one stone, we may distinguish the rook from the pigeon, but the act of throwing the stone was one and the same. The analogy is not precise, however, for the mental element involved often differs in criminal from civil liability. We may perhaps describe the characteristics of a crime as: (i) an act which the law prohibits (usually, if done with a

---

[9] But since 1982 a criminal court may make a compensation order which is not merely ancillary to some other order. Powers of Criminal Courts Act 1973; Criminal Justice Act 1982. Further provision has been made by the Criminal Justice Bill 1988.

[10] *Outlines of Criminal Law* (15th ed.), pp. 15–16.

[11] Habeas Corpus Act 1679. The Crown cannot pardon an unabated public nuisance, but here the offence is in substance civil though the proceedings are criminal in form.

[12] Below, Chap. 18. The same act may also constitute a breach of contract.

certain state of mind); (ii) the commission of which is prosecuted by a distinctive kind of legal proceedings; and (iii) which is generally punishable by law, even though because of the circumstances of a particular case, or the age of the offender, punishment is not inflicted and some other treatment (or none) is imposed.

2. CRIMINAL PROCEEDINGS[13]

The course of criminal proceedings is governed mainly by the consolidating Magistrates' Courts Act 1980, the Criminal Justice Act 1967, the Courts Act 1971, the Criminal Law Act 1977, practices preserved by those Acts and rules of court. Criminal proceedings are commenced normally by laying an information before a magistrate stating the name of the accused and the precise nature of the offence alleged. An accused person is brought before the court by the issue of either a summons directing him to appear at a specified time and place, or (if the offence is indictable) a warrant authorising a police officer to arrest him. In exceptional cases a person may be arrested without warrant, in which case he must be brought before a magistrates' court as soon as practicable.

Proceedings in the Magistrates' Courts[14] will normally be conducted by barristers or solicitors of the Crown Prosecution Service which has taken over the functions of local authorities and the police in this respect. The right of a citizen to bring a private prosecution is preserved.[14a] Police powers to stop and search suspects, to enter and search premises and to arrest and detain suspects, together with the questioning and treatment of persons detained by the police are now regulated by the Police and Criminal Evidence Act 1984. Under the Bail Act 1976 persons in custody are given, in principle, a right to bail (release, usually conditional upon the provision of sureties for their appearance at the trial) subject to a number of exceptions. In the case of imprisonable offences bail may not be granted if the court has substantial grounds for fearing that the accused may not surrender to bail or may commit an offence whilst on bail or may interfere with the course of justice. For non-imprisonable offences bail may only be refused if the accused

---

[13] For the jury, see Chap. 2; for committal proceedings and offences triable only on indictment, only summarily or either way, see Chap. 3; for appeals, see chapters on the various courts.

[14] Magistrates' Courts Act 1980. In serious fraud cases the Criminal Justice Act 1987, ss.4–6 makes provision for cases to be transferred to the Crown Court.

[14a] Prosecution of Offences Act 1985.

has previously failed to surrender and the court believes he would fail to do so again. Under the Criminal Justice Bill 1988 residence in a bail hostel may be made a condition of bail.

Summary Trial

Where a defendant pleads "Not Guilty," the prosecutor first addresses the magistrates, outlining the evidence he will produce to prove the alleged offence. The prosecutor then calls his witnesses. Each witness in turn is examined in chief by the prosecution, and may then be cross-examined by the defence (including an unrepresented defendant himself) and re-examined by the prosecution. At the close of the evidence for the prosecution, the defence may submit to the court that there is no case to answer, *i.e.*, that the evidence for the prosecution— even if true—is not sufficient in law to constitute the offence charged. The prosecution may reply to this submission. If the submission is accepted by the court, the case is dismissed. If no such submission is made, or the submission is rejected by the court, the case for the defence is then put.

Counsel or solicitor for the defendant (if he has one) or the defendant himself may make an opening speech where he intends to call evidence. The defendant is not obliged to give evidence on oath, which would subject him to cross-examination, but he may do so if he wishes. Any witnesses called by the defence are examined in chief by the defence, and may be cross-examined by the prosecution and re-examined by the defence. At the conclusion of the evidence for the defence the prosecution may call evidence in rebuttal. The accused may then address the court if he has not already done so. Either party may, with the leave of the court, address the court a second time but where one is given leave, the other must not be refused. Where both address the court, the prosecutor does so before the defendant.

A defendant who does not wish to dispute the facts alleged by the prosecution may plead "Guilty" by letter without having to attend court, provided the offence is triable only summarily and is not punishable by imprisonment for more than three months.[15] He may not be imprisoned or disqualified, however, without being given a further opportunity to appear, and in no case may he be sentenced to imprisonment in his absence.

[15] Magistrates Courts Act 1980, s.12.

Trial on Indictment

The defendant if in custody will be brought to the Crown Court from prison. If he has been released on bail he will be notified of the time and place of trial. Trial on indictment begins with arraignment, whereby the clerk of the court reads out the indictment and asks the accused whether he pleads "Guilty" or "Not Guilty" to the charge. The accused may move to quash the indictment, take a preliminary point of law or enter pleas of *autrefois convict* or *autrefois acquit* if he claims to have been already tried on the charges. Prior notice must be given if his defence is an alibi. Where the accused pleads "Not Guilty" a jury is empanelled. The proceedings then run on similar lines to those on summary trial, except that speeches of counsel and evidence of witnesses are addressed to the jury[16]; and defence counsel may make an opening speech if he is calling at least one witness other than the accused as to fact and at the conclusion of evidence for the defence the prosecution are entitled to address the jury first and the defence to address the jury last.[17] If the accused is unrepresented and either gives no evidence or only gives evidence himself the prosecution do not have a right to a closing speech. The judge then sums up the evidence to the jury. The jury retire to consider their verdict, which must be given in open court. If the accused is found not guilty he is discharged.

Sentence

When the accused pleads "Guilty," or is found guilty by a magistrates' court or by a jury in the Crown Court, he will be asked whether there is anything he wishes to say before sentence is passed. The court then goes on to consider the gravity of the offence, the defendant's "antecedents" or personal history (including previous convictions) and circumstances (including his means), and finally pronounces sentence.[18]

---

[16] Counsel address the judge on questions of law, including admissibility of evidence, the latter question being argued in the absence of the jury.

[17] Criminal Procedure (Right of Reply) Act 1964.

[18] For the various kinds of punishment or other treatment, see below, p. 274 *et seq.* The Attorney-General may refer a sentence which appears unduly lenient to the Court of Appeal for possible increase, Criminal Justice Bill 1988, above, p. 90.

3. CLASSIFICATION OF CRIMES

For procedural purposes, as we have seen,[19] criminal offences are classified into offences triable only on indictment, offences triable only summarily, and offences triable either way.

Indictable offences were divided at common law into treason, felonies and misdemeanours, treason sometimes being classed among the felonies. *Felonies* were originally the more heinous offences, conviction for which involved punishment by death or maiming and forfeiture of land and chattels to the lord or King, and a felon who fled from justice was outlawed. In the early nineteenth century conviction for felony still involved the death penalty,[20] forfeiture of property to the Crown and corruption of blood, though the number of capital offences was considerably reduced by statute. Forfeiture and corruption of blood were abolished by the Forfeiture Act 1870, except for misprision of treason. A *misdemeanour* was a breach of the King's peace other than felony, and was always punishable by imprisonment or fine or both. The term "misdemeanour" came to cover any indictable offence, or in some contexts any criminal offence (including offences triable summarily), other than treason or felony.

The Criminal Law Act 1967,[21] abolished the distinction between felony and misdemeanour, which had become illogical and inconvenient, and provided that the law and practice in relation to all offences, including mode of trial, should be those applicable at the commencement of the Act to misdemeanour. The Act defined a new category of *arrestable offence* (section 2) now covered by the Police and Criminal Evidence Act 1984. An arrestable offence is an offence to which the powers of arrest without warrant ("summary arrest") apply, *viz.*, an offence for which the *sentence is fixed by law, e.g.*, treason and murder, *or* for which a person (not previously convicted) may be sentenced to *imprisonment for five years* and attempts, conspiracies, incitements to commit such an offence or aiding and abetting it. The substantive law of treason was not affected, but the procedure on trials for treason was assimilated to the reformed procedure on trials for murder. The result (apart from treason) is a distinction between arrestable and non-arrestable offences

---

[19] Above, Chap. 3.
[20] Petty larceny (*i.e.*, where the thing stolen was worth 12d. or less) was not punishable by death.
[21] Based on Criminal Law Revision Committee, Seventh Report: *Felonies and Misdemeanours* (1965) Cmnd. 2659.

substantially similar to, but more logical and significant than, the former distinction between felonies and misdemeanours.

All crimes (in the wide sense) are offences against the State, but some are peculiarly of a public nature, such as treason, sedition, coinage offences, perjury, riot and unlawful assembly, while others closely affect private individuals. Of the second class of crimes some, such as murder, manslaughter, rape and assault, are committed in respect of persons; while others, such as theft, forgery and arson, are committed in respect of property. It is not easy to fit public nuisance, a common law offence, into this classification.

4. GENERAL PRINCIPLES OF CRIMINAL LIABILITY

Actus Reus

Two elements are required to constitute a crime, an act or omission (*actus reus*) and a state of mind (*mens rea*). A guilty mind alone is not sufficient in law, though it may be in ethics. To render a person criminally liable there must be some act or omission on his part forbidden by law; and what the accused did (or omitted to do) in the surrounding circumstances must have contributed directly or indirectly to the state of affairs which the law seeks to prevent. An act must be voluntary, which would exclude a state of automatism resulting from epilepsy or sleepwalking. The *actus reus* of theft is the appropriation of property belonging to another, while the *mens rea* is the dishonest intention of permanently depriving the other of it. For bigamy the *actus reus* is that a person, being validly married, during the lifetime of his or her spouse goes through a marriage ceremony with another person.

Not only completed crimes, but attempts to commit crimes are punishable.[22]

Mens Rea

Legal historians have studied the Anglo-Saxon Codes, the Year Books and medieval textbooks to try to discover the general principle of liability for wrongs in early English law. Some speak of "absolute liability" in early times, emphasising the general rule of liability for an act causing harm, but admitting exceptions in such cases as lunacy, infancy, self-defence, hostile compulsion and accident. Others, who emphasise the exceptions and contend that they imply some regard for intent even in the most

[22] Criminal Attempts Act 1981.

primitive law, prefer to use the expression "strict liability." However this may be, the development and refinement of the concept of wrongful intent, together with the extension of the idea of the King's peace and the increase in the number of offences which could not be atoned for merely by money payment, led to the distinction between criminal and civil liability which begins to be seen in the thirteenth century. In the reign of Edward IV a judge said that the thought of a man—that is, intention not manifested by words or conduct—was not triable.[23] It is clear by the time of Henry VII that in felony the intent was to be construed, so that it would be no felony "if a man is shooting in the butts and kills another."[24] Intent becomes the chief, though not the only, test; and the general rule is formed: *actus non facit reum nisi mens sit rea*, i.e., an act does not make the doer guilty unless his mind is guilty.[25] The old principle of strict liability remains generally for civil wrongs because, says Hale, the purpose of the injured party's proceedings is compensation, not punishment.[26] So the purpose of the proceedings, as well as the mental element, is a distinguishing mark between crime and tort.

"The full definition of every crime," said Stephen J. in *R. v. Tolson* (1889),[27] a case of bigamy, "contains expressly or by implication a proposition as to a state of mind." The requisite mental element may be either wrongful intent generally or recklessness, or such culpable negligence as amounts to criminal misconduct deserving of punishment[28]; or it may be a specific intent peculiar to a given class of crime, as "malice aforethought" in murder or "intent to do grievous bodily harm" in one species of assault. It usually involves foresight by the accused of the consequences of his conduct.

Some modern statutes have created offences which the courts have construed to involve "strict" liability. For example, on a charge of taking a female under the age of sixteen out of the possession of her father, it is not necessary to show that the accused knew or believed she was under sixteen.[29] Again, a butcher has been penalised for selling unsound meat although

---

[23] Brian C.J., Y.B. 17 Edw. 4, Pasch, pl. 2.
[24] Rede J., Y.B. 21 Hen. 7, Trin. pl. 5.
[25] Coke, 3 Inst. 6; *Younghusband* v. *Luftig* [1949] 2 K.B. 354, 370, *per* Lord Goddard C.J. The maxim in various forms can be traced back in English law at least as far as *Leges Henrici* (c. 1108).
[26] *History of the Pleas of the Crown*, i, 15, 16.
[27] 23 Q.B.D. 168, 187.
[28] *Andrews* v. *Director of Public Prosecutions* [1937] A.C. 576.
[29] *R.* v. *Prince* (1875) L.R. 2 C.C.R. 154.

he did not know that the meat was unsound[30]; and on a charge of selling intoxicating liquor to a drunken person it is not necessary that the licensee should have known that the customer was drunk.[31] On the other hand the House of Lords has confirmed the presumption that Parliament intends *mens rea* to be an essential ingredient of a statutory offence. Statutes creating criminal offences, said Lord Diplock in *Sweet* v. *Parsley*,[32] are "to be read as subject to the implication that a necessary element in the offence is the absence of a belief held honestly and upon reasonable grounds, in the existence of facts which, if true, would make the act innocent."

It is also presumed that, to be guilty, the accused must have been sane and not acting under duress or as the result of inevitable accident. It has recently been held by the House of Lords that duress is not a defence to a charge of murder in either the first or second degree (aiding and abetting).[33] Self-induced intoxication by drink or drugs is not a defence to a criminal charge where as in assault no special intent has to be proved.[34]

There is a conclusive presumption that a child under the age of ten years cannot be guilty of a criminal offence.[35] There is a presumption that a child between the ages of ten and fourteen years is incapable of committing a crime (*doli incapax*); but *malitia supplet aetatem*, and this presumption may (with certain exceptions) be rebutted by clear evidence that he knew he was doing wrong.[36] A person between the ages of fourteen and twenty-one is *doli capax*, though he is not always liable to be punished in the same way as a person over twenty-one.[37]

Sources of Criminal Law

Apart from contributions made by the Star Chamber to the law of perjury, forgery, libel and criminal attempts, and by the Court of Admiralty to the international crime of piracy, the basis of our criminal law has been common law. In the last hundred years, however, parts of the substantive law have been consolidated or codified by such statutes as the Theft Act 1968,

---

[30] *Hobbs* v. *Winchester Corporation* [1910] 2 K.B. 471.
[31] *Cundy* v. *Le Cocq* (1884) 13 Q.B.D. 207.
[32] [1970] A.C. 132; above, pp. 161–162.
[33] *R.* v. *Howe* [1987] A.C. 417.
[34] *D.P.P.* v. *Majewski* [1977] A.C. 443; *R.* v. *Bailey* [1983] 1 W.L.R. 760.
[35] Children and Young Persons Act 1963. At common law the age was under seven; this was raised to eight by the Children and Young Persons Act 1933.
[36] *R.* v. *Owen* (1830) 4 C. & P. 236.
[37] Below, pp. 276 and 277–278.

the Offences against the Person Act 1861, and the Sexual Offences Act 1956. Considerable additions have been made by the legislature in such statutes as the Official Secrets Acts, Public Order Acts and Race Relations Acts; and also many reforms, *e.g.*, Infanticide Act 1938, Suicide Act 1961, Criminal Damage Act 1971, Forgery and Counterfeiting Act 1981, Public Order Act 1986, a series of Criminal Justice Acts and Criminal Law Acts, and the Powers of Criminal Courts Act 1973.

5. SOME EXAMPLES OF CRIMES

The definitions of the various crimes, whether common law or statutory, are often long and precise. This is a corollary of the fundamental principle that the *prosecution* must prove the exact charge beyond all reasonable doubt.[38]

The definition of crimes may be illustrated by murder, and by theft and related offences.

Murder

The common law definition of murder is given by Coke:

> "Murder is when a man of sound memory, and of the age of discretion, unlawfully killeth ... any reasonable creature *in rerum natura* [*i.e.*, in being[39]] under the King's peace,[40] with malice aforethought, either expressed by the party, or implied by law, so as the party wounded, or hurt, etc., die of the wound or hurt, etc., within a year and a day after the same."[41]

Here every word counts. "Unlawfully" means not justifiably or excusably. "Malice aforethought" in murder means, generally, intent to cause the death,[42] or to inflict grievous bodily harm.[43]

At common law in the absence of any of the kinds of wrongful intent necessary for murder, unlawful killing constituted the crime of manslaughter, punishable by imprisonment for life.

---

[38] *Woolmington* v. *Director of Public Prosecutions* [1935] A.C. 462; *R.* v. *Hepworth and Fearnley* [1955] 2 Q.B. 600.

[39] *Cf.* child destruction: Infant Life (Preservation) Act 1929.

[40] The courts now have jurisdiction over murder committed by British subjects abroad: Offences against the Person Act 1861, s.9.

[41] Inst. 47.

[42] *Woolmington* v. *Director of Public Prosecutions*, above. See also *R.* v. *Cunningham* [1982] A.C. 566; *R.* v. *Moloney* [1985] A.C. 905; *R.* v. *Hancock* [1986] A.C. 455.

[43] *R.* v. *Cunningham*, above.

Manslaughter may be the consequence of criminal negligence,[44] recklessness[45] or killing in the course of an unlawful act. An accused who has killed with intent to kill or cause grievous bodily harm will, however, be guilty not of murder but only of manslaughter if he killed in circumstances covered by one of the defences in the Homicide Act 1957, namely provocation, diminished responsibility and killing in the course of a suicide pact. By statute unlawful killing may amount to the offence of infanticide, punishable as for manslaughter,[46] or "causing death by reckless driving," punishable by five years' imprisonment.[47]

Theft and Similar Offences

The law of larceny and kindred forms of fraud, which had long been recognised to be in need of reform, was referred to the Criminal Law Revision Committee in 1959, and the Theft Act 1968, substantially gives effect to their recommendations.

Basic definition of Theft

Section 1 of the Theft Act 1968, provides that "A person is guilty of theft if he dishonestly appropriates property belonging to another with the intention of permanently depriving the other of it." This definition simplifies the law, in particular by abolishing the requirement of "taking and carrying away" and the accompanying intention,[48] and by emphasising the dishonest appropriation of another person's property. The basic definition should be sufficient for most purposes, but the Act goes on to give further explanations to help the interpretation of section 1.

"Dishonestly," which replaces "fraudulently," does not include cases where a person appropriates property in the belief that he is legally entitled to it, or that the other person would consent if he knew about it, or that the owner cannot be discovered by taking reasonable steps. On the other hand, the appropriator may be dishonest although he is willing to pay for the property (section 2).

"Appropriates" includes the case where a person came by the property (innocently or not) without stealing it and later assumes the right to keep it or deal with it as owner (section 3).

---

[44] *Andrews* v. *Director of Public Prosecutions* [1937] A.C. 576, 583.
[45] *R.* v. *Seymour* [1983] 2 A.C. 493.
[46] Infanticide Act 1938.
[47] Road Traffic Act 1972, s.1; Criminal Law Act 1977, s.50.
[48] *Cf.* Larceny Act 1916, s.1, expanding the common law definition of larceny.

There must be some act of appropriation, and the definition seems to cover any dealing with the property that would formerly have constituted a taking, embezzlement or conversion.

"Property" includes money and all other property, real or personal, including things in action and other intangible property[49] (section 4(1)). But a person cannot steal land, or things forming part of land and severed from it by him, except (a) when he is a trustee or personal representative, etc. (formerly this would be fraudulent conversion); (b) when he is not in possession of the land and appropriates anything forming part of the land by severing it; or (c) when being tenant in possession he appropriates a fixture (subs. (2)). Picking wild mushrooms or wild flowers or fruit is not stealing unless it is done for sale (subs. (3)), and poaching wild animals is not generally stealing (subs. (4)), though these actions may constitute other offences.

"Belonging to another" for this purpose is not confined to the owner, but includes any person having possession or control (section 5). Thus it is possible to steal from an employee in possession of property as well as from the employer who owns it.

"With the intention of permanently depriving the other of it" includes the intention to treat the thing as one's own to dispose of, regardless of the other person's rights; and it may include borrowing or lending, but only if for a period or in circumstances making it equivalent to an outright taking or disposal, *e.g.*, if X borrows A's pen and then abandons it in such circumstances that it is very unlikely that A will ever get it back (section 6).

Robbery

A person is guilty of robbery if he steals, and immediately before or at the time of doing so, and in order to do so, he uses or threatens to use force on any person (section 8).

Burglary

The definition of burglary is considerably changed from the previous law by section 9 of the Theft Act. The previous definition involved the "breaking and entering" of a "dwelling-house" "in the night," (*i.e.*, between 9 p.m. and 6 a.m.),

---

[49] See below, p. 291.

accompanied by a complex intention.[50] The new definition provides that:

> "(1) a person is guilty of burglary if—(*a*) he enters any building or part of a building as a trespasser and with intent to commit any such offence as is mentioned in subsection (2) below; or (*b*) having entered any building or part of a building as a trespasser he steals or attempts to steal anything in the building or that part of it or inflicts or attempts to inflict on any person therein any grievous bodily harm. (2) The offences referred to in subsection (1)(*a*) above are offences of stealing anything in the building or part of a building in question, of inflicting on any person therein any grievous bodily harm or raping any woman therein, and of doing unlawful damage to the building or anything therein."

"Building" includes an inhabited vehicle or vessel, such as a caravan or houseboat, even though the inhabitant is not there. A more serious offence is "aggravated burglary," which is committed by a burglar who has with him any firearm (including an airgun or air pistol) or imitation firearm (whether capable of being discharged or not), or any weapon of offence or explosive (section 10).

Taking Motor Vehicle Without Authority

The offence of taking a motor vehicle *for use* without the owner's consent or other lawful authority (section 12), replaces the offence of taking *and driving away* a motor vehicle without such authority under the Road Traffic Acts.

Fraud and Blackmail

Certain cases of fraud are covered by the new definition of "obtaining property by deception" (section 15). Demanding with menaces is for the first time given the technical name of "blackmail" (section 21) and the Theft Act 1978 covers obtaining of services by deception, evasion of liability by deception and making off without payment.

Handling Stolen Goods

The former offence of "receiving" stolen goods *knowing* them to

---

[50] A similar offence committed otherwise than between 9 p.m. and 6 a.m., or with respect to a building other than a dwelling-house, constituted "housebreaking": Larceny Act 1916, s.26.

n stolen is replaced by that of "handling" stolen goods
, *or believing* them to be stolen goods.[51] Handling
in dishonestly receiving the goods (otherwise than in
the course of stealing), or dishonestly assisting in their reten-
tion, removal, disposal or realisation (section 22).

It might be thought that criminal law, with its strict definitions
of crimes each requiring the indictment to be drafted in the
appropriate language, was still in the state that civil law was in a
century ago before the forms of action were abolished. But it is
most necessary that a person accused of crime should know
exactly what charge he has to meet, and in any event
there are many cases where legislation or the common law
allows a prisoner charged with one offence to be convicted of
another similar offence. When it is said that X would not be
guilty of murder or theft in certain circumstances, it does not
necessarily mean that he is not guilty of any offence at all.

6. PUNISHMENT AND OTHER TREATMENT OF OFFENDERS

There is no one purpose or aim of punishment.[52] One or more of
the following three elements are present in varying degrees in
the different kinds of punishment or other treatment awarded to
offenders by English law today: (i) deterrence against further
crimes, both of the criminal himself and of potential criminals;
(ii) protection of the community from the criminal; (iii) reformation of the criminal. The last is the most modern idea, and has
not only affected the conditions of imprisonment but given rise
to other forms of treatment that are not properly punitive.[53]
Some would add as the purposes of punishment: (iv) revenge,
or the satisfaction of the desire for vengeance on the part of the
community or the persons primarily affected; (v) expiation or
retribution, a purging of the offender from his wrong or the
restoration of the balance between right and wrong.

The kinds of punishment or other treatment prescribed by
English law at the present day are various.[54] They are largely
contained in the Powers of Criminal Courts Act 1973, which

---

[51] The test is subjective: *Atwal* v. *Massey* [1971] 3 All E.R. 881; 56 Cr.App.R. 6 (D.C.).

[52] See H.L.A. Hart, *Punishment and Responsibility* (1968).

[53] And see Rehabilitation of Offenders Act 1974, designed to rehabilitate offenders who have not been reconvicted of any serious offence for periods of years, and which penalises unauthorised disclosure of previous convictions. Also *Practice Direction* [1975] 1 W.L.R. 1065 (D.C.).

[54] Walker, *Sentencing* (1985).

consolidated with amendments a number of statutes, in particular the Criminal Justice Acts 1948–72.[55] Judicial sentences of penal servitude, hard labour and corporal punishment, and also prison divisions, were abolished in 1948. Corporal punishment was then restricted to male prisoners guilty of mutiny or gross personal violence to a prison officer, but was abolished in 1967.

Criminal courts have been given power,[56] with the consent of the offender, to *defer* passing sentence for the purpose of enabling the court to have regard, in determining his sentence, to his conduct after conviction or to any change in his circumstances. Sentence may not be deferred for longer than six months. Such conduct or change of circumstances would include the making of reparation, marriage or finding work.

Death

The death penalty is now confined to treason, as to the passing of which sentence the court has no discretion but which is rarely prosecuted,[57] and piracy *jure gentium*[58] as to which the court must order the death sentence to be recorded. Murder until recently involved the death penalty, but after much controversy this was finally replaced by imprisonment for life from 1970.[59] The death penalty for arson or other destruction of H.M. ships, dockyards, stores, etc. was abolished in 1971.[60]

Imprisonment

In earlier times imprisonment was regarded generally as a temporary measure before bringing a person to trial. After the drastic reduction by statute in the number of capital offences and the ending of transportation to the colonies, imprisonment was developed in the nineteenth century as a form of punishment after conviction, together with the ideal that it might also be reformative. The term of imprisonment prescribed by Parliament is usually a maximum, the court having a discretion within that limit as to the term to be imposed;

---

[55] Part I of the Criminal Justice Act 1972 (powers for dealing with offenders) was repealed, except s.6 (restitution orders).

[56] Powers of Criminal Courts Act 1973, s.1, replacing Criminal Justice Act 1972, s.22.

[57] *Cf. Joyce* v. *D.P.P.* [1946] A.C. 347 (H.L.).

[58] Tokyo Convention Act 1967, s.4 and Schedule.

[59] Murder (Abolition of Death Penalty) Act 1965; resolutions of both Houses passed in 1969. And *cf.* Homicide Act 1957.

[60] Criminal Damage Act 1971, s.11(2), repealing Dockyards etc. Protection Act 1772.

and imprisonment is often an alternative to a fine or some less serious form of punishment or treatment. Since arrestable offences were substituted for felonies by the Criminal Law Act 1967, Parliament has been paying attention to the revision of the terms of imprisonment for various offences. Opportunity to do this for important classes of crimes was taken in the Theft Act 1968, the Criminal Damage Act 1971,[61] and the Criminal Justice Bill 1988.

A person under the age of twenty-one may not be imprisoned. A person who has not previously been imprisoned may not be sentenced to imprisonment unless he is legally represented or has had an opportunity to apply for legal aid.

Care is taken to ensure that there is no marked divergence in sentencing policy between courts and judges. The Court of Appeal (Criminal Division) provides guidance on the appropriate sentences for different offences.[61a]

Suspended sentences of imprisonment were introduced in 1967,[62] partly to relieve the pressure on our overcrowded prisons. A court that passes a sentence of imprisonment for a term of not more than two years may suspend the sentence for a period between one and two years, so that the sentence will not take effect unless during that period the offender commits another offence punishable with imprisonment and the later court orders that the suspended sentence shall take effect. A suspended sentence may not be imposed unless the court considers the case to be one where (apart from power to suspend sentence) imprisonment is the appropriate punishment.

Under the Repatriation of Prisoners Act 1984 a foreigner sentenced to imprisonment in this country may be repatriated to serve his sentence abroad and British subjects sentenced abroad returned to serve their sentences here.[62a]

The Criminal Law Act 1977, (as amended) provides that where a court sentences a person to imprisonment for not less than three months and not more than two years, it may order that, after he has served *part* of the sentence *in prison, the remainder* of it shall be held in *suspense.*[63]

---

[61] Criminal Justice Act 1982, s.1(1).
[61a] An element of public affront in vandalism R. v. *Davies* (1988) *The Times,* January 20 and a previous history of bad driving R. v. *Huty* (1988) *The Times,* February 29 will justify heavier sentences than usually imposed.
[62] See now Powers of Criminal Courts Act 1973.
[62a] When a prisoner is repatriated to this country it may be necessary to adapt the sentence to English standards R. v. *Home Secretary Ex p. Read* [1988] 2 W.L.R. 236.
[63] s.47 and the Criminal Justice Act 1982.

The Criminal Justice Bill 1988 provides that when the defendant is convicted on indictment of an either way offence and pleads guilty to associated summary offences, the Crown Court may sentence him for those offences.

Every prisoner sentenced for more than one month (except one sentenced to imprisonment for life) is eligible under the Prison Rules to be released after serving two-thirds of the sentence, subject to good conduct and industry. Such *remission* of sentence is now forfeited only as a punishment for a breach of prison discipline. The Home Secretary may now also release certain types of offenders up to six months earlier than otherwise in order to free prison places.[64]

The Criminal Justice Act 1967, provided that a prisoner may be considered for release on *parole* (*i.e.*, under licence) after serving one-third of his sentence or one year, whichever is the later. Parole is granted on the recommendation of the Parole Board,[65] an independent body composed of judges, psychiatrists, criminologists and after-care workers. The licence generally remains in force until the date on which the prisoner would have been released on remission if parole had not been granted. A prisoner on parole is normally under the supervision of a probation officer; and he is liable to recall by the Home Secretary on the recommendation of the Parole Board, or on revocation of his licence by the Crown Court if he is convicted of an offence punishable on indictment with imprisonment.

The Home Secretary may release a prisoner serving a life sentence at any time subject to conditions, including liability to recall; but in this case the Home Secretary must consult not only the Parole Board but also the Lord Chief Justice and (if available) the trial judge.

Youth Custody

Borstal training could formerly be imposed by the Crown Court for not more than two years on offenders between the ages of fifteen and twenty-one who were convicted of offences punishable with imprisonment. The system of Borstal training was introduced in 1908 as a reformative measure, though it contained a punitive element. It has now been replaced by youth custody.[66] Shorter sentences may be served in detention centres.

---

[64] Criminal Justice Act 1982, s.32.
[65] *Cf.* Criminal Justice Act 1982, s.33 (six months now basic period).
[66] Criminal Justice Act 1982. Only to be used if not other penalty appropriate *R. v. Reid and Cox* (1988) *The Times*, February 26.

Fines

Many minor offences are punishable by fine only, and for many more serious offences a fine is an alternative to, or may be imposed in addition to, imprisonment. The maximum fine is commonly prescribed by statute.[67] Within this maximum the court must consider the means of the offender,[68] as well as the gravity of the offence. Parents may be ordered to pay a fine imposed on a child or young person, unless this would be unreasonable.

The Criminal Justice Bill 1987 makes provision for new maxima and permits civilians employed in police stations to issue fixed penalty notices.

Time for payment, or payment by instalments, is often allowed by the court, which may, subject to certain conditions, fix a period of imprisonment in default, though this may not be put into operation until there has been an examination into the offender's means. In an endeavour to eliminate as far as possible imprisonment in default of payment of fines, provision has been made for the making of attachment of earnings orders[69]; but this is optimistic as regards magistrates' courts, since many of those convicted of minor offences have no settled employment.

Other Non-custodial Sentences

The court may discharge a person whom it has convicted of an offence (not being one for which the sentence is fixed by law), if it is of opinion, having regard to the nature of the offence and the character of the offender, that it is inexpedient to inflict punishment and that a probation order is not appropriate. The discharge may be absolute or conditional for a period of not more than three years. The condition is that the offender does not commit another offence within that period: if he does, he may be punished for the original offence as well as the new one.[70]

---

[67] The Criminal Law Act 1977, s.57, empowered the Home Secretary to take account of inflation by increasing certain of the fines prescribed by that Act. Criminal Justice Act 1982, s.48 provides a scale for these adjustments and see also the Criminal Justice Bill 1988, which requires parents to pay fines for non-compliance with supervision or community service orders.

[68] *R.* v. *Curtis* (1984) 6 Cr.App.R.(S.) 137.

[69] Attachment of Earnings Act 1971.

[70] Powers of Criminal Courts Act 1973, s.7.

The Crown Court may (except in the case of murder) instead of imposing punishment require an offender to enter into a recognisance (*i.e.*, to pledge a sum of money), with or without sureties, to come up for judgment when called upon; meanwhile the offender may be required to keep the peace and to be of good behaviour; if he fails to comply with this requirement the amount of the recognisance and sureties may be forfeited, and he may also be dealt with for the original offence. Magistrates' Courts also have power under certain conditions to "bind over" to keep the peace or to be of good behaviour, a power sometimes used as a method of preventive justice.[71]

Disqualification from driving for a prescribed period, and endorsement of driving licence, are additional sanctions for the more serious motoring offences (Road Traffic Act 1972).

The system of *probation* inaugurated by the Probation of Offenders Act 1907, has been extended by subsequent legislation.[72] An offender aged seventeen years or over may (except where the sentence is fixed by law) be put on probation if the court thinks that is the best way to deal with the case, and the offender—after the nature of a probation order has been explained to him—consents. A probation order requires the offender to be under the supervision of a probation officer for a period of not less than six months and not more than three years. If a person fails to comply with the requirements of the probation order he may be fined; or the court may deal with the offence in respect to which the order was made, in which latter case the probation order is terminated; or the court may make a community service order.

Where a person aged sixteen years or over is convicted of an offence punishable with imprisonment, the court may, with the consent of the offender, make a *community service order* requiring him to perform unpaid work for forty to 240 hours, under the supervision usually of a probation officer.[73] The work prescribed is of a kind normally undertaken by voluntary services.

Children and Young Persons[74]

The law relating to the care and other treatment of juveniles through court proceedings is being drastically reformed as the various provisions of the Children and Young Persons Act

---

[71] Justices of the Peace Act 1361; Magistrates' Courts Act 1980.
[72] Criminal Justice Act 1948; Powers of Criminal Courts Act 1973.
[73] Powers of Criminal Courts Act 1973, replacing Criminal Justice Act 1972.
[74] See also, Chap. 3 (Juvenile Courts).

1969,[75] come into force. Section 4 provides that criminal proceedings may not be brought in respect of offences (other than homicide) committed by children (*i.e.*, persons under the age of fourteen). The minimum age at which a person becomes liable to criminal proceedings was to be raised from ten to fourteen over a period of time. "Care proceedings" may be brought in Juvenile Courts by a local authority, constable or "authorised person" (*i.e.*, a person authorised by the Home Secretary) in respect of a child or young person in trouble, whether he is in need of care and protection, not receiving a proper education, or is guilty of an offence (excluding homicide) (section 1). A supervision order may be made putting him under the supervision of a local authority or probation officer (sections 11–19), or a care order putting him under the care of a local authority (sections 20–24). Care orders may be subject to a residential requirement, and the powers of the Court are to be strengthened by the Criminal Justice Bill 1988.

In respect of offences committed by young persons (over fourteen and under seventeen) an information was to be laid only by a "qualified informant," *i.e.*, a Crown servant, police officer or local authority, and then only if the informant was satisfied that the case could not be dealt with informally, *e.g.*, by parent, teacher, caution by constable, or care proceedings (section 5). Young persons under seventeen charged with indictable offences were to be triable summarily, except in the case of grave crimes or when charged jointly with a person over seventeen (section 6). The minimum age for probation order has been raised from fifteen to seventeen (section 7). A further limit was set on the publication of particulars of children and young persons (section 10). There is regional planning of "Community Homes," on the establishment of which Approved Schools, Remand Homes and similar institutions are being discontinued (sections 35–48). The various provisions of the Act are to come into force on dates appointed by the Home Secretary over a period of about twenty years from 1969.

Attendance centre orders may be made in respect of some offenders under twenty-one.

Ancillary Orders

The court may make certain ancillary orders in addition to dealing with a convicted person in any other way. These include the following.

---

[75] Based largely on *Children in Trouble* (1968) Cmnd. 3601.

Compensation

The court may make a compensation order requiring the offender to pay compensation for personal injury, loss or damage resulting from the offence. Since 1982 this need not be ancillary to some other order.[76]

Restitution

The court may order a person convicted of theft to restore the stolen goods or their proceeds to the person entitled, or to pay a sum out of any money found in his possession when he was arrested.[77]

Criminal Bankruptcy

The Crown Court may make a bankruptcy order where, as a result of the offence, loss or damage (not attributable to personal injury) has been suffered by other persons.[78]

Deprivation or Forfeiture of Property

This is property used or intended to be used for the purposes of crime.[79] The Criminal Justice Bill 1988 extends a general power of forfeiture to all criminal offences and makes elaborate provision for the confiscation of the assets of offenders convicted of highly profitable crimes. It also provides for the payment of compensation from proceeds of forfeiture.

Order for Costs

The prosecution (whether successful or not) may apply for an order for costs out of central funds or against a convicted defendant; and a defendant (if acquitted) may apply for an order for costs against the prosecution or out of central funds.[80] The award of costs is always within the discretion of the court in the light of the circumstances of the case; but generally the court should award costs out of central funds in favour of a successful defendant.

---

[76] Powers of Criminal Courts Act 1973; Criminal Law Act 1977, s.56. Criminal Justice Act 1982; Criminal Justice Bill 1988.

[77] Theft Act 1968; Criminal Justice Act 1972.

[78] To be abolished by Criminal Justice Bill 1988.

[79] Prevention of Crime Act 1953; Powers of Criminal Courts Act 1973. *R. v. Stratton* (1988) *The Times*, January 15 (a burglar's car may be forfeit).

[80] Prosecution of Offences Act 1985, Part II, ss.16, 17, 18.

CHAPTER 17

The Law of Property

1. PROPERTY: POSSESSION AND OWNERSHIP

Property

The word "property" when strictly used does not refer directly to things, but to certain kinds of rights in respect of things. This will not seem strange when it is realised that law regulates the relations between persons. A person's "property" is best described as his *proprietary rights in rem*, that is, such of his rights as are not personal in either sense of the word. Personal rights in one sense are those which are available only against a specific person or an ascertainable number of persons (rights *in personam*), in particular those created by obligation (contract and tort), and they are contrasted with real rights (rights *in rem*) which are available against persons generally. Personal rights in another sense are those which go to make up one's personal status but are not considered by law to have a pecuniary value, for example, rights in respect of one's life, personal freedom and reputation; these are contrasted with proprietary rights, which have money value, such as rights in respect of the use and enjoyment of land and goods, and debts. If "property" is confined to proprietary rights *in rem*, then it will be seen to exclude (a) rights *in personam* created by obligations (*e.g.*, payment of damages for tort or breach of contract, personal services due under contract), and (b) those rights *in rem* (*e.g.*, in respect of reputation) which—though they imply duties on the part of persons generally, for breach of which damages will be awarded—are not commercial assets.

In Roman law a very clear distinction was drawn between ownership as the ultimate right to property and possession. In practice, however, they often co-exist in the same person since a man very often possesses what he owns. Moreover strict proof of ownership as an ultimate right can be well-nigh impossible whereas proof of possession and of wrongful dispossession is comparatively simple. Hence it seems that Roman law in practice and English law in both theory and practice[1] protected ownership by giving remedies for wrongful dispossession. From this it followed that for English lawyers who reasoned from the remedy to the underlying right, ownership was essentially a better right to possession than any other that might be asserted against it if and when it came into dispute. This explains why it can be said that for the English lawyer possession is logically prior to and historically earlier than ownership, and why the question can be raised: "How did English law arrive at the conception of *ownership* as distinct from possession, if indeed it has such a conception?"

Possession

Possession in law is based on possession in fact, but it involves a mental as well as a physical element. It consists of certain rights *in rem* which arise when a person assumes control of a thing with intent to exclude others. Strictly, it is possible only of tangible things, whether land or chattels, and the nature of the control varies with the nature of the thing. One cannot sit on a whole field. Physical contact is the most obvious kind of control, but this is not necessary; in particular, the intention to exclude others is generally sufficient to retain possession once acquired, so that one does not lose possession of one's house and furniture by going away on holiday.

Possession is usually acquired by delivery from the owner, either with intent to pass the ownership or in order that the transferee may use it for himself or render some service in respect of it. English law accords possession to the lessee of land and to bailees of chattels, whether the bailment[2] be by way of

---

[1] See Nicholas, *Introduction to Roman Law*, pp. 107–109, 154–156; Salmond, *Jurisprudence* (12th ed.), pp. 294–297.

[2] A bailment is the delivery of goods on the undertaking that, when the purpose for which they are delivered has been fulfilled, they shall be returned to the bailor or otherwise dealt with in accordance with the terms of the undertaking.

pledge, loan, letting on hire, or for carriage or repair; also in certain conditions to the finder of chattels[3] and the squatter on land, and even to a thief; but not, for historical reasons, to a servant with regard to goods placed in his custody by his master.

There can be only one possession of the same thing: as the bailee has possession, the bailor has not.[4] And so, if the thing is wrongfully damaged by someone else, it is the bailee who can bring an action of trespass, the bailor having a remedy in such a case only if permanent damage is done to the thing so that his right to future possession is infringed.

Ownership

Ownership has been described as "the entirety of the powers of use and disposal allowed by law."[5] The phrase "allowed by law" implies that the powers of use and disposal may be limited by law; ownership, then, is relative to a particular legal system, but unless there were some powers of enjoyment and alienation we should not call it ownership. Though rights of ownership are not absolute, they are ultimate: what distinguishes them from other rights is that here is no greater right behind them. Owing to the doctrine of tenure and estates, which is discussed below,[6] the nearest approach to private ownership of land in English law is to hold the fee simple absolute in possession by socage tenure.

Not only has ownership grown out of possession, but the difference between them is seen on analysis to be a difference of degree rather than of kind. Indeed, the word "ownership" is not found in use before the year 1583, and the word "property" is uncommon in English before the nineteenth century: people got on quite well by talking about "possessions" and "estate."

Title to Land

An original and absolute title to land is occasionally granted by Act of Parliament, as when the Blenheim estate was given to the Duke of Marlborough; and sometimes the State guarantees a title which has been registered in due form. The latter has become more common since the Land Registration Act 1925,

---

[3] See *Parker* v. *B.A.B.* [1982] Q.B. 1004.
[4] But a bailor at will, who may call for the return of the thing at any time, retains his possession.
[5] Pollock, *First Book of Jurisprudence* (6th ed.), p. 179.
[6] Below, pp. 291–296.

made registration of title compulsory on a conveyance[7] in certain areas, and made provision for voluntary registration elsewhere. Registration of title is gradually becoming compulsory over the whole country. In such cases possession is comparatively unimportant. Otherwise the way of proving "title" to land in English law is to show continuous and undisturbed possession under a constant claim of title, for a time long enough to exclude any reasonable fear of adverse claims. It became the practice of conveyancers in an open contract for the sale of land to be satisfied with the production of deeds beginning with good root of title[8] showing such undisturbed possession under claim of right for not less than a fixed period, which was originally sixty years. In the nineteen century the period was fixed by statute at forty years, that is to say, in an "open" contract of sale, when nothing was said to the contrary, title had to be shown beginning not less than forty years before. The statutory period is now fifteen years.[9]

To eject from land by force without justification is a crime, and, even where justification exists, the use of more force than is reasonably necessary constitutes a tort. Therefore, if a person is wrongfully in possession of land and refuses to leave, the party entitled should bring an action. The action of ejectment, which superseded the possessory assizes and previous real actions, lay for the breach of the right to possess land. If the person wrongfully dispossessed of land omits to bring his action for a certain period, generally twelve years, he loses his remedy,[10] and in most cases his title.[11]

Incorporeal Property

The title to incorporeal property, such as an easement (*e.g.*, a right of way), can be acquired at common law not only by grant but by prescription, that is, continuous and uninterrupted user as of right from time immemorial (*i.e.*, 1189),[12] from which a grant will be presumed to have been made. The Prescription Act 1832, provides that such user for definite periods ranging from twenty to sixty years before action brought shall under certain conditions give a prescriptive right, which cannot be defeated

---

[7] On sale of the fee simple, or on assignment on sale of a lease having 40 years or more to run, or on grant of a leasehold for 40 years or more.

[8] A document such as a conveyance on sale covering the legal and equitable title and casting no doubt on it.

[9] Law of Property Act 1969.

[10] Limitation Act 1980, s.15.

[11] *Ibid.*, s.17.

[12] See above, Chap. 14, p. 226.

merely by showing that the easement or profit[13] could not have existed at some particular time since 1189. Such rights may also be acquired under the doctrine of "lost modern grant," by which the court will readily presume from user for twenty years that such a right has been granted in the past but documentary evidence has been lost. The presumption can only be rebutted by proof that the making of such a grant was impossible.[14] In effect it is a legal fiction.

Title to Goods

Although tenure never applied to goods, and limited estates in them were possible only in Equity under a trust, the common law ownership of goods has never really amounted to more than the fullest right to present possession or future possession, that is, the power to obtain possession or recover the value by legal means. This is shown by the fact that the remedies for wrongs to chattels were the actions of trespass for interference with possession, and detinue or conversion for infringement of the right to possess. Further, the wrongful possession of goods for six years bars the owner's right of action and extinguishes his title.[15]

Sources of the Law of Property

The basis of the land law is common law, though it has been affected by such important statutes as *De Donis* 1285, *Quia Emptores* 1290, the Statute of Uses 1535, the Tenures Abolition Act 1660, and the Law of Property Acts 1922–25. The modern "Property Statutes" culminating in the Law of Property Act 1925, the Settled Land Act 1925, the Land Charges Act 1925, and the Land Registration Act 1925, primarily concern conveyancing, for they deal with the manner in which estates and interests in land may be created and transferred, but do not interfere with rights of enjoyment. Some of the equitable rules relating to trusts and trustees have been codified and supplemented by the Trustee Act 1925,[16] and intestate succession has been modified

---

[13] A *profit à prendre* is a right to take something capable of ownership, *e.g.*, gravel or fish, from another's land. An easement is a right over another's land which does not allow such taking of property.

[14] See *Tehidy Minerals* v. *Norman* [1971] Q.B. 528. At p. 543 the court criticises the co-existence of three methods of prescription. In 1966 the Law Reform Committee recommended the abolition or reform of prescription. See Cmnd. 3100.

[15] Limitation Act 1939, ss.2 and 3, repealing Limitation Act 1623. See now, Limitation Act 1980, s.3.

[16] *Cf.* Trustee Investments Act 1961.

by the Administration of Estates Act 1925, and the Intestates' Estates Act 1952.

The law of chattels corporeal[17] is also based on common law; but the law relating to chattels incorporeal is much more recent and is mostly contained in such statutes as Copyright Acts, Patent Acts, Bills of Exchange Acts and Companies Acts.

The land law, as built up by the common law, says comparatively little about the rights of *enjoyment* which flow from the holding of the legal estate; it is concerned mostly with the power of disposing of property, the methods of alienation ("conveyancing") and the powers and duties of limited owners. There must be few owners of land who are exclusively entitled to the beneficial enjoyment free from incumbrances, for most estate owners are tenants for life or trustees for sale who hold the legal estate on the trusts of settlement or trust for sale, or else they have borrowed money on the security of their land and hold it subject to the rights of the mortgagee. The extent of rights of enjoyment is really seen in the law of tort (trespass, nuisance, etc.), which defines the duties of others in respect of one's property.

For the purposes of owning and succeeding to property the Family Law Reform Act 1969, s.1,[18] provides that a person attains full age on attaining the age of eighteen, instead of twenty-one as previously, and persons who had attained the age of eighteen but not twenty-one on January 1, 1970, attained full age on that date. A minor can own pure personalty, but a legal estate in land to which he is beneficially entitled will be held in trust for him. Section 9 provides that after January 1, 1970, a person attains the age of eighteen (or any other particular age) at the commencement of his relevant birthday, instead of (as at common law) the first moment of the preceding day.

The Social Control of Land

Recent statutes, however, do much to limit the rights of individual landowners in the wider interests of the community. Powers of planning the use of land in towns were first conferred by the Housing, Town Planning, etc., Act 1919. Such powers were extended to country districts by the Town

---

[17] Below, pp. 290–291.
[18] Based on *Report of the Committee on the Age of Majority* (Latey), (1967) Cmnd. 3342.

and Country Planning Act 1932. A comprehensive system of planning control has been imposed by a series of Town and Country Planning Acts from 1947 onwards. Permission for "development," that is, building or any change in the use of land, has to be obtained from the local planning authorities, which are county councils and district councils. Local authorities have power to acquire land compulsorily for planning purposes, on payment of the statutory compensation. There are additional controls relating to buildings of special architectural or historic interest and to the preservation of trees. It should be noted that planning control (apart from compulsory acquisition) does not affect estates or interests in land, but the use or enjoyment of it.

The Land Commission Act 1967, created the Land Commission, which collected from vendors of land a levy representing that part of the purchase price attributable to the increase in the value of the land due to development or potential development. This Act was repealed in 1971 but was followed by the Community Land Act 1975, which was intended to enable local and other authorities to acquire development land and the increase in the value of land resulting from permitted development—and this in turn was repealed in 1980.

Rent Acts and landlord and tenant legislation control the maximum rent of dwellings; and tenants of such premises are protected against eviction in certain circumstances by the creation of a "statutory tenancy," which is not a freely disposable interest. Tenants of certain categories of furnished dwellings may refer the rent to a Rent Tribunal; and tenants of agricultural holdings and of business premises whose tenancies have expired enjoy some security of tenure, and are entitled to compensation for improvements. The Leasehold Reform Act 1967, provided for the enfranchisement of long leases under a certain rateable value.

"The general nature of this development," it has been said,[19] "may perhaps be described as the gradual breaking down of the barrier which, in modern times, has tended to distinguish sharply between private law and public law, and as a consequence the reintroduction into land law of a conception of ownership which includes legal duties as well as legal rights."

[19] A. D. Hargreaves, *Introduction to the Principles of Land Law* (4th ed., G. A. Grove and J.F. Garner, 1963) p. 189.

2. REAL AND PERSONAL PROPERTY

Distinction between Real and Personal Property

The important distinction drawn by English law between real and personal *property* is not, unfortunately, the same as the distinction between real and personal *rights*. Real property is property which was formerly recoverable by what were called "real *actions*," and personal property is property which was not so recoverable but was protected by what were called "personal *actions*."

The most important real action of medieval times was that begun by writ of right, in which the lord of the manor of whom land in dispute was held was ordered to do full right between the rival claimants, and if he neglected to do so the matter was to be finally disposed of in the King's Court. The action was originally called "real" because the mesne process was against the thing in dispute (*res*),[20] that is to say, the land could be seized pending the trial of the action, to ensure that the person in possession appeared in court and abided by the judgment. The actions of debt and detinue (as also trespass and covenant) were called "personal" because the mesne process was against the person of the defendant, who could be taken into custody pending the trial of the action. Some time after the possessory assizes had superseded the writ of right as the means of recovering land they came to be called real actions, because, although the mesne process was against the defendant who had committed the wrong of dispossession, they resulted in the recovery of the land and the fact that the *res* in dispute was recovered came to be the distinguishing mark of real actions in the developed law. Not every action which resulted in the recovery of a thing, however, was a real action in English law, for the *res* was confined to certain estates and interests in land known as freeholds.[21] The actions of debt and detinue were personal actions although they resulted in the recovery of money or chattels: this was partly because they came into existence at a time when mesne process was the test and retained their personal character when the real actions came to confine their attention to the right to freeholds, and partly because the defendant in detinue was never (until the nineteenth century) compelled to restore a chattel but might choose to pay its value instead.

[20] "*realis*" being an adjectival form of "*res*."
[21] Below, p. 292.

Real Property

One of the chief effects of the forms of action on English law, then, was to develop the law of property in two distinct branches, real property and personal property, each having its peculiar characteristics. Only interests in land[22] can be real property and even they are not all so, for the leasehold or term of years came into existence when the kinds of real property had become fixed, and it was never received into that charmed circle.

Personal Property

The old term for personal property was "chattels." Chattels (*catalla*) is the same word as cattle, and the typical medieval chattel was the beast, though there were also ploughs, furniture, armour and jewels. We know little of the medieval law of chattels because, as they were movable, mostly perishable and largely consumed in use, possession was the chief consideration and that was probably protected in local courts whose records have been lost. This does not mean that chattels themselves were unimportant. "Not even in the feudal age did men eat or drink land," Maitland reminds us; "They owned flocks and herds, ploughs and plough-teams, and stores of hay and corn. A Cistercian abbot of the thirteenth century, who counted his sheep by the thousand, would have been surprised to hear that he had few chattels of any value."[23]

Leaseholds

Being interests in land, these are called "chattels real" to distinguish them from all other chattels, which are called chattels personal or pure personalty (below). The interest of the lessee was at first regarded merely as contractual, a right *in personam*, and his only protection was the action of covenant against the lessor who turned him out during his term. He was soon allowed to bring the action of trespass for damages against any other persons who interfered with his possession, and by the end of the fifteenth century he could recover the land itself from anyone by means of an action of ejectment. So the term of years became an estate in land; the lessee had rights *in rem*; he could even recover the thing (*i.e.*, the term of years). But the

---

[22] "Land" for most purposes includes mines, minerals, buildings, growing trees and plants, money held on trust to buy land, the proceeds of sale of settled land and certain rights over land such as easements and profits.

[23] Pollock and Maitland, *History of English Law*, Vol. II, p. 149.

action *de ejectione firmae* was an extension of trespass and was not a real action: nor was leasehold considered according to feudal notions to be a form of tenure. The significance of leaseholds being classed as personalty is mainly that until 1926 the rules of intestate succession to that kind of property were the same as those for pure personalty and differed from those for real property; until 1832 leaseholds were not a property qualification for the Parliamentary franchise; and if in a will or settlement even at the present day "realty" is given to A and "personalty" to B, leaseholds will go to B.

Chattels personal

These may be either in possession or in action. Choses in possession are corporeal things, such as goods or money. Choses in action are rights and other incorporeal things such as debts, negotiable instruments, stocks, shares and debentures, patents and copyright, trade marks, trade names and business goodwill, and sums payable under policies of insurance.

3. TENURE AND ESTATES IN LAND

The feudal doctrine that the Sovereign is "the lord paramount or above all."[24] and that subjects can only hold estates by some tenure, still remains in theory. The doctrine of tenure is in striking contrast to the ownership of chattels. Feudalism was of great importance also in medieval public law, which may almost be said to have been made up of criminal law and land law. It placed the Sovereign at the apex of the legal system; it largely determined the composition of those authorities of the central government, the Council and Parliament; it accounted for seignorial jurisdiction and the system of courts; and for centuries it restricted the Parliamentary franchise. In the thirteenth century the knights of the shire who attended Parliament were elected by the freeholders of the county, the suitors to the county court. The statute of Henry VI (1429) which limited the franchise to the "forty-shilling freeholders" continued in force with modifications for four hundred years, though Blackstone tells us that forty shillings in Henry VI's reign would be worth £20 in his own time.[25] The term "freehold," apart from its context, is ambiguous, for it may refer either to tenure or estates. Freehold tenure and freehold estates

---

[24] Blackstone, II, Comm. 59.
[25] Blackstone, I, Comm. 173.

were, however, largely coincident, and such was the case with the Parliamentary voter, for neither the copyholder (who held by unfree *tenure*) nor the leaseholder (who held an *estate* not of freehold) was given the vote until the Reform Act of 1832.

Tenures

Tenures were classified according to the nature of the "incidents" or services which the tenant had to render for his holding, these seignorial rights being a return for the lord's duty to protect those who held of him. The primary classification was into free and unfree tenures, the distinction of the later Middle Ages turning on the certainty (free) or uncertainty (unfree tenure) of the tenant's duties rather than on the personal condition of the tenant himself.

Freehold Tenures

The freehold tenures, or "freeholds" in one sense of that term, were (i) knight service by which the tenant had to provide a fraction of his lord's military service to the Sovereign[26]; (ii) frankalmoign by which religious houses undertook to say masses for the soul of the donor; (iii) serjeanty by which personal services mostly of an honorary nature were due, and (iv) socage which involved neither military, religious nor personal duties, but often an economic return. The Statute *Quia Emptores* 1290, by providing that on the conveyance of the fee simple no lordship was left in the grantor, had the effect of reducing the number of mesne lords, and eventually of making the majority of freeholders immediate tenants of the Sovereign. The grantee of land no longer became the feudal tenant of the grantor by subinfeudation but became the tenant of the grantor's lord by substitution, being substituted for the grantor in respect of the land when the grant was in fee simple. Long before Littleton's time the service rendered for military tenure was a substituted money payment called escuage (*scutagium*), and when the Tenures Abolition Act abolished military tenure in 1660 and converted it into socage, the latter became the only important free tenure. With military tenure disappeared the burdensome incidents of wardship and

---

[26] The unit was one knight's fee, *i.e.*, one armed horseman for forty days in the year, the monetary value being about £20 per annum. A tenant in chief would hold a number of knight's fees.

marriage, leaving escheat,[27] forfeiture,[28] the honorary incidents of grand serjeanty and the insignificant incidents of fealty[29] and suit of court.[30]

Copyhold Tenure

The incidents of unfree tenure varied according to the custom of the manor, and the unfree tenant in the Middle Ages might not know within the limits of an agricultural economy what services he would be called upon to render from week to week. This tenure was evidenced by copy of the Roll of the manorial court, and came to be called copyhold. It was not protected by the Royal Courts before the end of the fifteenth century. Copyholds might be enfranchised and so became freehold with the consent of the lord on payment of compensation; and by statute in the nineteenth century enfranchisement became compulsory against either party under certain conditions. But many copyholds remained until 1926 and involved annoying incidents, dues and sporting rights, as well as a different system of conveyancing, for copyholds were transferred by surrender and admittance in the Stewart's Court, even if that were merely the office of the lord's solicitor.[31]

The Law of Property Act 1922, abolished copyhold tenure and converted it into socage, provision being made for compensation for lords. Apart from certain manorial incidents which will continue to exist unless extinguished by mutual consent,[32] and the honorary incidents of grand serjeanty which manifest themselves chiefly at coronations and State banquets, the only vestige of the feudal system of tenure is socage. Such incidents of socage tenure as survived the statute of 1660 were abolished in 1925[33] except fealty, which had no commercial value and is not in practice exacted, escheat of real property being replaced by *bona vacantia*.[34]

The doctrine of tenure, however, remains as the peg on which to hang estates, to which also certain other interests cling, and is

---

[27] Land passing to the feudal lord on failure of heirs of the tenant or on his conviction for felony.

[28] The right of the Crown to land on a tenant's conviction for treason. Breach of obligation on the part of a tenant might also result in forfeiture to the lord.

[29] The obligation arising from the tenant's oath to perform his duties.

[30] The tenant's obligation to attend and assist in the lord's feudal court.

[31] But see Copyhold Act 1841.

[32] The most important of these are tenant's rights of common, lord's or tenant's rights to mines, minerals, etc., and lord's sporting rights.

[33] Law of Property Act 1922.

[34] The right of the Crown to the property of an intestate who has no relatives entitled under the law of intestacy. See below, p. 300.

thus of practical importance with regard to estates less than the
fee simple.

Estates

The word "estate" in this context does not primarily mean an
area of land but an interest in land limited by the time for which
a landowner, and in some cases his successors also, may hold
the land.[35] Estates may be classified in four different ways,
according as they are legal or equitable, absolute or conditional,
present or future, or according to their duration. The main
division of estates according to their duration is that into
freeholds which are of uncertain duration, and leaseholds which
are of certain duration. As freehold tenures were contrasted
with copyholds, so freehold estates were contrasted with
leaseholds.

Freehold Estates

There are four kinds of freehold estates.

(i) The *fee simple* before 1926 was an estate which lasted so
long as the owner had *heirs*, that is, persons capable of
inheriting according to the canons of descent.[36] At first
the fee simple would escheat on failure of heirs of the
last "purchaser" (*i.e.*, a person who acquired the
property by any transaction, whether for value or not,
e.g., sale or gift, and not merely by operation of law,
e.g., intestacy), but by the middle of the nineteenth
century only on failure of heirs of the person last
entitled to the land. Since the alteration in the law of
intestate succession by the Administration of Estates
Act 1925, the fee simple lasts so long as there are in
existence relatives entitled to succeed on an intestacy
under that Act.[37] It is the largest estate in land known
to English law, and if absolute and in possession is
practically equivalent to ownership.

(ii) A grant "to B and the heirs of his body" is an *estate tail*
(or fee tail), *i.e.*, an estate which, according to the

---

[35] *Walsingham's Case* (1579) 2 Plowd. 547, 555. "The land itself is one thing, and
the estate in the land is another thing, for an estate in the land is a time in the
land, or land for a time."

[36] Below, p. 301.

[37] The owner (strictly, tenant in fee simple) may, however, devise or grant the
estate to anyone he pleases and it will then last as long as the devisee or
grantee has successors.

statute *De Donis* 1285, lasts so long as there are in existence heirs of the body of B. This estate is less extensive than the fee simple, for it is liable to be cut off (*taillé*) on failure at any time of B's lineal descendants. Further, the heirs of the body may be restricted in the grant to males (or females) only, or to B's issue by a particular wife (or husband) only. It may be mentioned in passing that the Crown was vested by statutory entail in Sophia, Electress of Hanover, and the heirs of her body being Protestants. The purpose of creating an entailed interest (as it is now called) is to make a family settlement. In a settlement made on marriage it is normally preceded by a life interest to the settlor, the prospective husband. An estate tail came to be capable of being "barred" (*i.e.*, enlarged into a fee simple) under certain conditions, and so could be alienated or resettled on the family.

(iii) The third kind of freehold estate is the *life estate* (now called a life interest), which is a grant to A for his life. It comes to an end on A's death, but it is of uncertain duration for, although it is certain that he will die eventually, the date of his death is not certain. As we have said, it often precedes an entailed interest in a family settlement.

(iv) The other freehold estate is the estate *pur autre vie*, which exists where X holds for the life of A. This would most commonly arise where A conveys an estate held for his own life to X.

Leasehold Estate

The essence of a leasehold estate or term of years is that a certain ending (*terminus*)[38] is agreed upon between lessor and lessee. There is no maximum duration, and long leases of 999 years and 3,000 years are common in building leases and mortgages. The lessor retains a reversion, which entitles him at common law (apart from the covenants in the lease, but subject to statutory restrictions) to receive rent during the term, to bring an action or to distrain for rent in arrears, and to eject the tenant when the term expires. The lessee must have exclusive possession of the land. This distinguishes a lease from a licence, *i.e.*, mere

---

[38] Or ending capable of being rendered certain as in periodic, *e.g.* monthly leases.

permission to go onto or use land.[39] Although leasehold was never a tenure according to feudal notions, it is in practice as in popular language the most important kind of tenure at the present day.

Incorporeal Hereditaments

Attached to A's estate may be certain "interests" in respect of B's land, such as rights of ways and other easements. Being inheritable in the same manner as estates they were called "hereditaments," and being limitations on B's rights which did not give A exclusive possession of B's land, they were called "incorporeal."

4. LEGAL AND EQUITABLE PROPERTY

Just as we had to define real property as property which was formerly recoverable by real actions, so we must define equitable property as property which was formerly protected only in a Court of Equity. Conversely legal property is that which was formerly protected by the courts of common law. The most important kinds of equitable property are: (i) the interest of a beneficiary under a trust; (ii) the interest of the purchaser in land which has not yet been conveyed to him in pursuance of a specifically enforceable contract; and (iii) formerly a married woman's separate property.

It is only necessary here to speak of equitable property arising under a trust, the general nature of which has been mentioned in the first chapter. Side by side with the legal interest in trust property ordinarily held by the trustee, there exists a beneficial or equitable interest in the beneficiary. Equity allowed the beneficiary to hold this for the same estates and interests as could exist in the legal interest (*e.g.*, fee simple or life estate) and eventually for certain interests not at first possible at law.[40] The purpose of trusts is to give property by will or settlement *inter vivos* to persons in succession or for the benefits of minors, or (generally by will) to give property to charity.

Trusts

Trusts (formerly "uses") have a continuous history since medieval times; but the passive trust of freeholds as we know it today dates only from the seventeenth century, when the

---

[39] See *Street* v. *Mountford* [1985] A.C. 809.
[40] *Cf.* shifting and springing uses, below, p. 299.

ingenuity of lawyers found a way of utilising the provisions of the Statute of Uses 1535, to effect results very different from those intended by Henry VIII.

Trusts can be created in any kind of property, real or personal, legal or equitable. A trust of equitable property will arise where A, who is himself entitled to equitable property, conveys his interest to trustees to hold for B. But there must be an ultimate legal estate to which the trusts attach, for the Court of Chancery could no more invent wholly new kinds of estates than it could ignore those which existed at law—it acted on the conscience of the legal owner. Any estate in land which was possible at law could exist in Equity; further, life estates in personalty could be created by trust, though at common law estates could not be created in personalty except that the term of years itself was personal property.

Protection of Equitable Property

The limits to the protection by the Court of Chancery of the beneficiary's interest under a trust were settled in essentials by the time of Edward IV, though since then a number of refinements have been worked out. The beneficiary (*cestui que trust*) can take proceedings against the trustee himself to compel him to administer the trust or to compensate for breach of trust: lapse of time (although there is now a general statutory limit for the bringing of actions against trustees) does not bar his remedy if the breach of trust was fraudulent, or the trust property is still in the hands of the trustee, or the trustee has converted it to his own use. The beneficiary can enforce the trust against the trustee's personal representative, donee or creditors. He can "follow" the trust property itself or its proceeds into the hands of third parties, but not if it has lost its identity by being inextricably mingled with their own property.[41]

In effect, the beneficiary's interest is protected *against everyone except a bona fide purchaser of the legal estate for value and without notice of the trust*, for the latter's position is equal to his in Equity and superior at law.[42] This in essence is the modern distinction between legal and equitable property, for equitable property has frequently been recognised by statute, and since the Judicature Acts both kinds of property are protected in the same courts, though matters affecting equitable property are assigned generally to the Chancery Division.

---

[41] *Re Hallett's Estate* (1880) 13 Ch.D. 696; *Re Diplock* [1948] Ch. 465, *sub nom. Ministry of Health* v. *Simpson* [1951] A.C. 251.
[42] *Pilcher* v. *Rawlins* (1872) L.R. 7 Ch. 259.

Equity went further and developed the doctrine of "constructive" notice, by which a purchaser was deemed to have notice of such matters as he would have discovered if he had made such inspections and inquiries as the reasonable and prudent purchaser would make.[43] The doctrine of notice, however, has been modified by the Land Charges Act 1925, and the Law of Property Act 1925, by which certain charges on land are void unless registered, and registration of such charges is deemed to be actual notice.[44]

Legal Estates and Interests and Equitable Interests since 1925

Legal Estates

In order to facilitate the conveyance of the legal estate free from the incumbrance of third-party rights, the Law of Property Act 1925, provides that there shall be only two kinds of *legal* estates in land, namely, the fee simple absolute in possession and the term of years absolute. A fee simple is "absolute" if it is not determinable by any event other than the failure of appropriate successors in title. This excludes a determinable fee simple and a fee simple on condition.[45] The estate may, however, be absolute although it is subject to a legal or equitable right of re-entry.[46]

A "term of years absolute" excludes any term of years determinable with life or lives or with the cesser of a determinable life interest, but includes a term for less than a year. It may be mentioned that the term of years may be used for the creation of mortgages of land; it gives the mortgagee (lender) a legal estate while leaving a legal estate in the borrower.

Legal Interests

The Act of 1925 provides for a certain number of *legal* interests in land, such as easements and rentcharges, held in a similar manner to legal estates, and charges by way of legal mortgage.

Equitable Interests

All other interests in land or the proceeds of land are now equitable only. Equitable interests since 1925, therefore, include

---

[43] *Re Cox and Neve's Contract* [1891] 2 Ch. 109; *Re Nisbet and Potts' Contract* [1906] 2 Ch. 386.

[44] See now, Land Charges Act 1972.

[45] These are found when the fee simple is limited to end on the occurrence of some contingent event such as the ending of a particular use of the land, *e.g.* as a school or hospital.

[46] Law of Property (Amendment) Act 1926 (to enforce rentcharges).

all entailed interests (now allowed in personalty as well as realty), life interests and future interests.

With regard to future interests we may notice that at common law the only future estates were the "remainder" which vested in a grantee after the termination of a prior estate tail or life estate given in the same settlement, and the "reversion" or estate which returned to the settlor when all lesser estates of freehold granted in a settlement came to an end.[47] Other kinds of future interests were evolved in Equity by which estates might shift from one person to another ("shifting uses") or spring up at some future time on the happening of certain events ("springing uses"); and by an ingenious manipulation of the Statute of Uses such future estates could be created after 1535 at law ("executory interests").

Settlements

From the Restoration to the late nineteenth century much land was held under strict settlement to ensure that the person in possession of the land should only have a life interest and never be in a position to dispose of an unincumbered fee simple outside the family. In a settlement made on marriage the husband would reduce his fee simple to a life estate and the document would also contain provision for the support of his widow and for capital sums ("portions") for the younger children with provision for entailed interests for the eldest son and other children. When the eldest son came of age he would be persuaded, usually by the grant of an allowance, to reduce his entail to a life estate and this prevented him even partially barring the entail and taking the land outside the family. Settlement and re-settlement maintained the unity of great landed estates but had a crippling effect on powers of managing the land. To remedy this the Settled Land Act 1882 provided that a tenant for life should have power to dispose of the land itself and the limited interests of the settlement were to be transferred to the capital money arising on sale by a process known as "overreaching." The Settled Land Act 1925 improved conveyancing machinery for such land and extended the powers of the tenant for life, but such settlements are rarely created at the present day because of their serious tax disadvantages.

---

[47] This must be distinguished from the lessor's reversion (the interest retained by the lessor when he grants a lease), which is technically a present estate.

An alternative method for providing successive limited interests in property for members of a family is the trust for sale. Here trustees are instructed to hold property, which may be a mixed fund of real and personal property, on trust ultimately to sell the property, convert it into money and distribute it among the beneficiaries. By virtue of the equitable doctrine of conversion, an application of the maxim that equity regards that as already done which ought to be done, land comprised in the trust for sale is treated for many legal purposes as if it were already personal property. The trustees may, however, postpone the sale for an extended time and allow the beneficiaries to enjoy the property. Moreover, the effecting of the sale by the trustees may be subjected to the giving of various consents so that, paradoxically, there may now be greater certainty that the actual land will remain in a family under a trust for sale than under a strict settlement.

Where a settlement (whether a strict settlement or a trust for sale) is executed in the manner provided by the Settled Land Act 1925, and the Law of Property Act 1925, equitable interests will not appear on the title; and if the purchaser of the legal estate pays the purchase money to at least two trustees or a trust corporation, equitable interests arising under the trusts of the settlement are "overreached."

5. SUCCESSION TO PROPERTY ON DEATH

Succession on Death before 1926

In Norman times, when wills of land were not possible, it was probably the usual practice for the lord to grant merely a life estate to his tenant and, when the latter died, a new life estate to the eldest son or another relative as he thought fit. The term of years at that time seems to have been used only by way of mortgage. The development of estates of inheritance—the fee simple and the fee tail—shows that freehold tenants generally came to acquire a right that the land should pass on their death to their descendants; but a grant of land without express words of inheritance conferred only a life estate until 1926. As devises (*i.e.*, gifts by will) of real property became more common, intestacy became the exception among owners of large estates though still general among poorer people. Real property (except, of course, life estates) of a person who died intestate before 1926 descended to his heir. The meaning of the word *heir* in English law is the person who before 1926 succeeded to the *real* property of a person dying *intestate*. The identity of the heir

was determined by the canons of descent, which were fairly
well settled by the end of the thirteenth century, though
modified later by legislation.

A fee simple descended to the lineal descendants according to
the principles of primogeniture, which were originally framed to
suit military tenure. Male issue took before females, and the
eldest male excluded younger males in the same degree; but in
the absence of male descendants, all females in the nearest
degree took the land as coparceners. A descendant who had
already died was not passed over, but was represented by his
descendants. By the Inheritance Act 1833, on failure of lineal
descendants, lineal ancestors and their issue were admitted,
paternal ancestors being preferred to maternal. If none of these
persons existed, the land escheated, by the nineteenth century
almost invariably to the Crown, which in effect meant the State.
An estate tail, which was not devisable by will, descended in a
stricter manner to lineal descendants of the class named in the
grant. Copyholds descended on an intestacy to the customary
heir, who might, according to the local custom, be the eldest son
or the youngest son or all the sons.[48]

Testamentary dispositions of land were made from medieval
times by means of the use or trust, and the check imposed by
the Statute of Uses 1535, on such devises of freehold was
nullified by the Statute of Wills 1540, which allowed a written
will to pass all land held in socage tenure and two-thirds of land
held by military tenure, and the Tenures Abolition Act 1660,
which abolished military tenures. The executor, a personal
representative who was charged with carrying out the testator's
intentions as regards land and chattels, was controlled at first by
the Ecclesiastical Courts and later by the Court of Chancery.

The church courts were also interested in the disposition of
the personal property of one who, in spite of ecclesiastical
exhortation,[49] died intestate. They could appoint an administrator, and see that a proportion of the property was given to
charity and the residue distributed amongst his near relatives
and dependants. The Statutes of Distribution 1670 and 1685,
regulated the order of intestate succession to personalty, giving
the widow one-third after payment of debts, and dividing the
residue equally among the children or, failing them, passing to
the father or the nearest relatives. The administration of estates,
as distinct from the appointment of administrators (which was
retained by the Ecclesiastical Courts until the creation of the

---

[48] *Cf*. above, Chap. 14.
[49] *Cf. Book of Common Prayer*, rubric in the Order for the Visitation of the Sick.

Court of Probate in 1857), gradually passed to the Court of Chancery.

Intestate Succession after 1925

At the present day about 40 per cent. of people die intestate, *i.e.*, having made no (valid) will[50]; but the great majority of these leave estates of small value. The Administration of Estates Act 1925, abolished the old rules of descent, except with regard to an entailed interest not disposed of by will. This Act, as amended by the Intestates' Estates Act 1952, and the Family Provision Act 1966, provides that (with this exception) all the property, *real and personal*, in respect of which a person dies intestate shall vest in his personal representatives on trust for sale, the proceeds after payment of debts to be divided among his nearest relatives.

If the intestate leaves a husband or wife, but no issue and no parent, brother or sister or issue of brother or sister, than the surviving spouse is entitled to the whole estate. If the intestate leaves a husband or wife and issue (whether or not he also leaves parents, brothers or sisters), then the surviving spouse is entitled absolutely to all the "personal chattels" (*e.g.*, furniture, cars, books and jewellery, but not money or securities), and £40,000 absolutely; subject thereto, the spouse is entitled to a life interest in one-half of the residue, and the issue take the rest (*i.e.*, the other half and the remainder after the life interest has expired). The issue take on the "statutory trusts," that is to say, the property is held in trust for *all* the children (male and female) equally who attain the age of eighteen years or marry under that age, a deceased child being represented by his or her children. If the intestate leaves a husband or wife, and a parent, or brother or sister of the whole blood or their issue, but no issue, then the surviving spouse is entitled to the personal chattels and £85,000 absolutely; subject thereto, the spouse takes one-half of the residue absolutely, and the parent or parents or (if none) the brothers and sisters of the whole blood or their issue take the other half. If the intestate leaves issue but no husband or wife, the estate goes to the issue. If the intestate leaves no husband or wife and no issue, the estate goes to the parent or parents. If the intestate leaves no husband or wife, no issue and no parent, then the estate goes to the following persons living at his or her death in the following order: brothers and sisters of the whole blood or their issue, brothers and sisters of the half blood or

---

[50] If a will does not cover all the property of the deceased there is a partial intestacy, and the amounts mentioned below may be modified.

their issue, the grandparent or grandparents, uncles and aunts or their issue.

After January 1, 1970, an illegitimate child was entitled to share equally with legitimate issue in the intestacy of both his parents, and both parents of an illegitimate child were equally entitled to share in his intestacy (Family Law Reform Act 1969, s.14). Now, an illegitimate person is given the same rights on intestacy as one who is legitimate (Family Law Reform Act 1987, (s.18) and illegitimacy is generally to be disregarded in determining rights on intestacy.

If no person takes an absolute interest under these provisions, the property (real and personal) goes as *bona vacantia* to the Crown or the Duchy of Lancaster or the Duke of Cornwall. This in effect means the State, for *bona vacantia* are among the rights customarily surrendered by the Crown to the use of Parliament in exchange for the Civil List.

A knowledge of the old rules of inheritance remains of practical importance, for a purchaser of land may be concerned with a title which goes back before 1926; an entailed interest will continue to descend on an intestacy according to the old rules[51]; and if a testator devises land to "the heir of X," the person entitled to take will be, as a matter of interpretation, the person who would have been X's heir under the old rules if X had died intestate.

Wills

The form in which wills are to be made was laid down by the Wills Act 1837.[52] A will must be in writing, signed by the testator in the presence of two or more witnesses present at the same time, and attested and signed by the witnesses in the presence of the testator. Gifts to attesting witnesses are no longer void if the will is duly executed without their attestation.[53] The age at which a person can make a will has been reduced from twenty-one to eighteen.[54] A will is ambulatory, that is it does not take effect until death and revocable, though effect will be given to contracts to dispose of property in a particular way. Revocation may be by another will, destruction or marriage.

Soldiers, sailors and airmen in actual military service and members of the naval and marine forces and the merchant navy

---

[51] The new rules do not affect the descent of hereditary peerages and titles of honour.
[52] *Cf.* Administration of Justice Act 1982.
[53] Wills Act 1968.
[54] Family Law Reform Act 1969, s.3.

when at sea may make informal wills. These will be valid even if the testator is under eighteen.

Provision for Dependants of the Deceased

English law does not require a testator to make any provision for his dependants, nor indeed is a person required to make a will at all. The Inheritance (Family Provision) Act 1938, introduced a remedy for this defect as far as wills are concerned, and the Intestates' Estates Act 1952, extended these provisions to cases of intestacy.

These Acts have now been repealed by the Inheritance (Provision for Family and Dependants) Act 1975, which provides that the court, if it considers that the will or the law relating to intestacy does not make reasonable provision for specified dependants of the deceased, may on application order such provision out of the deceased's net estate. The dependants who may apply are the spouse or former spouse of the deceased, any child, legitimate or illegitimate, any person who was treated as a child of the family and any person who immediately before the death of the deceased was being maintained by him. In the case of a surviving spouse reasonable provision is not limited to maintenance; in other cases it is. In exercising its discretion the court must consider the financial resources and needs of the applicant, the size of the estate and any other relevant factors, including the conduct of the applicant and his or her expectations of education and maintenance. The court now has powers to set aside transactions intended to defeat applications. The court may order periodical payments, the payment of a lump sum, the transfer or settlement of property or the variation of settlements. The court may also vary orders for periodical payments in the event of a change in the financial circumstances of the applicant.

CHAPTER 18

The Law of Tort

1. THE NATURE OF A TORT

The word "tort" is not used in English except in the legal sense. It was borrowed through French from the Latin *tortum* (twisted), with the derived meaning of wrong (*i.e.*, wrung from the true). Curiously enough the equivalent in French law is *délit*, from the Latin *delictum*.

A tort may be defined for general purposes as *a civil wrong other than a breach of contract or a breach of trust*. The word "civil" distinguishes a tort from a crime, indicating that tort is primarily directed to compensation rather than punishment. The distinction was not drawn in early times: the greater part of the English law of tort is derived from the actions of trespass and trespass on the case, and trespass was originally quasi-criminal. The same act, however, may be both a tort and a crime, as in certain circumstances are trespass, nuisance, libel, fraud and negligence.

The word "wrong" in its wide sense means the breach of any duty, but in a narrower sense as applied to civil law it excludes a breach of contract and a breach of trust. The rights and duties which arise on the commission of a tort are in general created by operation of law and do not usually arise directly, as they do in contract, from the will of the parties. A tort further differs from a breach of contract in that, while the latter is the breach of a right *in personam*, a tort is the breach of a right *in rem*.[1] The distinction is not

[1] See above, p. 282.

older than the fifteenth century for, as we shall see in the next chapter, the law of simple contract was evolved by means of the action of assumpsit, which was originally tortious. The same act may be both a tort and a breach of contract: thus a wrongful refusal to return a chattel may be the breach of a contract of loan and also the tort of conversion; and the duty of care which is infringed by negligence is often created by contract, such as that between a transport company and its passengers or between a medical practitioner and his patients.[2] Where a plaintiff has causes of action both in tort and in contract against the same party, he may base his claim on either. The significance of the distinction between tort and breach of contract lies: (a) in the parties entitled to sue, for anyone injured by a tort has an action for damages,[3] but in general only a party to a contract may sue for its breach[4]; and (b) in the time within which actions must be brought, for although actions in tort or for simple contract must generally be brought within six years from the accrual of the cause of action, actions in respect of personal injuries must generally be brought within three years,[5] though the court may allow an action to proceed out of time if it is equitable to do so, and twelve years are allowed for an action on a contract under seal.[6]

In the case of latent damage other than personal injuries a plaintiff may now sue within three years from when he discovered or might reasonably have discovered the harm, subject to a final limit of fifteen years.[7]

A tort is distinguished from a breach of trust because the law of trusts was developed in the Courts of Equity separately from the Common Law Courts until 1875. Although the jurisdictions in common law and equity are now merged, their respective principles of liability and remedies remain different.

The characteristic remedy in tort is an action for unliquidated damages, that is, a claim for such amount of damages as the court in its discretion may award as compensation to the plaintiff for the damage or loss suffered, whether a particular sum is specified in the pleadings or not. Aggravated damages may be awarded where, for example, trespass to land is

---

[2] Solicitors may also be liable in tort and contract; *Midland Bank* v. *Hett Stubbs* [1979] Ch. 384.
[3] *Donoghue* v. *Stevenson* [1932] A.C. 562.
[4] *Tweddle* v. *Atkinson* (1861) 1 B. & S. 393.
[5] Limitation Act 1980, ss.2–7, 11–14.
[6] Limitation Act 1980, s.8.
[7] Latent Damage Act 1986.

aggravated by noise and disturbance.[8] The explanation given by Lord Devlin in *Rookes* v. *Barnard*[9] is that damages for mental injury to the plaintiff may be given when malevolence or spite or the manner of committing the wrong injure the plaintiff's proper feelings of dignity and pride.

The occasional award of exemplary or punitive damages as a form of punishment for the defendant's wrong which has a long history in our law, especially in actions of assault and libel,[10] was frowned upon by the House of Lords in *Rookes* v. *Barnard*.[11] Lord Devlin stated that exemplary or punitive damages, apart from rare statutory authorisation, would in future be awarded only: (a) where acts by Government servants are oppressive, arbitrary or unconstitutional, *e.g.*, *Wilkes* v. *Wood*[12] (jury award £1,000 damages in 1763 when plaintiff's house searched under a general warrant); and (b) where the defendant's conduct was calculated by him to make a profit for himself which was likely to be greater than the compensation payable to the plaintiff, *e.g.*, *Youssoupoff* v. *Metro-Goldwyn-Mayer Pictures Ltd.*[13] (defamation of Russian Princess in a film about Rasputin). This was not followed by the Privy Council on an appeal from Australia,[14] but the House of Lords reaffirmed its own view in *Cassell & Co.* v. *Broome*.[15]

There are other remedies for torts, such as injunction, abatement,[16] ejectment from land and restitution of goods; and in some cases these are the primary object of the proceedings; but unless damages may also be awarded the wrong is not classed as a tort.

---

[8] *Chamberlain* v. *Greenfield* (1772) 3 Wils.K.B. 292.

[9] [1964] A.C. 1129.

[10] In *Loudon* v. *Ryder* [1953] 2 Q.B. 202, the Court of Appeal upheld an award of £4,000 damages, including £3,000 exemplary damages, for assault. Heath J. in *Merest* v. *Harvey* (1814) 5 Taunt. 442, said: "I remember a case where a jury gave £500 damages for merely knocking a man's hat off; and the court refused a new trial."

[11] [1964] A.C. 1129.

[12] (1763) Lofft 1. And see *Huckle* v. *Money* (1763) 2 Wils.K.B. 205, where the plaintiff, who had been detained for a few hours under an illegal search warrant and treated the while with beefsteaks and beer, was awarded £300 damages.

[13] (1934) 50 T.L.R. 581.

[14] *Australian Consolidated Press Ltd.* v. *Uren* [1969] 1 A.C. 590.

[15] [1972] A.C. 1027. Captain Broome was awarded £25,000 exemplary damages for libel by the author and publishers of *The Destruction of Convoy PQ17*.

[16] The removal of a nuisance by the person aggrieved. The law does not favour this form of self-help.

Classification of Torts

Owing to the manner in which the law of torts has been developed in the Common Law Courts, and to the absence of any clear general principle of tortious liability, there is no classification of torts which is at once scientific and practical.

The type of classification most generally adopted in textbooks is: (a) torts committed in respect of personal safety and liberty *e.g.*, assault and battery, false imprisonment; (b) torts in respect of personal reputation, *viz.*, libel and slander; (c) torts committed in respect of property, *e.g.*, trespass to land and goods, nuisance and conversion; (d) interference with family, contractual and business relations, including conspiracy and slander of title; (e) deceit; (f) negligence, which may be in respect of person or property; and (g) abuse of legal procedure, *e.g.*, malicious prosecution.

Even if we included all those which have special names our classification would not exhaust all torts, for there are some torts which have no name, and there are other wrongs about which it is uncertain whether they are torts or not. "Thus," said Winfield,[17] "as a family group, torts may be divided into those which received names soon after birth, those which seem to be awaiting baptism in their riper years and those whose paternity is uncertain enough to make it doubtful whether they ought to be included in the family at all."

2. GENERAL PRINCIPLES OF LIABILITY IN TORT

There was no general theory of civil liability in Roman law, but a limited number of obligations created by wrongdoing (*ex maleficio* or *ex delicto*), which were added to from time to time by legislation and praetorian edict and never satisfactorily classified. These delicts consisted of breaches of rights *in rem* and gave rise to actions for penalties, which were in substitution for private revenge. Civil wrongs in Roman law thus remained as closely allied to crimes as were the civil wrongs of twelfth-century England. In French law a general principle has been developed, mainly by the courts aided by text-writers, of liability for wrong causing damage, this being obtained largely by interpretation of two sections of the Civil Code. The question for the court usually is whether there was a fault (*faute*) on the part of the defendant which caused the damage. If there was, the problems involved will relate chiefly to the various kinds of

---

[17] Winfield, *Tort* (6th ed.), p. 244. This passage has been omitted from later editions. See now *Winfield and Jolowicz on Tort*, 12th ed., pp. 563–570.

justification. Further, a plaintiff can recover damages for injury caused by the defendant's crime. The French law of delict, therefore, is not classified into separate wrongs, but consists of varied applications of the general principle of civil liability for wrong causing damage. The German Civil Code of 1900 has a general clause imposing liability for damage done by unlawful acts, and a number of subsidiary clauses dealing with particular instances such as defamation, seduction, unfair competition and damage by animals. On the other hand, a plaintiff will not be awarded nominal damages by merely asserting a right, as in the English law of trespass; he must prove a claim for substantial compensation or restitution of property.

Among English jurists there is a difference of opinion on the question whether there is any general principle of liability in tort. Liability for damage caused by intention (*dolus*) or negligence (*culpa*) was a general principle in Roman law, as it is in Scots law, Roman-Dutch law and French law. As regards English law, one view is that to make the defendant civilly liable the plaintiff has to bring his action under one of a limited number of specific torts recognised by the law and more or less corresponding to the old forms of action, for example, trespass, nuisance, libel and deceit. Another view is that a person is civilly liable for damage caused by him unless he has some just cause or excuse. Perhaps there is some truth in both theories. On either view the general condition of liability for an act causing damage is probably intention or negligence, except for certain cases of "absolute" or "strict" liability, including vicarious liability. And the exposition of this branch of the law based on either view will consist almost entirely of a description of specific torts, each with its peculiar history and rules.

The practical significance of the problem is that on it may depend the answer to the question whether the judges have power to create new torts at the present day, as they certainly did in the past.[18] Striking departures from established practice are, of course, only within the province of the legislature, but the combinations of facts with which the law of civil wrongs has to deal are infinitely various. If the plaintiff cannot bring his claim under one of the established torts, must he therefore necessarily go without remedy? The well-known rule in *Rylands* v. *Fletcher*,[19] imposing strict liability on an occupier for damage caused by potentially dangerous things escaping from his land,

---

[18] But see *Winfield and Jolowicz on Tort* (12th ed.), pp. 13–15.
[19] (1866) L.R. 1 Ex. 265, 279–280; (1868) L.R. 3 H.L. 330, 340. *Cf. Read* v. *Lyons & Co., Ltd.* [1947] A.C. 156: there must be an escape.

may be said to have been invented by Blackburn J.,[20] whose
judgment in the Court of Exchequer Chamber was approved by
Lord Cairns L.C. in the House of Lords. The Court of Appeal in
1951 held that there was no common law liability for pecuniary
damage caused by negligent misstatement in the absence of
contract or fiduciary relationship[21]; but the House of Lords in
Hedley Byrne & Co., Ltd. v. *Heller & Partners Ltd.*[22] has decided
that there may be liability for such negligent misstatement if
there is some "special relationship" between the parties.
As to what may constitute a special relationship for this
purpose, this is a matter for the courts to work out in particular
cases. "The creation of a new tort is now very rare," Lord
Devlin has said,[23]

> "and takes a very long time. It's rather like the process of
> canonisation. The cause is first of all fostered by academic
> well-wishers and then promoted in the lower courts.
> Eventually, if things prosper, the tort will be beatified by
> the Court of Appeal and then, probably after a long
> interval, it will achieve full sainthood in the House of
> Lords."[24]

Minors

A minor is generally liable for his torts. Thus in *Burnard* v.
Haggis[25] a minor who hired a mare expressly for riding and not
for jumping was held liable for lending it to a friend who caused
its death by jumping.

A parent is not liable as such for the torts of his child, but
he may be liable vicariously if the child was acting in the course

[20] Although Blackburn J. professedly relied on the judgment
of Holt C.J. in *Tenant* v. *Goldwin* (1704) 2 Ld.Raym. 1089.

[21] *Candler* v. *Crane, Christmas & Co.* [1951] 2 K.B. 164 (Denning L.J., dissenting).

[22] [1964] A.C. 465. Although the defendant had expressly excluded himself from
liability in that case, the considered statements by the House of Lords can
scarcely be regarded as *obiter*: see *per* Cairns J. in *W. B. Anderson & Sons* v.
Rhodes (Liverpool) [1967] 2 All E.R. 850. See now also, *Esso Petroleum* v. *Mardon*
[1976] Q.B. 801; *Lawton* v. *BOC Transhield* [1987] 2 All E.R. 608 (negligent
reference). As to damages for misrepresentation made by another party to a
contract, see Misrepresentation Act 1967, s.2.

[23] "Who is at fault when injustice occurs?" *The Listener*, December 12, 1968, p.
779, at p. 780.

[24] *Cf.* the refusal of the courts to allow an action for purely economic loss
negligently caused: *Spartan Steel* v. *Martin* [1973] Q.B. 27; *Junior Books* v. *Veitchi*
[1983] 1 A.C. 520, but see cases at p. 313, n. 33 which restrict the scope of this
case.

[25] (1863) 14 C.B.(N.S.) 45. *Cf. Jennings* v. *Rundall* (1799) 8 T.R. 335 (attempt to
enforce indirectly a contract made by a person under age).

of employment,[26] or as a tortfeasor himself if, for example, he was personally negligent in allowing the child to handle a dangerous thing, such as an airgun.[27]

Trade Unions

A very important immunity was the exemption of trade unions from actions in tort, originally created by section 4 of the Trade Disputes Act 1906, passed in order to nullify the decision of the House of Lords in the *Taff Vale* case.[28] This protection was removed by the Industrial Relations Act 1971, which in its turn was repealed by the Trade Union and Labour Relations Act 1974. The Employment Act 1982 then abolished this regained immunity of unions, though they may rely on the same defences as an individual for certain torts committed in contemplation or furtherance of a trade dispute and the unions will only be liable if the tort was authorised by some responsible official or body and there are restrictions on the amounts recoverable from the unions, but they may be sued without limit for negligence, nuisance or breach of duty resulting in personal injury or for torts connected with property. There are also certain immunities for individuals doing acts in contemplation or furtherance of a trade dispute covered by the Act of 1974 and as limited in the case of "secondary action" by the Employment Act 1980.

It is not possible here to attempt any full account of the law of tort, so we will confine ourselves to a brief description of the more important torts, giving priority to negligence as the most important at the present day and thereafter roughly in the order in which they acquired a separate existence in something like their modern form.

3. SOME SPECIFIC TORTS

Negligence

In one sense negligence means undue indifference towards the consequences of one's act. The negligent person is one who is wholly, or unduly, careless whether the consequences in question follow or not. It is not necessary that he should be entirely thoughtless or inadvertent towards the consequences[29]:

---

[26] *Moon* v. *Towers* (1860) 8 C.B.(N.S.) 611.
[27] *Bebee* v. *Sales* (1916) 32 T.L.R. 413; *Newton* v. *Edgerley* [1959] 1 W.L.R. 1031.
[28] *Taff Vale Ry.* v. *Amalgamated Society of Railway Servants* [1901] A.C. 426 (H.L.).
[29] *Vaughan* v. *Menlove* (1837) 3 Bing.N.C. 468.

indifference is sufficient, though the habit of indifference often leads to inadvertence. It will be seen that negligence and intention are mutually exclusive states of mind.

The word "negligence" is also applied to the conduct of a negligent person, and this transferred meaning is of greater significance for lawyers because the law takes no account of carelessness, except when it is manifested in action or in omission where action was obligatory; and no liability attaches unless the negligent act (or rather the act of a negligent person) causes harm.

Negligence as a state of mind is often an ingredient in tort (*e.g.,* in trespass, nuisance and defamation), as well as in crime (*e.g.,* in manslaughter) and breach of contract. It is now generally agreed that negligence as conduct, where there is a duty of care, also emerged as a specific tort in the nineteenth century; and it was recognised as such in *Donoghue* v. *Stevenson*[30] which provides a general test for ascertaining the existence of a common law duty of care.

In that case a manufacturer sold ginger-beer in an opaque bottle to a retailer, who sold it to X, who gave it to the plaintiff. A decomposed snail, which had found its way into the bottle before it left the factory, was said to have made the plaintiff seriously ill, and she sued the manufacturer for damages. There was no contract between the manufacturer and the plaintiff, but the House of Lords held that the law imposed on the manufacturer a duty of care to the plaintiff to ensure that the bottle did not contain any harmful substance, breach of which duty entitled the plaintiff to a remedy. Lord Atkin said:

> "You must take reasonable care to avoid acts or omissions which you can reasonably foresee would be likely to injure your neighbour. Who, then, in law is my neighbour? The answer seems to be—persons who are so closely and directly affected by my act that I ought reasonably to have them in contemplation as being so affected when I am directing my mind to the acts or omissions which are called in question."

New cases may arise in which it is held that a duty of care was owed to the plaintiff, for, as Lord Macmillan said, "the categories of negligence are never closed." There are, however, some situations where the courts for reasons of policy have decided that there is no duty of care. An example is the

---

[30] [1932] A.C. 562 (H.L.).

immunity of judges and barristers.[31] There are other situations such as nervous shock,[32] economic loss[33]; negligent misrepresentation,[34] where the duty of care seems to be somewhat more restricted than in the generality of cases.

The courts are conscious that in these cases to impose the ordinary "neighbour" duty of care might "open the floodgates" of liability and, in imposing too wide a liability check desirable ventures and render insurance difficult to obtain.

A formula of Lord Wilberforce in *Anns* v. *Merton Boro. Council*[35] that the court should first ask whether there is a sufficient relationship of proximity between the parties, in which case there would be a prima facie duty of care and then ask whether there were any policy reasons for excluding the duty led to many decisions establishing new duty situations but a more cautious and restrictive approach to this has now appeared.[36]

Negligence involves not only a legal duty of care owed by the defendant to the plaintiff, but also a breach of that duty by the defendant in failing to observe the prescribed standard of care; and resulting harm to the plaintiff which is not too remote a consequence of the breach.

The standard of care expected by the common law is that of *the reasonable man in the circumstances*. It is not that of the particular person himself, which may be higher or lower,[37] nor that of the ideal man, but that of the reasonable and prudent man; and it is immaterial that the defendant thought he was acting as a reasonable man would act. The degree of care shown

[31] *Rondel* v. *Worsley* [1969] 1 A.C. 191 (H.L.); *Saif Ali* v. *Mitchell* [1980] A.C. 198; *Sirros* v. *Moore* [1975] Q.B. 115.
[32] *McLoughlin* v. *O'Brian* [1983] A.C. 410; *Attia* v. *British Gas* [1988] Q.B. 304 (loss of home). *pet* dis.H.L. [1988] 1 W.L.R. 307.
[33] See *Spartan Steel* v. *Martin* [1973] Q.B. 27; *Junior Books* v. *Veitchi* [1983] A.C. 520; *Candlewood* v. *Mitsui* [1986] A.C. 1; *Muirhead* v. *Industrial Tank Specialities* [1986] Q.B. 507; *Leigh & Sillivan* v. *Aliakmon* [1986] 1 A.C. 785. Recovery will only be allowed if there is a very close relationship of reliance between the parties or the economic loss accompanies physical harm or is incurred to prevent physical harm. See also *Simaan* v. *Pilkington* [1988] 2 W.L.R. 761.
[34] *Hedley Byrne* v. *Heller* [1964] A.C. 465 (H.L.).
[35] [1978] A.C. 728.
[36] *Peabody* v. *Parkinson* [1985] A.C. 210; *Leigh & Sillivan* v. *Aliakmon* [1986] 1 A.C. 785; *Curran* v. *Northern Ireland Co-ownership Housing Association* [1987] A.C. 718; *Clarke* v. *Bruce Lance* [1988] 1 All E.R. 364; *Jones* v. *Dept. of Employment* (1987) *The Times*, November 27; *Rowling* v. *Takaro Properties* [1988] 2 W.L.R. 418; *Business Computers* v. *Company Registrar* [1987] 3 W.L.R. 1134; *Yuen Kun Yeu* v. *A.G. for Hong Kong* [1988] A.C. 175; but see *Lawton* v. *BOC Transhield* [1987] 2 All E.R. 608 (reference for employee).
[37] *Wimpey* v. *Poole* [1984] 2 Lloyds Rep. 499.

by the reasonable and prudent man varies according to the circumstances, for it depends on the probability of harm resulting from the act in the known circumstances. The seriousness of the injury risked must also be taken into account, so that an employer would be expected to take greater care to prevent eye injury to a one-eyed employee than need be taken with regard to employees with both eyes.[38] It is that reasonable degree of care in those circumstances which forms the standard by which the defendant will be judged. But if a person holds himself out as having some special skill, *e.g.*, a surgeon, then he will be expected to show the average competence (as well as reasonable care) associated with that profession or calling.[39] The court will also take account of the utility of the defendant's activity,[40] the expense of precautions when set against the extent of the risk[41] and a defendant who follows normal and approved practice will usually, but not always, escape liability.[42]

Special damage must, however, be proved in addition to the breach of duty.

Provided there is a duty of care owed by the defendant to the plaintiff in the circumstances of the case, the criterion for establishing liability in negligence, then, is reasonable *foreseeability* that damage would probably be caused if there was a breach of that duty. The damage, in order that the defendant may be liable to compensate for it, must be capable of being legally regarded as caused by the defendant's act or omission.[43] If the

---

[38] *Paris* v. *Stepney Borough Council* [1951] A.C. 367 (H.L.). *Cf. Haley* v. *London Electricity Board* [1965] A.C. 778 (H.L.), blind persons more likely to trip over obstacle on highway than sighted persons.
[39] *Bolam* v. *Friern Hospital Management Committee* [1957] 1 W.L.R. 582. See now *Sidaway* v. *Bethlem Royal Hospital* [1985] A.C. 87; *Maynard* v. *W. Midlands Health Authority* [1984] 1 W.L.R. 634; *Gold* v. *Haringey Health Authority* [1987] 3 W.L.R. 649.
[40] *Daborn* v. *Bath Tramways* [1946] 2 All E.R. 333 (C.A.).
[41] *Latimer* v. *A.E.C.* [1953] A.C. 643.
[42] *Cavanagh* v. *Ulster Weaving* [1960] A.C. 145.
[43] The prime question asked on causation is whether the harm would have occurred "but for" the defendant's breach, *Barnett* v. *Chelsea and Kensington Hospital* [1969] 1 Q.B. 428 and in *McGhee* v. *N.C.B.* [1973] 1 W.L.R. 1 it was held to be sufficient proof of cause if the defendant had materially increased the risk of harm. This has been followed by the Court of Appeal in *Fitzgerald* v. *Lane* [1987] Q.B. 781 but was distinguished in the House of Lords in *Hotson* v. *East Berkshire* [1987] A.C. 750 and *Kay* v. *Ayrshire and Arran Health Board* [1987] 2 All E.R. 417. In *Wilsher* v. *Essex* [1988] 2 W.L.R. 557, the House of Lords held it was not enough to show that negligence might have been one of several possible causes.

above conditions are complied with, does that mean that the defendant is liable for *all* the damage so caused?

In *Re Polemis and Furness, Withy & Co.*,[44] the charterers of *SS. Thrasyvoulos* had loaded the ship with tins of petrol, and the tins leaked during the voyage so that there was a considerable quantity of petrol vapour in the hold. At one of the ports of call stevedores, in order to shift some cases of benzene, made a platform of planks. One of the planks was dropped into the hold, its fall caused a spark which ignited the petrol vapour and the ship was destroyed by fire. It was held by the Court of Appeal that the dropping of the plank constituted a breach of the duty to take care owed by the stevedores (servants of the charterers) to the owners of the vessel: it could reasonably have been foreseen that some damage to the ship would result; and so, once negligence was established, the stevedores (and through them the charterers) were liable for *all* the physical damage which in fact resulted directly from it. But in *The Wagon Mound (No. 1)*[45] a strong Judicial Committee of the Privy Council, on an appeal from New South Wales, disagreed with the decision in *Re Polemis* and declined to follow it. The defendants were charterers of an oil-burning ship, *The Wagon Mound*, which was refuelling at a wharf in Sydney Harbour. Owing to the defendants' carelessness, fuel oil was spilt on to the water and spread to the plaintiff's wharf where oxy-acetylene welding was being carried on. Floating cotton waste impregnated with the oil was ignited by hot metal falling from the welding, and the fire did serious damage to the plaintiff's wharf and equipment. It was found as a fact that some kind of damage to the plaintiff's wharf by the spillage of oil (*i.e.*, fouling of the slipways) was foreseeable by the reasonable man, but it was not foreseeable that the oil on the water would catch fire. Although there was a breach of duty and direct damage, the kind of damage caused was not foreseeable and therefore the defendants were not liable.

The Court of Appeal in *Doughty* v. *Turner Manufacturing Co., Ltd.*[46] followed *The Wagon Mound (No. 1)* and treated *Re Polemis* as being "no longer law." An important qualification to this test of foresight is the "egg-shell skull" rule. Whilst no special duty is owed to an exceptionally susceptible plaintiff unless his

---

[44] [1921] 3 K.B. 560. *Cf. Liesbosch Dredger* v. *Edison S.S.* [1933] A.C. 449 (H.L.).

[45] *Overseas Tankship (U.K.) Ltd.* v. *Morts Dock & Engineering Co. Ltd.* [1961] A.C. 388.

[46] [1964] 1 Q.B. 518. *Cf. Hughes* v. *Lord Advocate* [1963] A.C. 837; *Overseas Tankship (U.K.) Ltd.* v. *Miller Steamship Co. Pty.* (*Wagon Mound, No. 2*) [1967] 1 A.C. 617 (P.C.).

weakness is known to the defendant, if the defendant so acts
that he would be in breach of duty to a normal person but
because of the plaintiff's special physical weakness or sensitivity
the consequences are far more catastrophic than could have
been foreseen, the defendant is liable for all those consequences
to the plaintiff.[47] For remoteness the courts have used an
extended range of foreseeability so that in practice there is now
little difference from the *Polemis* test.[48] Difficult questions have
also arisen as to how far a defendant may be liable for the
subsequent conduct of a third party which the defendant may
have foreseen or facilitated. It seems he will only be liable if this
conduct is very likely or almost inevitable.[49]

Volenti non fit injuria (To a consenting person a legal wrong
does not occur) When a person consents to run the risk of injury
or harm without compensation he will be barred from recovery
under this maxim.[50] Full and free consent is required and if a
plaintiff was acting under the compulsion of a legal or moral
duty as in the case of a rescuer he will not be barred.[51]

Contributory Negligence

If A was injured by B in such circumstances that both A and B
showed some degree of carelessness, the common law either
awarded A the whole of the damages suffered, or no damages at
all, according to somewhat artificial principles of causation.[52]
The Law Reform (Contributory Negligence) Act 1945, provides
that:

> "Where any person suffers damage as the result partly of
> his own fault and partly of the fault of any other person or
> persons, a claim in respect of that damage shall not be
> defeated by reason of the fault of the person suffering the
> damage, but the damages recoverable in respect thereof
> shall be reduced to such extent as the court thinks just and

---

[47] *Smith* v. *Leech Brain & Co. Ltd.* [1962] 2 Q.B. 405 (Lord Parker C.J.); *Brice* v. *Brown* [1984] 1 All E.R. 997.

[48] *Stewart* v. *West African Terminals* [1964] 2 Lloyds Rep. 371; *Bradford* v. *Robinson Rentals* [1967] 1 W.L.R. 337.

[49] *Lamb* v. *Camden Boro. Council* [1981] Q.B. 625 (squatters); *Perl* v. *Camden Boro. Council* [1984] Q.B. 342 (burglars); *Ward* v. *Cannock Chase* [1986] Ch. 546; *King* v. *Liverpool City Council* [1986] 1 W.L.R. 890; *Smith* v. *Littlewoods* [1987] A.C. 241.

[50] *I.C.I.* v. *Shatwell* [1965] A.C. 656.

[51] *Haynes* v. *Harwood* [1935] 1 K.B. 146; *Harrison* v. *B.R.B.* [1981] 3 All E.R. 679.

[52] *Davies* v. *Mann* (1842) 10 M. & W. 546; *cf. Butterfield* v. *Forrester* (1809) 11 East 60; *McLean* v. *Bell* (1932) 147 L.T. 262.

equitable having regard to the claimant's share in the responsibility for the damage."

Thus the Act altered the legal consequences of contributory negligence and applied to them the same principle as in the Admiralty law.[53]

There is no need for a plaintiff to be in breach of a legal duty for him to be contributorily negligent. It is enough if he fails to take reasonable care for his own safety. He need not contribute to the happening of the tort; it is enough if he contributes to his damage or injury as by failing to wear a crash helmet[54] or a seat belt.[55] Action taken in the grip of an emergency or "the agony of the moment" will at most be regarded as only partially contributing to the damage.[56]

This defence may apply to some intentional torts[57] but does not apply to conversion[58] except for certain banking cases.[59] It may apply to contract.[60] A person in serious breach of the law, such as a criminal injured by a fellow-criminal, may not recover damages, being barred under the maxim *ex turpi causa non oritur actio*.[61]

Civil Liability for Breach of Statutory Duty

An action in tort for damages may be brought for a breach of statutory duty, if it appears that Parliament so intended. The duty must be owed to the plaintiff.[62] This is sometimes called "statutory negligence," and it may be equivalent to negligence if the duty is to take care not to injure.[63] Statutory duties, *e.g.* to

---

[53] Maritime Conventions Act 1911, s.1(1): "Where by the fault of two or more vessels, damage or loss is caused . . . the liability to make good the damage or loss shall be in proportion to the degree in which each vessel was in fault."
[54] *O'Connell* v. *Jackson* [1972] 1 Q.B. 270 (C.A.).
[55] *Froom* v. *Butcher* [1976] Q.B. 286.
[56] *Jones* v. *Boyce* (1816) 1 Stark. 493; *The Bywell Castle* (1879) 4 P.D. 219; *Sayers* v. *Harlow U.D.C.* [1958] 1 W.L.R. 623 (C.A.).
[57] *Barnes* v. *Nayer* (1986) *The Times* December 19.
[58] Torts (Interference with Goods) Act 1977, s.11(1).
[59] Banking Act 1979, s.47.
[60] *Forsikringsaktieselkapet Vesta* v. *Butcher* [1988] 2 All E.R. 43.
[61] *Ashton* v. *Turner* [1981] Q.B. 137; *N.C.B.* v. *England* [1954] A.C. 403; (The maxim may be translated "no action arises from an evil cause") *Saunders* v. *Edwards* [1987] 2 All E.R. 651.
[62] *Groves* v. *Lord Wimborne* [1898] 2 Q.B. 402; *Phillips* v. *Britannia Hygienic Laundry* [1923] 2 K.B. 832. *Thornton* v. *Kirklees Metropolitan Borough Council* [1979] Q.B. 626; *McCall* v. *Abelesz* [1976] Q.B. 585.
[63] *Lochgelly Iron & Coal Co.* v. *M'Mullan* [1934] A.C. 1 (H.L.); *London Passenger Transport Board* v. *Upson* [1949] A.C. 155 (H.L.).

fence dangerous machinery,[64] however, are often absolute.[65] To be actionable, the breach of duty must be shown to have caused damage to the plaintiff, and the principles of causation are generally the same as for common law negligence. The damage must also be of a type that the statute was intended to guard against.[66]

Negligence, Fault and Insurance

The law of negligence is intended to compensate casualties incident to the activities of a modern industrial society, and operates in conjunction with both State and private insurance. As society approves of many activities involving risk, *e.g.*, motor traffic, it has been felt that the resultant loss should be spread over society as a whole. This is achieved by imposing liability and obligations to insure on motorists, and on employers and others who can pass on their costs in increased prices. It has further been thought by many that the combination of fault liability and insurance is expensive, capricious and inefficient. Proof of negligence may be very difficult. Contributory negligence may be unjust in operation. In New Zealand and North American jurisdictions negligence has been replaced in whole or in part by "no fault" insurance schemes, and in 1973 a Royal Commission under the chairmanship of Lord Pearson was appointed to investigate these problems in relation to this country.[67] It reported in 1978 but effect has not been given to its limited recommendations to extend "no fault" compensation. Part I of the Consumer Protection Act 1987, passed to give effect to an E.E.C. Directive, is designed to extend strict liability to product liability. It is, however, subject to many defences including a "state of the art" defence, which permits a defendant to escape liability if in the light of available scientific and technical knowledge he might not have been expected to have discovered the defect. Hence the "no fault" element is qualified.

Trespass

Trespass is a direct and forcible injury to person, land or goods. The writ appears in the twelfth century and is the parent of most

---

[64] Factories Act 1961, s.14; Health and Safety at Work Act 1974, s.47.
[65] *John Summers* v. *Frost* [1955] A.C. 740 (H.L.).
[66] *Gorris* v. *Scott* (1874) L.R. 9 Ex. 125.
[67] See Atiyah and Cane *Accidents, Compensation and the Law* (4th ed.); "No Fault on the Roads," *Justice* (1974); Glanville Williams and B.A. Hepple, *Foundations of the Law of Tort* (2nd ed.) Royal Commission on Civil Liability and Personal Injury Cmnd. 7054; Fleming *Introduction to Torts* (2nd ed.).

other torts. Trespass is itself a wrong for which the plaintiff is entitled at least to nominal damages[68] and usually costs. If special damage is suffered it may, of course, be pleaded. There must be intention, but this means intention to do the act complained of, not necessarily intention to harm or knowledge that property belongs to another[69]; and it excludes an involuntary act as where one is pushed over the boundary of another's land. "Force" was a term of pleading which has long ceased to have any meaning other than against the wishes of the other party[70]; but "direct" is important, for if the damage was consequential (indirect) or was caused by the defendant's servant, the action (if any) would be on the case.

Trespass to land

This is a wrongful interference with the possession of land.[71] It includes an unjustified entry or remaining on land in the possession of another, or placing any object on it or throwing any object upon it, or building a projection in the air space over another's land.[72] It follows from the principles stated that no special damage need be proved, and that the action can be brought by the person in possession although he is not the owner.

Trespass to goods

The principles relating to trespass to goods (or chattels) are similar to those for trespass to land,[73] except that in modern law wrongful intention or negligence may be necessary for the former.[74] As trespass to land has to be distinguished from nuisance,[75] so trespass to goods is to be distinguished from conversion.[76]

---

[68] *Ashby* v. *White* (1703) 2 Ld.Raym. 938, 955; *Entick* v. *Carrington* (1765) 19 St.Tr. 1030, 1066.

[69] *Morriss* v. *Marsden* [1952] 1 All E.R. 925.

[70] *Rawlings* v. *Till* (1837) 3 M. & W. 28.

[71] *Smith* v. *Milles* (1786) 1 T.R. 475.

[72] *Kelsen* v. *Imperial Tobacco Co.* [1957] 2 Q.B. 334. The Civil Aviation Act 1982, provides that the flying of aircraft over another person's land at a reasonable height is not in itself trespass, but imposes strict liability on civil aviators for actual damage caused.

[73] *Fouldes* v. *Willoughby* (1841) 8 M. & W. 540, at p. 549.

[74] See *National Coal Board* v. *J. E. Evans & Co.* [1951] 2 K.B. 861. Either intention or negligence may now be necessary for all forms of trespass. For straying animals see now Animals Act 1971, s.4, which imposes a strict liability.

[75] p. 322 below.

[76] Below, p. 320.

Trespass to the Person

The least touching of a person by hand or with an instrument or by throwing something at him is a battery, though commonly called an assault.[77] An assault strictly is the putting of another in reasonable apprehension of the immediate commission of a battery by one who appears to have the power and intention to commit it.[78] Serious assault and battery would usually be prosecuted by criminal proceedings under the Offences against the Person Act 1861. In modern law, the plaintiff in an action for trespass to the person must allege and prove intention or negligence.[79] The view formerly was that, except in highway collisions, it was for the defendant to disprove them, and in *Letang* v. *Cooper*[80] a majority of the court took the view that trespass to the person must be intentional and that actions for injuries negligently inflicted come under the tort of negligence.

A form of trespass to the person which is very important in public law, though it may be committed by any private individual, is false imprisonment. It covers any deprivation of personal freedom without lawful justification or judicial order so that there is no direction in which the person is free to go, and does not necessarily involve arrest and incarceration in a building.[81] The specific remedy, apart from damages, is the writ of habeas corpus. But where the arrest is by order of a judge or magistrate as the result of a prosecution which turns out to be unsuccessful, an action will only lie against one who instituted it maliciously (*i.e.*, for an improper motive) and without reasonable and probable cause.[82] This tort of malicious prosecution was an action on the case.

Conversion

Conversion is a dealing with goods which constitutes an unjustifiable denial of the plaintiff's rights.[83] The essence of conversion is that the defendant exercised some act of dominion over the goods. When this element is not present the act may be trespass, but it cannot be conversion. Conversion overlaps

---

[77] *Pursell* v. *Horn* (1838) 8 Ad. & El. 602; *Wilson* v. *Pringle* [1987] Q.B. 237.

[78] *Read* v. *Coker* (1853) 13 C.B. 850.

[79] *Fowler* v. *Lanning* [1959] 1 Q.B. 426, *per* Diplock J.

[80] [1965] 1 Q.B. 232.

[81] *Meering* v. *Grahame-White Aviation Co.* (1920) 122 L.T. 44. Arrest without a warrant and detention at a police station are now governed by the Police and Criminal Evidence Act 1984, ss.25–46.

[82] *Abrath* v. *North Eastern Ry.* (1886) L.R. 11 App.Cas. 247.

[83] *Winfield and Jolowicz on Tort* (12th ed.), p. 79 *Howard Perry* v. *B.R.B.* [1980] 1 W.L.R. 1375.

trespass where the act is a wrongful taking out of the plaintiff's possession; but there are forms of conversion which are not trespass, for example, refusal to deliver up on demand or purporting to transfer the property to another. It is not necessary that the defendant should know he was not entitled to the goods.

In *Hollins* v. *Fowler*[84] the defendant, a cotton broker, honestly purchased from a third party, who had obtained possession by fraud, a quantity of cotton belonging to the plaintiff, and sold it to a manufacturer. The defendant's act of selling and delivering the cotton was held to be a conversion, an act inconsistent with the plaintiff's title, and it was immaterial that he did so in good faith. In *Fouldes* v. *Willoughby*,[85] decided in 1841, when it was still necessary in a personal action to mention a form of action in the writ, a plaintiff unsuccessfully sued for conversion when he might have succeeded in trespass. The defendant was the owner of a ferry, who had agreed to carry the plaintiff and his horses across a river. The plaintiff having misconducted himself, the defendant put the horses ashore to induce the plaintiff to get off. It was held that this did not amount to a denial of the plaintiff's title to the horses.

An action for conversion can be brought not only by the owner or possessor of goods, but also by one who has an immediate right to possess, such as a master in respect of goods received by his servant from a third person on his behalf before the servant has transferred them to the master. Now whether or not the plaintiff was in possession, the defendant may prove that some other person has a better title.[86]

The action is also called trover, having evolved as an action of trespass on the case by alleging a fictitious loss and finding.

The Torts (Interference with Goods) Act 1977, now gives the generic name of wrongful interference to conversion, trespass and negligent harm to goods. Mere denial of title does not of itself amount to conversion. Detinue (for wrongful detention of goods) is abolished and replaced by a new procedure.

---

[84] (1875) L.R. 7 H.L. 757.
[85] 8 M. & W. 540, p. 319.
[86] The old rules as to *jus tertii* have been abolished by the Torts (Interference with Goods) Act 1977.

Private Nuisance

As a tort, private nuisance consists of unlawful interference with a person's use or enjoyment of land, or of some right over or in connection with it.[87]

The most common ways of interfering with the use or enjoyment of land are by unreasonable noise,[88] obnoxious fumes,[89] pollution of water, overhanging trees,[90] and the unreasonable collection of queues.[91] The question whether the defendant's use of his land was reasonable in relation to his neighbours is one which involves a consideration of the time, place and all the other circumstances. Malice, in the sense of improper motive, does not turn a lawful act—such as abstracting underground water flowing under one's own land otherwise than in defined channels—into a tort even though it causes damage[92]; but malice (in this sense) on the part of the defendant in doing something—such as making a noise—which may *prima facie* be a nuisance, will defeat the defence of "live and let live"[93] normally available in such cases.[94]

The most important kind of interference with a right over land is obstruction of a right of way, whether it be a private right of way[95] or the right of members of the public to pass along a highway, in the latter case it being also the common law misdemeanour of public nuisance.[96] The interference to be actionable as a nuisance, must not be purely evanescent,[97] as there must be mutual give-and-take in the affairs of everyday life. Thus if, in the course of a game of cricket, a batsman hits the ball out of the ground and injures a passer-by in the highway, this isolated act may not constitute a nuisance, though it might,

---

[87] Winfield, *op. cit.*, p. 380; description adopted by Scott L.J. in *Read* v. *Lyons & Co., Ltd.* [1945] K.B. 216, 236; by Lord Goddard C.J. in *Howard* v. *Walker* [1947] 2 All E.R. 197; and by Evershed J. in *Newcastle-under-Lyme Corporation* v. *Wolstanton, Ltd.* [1947] Ch. 92, 107.

[88] *Soltau* v. *de Held* (1851) 2 Sim.(N.S.) 133. The Civil Aviation Act 1982 provides that the flying of aircraft over another person's land at a reasonable height is not in itself nuisance.

[89] *St. Helens Smelting Co.* v. *Tipping* (1865) 11 H.L.C. 642.

[90] *Lemmon* v. *Webb* [1895] A.C. 1.

[91] *Dwyer* v. *Mansfield* [1946] K.B. 437.

[92] *Mayor of Bradford* v. *Pickles* [1895] A.C. 587.

[93] *Bamford* v. *Turnley* (1862) 3 B. & S. 62, *per* Bramwell B. at pp. 83–89.

[94] *Hollywood Silver Fox Farm Ltd.* v. *Emmett* [1936] 2 K.B. 468; *Christie* v. *Davey* [1893] 1 Ch. 316.

[95] *Thorpe* v. *Brumfitt* (1873) L.R. 8 Ch. 650.

[96] *Winterbottom* v. *Lord Derby* (1867) L.R. 2 Ex. 316; *Fabbri* v. *Morris* (1947) 63 T.L.R. 34.

[97] *Benjamin* v. *Storr* (1874) L.R. 9 C.P. 400.

according to the facts, show negligence on the part of the managers of the ground.[98] In the Court of Appeal the view was expressed that in a case of this type "causing or permitting a state of affairs to *exist*" from which danger might result, might constitute a nuisance. An occupier may now be liable in nuisance for an operation of natural forces, *e.g.* a landslide on his land, which interferes with his neighbour's land.[99]

The action of nuisance was developed from the early fifteenth century as an action on the case, so that special damage would generally have to be proved. The action can be brought by the occupier of land,[1] or by a person entitled to future possession if the land is permanently injured,[2] or by a member of the public suffering special damage peculiar to himself from obstruction of the highway.[3] The person liable for a private nuisance is generally the occupier of the land from which the nuisance proceeds not the owner as such.[4]

The specific remedies for private nuisance, apart from damages, are abatement (*i.e.*, removal of nuisance by the injured party[5]) and injunction. An occupier of premises who is aggrieved by noise amounting to a nuisance may now by statute bring summary proceedings in a magistrates' court against the person responsible, and the court may order an abatement of the nuisance and/or prohibit a recurrence of it.[6]

Defamation[7]

Winfield defines defamation[8] as "the publication of a statement which reflects on a person's reputation and tends to lower him

---

[98] *Bolton* v. *Stone* [1951] A.C. 850. Point reserved at p. 868. *Cf. Miller* v. *Jackson* [1977] Q.B. 966.

[99] *Leakey* v. *National Trust* [1980] Q.B. 485. But see *Home Brewery Co.* v. *William Davis* [1987] 2 W.L.R. 117 (no liability for outflow of natural unchannelled water and a neighbour must not act unreasonably in diverting the flow).

[1] *Inchbald* v. *Robinson* (1869) L.R. 4 Ch. 388.

[2] *Jesser* v. *Gifford* (1767) 4 Burr. 2141.

[3] *Rose* v. *Miles* (1815) 4 M. & S. 101. It was held in *Overseas Tankship (U.K.) Ltd.* v. *Miller Steamship Co. Pty. Ltd.* (*Wagon Mound, No.* 2) [1967] 1 A.C. 617 (P.C.) that where the act complained of constituted a public nuisance, the plaintiff is entitled to damages only if the damage was reasonably foreseeable. There are *dicta* to the effect that the principle of foreseeability is also applicable to private nuisance.

[4] *Russell* v. *Shenton* (1842) 3 Q.B. 449.

[5] *Bradburn* v. *Lindsay* [1983] 2 All E.R. 408.

[6] Control of Pollution Act 1974, s.59, replacing Noise Abatement Act 1960.

[7] Very far-reaching changes in the law of defamation, including the abolition of the distinction between libel and slander, were proposed in the *Report of the Committee on Defamation* (1975) Cmnd. 5909 (Faulks Committee).

[8] Winfield, *op. cit.*, p. 293.

in the estimation of right-thinking members of society generally; or which tends to make them shun or avoid him." The first part of this definition was suggested by Lord Atkin in *Sim* v. *Stretch*,[9] where he considered that the conventional phrase "exposing the plaintiff to hatred, contempt or ridicule" was too narrow. The latter part of the definition is meant to cover such cases as *Youssoupoff* v. *Metro-Goldwyn-Mayer Pictures Ltd.*,[10] where the imputation was that the female plaintiff had been ravished by Rasputin, for ravishment would not involve moral turpitude on the plaintiff's part.

Libel and Slander

Defamation may take either of two forms, (a) libel (permanent form, especially writing), and (b) slander (transitory form, especially spoken words).

There are two main consequences of this distinction. First, libel is actionable *per se*, that is, without proof of any damage; while slander—with several important exceptions—requires proof of special damage. The historical reason is that civil libel, though it was an action on the case, was developed in the King's Bench from the seventeenth century in close association with criminal libel, which that court had taken over from the defunct Star Chamber, and the gist of the latter offence was not damage to the plaintiff but the tendency to cause a breach of the peace. Slander, on the other hand, acquired the characteristic common to actions on the case of requiring special damage when the King's Bench took it over from the Ecclesiastical Courts by granting an action on the case.[11]

Secondly, libel which tends to cause a breach of the peace may also be a criminal offence, while slander as such is only a tort.[12] The historical reason is that the Court of Star Chamber was concerned with defamation of officers of State under the Statutes *De Scandalis Magnatum* 1275–1559. Offences of this nature were dealt with criminally and called "libel," whether the words were written or spoken; but the Star Chamber heard very few cases of spoken words, as it was concerned almost entirely with the danger to public order let loose by the new art of printing. It was only when the King's Bench took over defamation from the Star Chamber in the seventeenth century

---

[9] [1936] 2 All E.R. 1237.

[10] (1934) 50 T.L.R. 581.

[11] *Davis* v. *Gardiner* (1593) 4 Co.Rep. 16b.

[12] But if a slanderous statement is seditious or blasphemous, it may be prosecuted as seditious words or blasphemy.

that the distinction between libel and slander came to be, not that between criminal and civil proceedings, but between written and spoken words.

Civil and Criminal Libel

There are two main differences between civil and criminal defamation. First, the truth of a defamatory statement is a complete defence to a civil action, but it is not by itself a defence to a criminal prosecution. This is because the gist of the former is injury to a person's reputation, which he cannot sustain if he does not deserve his reputation; while the gist of the latter is a tendency to cause a breach of the peace. That truth is no defence to a criminal prosecution was laid down by the Star Chamber in *Case de Libellis Famosis*,[13] where an "infamous libel in verse" was published of the former Archbishop of Canterbury (Bancroft) and the then Archbishop, by which they were "traduced and scandalised." The Libel Act 1843 ("Lord Campbell's Act"), however, allows the defence of justification in criminal libel if it is also proved that publication was for the public benefit.[14] Secondly, publication (*i.e.*, any communication) to a third person (other than the defendant's spouse) is necessary for a civil action, but not for a criminal prosecution. This is because a person cannot suffer damage if the defamatory statement is not communicated to a third person, but communication to the person defamed may cause a breach of the peace.

Defences

It is not possible here to describe in any detail the various defences to an action for defamation. The defences are "justification" (*i.e.*, that the statement was true in substance and in fact),[15] "fair comment" on a matter of public interest, and "privilege" (*i.e.*, that the statement was made on a privileged occasion). Privilege, according to the circumstances, is either absolute or qualified, the latter defence being rebutted by malice normally in the sense of personal spite or ill-will. These defences are designed to strike a balance between the claims of free speech and the plaintiff's interest in the integrity of his

[13] (1605) 5 Co.Rep. 125.

[14] This does not apply to *seditious* libel.

[15] This defence has been affected by the Rehabilitation of Offenders Act 1974, which provides that after the lapse of specified periods offences will be regarded as "spent" and legally non-existent. A defendant who discloses the "spent" offences of the plaintiff can only rely on justification if the publication was without malice.

reputation. This is clearly seen in the example of the absolute privilege of persons taking part in judicial proceedings,[16] and in the fact that fair comment is linked to matters of public interest. At common law it was immaterial that the defendant did not intend to defame the plaintiff or even that he was ignorant of the plaintiff's existence, so long as he intended to publish the statement and some persons reasonably thought that it referred to the plaintiff.[17]

Defamation Act 1952

Important reforms were introduced by the Defamation Act 1952.[18] Where B has published a defamatory statement of A, it is now in certain circumstances a defence to publish a correction and apology, if the statement was made without intent to defame A and without negligence.[19] In an action for a slander (*sic*) calculated to disparage the plaintiff in any office, profession or business, it is no longer necessary to allege and prove special damage, whereas at common law it was necessary to do so unless the words were spoken of the plaintiff *in the way of* his calling.[20] The occasions of qualified privilege enjoyed by newspapers, already largely statutory, are extended. Broadcasts by radio are to be treated as publication in permanent form, so that if defamatory they will constitute libel, and thus be actionable without proof of special damage.

Deceit or Fraud

The common law definition of deceit or fraud is a false representation of fact made by the defendant with knowledge of its falsity, or "recklessly" not caring whether it be true or false,[21] with intention that it should be acted upon by the plaintiff[22] and actually inducing him to act upon it[23] so that he thereby suffers damage. Fraud involves a statement and not merely non-disclosure, save in exceptional cases, as where a half-truth may

---

[16] *Munster* v. *Lamb* (1883) 11 Q.B.D. 588.
[17] *Hulton* v. *Jones* [1910] A.C. 20; *Newstead* v. *London Express Newspaper, Ltd.* [1940] 1 K.B. 377. A non-negligent distributor, e.g. newsagent, would have a defence. *Emmens* v. *Pottle* (1885) 16 Q.B.D. 354.
[18] Based on report of Lord Chancellor's Committee on Law of Defamation: (1948) Cmd. 7536.
[19] *Cf. Hulton* v. *Jones*; *Newstead* v. *London Express Newspaper, Ltd.*, above.
[20] *Jones* v. *Jones* [1916] 2 A.C. 481; *Hopwood* v. *Muirson* [1945] K.B. 313.
[21] *Derry* v. *Peek* (1889) 14 App.Cas. 337.
[22] *Langridge* v. *Levy* (1837) 2 M. & W. 519.
[23] *Horsfall* v. *Thomas* (1862) 1 H. & C. 90.

mislead; a statement of fact and not merely of opinion[24]: and the deceit lies in knowledge of its untruth as opposed to belief in its truth, or reckless disregard for its truth as opposed to merely careless ignorance.[25] The plaintiff must have suffered damage in acting on the statement, for the action of deceit was an action on the case, though probably not derived from trespass.

The action of deceit was developed from the fourteenth century in connection with contracts of sale, and was not used independently of a contract between the parties until the end of the eighteenth century.[26] It was established in the nineteenth century that knowledge of the untruth of the statement is not necessary to make the defendant liable; while on the other hand, *Derry* v. *Peek*[27] finally settled the common law rule that belief in its truth cannot be fraud even though the defendant had no reasonable grounds for his belief,[28] though both case law and statute have now established wide liability for negligent misrepresentation.

4. VICARIOUS LIABILITY IN TORT

A person is always liable for torts committed by himself. If he is in employment, his employer may also be liable vicariously. Liability is said to be "vicarious" when one person is liable for what someone else has done. For the purpose of vicarious liability in tort a distinction is drawn between servants and other kinds of agents, who are often called independent contractors. The legal distinction turns on whether the employer retains the control and the direction of the method as well as of the result (master and servant), or whether he merely requires a certain result while leaving it to employee's discretion within that limit to determine the appropriate means (employer and independent contractor).[29] Thus a man employed as a chauffeur is the servant of his employer, while a taxi-driver is the independent contractor of his passenger: his gardener is the householder's servant, but the builder who mends his roof is an independent contractor; or, as Denning L.J. put it, "under a contract of

[24] Cf. *Anderson* v. *Pacific Fire & Marine Insurance Co.* (1872) L.R. 7 C.P. 65, 69.
[25] *Derry* v. *Peek*, above.
[26] *Pasley* v. *Freeman* (1789) 3 T.R. 51.
[27] (1889) 14 App.Cas. 337.
[28] Cf. Companies Act 1985, ss.67–69 (substantially reproducing Directors Liability Act 1890, passed in consequence of *Derry* v. *Peek*); Misrepresentation Act 1967; *Hedley Byrne & Co. Ltd.* v. *Heller & Partners Ltd.* [1964] A.C. 465; below, p. 345.
[29] *Mersey Docks and Harbour Board* v. *Coggins & Griffiths, Ltd.* [1947] A.C. 1.

service, a man is employed as part of the business, and his work is done as an integral part of the business; whereas, under a contract for services, his work, although done for the business, is not integrated into it but is only accessory to it."[30]

Torts Committed by Independent Contractors

If P (the principal) expressly or impliedly *authorised* A (an independent contractor) to commit a tort which injures X, then P and A are jointly and severally liable to X. By the phrase "commission of a tort" we include not merely an act which is tortious in its nature, such as libel, but the commission of a lawful act negligently or fraudulently or so as to cause a nuisance. But if, as would usually be the case, P did not authorise the commission of the tort, and was not negligent in employing A as his contractor for the kind of work in hand, then A only and not P is liable.[31]

There is an apparent exception where a person is under a duty by statute or at common law either to do an act himself or to see that it is done properly. In such cases the principal may be liable, not indeed vicariously, but because he is himself in default of his duty, *e.g.*, to ensure that a building adjoining the highway does not become a nuisance,[32] or to ensure that operations involving fire do not cause a conflagration.[33]

Torts Committed by Servants

If S (a servant) commits a tort *in the course of his employment* with M (the master), then M and S are jointly and severally liable to X, the injured party. It is immaterial that M did not authorise the commission of the tort: if he employs S to do a certain kind of work, he is liable if it is done negligently or so as to cause a nuisance or even fraudulently. Indeed it is immaterial that M may have expressly forbidden S to do the act in question, if what was done was done in the course of his employment, though such prohibition may be relevant in determining what was the scope of his employment. M is not necessarily liable for acts done by S *at the time when* he is engaged on M's business; the phrase "in the course of his

---

[30] Stevenson, Jordan & Harrison, Ltd. v. Macdonald and Evans [1952] 1 T.L.R. 101, 111.
[31] Salsbury v. Woodland [1970] 1 Q.B. 324 (C.A.).
[32] Tarry v. Ashton (1876) 1 Q.B.D. 314.
[33] The Pass of Ballater [1942] P. 112, 117.

employment" does not refer to time, but means pursuant or incidental to his employment.[34]

These principles may be illustrated by the following cases. A firm of solicitors was held liable for the fraud of their managing clerk committed in the course of conveyancing work undertaken for one of the firm's clients, although the fraud was committed for the clerk's own benefit and did not benefit the firm, because the firm had held out the clerk as a person who might do that kind of work and whom the client could trust.[35] And an omnibus company was held liable where one of its drivers, in racing another omnibus against the express instructions of the company, caused the rival omnibus to overturn.[36] On the other hand, the company was not liable where one of its conductors negligently drove an omnibus into the plaintiff, for driving was outside the scope of his employment.[37] Where the master is not liable, of course, the servant remains so.[38]

Where M and S (or P and A) are jointly and severally liable to X, they are called joint tortfeasors. In such cases X may sue M separately for the full amount of the damage, *or* he may sue S separately for the full amount of the damage, *or* he may sue M and S jointly for the aggregate amount of damage and recover the full sum from either. X will usually wish to sue M if he can, because M is more likely than S to be able to satisfy judgment. It is generally wise to sue them jointly, in case there is doubt whether S was M's servant, or whether the tort was committed in the course of his employment. Since the Law Reform (Married Women and Tortfeasors) Act 1935, an unsatisfied judgment against either M or S no longer bars an action by X against the other.

M had a common law right under the contract of employment to be indemnified by S for the damages he had to pay to an injured party under his vicarious liability for S's tort.[39] Under the Law Reform (Married Women and Tortfeasors) Act 1935, however, the court could order any contribution or indemnity between M and S as might be found by the court to be just and

---

[34] See *Poland* v. *Parr* [1972] 1 K.B. 236; *Staton* v. *N.C.B.* [1957] 1 W.L.R 893 (master may even be liable for acts outside working hours). *Heasmans* v. *Clarity Cleaning Co.* (1987) *The Times* January 23, (misuse of telephone by cleaner not in course of employment).

[35] *Lloyd* v. *Grace, Smith and Co.* [1912] A.C. 716. See also, *Morris* v. *Martin* [1966] 1 Q.B. 716.

[36] *Limpus* v. *London General Omnibus Co.* (1862) 1 H. & C. 526. See also, *Rose* v. *Plenty* [1976] 1 W.L.R. 141; *Stone* v. *Taffe* [1974] 1 W.L.R. 1575.

[37] *Beard* v. *London General Omnibus Co.*, [1900] 2 Q.B. 530.

[38] *Stephens* v. *Elwall* (1815) 4 M. & S. 259.

[39] *Semtex* v. *Gladstone* [1954] 1 W.L.R. 945.

equitable having regard to the extent of their responsibility for the damage[40] and this continues under the Civil Liability (Contribution) Act 1978. Where S has been solely to blame, the effect of the statute is the same as the common law.[41]

The reason why the law imposes vicarious liability in tort has been variously explained on the grounds of extension of the master's personality, implied undertaking to accept responsibility, presumed authorisation of the wrong, negligence in employing a careless or dishonest servant, or the benefit derived by the master from his servant's activities. The rule seems to have its origin in the semi-servile status of servants in early times, and it has been retained for reasons of public policy.[42] In any event, the burden on the master at the present day is mitigated by the fact that he can cover his risk by insurance. He can then in effect distribute the loss among the public by raising his prices to cover the premiums.

---

[40] *Jones* v. *Manchester Corporation* [1952] 2 Q.B. 852.
[41] *Lister* v. *Romford Ice and Cold Storage Co.* [1957] A.C. 555: insurance companies made a "gentleman's agreement" not to enforce a master's indemnity against a servant tortfeasor. See also *Morris* v. *Ford Motor Co. Ltd.* [1973] Q.B. 792 holding that the master's right to an indemnity from the servant is excluded in an industrial setting.
[42] *Per* Holt C.J. in *Hern* v. *Nichols* (1700) 1 Salk. 289; *I.C.I. Ltd.* v. *Shatwell* [1965] A.C. 656, 686 (H.L.).

CHAPTER 19

The Law of Contract

1. THE NATURE OF A CONTRACT

Definition

A contract is *an agreement enforceable by law.* "Enforceable" does not necessarily—or, indeed, usually—mean enforceable specifically according to its terms; the definition is satisfied if damages will be awarded for breach of the contractual duty. The law is primarily concerned, of course, with the external or objective manifestations of agreement in writing, words or conduct, and not with the undisclosed mental states of the parties at the time of contracting.[1]

Intention to create legal relations

There must be an intention to create a legal obligation. Even a business engagement may contain an express clause that it is not entered into as a formal or legal arrangement.[2] But, of course, a party to what is in law a contract cannot evade his obligations by saying that he never intended to fulfil them.[3]

---

[1] *Tamplin* v. *James* (1880) 15 Ch.D. 215; *Smith* v. *Hughes* (1871) L.R. 6 Q.B. 597, 607.

[2] *Rose and Frank Co.* v. *J.R. Crompton & Bros., Ltd.* [1925] A.C. 445; *Jones* v. *Vernon's Pools, Ltd.* [1938] 2 All E.R. 626. In a commercial agreement the presumption is that there is intent to create legal relations, *Kleinwort Benson* v. *Malaysian Mining* [1988] 1 All E.R. 714 (letter of comfort).

[3] *Carlill* v. *Carbolic Smoke Ball Co.* [1893] 1 Q.B. 256.

Whether a social or domestic arrangement is intended to create legal relations is a question of interpretation: thus a paying boarder has been held entitled to share with his landlady a prize won in a newspaper competition in which they took part together[4]; but a wife failed in her claim to enforce a promise by her husband to pay her a certain monthly sum as maintenance while he was stationed abroad.[5]

Offer and Acceptance

It is commonly said that an agreement consists of an offer and an acceptance. Where these elements are not actually present, the agreement may usually be analysed into a notional offer and acceptance in order to determine the time when, and the place where, the contract came into existence; but this analysis is necessarily artificial. It is not always easy, for example, to distinguish between an offer and a mere invitation to treat. Where the defendants advertised for the tenders for the sale of stock, it was held that the advertisement for tenders was an invitation to negotiate, that the defendants were not bound to accept the highest or indeed any tender, but that the tenders themselves were offers which the defendants were free to accept or not as they pleased.[6] A shopkeeper who displays an article in the window or on the counter has been held to be merely inviting offers to buy,[7] but it is probable that where he places goods in an automatic machine outside his shop this would be construed as an offer to sell.[8] Difficulty also arises where acceptance of an offer is communicated by post. The rule is that, if the post is expressly or impliedly a proper means of communicating acceptance, the acceptance of the offer, and therefore the formation of the contract, is complete as soon as the letter is posted. Where an allotment letter (*i.e.*, the acceptance of an offer to buy shares) was lost in the post and never reached the applicant (the offeror), he was nevertheless held liable as a shareholder when the company went into liquidation three years later.[9]

---

[4] *Simpkins* v. *Pays* [1955] 1 W.L.R. 975.
[5] *Balfour* v. *Balfour* [1919] 2 K.B. 571.
[6] *Spencer* v. *Harding* (1870) L.R. 5 C.P. 561.
[7] *Pharmaceutical Society of Great Britain* v. *Boots Cash Chemists (Southern) Ltd.* [1953] 1 Q.B. 401.
[8] *Thornton* v. *Shoe Lane Parking Ltd.* [1971] 2 Q.B. 163.
[9] *Household Fire Insurance Co.* v. *Grant* (1879) 4 Ex.D. 216.

Mistake

The question of the effect of mistake in the law of contract is extremely difficult, and it is only possible here to state a few broad generalisations. Some kinds of mistake at common law will make a contract "void" *ab initio, i.e.,* there is no contract. (1) A and B are in agreement, but they are mutually mistaken as to the existence of some fact or as to an assumption that goes to the root of the contract (*Bell* v. *Lever Bros.*[10]); the mistake may be as to the existence of the subject-matter, such as cargo (*Couturier* v. *Hastie*[11]), or as to title or the quality of a thing. (2) A and B appear to be in agreement, but: (a) the offer and acceptance do not really coincide: *Raffles* v. *Wichelhaus*[12] (sale of cargo "to arrive *ex Peerless* from Bombay": two ships of that name due to sail from Bombay in different months, A meant one ship and B the other); (b) there is a mistake by one party as to the identity of the other contracting party which is known or ought to be known to that other: *Boulton* v. *Jones*[13] (A orders goods from C, with whom he is accustomed to deal and against whom he is entitled to a set-off; B supplies the goods without telling A that he has taken over C's business; held, no contract between A and B): (c) B mistakes A's promise, and A knows of the mistake: *Smith* v. *Hughes*[14] (A offered to sell oats; B thought A's offer was to sell *old* oats; A did not intend to sell old oats, but he knew that B thought he did; the oats were in fact new and useless for B's purpose; the contract was held void); (d) one party who is mistaken to the knowledge of the other as to the fundamental character of a document, which he is not careless in signing, may plead *non est factum,*[15] (in which case the document is void).

Equity may grant relief in certain cases of mistake where the common law would not intervene. Thus the court may grant rectification of a deed or written contract where, owing to mutual mistake, there is a discrepancy between the original agreement and the written instrument, as where a conveyance includes more property than the contract of sale[16]; and in certain cases the court may grant rescission of the contract, as in unilateral mistake where the conduct of the other party

[10] [1932] A.C. 161 (H.L.); *Associated Japanese* v. *Crédit du Nord* [1988] N.L.J. 109.
[11] (1856) 5 H.L.C. 673 (H.L.).
[12] (1864) 2 H. & C. 906.
[13] (1857) 2 H. & N. 564; *Cundy* v. *Lindsay* (1878) 3 App.Cas. 459 (H.L.). See also *Lewis* v. *Averay* [1972] 1 Q.B. 198.
[14] (1871) L.R. 6 Q.B. 597 (there was a conflict of evidence as to whether A said "old oats"); *Hartog* v. *Colin & Shields* [1939] 3 All E.R. 566.
[15] *Saunders* v. *Anglia Building Society* [1971] A.C. 1004 (H.L.).
[16] *Craddock Bros.* v. *Hunt* [1923] 2 Ch. 136.

is unconscionable,[17] or in common mistake as to the parties' respective rights.[18]

Privity of Contract

A contract in itself creates rights *in personam* enforceable only against the òther party or parties,[19] though there is also a right *in rem* that other persons should not interfere unjustifiably with the performance of the contract, breach of which right *in rem* is a tort.[20] The common law doctrine of "privity of contract" means that if A and X contract that X shall do something for M, M acquires no rights under the contract.[21] In equity, however, A may be able to obtain specific performance against X,[22] and M might himself be able to enforce the promise if it could be construed as a trust.[23]

Contract and Conveyance

A contract must be distinguished from a conveyance, which creates or transfers immediate rights *in rem*; and from the creation of a trust, which is enforceable in Equity by any beneficiary. The distinction can be seen in private international law, where a contract to convey immovables may be governed by a different system of law from the conveyance itself. Again, the Law of Property Act 1925, requires that a conveyance of land shall be by deed, while a contract to convey land need only be evidenced by writing. The same transaction, however, may be both a contract and a conveyance, and it may also create a trust. Thus a "sale" of goods in English law is often at the same time a contract to sell and a transfer of the property to the buyer; a lease, which vests a term of years in the lessee, invariably contains contractual promises or "covenants" relating to rent, repairs and so on; a contract to sell land might have the effect in Equity of giving the purchaser proprietary rights enforceable against everyone except a bona fide purchaser of the legal estate

---

[17] *Torrance* v. *Bolton* (1872) L.R. 8 Ch.App. 118.

[18] *Solle* v. *Butcher* [1950] 1 K.B. 671; *Grist* v. *Bailey* [1967] Ch. 532; *Magee* v. *Pennine Insurance* [1969] 2 Q.B. 507.

[19] *Dunlop Pneumatic Tyre Co.* v. *Selfridge & Co.* [1915] A.C. 847 (H.L.).

[20] *Lumley* v. *Gye* (1853) 2 E. & B. 216.

[21] *Dunlop Pneumatic Tyre Co.* v. *Selfridge & Co.*, above, p. 337. *Beswick* v. *Beswick* [1968] A.C. 58 (H.L.). *Cf.* agency for undisclosed principal, below, p. 351.

[22] *Beswick* v. *Beswick*, above.

[23] *Les Affréteurs Réunis Société Anonyme* v. *Leopold Walford (London) Ltd.* [1919] A.C. 801 (H.L.). And see Road Traffic Act 1972, third party motor insurance.

for value and without notice[24]; and A may convey property to B who promises A to hold it in trust for X.

Contracts under Seal

When a person signs, seals and delivers a document it is called a deed, specialty or covenant. Any promise included in a deed, for example, a promise to give property to charity, is binding even in the absence of consideration, for the action of covenant lay on such a promise because of the solemnity of the form long before the doctrine of consideration[25] was evolved for informal promises. "Whatever truth there may have been in this view in medieval times," Lord Goddard has said,[26] "a seal nowadays is very much in the nature of a legal fiction. The seal is no longer a wax impression of a man's crest or coat of arms; it is usually no more than an adhesive wafer attached by the law stationer when the document is engrossed. It is the party's signature, and not his seal, which in fact authenticates the document." In all but theory we have reverted to the practice of our Anglo-Saxon ancestors, who signed their documents; sealing was introduced by the Normans.

The use of the common seal was required by common law to authenticate the contracts of a corporation, but the rule has been abrogated by statute. Most of the so-called "contracts" which are required by statute to be under seal are really grants or conveyances—for example, a lease for more than three years,[27] and the transfer of a British ship or of any share therein.[28]

Simple Contracts

Every contract which is *not under seal* is called a simple or parol contract, and requires "consideration."[29] The terms "simple" and "parol" here are synonymous. "Simple" does not mean unconditional, and "parol" does not mean oral. The terminology dates from the time when the only enforceable contract was the contract under seal, or specialty as it was called, with which was contrasted the simple contract. There was little object in

---

[24] But a contract to sell land is registrable as an estate contract under the Land Charges Act 1972; if it is registered the purchaser is protected as registration constitutes actual notice; if it is not registered it is void against a third party who purchases the legal estate for money or money's worth.

[25] Below, pp. 338–340.

[26] Sixth Interim Report of Law Revision Committee (1937), Cmd. 5449, p. 35.

[27] Law of Property Act 1925.

[28] Merchant Shipping Act 1894.

[29] Below, pp. 338–340.

taking quill and parchment to write laborious promises which would not be enforced, and so *most* of the promises made which were not binding at law—though they might be enforced in the Church courts—were oral ("parol").

There is said to be a written contract where the parties agree to put the contract into writing and sign it, thereby showing their intention to be bound by the terms as expressed in the instrument. Oral evidence is not normally admissible by one party to contradict or vary its terms, though it may be orally rescinded by both parties.[30] It is not always easy to tell whether the parties intended that no legal obligation should be created until a contract in writing should be drawn up and signed ("written contract"); or whether they intended to be bound by an oral agreement, the subsequent writing being merely for a permanent record ("contract evidenced by writing"). In either event, of course, it may be proved—by oral evidence—that the contract is void owing to mistake[31] or illegality,[32] or voidable owing to fraud.[33]

Certain contracts are required by statute to be in writing in order that they may have legal effect, for example, bills of exchange and promissory notes,[34] and policies of marine insurance.[35]

2. GENERAL PRINCIPLES OF CONTRACTUAL LIABILITY

General Theory

It is for each system of law to decide for itself the conditions under which it will clothe an agreement with a legal obligation. No legal system enforces all agreements which are intended to be binding, for at least it will stop short at those which contemplate an illegal purpose. Beyond this there was no general theory of contract in classical Roman law. An agreement was not enforceable unless there was some legal reason (*causa*) why it should be, and that in practice meant unless it fell within one of the recognised classes of enforceable agreements. These were classified into those created by formal words, formal writing, transfer of a thing for one of a limited number of purposes, and mere agreement with one of a limited number of

[30] *Jacobs* v. *Batavia and General Plantations Trust* [1924] 1 Ch. 287, 295; 2 Ch. 329.
[31] Above, pp. 333–334.
[32] *Benyon* v. *Nettlefold* (1850) 3 Mac. & G. 94.
[33] *Kennedy* v. *Panama Royal Mail Co.* (1867) L.R. 2 Q.B. 580.
[34] Bills of Exchange Act 1882.
[35] Marine Insurance Act 1906.

purposes. An agreement which did not fall into any of the recognised classes was *nudum pactum*; there was no *causa* and therefore no legal obligation. Although the classes of enforceable agreements in Roman law were eventually very numerous, and almost the only kind of agreement which remained unenforceable was one for personal services unperformed on both sides, we can scarcely say that a general theory of contract was attained even in the time of Justinian.

In English law there is such a general theory. An agreement made with intention to create a legal obligation and with the presence of "consideration" is a contract, and a contract is enforceable unless there is some legal reason (such as illegality or mistake) why it should not be. Consideration is an element in an agreement essential to its existence as a contract, and therefore it is not the same as the Roman *causa*, which in effect meant enforceability. No special form is necessary unless it is required in particular cases by statute, or it is desired to bind oneself by a gratuitous promise. Certain kinds of contracts, particularly mercantile contracts, have special rules which are mostly statutory, but the general common law principles are the same for all kinds of contracts. We do not study the rudiments of this branch of English law under the headings of separate contracts, as we do with the Roman law of obligations or the English law of torts, but under topics of general application such as consideration, mistake, fraud and illegality of purpose.

Historical Development

The general remedy which was developed from the fourteenth to the seventeenth centuries for enforcing informal undertakings was the action of *assumpsit*, which was a form of trespass on the case, sometimes containing also an element of deceit. In early medieval times the only actions of a contractual nature were those begun by writ of debt, detinue, account or covenant. Debt lay only for the recovery of a specific sum of money, as where A had sold and delivered a horse to B and had not yet been paid; detinue lay only for the recovery of a specific chattel, and would be available against a carrier or borrower, or against a seller who had been paid for the chattel but had not yet delivered it; account lay only between persons in a special relationship with one another, as between the lord of a manor and his bailiff; while no action lay in covenant unless the plaintiff could produce a deed under the defendant's seal. These remedies were found inadequate, for they did not cover either the mere failure to fulfil a promise or an agreement consisting of mutual promises. It was to the law of tort that lawyers looked to fill in this gap in the legal system, and this development was summed up in 1603 in *Slade's Case*.[36] Thereafter *assumpsit*, which was not abolished as a form of action until the nineteenth century, was regarded as contractual and not tortious in nature, and damages for breach of contract came to be assessed no longer as if they were compensation for damage incurred by trespass or deceit but as compensation for failure to obtain what had been promised. It was then left to the eighteenth and early nineteenth centuries to refine the doctrine of consideration as the test whether an agreement should be recognised as a contract and so enforced.

Doctrine of Consideration[37]

The nature of the "consideration" that English law makes an essential element for an enforceable agreement was not defined in its present form until the middle of the nineteenth century. Since then the cases on this topic have turned rather on the question whether the particular facts amount to consideration. There is some difference of opinion among legal historians concerning the origin of the doctrine, which need not trouble us here. Consideration in some form seems always to have been necessary in an action of *assumpsit*, though it began by being a precedent debt or transfer; and as a contractual measure of damages displaced a tortious measure of damages, so a contemporaneous act or promise displaced a precedent debt or grant.

Consideration may be defined as *an act (including a forbearance or promise) done by the promisee in exchange for the contemporaneous promise which he seeks to enforce.* It may be the performance of any act or any forbearance from acting or any promise to act, so that the promisee is in a different position in reliance on the promise of the other party from that in which he would be if the promise had not been made. The "promisee" may be either party, for he is the person to whom the promise was made which it is sought to enforce. In more general words, consideration may be described as the price for which the promise of the other party is

---

[36] 4 Co.Rep. 92b.

[37] Lord Mansfield, a Scotsman, tried to establish the principle that consideration, a peculiarly English concept, was alternative to writing (*Pillans* v. *Van Mierop* (1765) 3 Burr. 1663), but he was overruled by the House of Lords in *Rann* v. *Hughes* ((1778) 4 Bro.P.C. 27). The doctrine of consideration has long been the object of criticism, notably by the Law Revision Committee in (1937) Cmd. 5449.

bought.[38] Some of the most frequent examples of consideration
are the promise to pay, or the payment of, money: the promise
to perform, or the performance of, personal services: the
promise to transfer, or the transfer of, the ownership or
possession of land or goods: giving permission to enter land or
to do something with respect to goods: promising not to enter
land or not to do something with respect to goods: and
promising not to work for anyone else or not to buy goods from
anyone else.

The promise to perform, or the performance of, an act which
the promisee was already legally bound to do—at least if it was a
public duty[39] or a contractual duty owed to the promisor[40]—is
no consideration, for the promisee has not thereby suffered
what the law calls a "detriment" in respect of the promise he is
seeking to enforce. Further, an act done or a promise given by
the promisee previously to the making of the promise sought to
be enforced ("past consideration") is no consideration, for it was
not done in exchange for that promise.[41]

Apart from these principles, the most important characteristic
of consideration is that the law is concerned only with its
existence (reality) and not with its value. A party is free to place
his own value on the services rendered by another. It is
sometimes said that consideration must be "valuable." The
courts do not recognise as consideration a promise to pay a
smaller sum in full settlement of a larger sum already due; with
the result that a debtor, whose creditor agrees to accept £45 in
full settlement of a debt of £50, cannot hold the creditor to that
promise because the debtor has not furnished consideration.[42]
On the other hand it would be good consideration if the creditor
agreed to accept in full settlement the smaller sum a day
before it was due or at a different place, or if he accepted
the smaller sum together with something other than money,
e.g., "a horse, or a canary, or a tomtit."[43] This is another
way of saying that consideration must be *real.* But the law
takes no account of its *adequacy,* so that a promise to pay a
rent of £1 a year has been held good consideration for an
agreement to let a house.[44]

[38] *Dunlop Pneumatic Tyre Co.* v. *Selfridge & Co.* [1915] A.C. 847, 855.
[39] *Collins* v. *Godefroy* (1831) 1 B. & Ad. 950.
[40] *Stilk* v. *Myrick* (1809) 2 Camp. 317.
[41] *Roscorla* v. *Thomas* (1842) 3 Q.B. 234; *cf. Re Casey's Patents, Stewart* v. *Casey* [1892] 1 Ch. 104.
[42] *Pinnel's Case* (1602) 5 Co.Rep. 117a; *Foakes* v. *Beer* (1884) 9 App.Cas. 605.
[43] *Couldery* v. *Bartrum* (1881) 19 Ch.D. 394, 399, *per* Jessel M.R.
[44] *Thomas* v. *Thomas* (1842) 2 Q.B. 851.

Some inroad into the doctrine of consideration seems to have been made in recent years by the application of the equitable doctrine of estoppel. This application was suggested *obiter* by Denning J., as he then was, in *Central London Property Trust, Ltd.* v. *High Trees House, Ltd.*,[45] and it was later explained by Denning L.J. in the Court of Appeal in *Combe* v. *Combe*[46] as follows:

"Where one party has, by his words or conduct, made to the other a promise or assurance which was intended to affect the legal relations between them and to be acted on accordingly, then, once the other party has taken him at his word and acted on it, the one who gave the promise or assurance cannot afterwards be allowed to revert to the previous legal relations as if no such promise or assurance had been made by him, but he must accept their legal relations subject to the qualification which he himself has so introduced, even though it is not supported in point of law by any consideration but only by his word."

It should be noted that equitable estoppel may be used as a defence to show that a contract has been modified; but it does not give a cause of action; still less does it obviate the necessity of consideration for the formation of a contract, and it may only suspend not extinguish obligations.

Requirement of Written Evidence

Certain contracts are by statute unenforceable by action unless there is written evidence of their terms signed by the party to be charged. The requirement of a written memorandum in such cases does not make writing essential for the validity of a contract, but means that the plaintiff cannot enforce it by action for damages unless he can produce a memorandum in writing signed by the defendant or his agent.[47] The most important are contracts for the sale or other disposition of land or any interest in land.[48] If such contracts are not evidenced in writing they cannot be enforced by a direct action for damages; but if money has been paid they will operate as a defence to an action for repayment, and in the case of land they will be specifically

---

[45] [1947] K.B. 130.
[46] [1951] 2 K.B. 215; see also, *Tool Metal Manufacturing Co., Ltd.* v. *Tungsten Electric Co., Ltd.* [1955] 1 W.L.R. 761; [1955] 2 All E.R. 657 (H.L.), and *Ajayi* v. *Briscoe* [1964] 1 W.L.R. 1326; [1964] 3 All E.R. 556 (P.C.). *The Post Chaser* [1982] 1 All E.R. 19.
[47] *Maddison* v. *Alderson* (1883) 8 App.Cas. 467.
[48] Law of Property Act 1925, s.40, replacing part of the Statute of Frauds 1677, s.4. *Tiverton Estates Ltd.* v. *Wearwell Ltd.* [1975] Ch. 146 (C.A.).

enforced in equity if the plaintiff can show an act of part performance on his part.[49]

A miscellaneous collection of other contracts were required by section 4 of the Statute of Frauds 1677, to be evidenced by a written memorandum, but these provisions were abolished by the Law Reform (Enforcement of Contracts) Act 1954, s.1, except for a contract to guarantee a third party.[50] The Sale of Goods Act 1893, s.4 (replacing the Statute of Frauds, s.17), required a written memorandum for a contract for the sale of goods of the value of £10 or upwards, but this requirement was also repealed by the Law Reform (Enforcement of Contracts) Act 1954, s.2.

The Employment Protection (Consolidation) Act 1978, requires an employer to give an employee written particulars of the terms of employment. If the employer fails to do so the contract is not invalidated but the matter can be referred to an Industrial Tribunal. The Hire Purchase Acts 1938 and 1965, imposed complex formalities on contracts governed by them, and the Consumer Credit Act 1974, now requires a "regulated agreement" to be in prescribed form, otherwise it can only be enforced against the debtor by order of the court. The court is given a wide discretion in making such orders.

Contribution of Equity

Equitable Remedies

The main contributions of Equity to the law of contract are the decree of specific performance and the injunction, for disobedience to which the sanction is imprisonment for contempt of court. Being equitable remedies, they are granted at the discretion of the judge,[51] though the discretion has long been judicially exercised according to precedent.[52]

Specific performance, by which a party is ordered to carry out a contract according to its terms, will not be granted if damages would be an adequate remedy,[53] and the cases in which it is most commonly granted are contracts for the sale or lease of land.

An injunction is most commonly granted to restrain such torts as nuisance and defamation; but it may be granted to enforce a

---

[49] Below, p. 342.
[50] See *Eastwood* v. *Kenyon* (1840) 11 Ad. & E. 438.
[51] *Lamare* v. *Dixon* (1873) L.R. 6 H.L. 414, 423. See below, pp. 348–349 for further details.
[52] *Stickney* v. *Keeble* [1915] A.C. 386, 419.
[53] *Cud* v. *Rutter* (1720) 1 P.Wms. 570.

promise not to do something, as in a restrictive building covenant,[54] and in exceptional cases to enforce the negative of a promise.[55] Thus where a publican covenants to buy beer exclusively from his lessor, the court can restrain him from buying beer from anyone else though it cannot compel him to buy from the lessor.

Part Performance

The Court of Chancery construed the Statute of Frauds 1677, freely as a statute designed to prevent fraud and perjury. Equity will not allow a party to rely on the absence of a memorandum where to do so would be unconscionable. Thus in an oral contract of the type that Equity will specifically enforce, such as a contract to sell land or to grant a lease of land, where A has with B's knowledge partly performed the contract by doing something referable to the contract, *e.g.*, making alterations to the premises, Equity could compel B to provide the written memorandum and so will specifically enforce the contract.[56]

Contracts by Minors

A person attains full age for the purpose of making contracts at the age of eighteen by the Family Law Reform Act 1969, s.1, instead of at the age of twenty-one as at common law.[57] Persons not of full age, who were called "infants" by the common law, may now be described as "minors" (section 12). A minor is bound at common law by a beneficial contract of employment, education or training[58]; and he is bound to pay a reasonable price for the provision of "necessaries," *e.g.*, board and lodging, suitable clothes and professional advice.[59] A contract by a minor for the acquisition of a permanent interest in property, *e.g.*, the purchase of land, or company shares or a partnership agreement, is *voidable*, that is, valid unless and until the minor repudiates it during minority or within a reasonable time after coming of age.[60]

Otherwise, at common law contracts made by a minor were voidable but could be ratified by him on attaining majority. The law was appreciably altered, however, by the Infants Relief Act

---

[54] *Tulk* v. *Moxhay* (1848) 2 Ph. 774.
[55] *Catt* v. *Tourle* (1869) L.R. 4 Ch.App. 654.
[56] *Rawlinson* v. *Ames* [1925] Ch. 96; *Steadman* v. *Steadman* [1976] A.C. 536.
[57] Above, p. 287.
[58] *Roberts* v. *Gray* [1913] 1 K.B. 520; *Doyle* v. *White City Stadium* [1935] 1 K.B. 110.
[59] *Nash* v. *Inman* [1908] 2 K.B. 1; Sale of Goods Act 1979, s.3.
[60] *Goode* v. *Harrison* (1821) 5 B. & Ald. 147.

1874. Three classes of contracts entered into by a minor were *void*, namely: (a) contracts for the repayment of money lent or to be lent; (b) contracts for goods supplied or to be supplied, other than necessaries; and (c) accounts stated[61] (section 1); and a minor did not render himself liable by ratifying after coming of age any promise or contract by which he was not bound during minority (section 2).

Despite the use of the word "void" it was generally thought that these contracts were voidable by the infant. The Minors' Contracts Act 1987 has now "disapplied" the 1874 Act to the contracts within it, thus, it would seem that an adult may now sue unless and until the infant avoids. A guarantee given in respect of an infant's contract is not invalidated if the infant avoids his contract and a former minor may be liable on a ratification or a new contract to perform after majority a contract entered into during minority. Where an infant avoids a contract the court may, if it thinks it just and equitable, order the defendant to transfer to the plaintiff any property acquired under the contract or any property replacing it.

"Freedom of Contract"

In the nineteenth century much emphasis was placed on the idea of freedom of contract. The theory was that one was free, not only to choose whether to enter into a contract or not, but also to bargain over the terms. This freedom had certain well-defined limits, marked off by illegality of purpose,[62] immorality,[63] infringement of public policy,[64] and contravention of specific statutes, such as Gaming Acts.

In the conditions of modern society freedom of contract, never in fact so complete as was supposed, is becoming more and more restricted in various ways. Thus the form in which the terms of a contract are stated may be prescribed by statute, *e.g.*, Moneylenders Act 1927, the Hire-Purchase Act 1965, and now the Consumer Credit Act 1974. Some of the terms themselves may be prescribed, *e.g.*, the right to a minimum period of notice under the Employment Protection (Consolidation) Act 1978. It may even be compulsory to enter into a contract, *e.g.*, insurance by a motorist against third party risks under Road Traffic Acts. Conversely, a party may be forbidden to enforce some of the

---

[61] Account stated is an acknowledgment by one person that he owes a certain sum to another, and is only *prima facie* evidence of a debt in modern law.

[62] *Begbie* v. *Phosphate Sewage Co.* (1875) L.R. 10 Q.B. 491.

[63] *Ayerst* v. *Jenkins* (1873) L.R. 16 Eq. 275.

[64] *Nordenfelt* v. *Maxim Nordenfelt Guns and Ammunition Co.* [1894] A.C. 535.

rights under a contract, *e.g.*, by Rent Acts. The Restrictive Trade Practices Act 1976, and the Resale Prices Act 1976, enforced by the Restrictive Practices Court, are further striking examples of statutory regulation in the field of contract.

Economic conditions resulting from the industrial revolution led to standard form contracts with large monopolies like railway, electricity and gas corporations, and highly organised trades or businesses like builders and laundries. These contracts are of the take-it-or-leave-it kind, for here the consumer or customer cannot bargain over the terms: his only choice is to accept the terms *in toto* or to reject the service altogether. Such standard form contracts, as well as ordinary contracts, may contain unfair exemption clauses printed on a ticket, receipt or notice. The courts developed a doctrine of "fundamental breach" or "breach of a fundamental term," that is, a term the breach of which amounted to a non-performance of the contract. So it was held in *Alexander* v. *Railway Executive*[65] that a clause exempting the railway corporation from liability for loss of luggage deposited in a cloakroom did not prevail against the defendant's fundamental breach in permitting an unauthorised person to remove the plaintiff's luggage without producing a cloakroom ticket. But the House of Lords in the *Suisse Atlantique Case*[66] checked this development by holding that the doctrine of the fundamental term or fundamental breach is not a substantive rule of law, but a matter of construction of the contract. There may be a presumption that an exemption clause is not intended to apply to a fundamental breach, but the court may find that the parties did intend the clause to cover the breach of a fundamental term.

These common law devices may still be used but after piecemeal statutory intervention there came the Unfair Contract Terms Act 1977. This Act applies to "business liability" and provides that contract terms designed to exclude liability for negligence causing death or injury, or for loss or damage caused by defective consumer goods when the term is in a guarantee or for breach of implied terms in sale of goods and analogous contracts when one party is dealing as a consumer are void. Otherwise exclusion clauses relating to negligence causing harm other than death and injury, or in standard term contracts or excluding liability in sale and similar contracts when neither party is a consumer or excluding liability for misrepresentation

---

[65] [1951] 2 K.B. 882.
[66] *Suisse Atlantique Société d'Armement Maritime S.A.* v. *N.V. Rotterdamsche Kolen Centrale* [1967] 1 A.C. 361; *Photo Production* v. *Securicor* [1980] A.C. 827.

must satisfy a test of reasonableness, for which the Act provides guidelines, if they are to be effective.[67] The Act is subject to numerous and complex exceptions.

The final state, where the monopolies are controlled by the Government or Public Corporations, is to prescribe the prices to be charged by statutory regulation.[68]

It is not only the manufacturer or producer who lays down the terms, for trade unions have powerful weapons in collective bargaining about wages and conditions of work.

Misrepresentation

A misrepresentation of fact made by B to A during negotiations for a contract between them, and inducing A to enter into the contract, may have varying effect according to B's state of mind.

Fraudulent Misrepresentation

If B's misrepresentation was fraudulent, *i.e.*, B knew it was untrue, or did not believe it to be true, or was recklessly careless whether it was true or false (*Derry* v. *Peek*[69]), the contract is "voidable" at A's option. A may choose whether to affirm and bring an action for damages for fraud or deceit, or to rescind the contract in Equity and claim damages for the loss suffered; or else he may set up fraud as a defence to an action brought against him by B and counterclaim for damages.

Negligent Misrepresentation

Before 1967 if B's misrepresentation was negligent, A could rescind the contract in Equity but he could not generally claim damages at common law.[70] The Misrepresentation Act 1967, s.2, now makes B liable to A for damages for negligent misrepresentation inducing the contract between them, unless B proves that he had reasonable ground to believe, and did believe up to the time the contract was made, that the facts represented were true.[71] A may both claim damages and rescind, but the court may also award damages in lieu of rescission.

---

[67] *Phillips Products* v. *Hyland* [1987] 2 All E.R. 620.

[68] *e.g.*, Post Office Act 1969, s.28.

[69] (1889) 14 App.Cas. 337; above, pp. 326–327.

[70] But damages could be claimed if there was a fiduciary relationship, *e.g.*, solicitor: *Nocton* v. *Lord Ashburton* [1914] A.C. 932 (H.L.); or there was a "special relationship," between the parties: *Hedley Byrne & Co., Ltd.* v. *Heller & Partners, Ltd.* [1964] A.C. 465 (H.L.).

[71] The burden of proof favours the plaintiff as compared with a claim under *Hedley Byrne*. See *Howard Marine* v. *Ogden* [1978] Q.B. 574.

Innocent Misrepresentation

This expression was formerly used for any misrepresentation that was not fraudulent. Now it may conveniently be used to mean any misrepresentation that is neither fraudulent nor negligent. No damages lie at common law for such a representation, but rescission may be allowed in Equity. The plaintiff may be awarded a financial indemnity against obligations created by the contract,[72] or the court may under the 1967 Act award damages in lieu of rescission.

A contract may also be set aside where one party has exercised undue influence over the other.[73]

Frustration of Contract

A contract may be discharged by impossibility of performance, as where there is an implied condition that B's performance will be excused if some person or thing ceases to exist without the default of B, *e.g.*, B agrees to hire A's music-hall for an entertainment and before the day fixed the hall is burnt down (*Taylor* v. *Caldwell*[74]). A contract for personal services by B, *e.g.*, to perform at a concert, will be frustrated by the death or serious illness of B (*Robinson* v. *Davison*[75]). Again the non-occurrence, through the fault of neither party, of an event on which the contract depends amounts to "frustration of the adventure," *e.g.*, the hire of a flat from which to view the coronation of Edward VII, which was cancelled (*Krell* v. *Henry*[76]).

The now accepted test for frustration is whether continuance of the contract in the new circumstances would be entirely different from what was originally agreed by the parties.[77] A lease may be frustrated, though this will rarely happen.[78]

The Law Reform (Frustrated Contracts) Act 1943, provides that where a contract between A and B is frustrated through impossibility of performance or otherwise, sums paid by A to B in pursuance of the contract before the time of discharge shall be recoverable, and sums payable at that time shall cease to be payable; but if B incurred expenses before the time of discharge in connection with the contract, the court may allow B to retain

---

[72] *Whittington* v. *Seale-Hayne* (1900) 82 L.T. 49.
[73] *National Westminster Bank* v. *Morgan* [1985] A.C. 686; *Goldsworthy* v. *Brickell* [1987] Ch. 378.
[74] (1863) 3 B. & S. 826.
[75] (1871) L.R. 6 Ex. 269.
[76] [1903] 2 K.B. 740; *Herne Bay Steamboat Co.* v. *Hutton* [1903] 2 K.B. 683.
[77] *Davis* v. *Fareham* [1956] A.C. 696; *Pioneer Shipping* v. *B.T.P.* [1982] A.C. 724.
[78] *National Carriers* v. *Panalpina* [1981] A.C. 675.

or recover the whole or part of such sums up to the amount of the expenses so incurred. The Act further provides that either party may be awarded compensation from the other party for any valuable benefit obtained in connection with the contract, such as delivery of goods.[79] The Act does not apply to contracts of insurance or certain contracts for the sale of specific goods.

Discharge by Breach

If B renounces his contract with A, or makes it impossible for B himself to perform it, or in certain conditions if B fails to perform it (*e.g.*, where the promises of A and B are interdependent, and where the contract is "entire" and indivisible, so that B's breach is fundamental) A may choose whether to treat the contract as still subsisting or to regard himself as discharged from (further) performance.

Remedies for Breach of Contract

Damages

The commonest remedy for breach of contract is the common law action for damages. The first requirement is that *the damage must not be too remote*. The leading case is *Hadley* v. *Baxendale*.[80] The plaintiff's mill was stopped by a broken crankshaft, and the shaft had to be sent to the manufacturers as a pattern for a new one. The plaintiffs asked the defendants, who were carriers, to send it immediately, and the defendants' clerk replied that they would deliver it to the manufacturers the day after they received it from the plaintiffs.[81] The defendants' clerk knew that the plaintiffs were millers and that the article to be carried was a broken mill shaft, but he was not told that the mill had stopped and that immediate delivery of the shaft was necessary. Owing to the defendants' neglect delivery of the shaft to the manufacturers was delayed for several days, and the plaintiffs claimed

---

[79] Cf. *Fibrosa Spolka Akcyjna* v. *Fairbairn Lawson Combe Barbour, Ltd.* [1943] A.C. 32 (H.L.); *B.P.* v. *Hunt* [1979] 1 W.L.R. 783.

[80] (1854) 9 Exch. 341; *Victoria Laundry (Windsor), Ltd.* v. *Newman Industries, Ltd.* [1949] 2 K.B. 528 (C.A.), *per* Asquith L.J. See now *Koufos* v. *Czarnikow* (C.) [1969] 1 A.C. 350; *sub nom. Heron II, The* [1967] 3 All E.R. 686 (H.L.).

[81] Even if the undertaking to deliver the shaft the following day is regarded as part of the contract, time is not generally of the essence of a contract, unless the contract expressly states that time is of the essence (*Steedman* v. *Drinkle* [1916] 1 A.C. 275), or where it is implied by the nature, subject-matter or circumstances of the contract: *Tadcaster Tower Brewery Co.* v. *Wilson* [1897] 1 Ch. 705; *Hare* v. *Nicoll* [1966] 2 Q.B. 130; Law of Property Act 1925, s.41; Sale of Goods Act 1979, s.10.

damages for the consequent loss of profits. It was held that damages for breach of contract must be such as may fairly and reasonably be considered *either* arising naturally, *i.e.*, according to the usual course of things, from such breach, *or* such as may reasonably be supposed to have been in the contemplation of both parties, at the time they made the contract, as the probable result of its breach. In this case the special circumstances had not been communicated to the defendants—the plaintiffs might have had a spare shaft, or the stoppage might have been due to some other cause: the defendants were therefore liable for the amount of injury that would arise in an ordinary case not affected by special circumstances.

The question of the *measure of damages* only arises if the principles of *Hadley* v. *Baxendale* as to remoteness of damage are satisfied. The damage being sufficiently proximate, the object of the remedy is *restitutio in integrum*, that is, the defendant must—as far as money can do so—restore the plaintiff to the position in which he would have been if that damage had not occurred (*Robinson* v. *Harman*[82]). In contract damages are normally[83] to put the plaintiff in the same position as if the contract had been performed, so that he recovers for "loss of bargain" or profit that he would have made, whereas in tort damages are to place the plaintiff in the same position as if the tort had not been committed. The parties may make a reasonable pre-estimate of loss which might be caused by breach, known as liquidated damages. These will be recoverable whatever the actual loss but if they agree upon a sum which is grossly excessive this is a "penalty" and not recoverable.[84] The doctrine of "mitigation of damage" further requires that the plaintiff must take such reasonable steps as are available to mitigate the loss caused by the breach, and he will only be awarded compensation for the balance which cannot be eliminated.[85]

Specific Performance

This is an equitable remedy granted at the discretion of the court in certain cases where damages would be inadequate.[86] Thus it

---

[82] (1848) 1 Ex. 850.

[83] Under the rule in *Bain* v. *Fothergill* (1874) L.R. 7 H.L. 158 on a vendor's failure to make title to land the intending purchaser cannot recover loss of bargain but merely expenses of investigating title. See *Sharneyford Supplies* v. *Edge* [1987] Ch. 305.

[84] *Dunlop* v. *New Garage Co.* [1915] A.C. 79.

[85] *Brace* v. *Calder* [1895] 2 Q.B. 253; *Payzu Ltd.* v. *Saunders* [1919] 2 K.B. 851.

[86] *Cud* v. *Rutter* (1720) 1 P.Wms. 570 (shares); but *Pusey* v. *Pusey* (1684) 1 Vern. 273 (ancient horn); *Somerset* (*Duke of*) v. *Cookson* (1735) 3 P.Wms. 390 (ancient altar).

will not be granted in respect of ordinary articles of commerce when equivalents could easily be purchased with a sum of damages, but only in respect of subject-matter of special or unique character. By an order of specific performance the court directs the defendant to perform his part of the contract according to its terms. Breach of the order would be contempt of court. Specific performance would generally be granted of a contract for the sale of land, which is always regarded as being unique; and it is granted to the vendor (although he could usually sell to someone else) as well as to the purchaser.[87] Specific performance is never granted of contracts for personal services, whether domestic, professional, artistic or social[88]; and in general the remedy will not be granted when the court cannot supervise the performance, for "Equity does nothing in vain."[89] Again Equity will not grant specific performance of a gratuitous promise under seal, though it deems marriage to be consideration.[90]

Injunction

A court will occasionally in its discretion grant the equitable remedy of injunction to forbid the breach of an express negative promise, that is, a promise not to do something. Thus although the court will not specifically enforce a promise to sing at the plaintiff's theatre or to act for the plaintiff's film company, it may grant an injunction to restrain the defendant from breaking an express promise not to sing at any other theatre for a certain time,[91] or not to act for any other film company.[92] The court, however, will not grant an injunction when to enforce the negative terms of a contract would be tantamount to specifically enforcing the positive terms.

3. LIABILITY OF PRINCIPAL AND AGENT IN CONTRACT

Agency is a contract whereby one party (called the agent) agrees to perform a certain act or series of acts on behalf of the other party (called the principal) and those acts are treated in law as if they were the acts of the principal. With the contract of agency

---

[87] *Hope* v. *Walter* [1900] 1 Ch. 257.
[88] *Rigby* v. *Connol* (1880) 14 Ch.D. 482; *cf. Lumley* v. *Wagner*, below. An order for reinstatement may be made under the Employment Protection (Consolidation) Act 1978, s.69: *Hill* v. *C.A. Parsons* [1972] Ch. 305.
[89] *Ryan* v. *Mutual Tontine Assn.* [1893] 1 Ch. 116.
[90] *Jefferys* v. *Jefferys* (1841) Cr. & Ph. 138.
[91] *Lumley* v. *Wagner* (1852) 1 De G.M. & G. 604.
[92] *Warner Brothers Pictures Incorporated* v. *Nelson* [1937] 1 K.B. 209.

itself, as creating rights and duties between principal and agent, we are not here concerned. It forms part of the more detailed study of the law of contract. Our attention will be confined to the contractual liability of principal and agent to third parties, *i.e.*, persons who deal with the agent.

Under the doctrine of "holding out," where P puts A in a position from which other persons may reasonably suppose that A has authority to act as his agent for a certain class of transaction, P cannot escape liability in contract—any more than he can in tort—by saying that he had not actually conferred that authority or that he had secretly withdrawn an authority which he had given. If X goes into P's shop and buys an article over the counter from A, a shop assistant, it is clear that the contract is made with P.

There is a presumption arising out of cohabitation that a wife who is living with her husband has implied authority to pledge his credit for "necessaries," *i.e.*, the supply of necessary goods and services for herself, her husband, children and the household, suitable to the husband's style of living.[93]

Apart from presumptions such as these, there are three types of agency to be noticed:

(i) Where an agent (A) expressly contracts *as agent* for a principal (P) whom he *names* ("named principal"), it is clear as a general rule that the other party to the contract (X) relies on the credit of P and not of A. The contract when completed is accordingly considered to be a contract between X and P only. A, who was engaged merely as an intermediary to bring the parties together, drops out entirely. The rights and duties under the contract, and the mutual actions for breach of contract, lie exclusively between X and P.[94] It should be noticed, however, that where the contract is in writing the intention to contract *as agent* must be clearly expressed,[95] and where it is under seal all persons expressed to be parties to the deed, and only they, are liable.[96]

(ii) Where A expressly contracts *as agent* for a principal whom he *does not name* ("unnamed principal"), the

---

[93] *Debenham* v. *Mellon* (1880) 6 App.Cas. 24; *Miss Gray, Ltd.* v. *Cathcart (Earl)* (1922) 38 T.L.R. 562.

[94] *Fairlie* v. *Fenton* (1870) L.R. 5 Ex. 169; *Paquin* v. *Beauclerk* [1906] A.C. 148.

[95] *Universal Steam Navigation Co.* v. *McKelvie* [1923] A.C. 492.

[96] *Schack* v. *Anthony* (1813) 1 M. & S. 573; *cf.* Law of Property Act 1925, s.123; *Harmer* v. *Armstrong* [1934] 1 Ch. 65.

rule is the same as in the first type of case, for X can generally be taken to have looked beyond A to the unnamed principal. In such a case A drops out altogether, and the contract is considered to be one between X and P only. The difference between the two cases is that where the principal is not named greater care must be taken by an agent, who wishes to exclude himself from liability, to indicate that he is contracting only "as agent."[97]

(iii) The position is different where A contracts with X on behalf of a principal whose *existence* he does not disclose ("undisclosed principal"). The contract here is between X and A, for X intended to contract with A and it cannot be shown that he would have contracted with anyone else. When X discovers that A was really acting on behalf of P, he may enforce the contract against *either* A (the supposed principal) *or* P (the real principal)[98]; and if he has already sued A and obtained judgment against him, although it remains unsatisfied, he can now sue P without first having the judgment against A set aside.[99]

Ratification

If a person purports to act as agent on behalf of an identified principal but without actual or apparent authority to do so, the alleged principal will not be liable or entitled as against the third party. The alleged principal may, if he wishes, ratify the transaction professedly done on his behalf, and will then be entitled and bound just as if he had originally authorised the transaction.[1] If the alleged principal does not ratify, the professed agent will be liable to the third party for breach of warranty of authority.[2]

Agency of necessity

An agency relationship may also come into existence in a case of emergency, as where a carrier or other bailee is in charge of another's perishable goods which are threatened with destruction. The bailee will then be regarded as having an implied

---

[97] *Southwell* v. *Bowditch* (1876) 1 C.P.D. 374.
[98] *Thomson* v. *Davenport* (1829) 9 B. & C. 78; *Keighley Maxsted & Co.* v. *Durant* [1901] A.C. 240, 261.
[99] Civil Liability (Contribution) Act 1978.
[1] *Keighley Maxsted & Co.* v. *Durant* [1901] A.C. 240.
[2] *Collen* v. *Wright* (1857) 8 E. & B. 647.

authority to sell the goods so as to preserve the value of the owner's interest.[3] This is known as agency of necessity. At one time a deserted wife might be treated as an agent of necessity in pledging her husband's credit for her support, but this has now been abolished by statute.[4]

Delegation

The general rule is that an agent may not delegate performance of his duties to another, and the principal will not be bound by the acts of an unauthorised sub-agent. This rule is embodied in the maxim *delegatus non protest delegare*.[5] Authority to delegate may be express or implied, real or apparent. Sometimes an agent may have authority to appoint a substitute for himself, in which case the principal is fully entitled and bound by the acts of the substitute.[6] In other cases the agent may appoint a sub-agent, whose dealings with third parties may bind the principal, but who is primarily entitled to payment from and liable to the appointing agent,[7] and is in effect the latter's agent.

[3] *Springer* v. *G.W.R.* [1921] 1 K.B. 257; *Sachs* v. *Miklos* [1948] 2 K.B. 23.

[4] Matrimonial Proceedings and Property Act 1970, s.41. This was repealed and not re-enacted by the Matrimonial Causes Act 1973, Sched. 3.

[5] A delegate cannot delegate.

[6] *Schwensen* v. *Ellinger, Heath Western & Co.* (1949) 83 Ll.L.R. 79.

[7] *Calico Printers Assn.* v. *Barclays Bank* (1931) 145 L.T. 51.

CHAPTER 20

Family Law

Family Law covers the legal aspects of the formation and termination of marriage and the relationship of parent and child.

Marriage

Until 1857 much of the law relating to marriage was to be found in the Canon Law administered by the ecclesiastical courts.[1] The Canon Law required little by way of formality for the formation of marriage, but clandestine unions proved so troublesome that Lord Hardwicke's Act of 1753 made secular provision for necessary formalities. At the present day legally valid marriages in this country must normally be celebrated in a church or other place of worship registered for the purpose, with a registrar in attendance, or at a Register Office.[2] The principal substantive requirements are that the parties must be over the age of sixteen, not at the time lawfully married to some third party, not within the prohibited degrees of relationship, and must give free consent uninfluenced by duress, mistake or unsoundness of mind.[3] The consent of parents or guardians is required for the marriage of parties under eighteen, but absence of this consent does not invalidate the marriage.

---

[1] Above, p. 105.
[2] See Marriage Acts 1949 to 1986.
[3] Matrimonial Causes Act 1973, ss.11 and 12, provide for certain other grounds of invalidity. See also, Marriage (Prohibited Degrees of Relationship) Act 1986.

Until the Matrimonial Causes Act 1857, the ecclesiastical courts granted decrees of nullity declaring an apparent marriage to be null and void, and divorce *a mensa et thoro* (from bed and board) which amounted to judicial separation and did not allow the parties to remarry. Divorce *a vinculo* (from the bond of a valid marriage), allowing remarriage, could only be obtained through the cumbersome and expensive mechanisms of a private Act of Parliament.[4] Some aspects of Family Law were controlled by the Court of Chancery, when children were made wards of courts and wives were protected in the enjoyment of their separate property through the machinery of trusts.[5] Other aspects were regulated by the common law courts which entertained actions in tort for criminal conversation (adultery with the plaintiff's spouse), enticement of a spouse and seduction, and in contract for breach of promise of marriage.

When the judicial regulation of divorce and nullity was transferred to a secular Divorce Court by the Act of 1857 and divorce *a vinculo* could be obtained by judicial process, grounds for divorce remained restricted to adultery and continued to be based on Canon Law concepts of matrimonial fault. Though these grounds were eventually relaxed and widened, notably by the Matrimonial Causes Act 1937, which added cruelty, desertion and supervening incurable insanity, there were insistent complaints that the law was widely abused and the courts frequently deceived especially on evidence of adultery. Following reports published in 1966 by the Law Commission and a group appointed by the Archbishop of Canterbury, the Divorce Reform Act 1969, was passed and was re-enacted in the Matrimonial Causes Act 1973. The 1969 Act appeared to make a striking departure in basing divorce on the single ground of irretrievable breakdown of the marriage, but this breakdown must be shown by proving conduct which in large measure would formerly have constituted matrimonial fault. Moreover, if the parties have lived apart for two years the marriage may be terminated by consent, and if they have lived apart for five years a divorce may be obtained by either party even though the other party objects. The Act includes provisions designed

---

[4] The first such Act was obtained by Lord de Roos in 1669 and the first by a woman in 1801. See the ironic comments attributed to Maule J. in Holdsworth, *History of English Law*, Vol. I. (7th ed.), pp. 623–624. In old reports decrees of nullity are sometimes referred to as divorce *a vinculo*. See Bromley, *Family Law* (7th ed.), p. 170.

[5] See Megarry and Wade, *The Law of Real Property* (5th ed.), pp. 1020–1024.

to encourage reconciliation[6] and to secure the welfare of children of the marriage.[7] The courts also have wide discretionary powers in cases of divorce, nullity and judicial separation to make orders relating to the income and property of the parties.[8]

Actions for criminal conversation were abolished in 1857, and actions for enticement, seduction and breach of promise of marriage by the Law Reform (Miscellaneous Provisions) Act 1970.[9] Increasing numbers of petitions led to divorce proceedings being heard at assizes in the inter-war years; after the Second World War County Court Judges sitting as Divorce Commissioners with the status and powers of a High Court judge also heard many cases. In 1967 it was provided that all divorce cases should be commenced in designated County Courts and undefended cases determined there.[10] Divorce Commissioners were no longer appointed after the Courts Act 1971. As the original Roman and Canon Law background which had explained the creation of the Probate, Divorce and Admiralty Division became of less importance, it was felt that some re-arrangement of the High Court was required. This was brought about by the Administration of Justice Act 1970, which was put into effect in 1971. The new Family Division retained the matrimonial and uncontested probate jurisdiction (common form) of the former Division, and took over wardship proceedings from the Chancery Division which, in its turn, took over contested probate proceedings (solemn form). Magistrates' courts also have an extensive matrimonial and domestic jurisdiction involving such matters as financial provision, guardianship and adoption,[11] but not divorce.

Nullity

Apart from terminating the legal effects of an existing marriage by divorce or suspending its obligations by separation, a court may be asked to decide that an apparent marriage is in fact a

---

[6] *e.g.*, in calculating the periods of two and five years of non-cohabitation no account is to be taken of any periods not amounting to more than six months during which the parties may have lived together.

[7] Matrimonial Causes Act 1973, s.41.

[8] Matrimonial Causes Act 1973, ss.21–25. Matrimonial Homes Act 1983; Matrimonial and Family Proceedings Act 1984.

[9] See Winfield and Jolowicz, *Tort* (12th ed.), pp. 506–507.

[10] See above, p. 69 and Matrimonial Causes Act 1967. Under new rules, undefended divorces may be obtained by correspondence without a court hearing. Property and custody of children will be dealt with in chambers.

[11] See above, pp. 69–72. Domestic Proceedings and Magistrates Courts Act 1978.

nullity. It may be void from the outset because, for example, the parties were under age or within the prohibited degrees.[12] On the other hand it may be voidable, that is to say valid until declared void as to the future. A petitioner may lose the right to avoid by approbating the marriage. Examples of grounds of voidability are non-consummation, duress, mistake or unsoundness of mind.[13] Decrees of nullity may be granted by the Family Division. Matrimonial proceedings involving a foreign element sometimes raise difficult questions of conflict of laws as, for example, the extent to which the courts of this country will recognise polygamous unions contracted abroad.[14]

Property

At common law all the personal property (including leaseholds) of a married woman, owned at marriage or acquired later, became her husband's property. He also controlled her real property, being entitled to the rents and profits during her life; and he might have a life interest, known as tenancy by the curtesy, after her death. A married woman could not make a contract, and her husband was liable for her antenuptial debts and her torts.

In the eighteenth century, however, equity intervened to protect the wife's beneficial interest in property settled in trust for her "separate use." If a "restraint on anticipation" was employed in the settlement the wife was only permitted to control the annual income and was not allowed to dispose of the capital. This, as one Lord Chancellor said, was to prevent the husband from "kicking or kissing" her out of her fortune. In the late nineteenth century Married Women's Property Acts, the most important of which came in 1882, gave all married women that control over their property which had hitherto only been secured for wealthier women through equity's trust devices. The Law Reform (Married Women and Tortfeasors) Act 1935, went far to assimilating the civil capacity of a married woman to that of a single woman (*feme sole*). Surviving restraints on anticipation were swept away in 1949.

Husband and wife could not sue each other in tort at common law but may now do so under the Law Reform (Husband and Wife) Act 1962. The court may stay the action, however, if it

---

[12] Matrimonial Causes Act 1973, s.11.
[13] Matrimonial Causes Act 1973, ss.12 and 13. Approbation has in strictness been abolished but replaced by a statutory bar which closely resembles it.
[14] Bromley, *Family Law* (7th ed.), pp. 56–64. Family Law Act 1986. Recognition of Divorces and Legal Separation Act 1971.

appears that no substantial benefit would accrue from the proceedings or that the question could more conveniently be dealt with under the Married Women's Property Act 1882, section 17 of which gives the court wide discretionary powers in regard to property. At one time also the choice of the location of the matrimonial home was within the husband's sole control, but now he must not disregard the wife's wishes.[15]

At common law a wife has a right, as against her husband, to occupy the matrimonial home and the Matrimonial Homes Acts 1967 and 1983 reinforced this right and conferred similar rights on husbands. These rights of themselves do not affect third parties and to remedy this the courts invented the "deserted wife's equity" which could be used against anyone to whom the husband disposed of the house, but this created problems for conveyancers and was rejected by the House of Lords.[16] The Matrimonial Homes Act 1967 then allowed these rights to be registered as land charges, so binding third parties. Grave difficulties would have been caused if all such rights had been registered and in fact the legislation works on the basis of "mass invalidation" for non-registration.[17] This problem would disappear if co-ownership was an automatic consequence of marriage.[18] In practice, however, many spouses are nowadays beneficial joint tenants by agreement and do not have to rely on these special rights to occupy.

The old strict settlement which once gave limited successive interests in land to members of a family, though provided with elaborate legal machinery by the Settled Land Act 1925, is now carefully avoided by conveyancers because of its tax disadvantages and such settlements are now only created unwittingly by home-made wills. A preferred method is the trust for sale under which the trustees are ultimately obliged to sell the trust property and, if it is land, convert it into money but may postpone the sale for an extended time and allow the beneficiaries to manage and enjoy the property in kind. If there is a difference of opinion between the trustees whether to defer or sell, the basic rule is that the sale must take place but where the property in question is a family home the court has developed a discretion under the Law of Property Act 1925, s.30 which enables them to refuse to order a sale when the purpose

---

[15] *Dunn* v. *Dunn* [1949] P. 98.
[16] *National Provincial Bank* v. *Ainsworth* [1965] A.C. 1175. See Gray, *Elements of Land Law*, Chap. 22, pp. 781–791.
[17] *Wroth* v. *Tyler* [1974] Ch. 30.
[18] Gray, *op. cit.* pp. 790–791.

of providing a family home is still in existence.[19] The section allows the court to make such order as it thinks fit when trustees for sale refuse to exercise their powers and the factors which will be taken into account by the court include the state of family relationships, the size of the property in relation to the needs of the family and, where it is leasehold, its declining value as an asset.

More informal family arrangements have also posed problems. Decisions of the House of Lords have restricted the use of the trust to resolve these[20] and recourse has been had to the law of licences[21] and proprietary estoppel[22] in order to protect occupation and give compensation for services.

Children

Parents are legally bound to support their children[23] and to ensure that they receive suitable education to school leaving age, now sixteen.[24] Parents as parents are not, however, liable on their children's contracts and torts though they may incur liability if their children act as their servants or agents, or if the parents' own negligence in controlling a child results in tortious harm to another.[25] The custody of minors is generally vested in both parents or the survivor of them. Either parent may appoint a guardian by deed or will to act after their death. The court also has power in certain circumstances to appoint any person as guardian or to supervise a guardian.[26] A doctor need not always inform parents of treatment for their child.[27]

Adoption

Adoption, by which an adopted child is placed for almost all legal purposes, including succession to property on death, in

[19] *Ibid.* pp. 819–827.
[20] *Pettitt* v. *Pettitt* [1970] A.C. 777; *Gissing* v. *Gissing* [1971] A.C. 886.
[21] Permission, contractual or non-contractual, to enter and use land. See Gray, *op. cit.* pp. 799–800.
[22] A doctrine of evidence which debars a person from revoking an assurance on which the party to whom it was given has relied to his detriment. Remedies for infringing this form of estoppel may be the grant of an interest in land, a right to occupy or compensation.
[23] Supplementary Benefits Act 1976.
[24] Education Act 1944, s.36; Raising of School Leaving Age Order 1972.
[25] *Mortimore* v. *Wright* (1840) 6 M. & W. 482; *Bebee* v. *Sales* (1916) 32 T.L.R. 413.
[26] Guardianship of Minors Act 1971; Guardianship Act 1973. Family Law Act 1986. See also, Matrimonial Causes Act 1973, s.41 and above pp. 279–280 for care proceedings and other regimes in criminal law.
[27] *Gillick* v. *West Norfolk Health Authority* [1986] A.C. 112.

the same position as a natural legitimate child, was a late introduction into English law. Though informal adoption had long been known, statutory recognition giving full legal effect only came with the Adoption of Children Act 1926.[28]

Legitimation

Legitimation by the subsequent marriage of a child's parents, though known to both Roman and Canon Law, was similarly a latecomer to English law, also being introduced as a process of law in 1926 by the Legitimacy Act. The Barons at Merton in 1235 had declared they did not wish to change the laws of England in this matter, so until 1926 legitimation could only be achieved by private Act of Parliament. More recent legislation has extended the availability and effect of legitimation, so that it is no longer a bar to legitimation that one or both of the parents was or were married at the time of the child's birth.[29]

The law relating to illegitimacy has been substantially altered by the Family Law Reform Act 1987. The status remains but almost all the legal consequences which discriminated against the illegitimate have been abolished.

The putative father of an illegitimate child could formerly have been compelled to provide for the child's support up to the age of sixteen by affiliation proceedings brought by the mother in a magistrates' court.

Now, all orders for financial provision for children, whether legitimate or illegitimate, are to be obtained under the Guardianship of Minors Act 1971.[30] After some piecemeal alterations in the law, illegitimate children now have full rights on intestacy,[31] and they have also been included amongst the classes of persons entitled to bring a claim in tort for the death of "a breadwinner" under the Fatal Accidents Acts 1976.[32]

At common law persons under the age of twenty-one were known as infants and had only a limited capacity to render themselves liable in contract and tort. By the Family Law Reform Act 1969, the age of majority for the purposes of civil law was reduced to eighteen, and persons below that age may now be referred to as minors, and their incapacities in contract have been altered by the Minors Contracts Act 1987.[33]

---

[28] See now Children Act 1975; Adoption Act 1976.
[29] Legitimacy Act 1959. Legitimacy Act 1976.
[30] Family Law Reform Act 1987, s.17.
[31] Family Law Reform Act 1987, s.18.
[32] Fatal Accidents Acts 1846–1959. Fatal Accidents Act 1976.
[33] As to the effect of age in criminal law see above Chap. 16, pp. 277 and 279–280. For tort see above, Chap. 18, pp. 310–311 and for contract Chap. 19, pp. 342–343.

CHAPTER 21

Evidence and Civil Procedure

The law of evidence regulates the means by which the allegations of parties to civil or criminal proceedings may be proved or disproved and other incidental matters. The rules of civil procedure regulate the methods by which a question for civil adjudication may be brought before a court, and by which effect may be given to the decision of the court or any settlement of the proceedings which the parties may have arrived at between themselves. Evidence and procedure are often described as adjective law in contrast to substantive law, which comprises the duties and liabilities to which evidence and procedure are subservient.

1. EVIDENCE

The law of evidence primarily governs the proof and disproof of assertions of fact made by parties to legal proceedings. It also specifies when proof of relevant facts is either not required or not allowed.

The means of proof are witnesses, documents and real evidence. This last is evidence provided by material things, such as weapons and other instruments of crime or goods the subject of litigation in a civil case.[1]

---

[1] See R. v. Hunt (1820) 3 B. & Ald. 566 (banners with inscriptions held to be things), Line v. Taylor (1862) 3 F. & F. 731 (a dog). On fingerprints, see Police and Criminal Evidence Act 1984, s.61.

Witnesses

The law of evidence specifies when a witness is competent and compellable to give evidence, whether his evidence should be on oath or affirmation and whether it requires corroboration. Normally the evidence of a single witness who is believed is sufficient for a court to arrive at a decision; but in certain cases where experience has shown such evidence to be often unreliable, as with opinion evidence as to speed limits, corroboration in a material particular or by other material evidence, which may not necessarily be the evidence of a second witness, is required as a matter of law. In other cases, such as very many sexual offences and the evidence of accomplices in crime, the judge must warn the jury of the danger of convicting on uncorroborated evidence.[2]

Witnesses must normally speak to matters of fact which they have perceived with their senses and not as to their opinion.[3] There are, however, some matters such as age[4] and speed[5] on which ordinary witnesses may speak to their opinion; and expert witnesses, qualified by virtue of special skill in some art or science, may give their opinion on matters within their special field.[6] Matters of expert knowledge which frequently come before the courts include medical, scientific and engineering evidence, comparison of handwriting in cases of alleged forgery,[7] and matters of foreign law when this is material in a case involving a foreign element.[8] The Police and Criminal Evidence Act 1984 provides for the tape recording of police interviews with suspects and codes of practice cover identification parades. The Criminal Justice Bill 1988 provides that, with leave of the court, the evidence of witnesses who are abroad and of children may be given by live video link in cases involving violence and sexual offences. An expert witness need not give oral evidence in support of his report, and procedures for obtaining evidence from witnesses abroad are also covered.

[2] As to children abolished by Criminal Justice Bill 1988.
[3] R. v. *Loake* (1911) 7 Cr.App.R. 71.
[4] R. v. *Cox* [1898] 1 Q.B. 179.
[5] Road Traffic Regs. Act 1967. See also, Civil Evidence Act 1972, s.3(2).
[6] *Folkes* v. *Chadd* (1782) 3 Douglas 157. See Civil Evidence Act 1972, s.3(1) and Police and Criminal Evidence Act 1984, s.81 on the need for prior disclosure of an expert witness in criminal cases.
[7] R. v. *Silverlock* [1894] 2 Q.B. 766.
[8] See Civil Evidence Act 1972, s.4(1); *Brailey* v. *Rhodesia Consolidated* [1910] 2 Ch. 95. As to E.E.C. law, see above, p. 20. Under the European Communities Act 1972 s.3(2) it is to be judicially noticed and does not require proof.

Documents

"Ancient documents," more than twenty years old and produced from proper custody, are said to prove themselves.[9] Some documents such as wills, require to be attested (formally signed by witnesses),[10] or to comply with other formalities such as revenue stamping if they are to be produced in evidence in civil cases.[11] If a document is lost or in the possession of an opponent or third party who will not produce it, difficult questions will arise as to whether secondary evidence of its contents can be given. Another fertile source of difficulty is the extent to which evidence of matters extrinsic to a document can be given to assist in its interpretation.[12] The Police and Criminal Evidence Act 1984 makes provision for the admissibility of documentary records, computer records and microfilms.[13] The Criminal Justice Bill 1988 provides that in criminal cases documents are generally to be admissible to the same extent that the same evidence would be admissible if given orally as are business records but documents produced specifically for the purposes of criminal proceedings are only to be admissible with leave of the court.

Judicial Notice

The court will take "judicial notice" of a wide range of matters of common knowledge and of a legal, constitutional and administrative nature. Such matters do not require to be proved.[14]

The Burden of Proof and Presumptions

The task of the tribunal in according proper weight to the evidence adduced by the parties is facilitated by rules relating to the burden and standard of proof, and by various presumptions both of law and fact. Both in civil and criminal cases the burden of proof normally lies on the party instigating the proceedings,

[9] *Meath* v. *Winchester* (1836) 3 Bing.N.C. 183.
[10] Wills Act 1837, s.9.
[11] Unstamped documents may be produced in criminal cases.
[12] *De Lassalle* v. *Guildford* [1901] 2 K.B. 215.
[13] ss.68–71.
[14] *e.g.* the streets of London are crowded and dangerous, *Dennis* v. *White* [1916] 2 K.B. at p. 6; the time difference east and west of Greenwich, *Curtis* v. *Marsh* (1858) 3 H. & N. 866; likelihood of war, *Monarch S.S. Co.* v. *Karlshamms Oljefabriker* [1949] A.C. 196, 234; procedure and privileges of Parliament, *Stockdale* v. *Hansard* (1839) 9 A. & E. 1. In matters involving the foreign relations of this country the court will act on a certificate from the Foreign Office: *Duff Development* v. *Kelantan* [1924] A.C. 797. In other matters it may wish to make inquiry before taking judicial notice.

the plaintiff in a civil case and the prosecution in criminal proceedings.[15] This burden will be satisfied by the party producing evidence which attains to the appropriate standard of proof. In criminal cases the prosecution must prove its case beyond reasonable doubt, and in civil cases the plaintiff must prove that on balance of probabilities his case is more likely to be true than that of the defendant.[16] Again when certain frequently recurring types of fact are proved to have occurred, the conclusion will be drawn, in the absence of rebutting evidence to the contrary, that certain other facts often found to accompany the first have also occurred. Sometimes, indeed, the inference must be drawn and cannot be negated. There is then said to be a conclusive or irrebuttable presumption, such as the rule that a child under ten cannot be guilty of crime.[17] This is in effect not a presumption but a rule of substantive law.

If, however, the law allows the usual inference to be contradicted, then the presumption is said to be rebuttable. If the court is obliged by a rule of law to draw a prescribed conclusion, whether rebuttable or not, the presumption is said to be one of law. If, however, the court may, but need not, draw the usual inference the presumption is one of fact. Indeed presumptions of fact are perhaps best regarded as frequently recurring pieces of "circumstantial evidence." This consists of circumstances from which the occurrence of some event or the existence of some further state of fact may be inferred, and is normally contrasted with "direct evidence," a statement by a witness or in a document that the event in question happened or the state of fact existed. Thus on a criminal charge, when there is no confession and no witness available to testify directly to the commission of the crime by the accused, the fact that the accused had a motive, that he had prepared for or equipped himself for the crime, that he was present at the time of the offence, that his fingerprints or fragments of his clothing were found on or near the scene of the crime or on objects connected with it, the fact that property involved in the crime was later found in his possession, the fact that he attempted to suborn witnesses as to his whereabouts at the time of the offence or the fact that he attempted to hamper investigation of the offence, may all be circumstantial evidence tending to prove his guilt.

[15] *Woolmington* v. *D.P.P.* [1935] A.C. 462; *Abrath* v. *North Eastern Rail Co.* (1883) 11 Q.B.D. 440.
[16] *R.* v. *Carr-Briant* [1943] K.B. 607; *Hornal* v. *Neuberger Products* [1957] 1 Q.B. 247.
[17] Children and Young Persons Acts 1933 and 1963.

Some examples of presumptions of law are the presumption of death arising from seven years' absence when the subject's whereabouts are unknown,[18] and the presumption of regularity and legality embodied in the maxim *omnia praesumuntur rite ac sollemniter esse acta*.[19] Examples of presumptions of fact occur when some normally continuing state of affairs is shown to have existed at a given time and is then presumed to have continued for some further time,[20] and the inferences to be drawn from the fact that a person is in possession of recently stolen goods.[21]

The growth of much of our law of evidence was historically conditioned by the undesirability of allowing an untrained tribunal, the jury, to be acquainted with evidence the prejudicial character of which might far outweigh its probative value. One product of this was a general rule against the admissibility of "hearsay" evidence. Such evidence occurs when a witness recounts some statement made by a third or more remote party, not merely to show that it was in fact made but as proof of the truth of its contents.[22] There had always been many exceptions to this general exclusionary rule, and with the decline of jury trial in civil cases these exceptions were much extended by the Evidence Act 1938, and the Civil Evidence Act 1968. Indeed the latter Act has gone far to make all "first-hand" hearsay admissible in *civil* proceedings. The Criminal Justice Bill 1988 makes provision for the admissibility in criminal cases of first-hand documentary hearsay and business records.

Similar Facts

Again because of its prejudicial character, the courts were always reluctant to admit evidence of facts similar to those in issue, when the only effect of this "similar fact" evidence was to show that the party against whom it was proffered was the sort of person who might have engaged in the kind of conduct alleged against him.[23] Evidence of similar facts may, however, be admitted when there is such a connecting link between the similar facts and the facts in issue that the similar facts show a *system*, so as to rebut a defence of accident or coincidence[24] or

---

[18] *Re Phene's Trusts* (1869) L.R. 5 Ch.App. 139.
[19] Everything is presumed to have been done properly and in due form. See *Berryman* v. *Wise* (1791) 4 T.R. 366; *Johnson* v. *Barnes* (1873) L.R. 8 C.P. 527.
[20] *R.* v. *Lumley* (1869) L.R. 1 C.C.R. 196.
[21] *R.* v. *Schama and Abramovitch* (1914) 84 L.J.K.B. 396.
[22] *Subramaniam* v. *Public Prosecutor* [1956] 1 W.L.R. 965.
[23] *Harris* v. *D.P.P.* [1952] A.C. 694.
[24] *Makin* v. *Att.-Gen.* (*N.S.W.*) [1894] A.C. 57; *R.* v. *Rhodes* [1899] 1 Q.B. 77. *Berger* v. *Raymond Sun* [1984] 1 W.L.R. 625. See also, Theft Act 1968, s.27(3).

serve to identify a party.[25] When matters which might in strictness be regarded as hearsay or similar fact are so closely associated in time and circumstances with the principal matter at issue in the case that all may be regarded as one single event, then all may be proved as part of the *res gestae*.[26]

Until the Criminal Evidence Act 1898, an accused in a criminal case was in general not allowed to give sworn evidence on his own behalf, but could only make an unsworn statement from the dock. When that Act allowed sworn evidence to be given by the accused it counterbalanced this relaxation by providing that, if the accused attacked the character of the prosecutor or gave evidence against a co-accused or gave evidence of his own good character, then evidence of previous convictions could be given against him.[27] The jury in a criminal case and magistrates are otherwise not told of previous convictions of the accused until after verdict or decision, and the accused is protected against questions tending to reveal them.[28]

The Criminal Evidence Act 1898, was the culmination of a number of nineteenth-century statutory reforms in the law of evidence which abrogated many exclusionary rules, such as those which prevented the parties to a civil case and their spouses from giving evidence in the case. Matters which had hitherto gone to admissibility were in future merely to go to weight of evidence.

Privilege

The law of evidence also recognised that many documents and communications might be privileged from production as evidence. Thus, for example, a party may not be compelled to give evidence of matters he has communicated to his legal advisers,[29] nor may evidence ordinarily be given of "without prejudice"

---

[25] *R.* v. *Straffen* [1952] 2 Q.B. 911. *D.P.P.* v. *Boardman* [1975] A.C. 421.

[26] *R.* v. *Ellis* (1826) 6 B. & C. 145; *R.* v. *Birdseye* (1830) 4 C. & P. 386; *Thompson* v. *Trevanion* (1693) Skinner 402; *R.* v. *Foster* (1834) 6 C. & P. 325. *Ratten* v. *R.* [1972] A.C. 378. *R.* v. *Turnbull* (1985) 80 Cr.App.R. 104. *Res gestae* = things done, *i.e.*, some conduct or transaction.

[27] See Criminal Evidence Act 1979. When a defendant reveals offences in his defence he may be asked if he was wanted by the police. *R.* v. *Anderson* (1988) *The Times*, February 4.

[28] See Police and Criminal Evidence Act 1984, s.74 and *R.* v. *Robertson* (1987) *The Times*, June 13 on proof of conviction as proof of the commission of an offence.

[29] *Wheeler* v. *le Marchant* (1881) 17 Ch.D. 675; *R.* v. *Cox and Railton* (1884) 14 Q.B.D. 153.

communications to the other party in civil proceedings.[30] The purpose of these exceptional privileges is to facilitate the proper operation of the law. This explains why they are not accorded to other professional communications. It came to be recognised, however, that the ends served by many of the old heads of privilege scarcely warranted the obstruction they put in the way of ascertaining the truth. Hence the Civil Evidence Act 1968, abolished many cases where privilege might hitherto have been claimed in civil cases.[31]

Estoppel

Another very important topic of the law of evidence is estoppel. It is sub-divided into three types—estoppel by judgment, by deed and by conduct. The essence of estoppel is that some person is precluded or barred from contradicting matters declared in a judgment of a court or in a deed, or which have been represented by word or conduct by that person to another with a view to that other acting on the facts as represented, where he does act on the representation to his prejudice.[32] Common law estoppel, which may wholly bar the representor from going back on his representation, must involve a representation of fact.[33] Equitable or promissory estoppel, which involves a promise as to the future, may have a less absolute effect, though it cannot be said that all the implications of this topic, which in its modern form derives from a famous judgment of Denning J. in *Central London Property Trust* v. *High Trees House*[34] and which was designed to mitigate some of the less satisfactory features of the doctrine of consideration in contract, have been fully worked out.

For obvious reasons of policy the courts refuse to admit confessions of guilt made by accused persons under the influence of fear or favour exerted by some person in authority.[35] The well-known Judge's Rules, which were rules of

---

[30] *Paddock* v. *Forrester* (1842) 3 Man. & G. 903. *Cutts* v. *Head* [1984] Ch. 290; *South Shropshire District Council* v. *Amos* [1986] 1 W.L.R. 1271. *Rush & Tomkin* v. *G.L.C.* [1988] 2 W.L.R. 533 (privilege ends when settlement achieved).

[31] s.16. See also, s.14. See also, Police and Criminal Evidence Act 1984, s.80(9) abolishing two heads of marital privilege in criminal cases. Civil privilege will still operate even though documents may have been revealed for a criminal trial. *British Coal Corp.* v. *Dennis Rye* (1988) *The Times*, March 7. Public interest immunity attaches to police reports to the Director of Public Prosecutions *Evans* v. *Chief Constable of Surrey* (1988) *The Times*, January 21.

[32] *Freeman* v. *Cooke* (1848) 18 L.J.Ex. 114.

[33] *Jorden* v. *Money* (1854) H.L.Cas. 185.

[34] [1947] K.B. 130.

[35] *R.* v. *Baldry* (1852) 2 Den. 430. *D.P.P.* v. *Ping Lin* [1976] A.C. 574.

practice rather than law, were designed to protect those suspected of crime from unfair interrogation. In any event the judge has an overriding discretion to reject an unfairly obtained confession. These matters are now covered by the Police and Criminal Evidence Act 1984 and Codes of Practice made under the Act.[36] On the other hand there is no general rule of English law excluding illegally obtained evidence, though the judge has a discretion to reject it if he thinks fit.[37]

Attendance of Witnesses

A compellable witness may be required to attend a magistrates' court by summons or warrant, the county court by witness summons, criminal proceedings in the Crown Court by witness summons or witness order and the High Court by *subpoena ad testificandum*. If he is required to attend with a document he will be summoned by a *subpoena duces tecum*. Failure to attend may then be punished as contempt of court, but the witness summoned may apply to have the subpoena set aside if it is an abuse of process and he has no relevant evidence to give, as in *R. v. Baines*[38] where the then Prime Minister and Home Secretary were called to give evidence in a trial for breach of the peace and unlawful assembly. In a civil case it is for the parties to call their witnesses and a judge must not call a witness without the parties' consent[39]; it is otherwise, however, in criminal trials where the judge may himself call witnesses when the interests of justice require.[40]

2. CIVIL PROCEDURE[41]

One of the chief ends here is to ensure that each party to proceedings has fair notice of the case against him and that the issues between the parties are reduced to as well-defined a form as possible. This facilitates the tribunal's task of arriving at a just decision, reduces expense and may go some way to assist the parties to compromise their claims before the case comes to a full hearing.

[36] See ss.76 and 82.
[37] *Kuruma, Son of Kaniu* v. *R.* [1955] A.C. 197. See also *R.* v. *Voisin* [1918] 1 K.B. 531 and *R.* v. *Gould* (1840) 9 C. & P. 364. *R.* v. *Sang* [1980] A.C. 402. Police and Criminal Evidence Act 1984, ss.76 and 82.
[38] [1909] 1 K.B. 258.
[39] *Re Enoch* [1910] 1 K.B. 327.
[40] *R.* v. *Holden* (1838) 8 C. & P. 606; *R.* v. *Harris* [1927] 2 K.B. 587.
[41] For Criminal Procedure see Chaps. 3 and 16; Jacob, *Fabric of English Civil Justice* (1986).

Until the reforms of the nineteenth century English civil procedure was a complex labyrinth of intricate devices, some of great antiquity, which varied widely not only from court to court but from one type of claim to another, as the old forms of action demonstrate. Whilst it cannot be said that procedure is now simple or always logical it is nevertheless more straightforward and flexible than it once was.[42] There are substantial differences between High Court and county court procedure and between the procedures of the various Divisions of the High Court, and the whole field cannot be examined in detail. Thus in order to illustrate the operation of civil procedure at the present day, the chief steps in an action commenced by writ in the Queen's Bench Division will be described since this exemplifies a pattern from which other forms of proceedings may, to a greater or lesser degree, be regarded as variants. The chief steps in a county court action will also be outlined.

Rules of the Supreme Court

All procedural steps in the High Court are governed by Rules of the Supreme Court made by a Rule Committee of judges and others first set up under the Judicature Act.[43] The preliminary procedural steps in an action, known as interlocutory proceedings, are supervised by an official of the Court, a Master in London or a District Registrar in the Provinces.

Compromise

Settlement or compromise of a dispute before proceedings have commenced is assisted by allowing the parties to negotiate by means of letters marked "without prejudice." Such letters cannot subsequently be used as admissions in evidence between the parties if the negotiations fail and the case goes to trial.[44] Settlement is encouraged by allowing a defendant to pay into court a sum he judges adequate to meet the plaintiff's claim. If the plaintiff, having been notified of this, continues the action and fails to recover more than the sum paid in, he will be deprived of his costs and condemned to pay the defendant's costs from the date of payment in.

---

[42] See "Going to Law" by *Justice* (1974) for a criticism of modern procedure.
[43] Supreme Court Act 1981, ss.84–87.
[44] *Paddock* v. *Forrester* (1842) 3 M. & G. 903. *Cutts* v. *Head* [1984] Ch. 290; *South Shropshire District Council* v. *Amos* [1986] 1 W.L.R. 1271. *Rush & Tomkin* v. *G.L.C.* [1988] 2 W.L.R. 533.

The Writ

When a plaintiff has decided to commence proceedings he or his advisers must first decide who are the proper parties to the action, whether as co-plaintiff with him or co-defendants, since all necessary parties must be named in the writ. The plaintiff must then complete two writ forms. These summon the defendant or defendants to answer the case alleged against them.[45] The writ may carry a concise statement of the plaintiff's claim and remedies sought. This is commonly known as a "general endorsement." Alternatively it may be "specially endorsed" with a full statement of the matters of fact upon which the plaintiff relies.

The writ forms must be taken or posted by a solicitor to the Central Office of the Supreme Court in London or a District Registry in the Provinces, where a fee will be paid and one of the forms filed away. The other will be sealed and returned to the plaintiff. The writ is then regarded as issued and the action commenced for the purpose of the law of limitation. In order to prevent the litigation of stale claims this prescribes time limits within which various types of action must be commenced.[46]

The plaintiff must then serve the writ on the defendant personally or by post or more usually by sending it to his solicitor. If the defendant is out of the jurisdiction, leave of the court must be obtained to effect service,[47] and if the defendant cannot be found leave may be given for various forms of substituted service, as by newspaper advertisement.

If the defendant wishes to defend the action he must, after being served with the writ, "acknowledge service" within fourteen days by completing a form of acknowledgment of service which accompanies the writ and by delivering or posting it to the court offices. Until 1980 this stage was represented by the "entry of an appearance." Otherwise judgment may be entered against him by default.

Order 14

If the plaintiff believes that there is no substantial defence he may apply for summary judgment under Order 14 if he has "specially endorsed" the writ. The case will be heard by a Master or Registrar, who may give judgment for the plaintiff if he agrees that there is no real defence or may if he thinks that

---

[45] The present form dates from 1979.
[46] See Limitation Acts 1980. Latent Damage Act 1986.
[47] R.S.C., Ord. 11.

there is a weak or dubious defence, impose conditions on its presentation. If there is a good defence no conditions will be imposed on the defendant and the plaintiff may be penalised in costs for having proceeded under Order 14.

Pleadings

If there is no substantial dispute as to facts there may be trial without pleadings. Otherwise the parties must exchange pleadings. These are written statements of the facts (not law nor the evidence by which the facts are to be proved) upon which the parties rely.

The first pleading comes from the plaintiff in his statement of claim if he has not specially endorsed the writ; such an endorsement is itself a statement of claim. The defendant in his turn delivers a defence, and to that there may be a reply from the plaintiff or, if the defence raises a counterclaim, a defence to that counterclaim. These are the pleadings normally used at the present day and leave will be required if more are to be exchanged. The drafting of pleadings is a highly technical task, and although it is now far less easy to shipwreck a good case than in the past by defective pleading and although the courts are fairly liberal in allowing amendments, these may be expensive in terms of costs. It has been said that caution induced by this has meant that pleadings, instead of closely defining the matters at issue between the parties, are usually drafted to preserve the widest possible field of manoeuvre, thus defeating their chief purpose.[48]

If a party is dissatisfied with his opponent's pleadings he may ask for further and better particulars. Parties may also seek to delimit the field of conflict before trial by administering "interrogatories" or questions to be answered on oath by their opponents. "Discovery of documents" has since 1964 automatically ensured that parties will have an opportunity of examining documents relevant to the case which are in the possession of their opponents.

A party may wish to restrain another from some course of action prior to the hearing. This can be done by an interlocutory injunction. The test for granting this is now balance of convenience.[49] A plaintiff may obtain a *Mareva*

[48] See "Going to Law," pp. 12–13.
[49] *American Cyanamid* v. *Ethicon* [1975] A.C. 396 but see *Cayne* v. *Global Resources* [1984] 1 All E.R. 225. *Mail Newspapers* v. *Insert Media* (1987) *The Times*, April 21.

injunction[50] to restrain a defendant from removing assets from the jurisdiction which would otherwise be available to satisfy judgment against him and in patent, copyright and similar intellectual property cases an *Anton Piller*[51] order to search the defendants' premises for infringing articles.

Summons for Directions

Within a month of the close of pleadings the plaintiff should, except in certain personal injury actions, take out a summons for directions to be heard by the Master or District Registrar. This is intended to be a "general stocktaking" of the action as far as it has proceeded, and the Master or Registrar may make a variety of orders as to the location and type of trial and as to any further interlocutory steps to be taken by the parties. In 1980 a system of automatic standard directions relating to matters such as expert evidence and the place of trial was introduced for all personal injury cases other than in Admiralty or where medical negligence was alleged.

The Trial

When the trial commences, in the ordinary course counsel for the plaintiff will open his case with an explanatory speech and then elicit their evidence from his witnesses by means of brief questions in examination-in-chief. Counsel for the defendant may cross-examine each of the plaintiff's witnesses after he has been examined-in-chief, and counsel calling the witness may then endeavour to counteract the effect of the cross-examination by re-examining the witness. "Leading questions," which may suggest a desired answer, may not be put by counsel in examination-in-chief or re-examination but may be freely used in cross-examination.

When the plaintiff's case has concluded, counsel for the defendant may submit that there is no case to answer, but this is a course fraught with danger since in the case of a non-jury trial counsel will be required to "stand on his submission," so that if

[50] *Mareva Compania* v. *International Bulk Carriers* [1980] 1 All E.R. 213; Supreme Court Act 1981, s.37 (allowing an injunction when the defendant is not in the jurisdiction); Civil Jurisdiction and Judgments Acts 1982, s.25 (applying the procedure to litigation in other contracting States). Flouting the injunction may result in immediate imprisonment. *Popischal* v. *Phillips* (1988) *The Times*, January 20.
[51] *Anton Piller* v. *Manufacturing Processes Ltd.* [1976] Ch. 55; Supreme Court Act 1981, s.72.

the court rules against him he will not be allowed to call evidence.[52]

If there is no such submission, counsel for the defendant will make an opening speech and call his witnesses, who will be examined-in-chief, cross-examined and re-examined. Counsel for the defendant will then make a closing speech, followed by a closing speech from counsel for the plaintiff. If the defendant does not call evidence, counsel for the plaintiff will make his closing speech after he has called his witnesses and before the defendant's case is put to the court.

When the parties' cases are concluded the judge will sum up and direct the jury, if it is one of the now rare civil cases heard with a jury. Otherwise he will determine the law and the facts and give judgment. In a difficult case he may reserve judgment to consider his decision.

Costs

The judge will normally award costs to the successful party. This means that he may recover costs he has incurred from the other party. The actual disbursements will be "taxed" by an official known as a Taxing Master to reduce them to a figure regarded as reasonably necessary for running the action. "Taxation" here means "assessment" and has no revenue connotation.

Appeal

Appeal to the Court of Appeal (Civil Division) is normally as of right (no leave being required), and may be on questions of fact, law, damages or costs. A point of law must normally have been taken at the trial.[53] On fact the Court of Appeal draws a distinction between "the perception and the evaluation of fact"[54] and is reluctant to interfere on questions of "direct fact" or "perception of fact," that is to say, whether witnesses are to be believed or not, since it does not see the witnesses. The Court is not so inhibited, however, in regard to matters of inference drawn from established facts, that is to say, the "evaluation" of fact.[55] On damages the Court of Appeal will not alter the award

---

[52] See *Alexander* v. *Rayson* [1936] 1 K.B. 169, 178–180. The rule is less strict in jury trials. *Young* v. *Rank* [1950] 2 K.B. 510, 514. See Langan, *Civil Procedure* (3rd ed.), pp. 222–225.

[53] *Clouston* v. *Corry* [1906] A.C. 122; *U.D.T.* v. *Bycroft* [1954] 1 W.L.R. 1345.

[54] *Benmax* v. *Austin* [1955] A.C. 370.

[55] *S.S. Hontestroom* v. *S.S. Sagaporack* [1927] A.C. 37.

merely because it would have awarded a different sum, but it will interfere only when the award is so large or so small that the court below must have acted on some wrong principle.[56] Appeal on costs requires leave, and the Court of Appeal will only interfere if the appeal, though in form on costs, in fact involves the merits of the case or it is clear that the court's discretion was misused.[57]

Appeal from the Court of Appeal (Civil Division) to the House of Lords requires leave either from the Court of Appeal or the House of Lords.[58]

Instead of appealing to the Court of Appeal the parties may, under certain conditions, take a "leapfrog" appeal to the House of Lords directly from the High Court.[59]

When an appeal is from a judge sitting alone the Court of Appeal may make any determination or order that was open to the court below and substitute its decision for that of the judge.[60] An appeal from a jury takes the form of an application for a new trial, though there are cases where the Court of Appeal has itself determined the case.[61]

Enforcement

If a party refuses to comply with a judgment various methods of enforcement are available. An award of damages may be enforced by execution, *i.e.* the seizure and sale of so much of the defendant's property as is necessary to satisfy the judgment. If a party fails to obey an injunction he may be imprisoned for contempt of court.[62] Imprisonment for negligent or wilful failure to pay a debt following a judgment has been much restricted since 1970, though it has not completely vanished.[63] By means of a garnishee order a debtor of the judgment debtor (unsuccessful party) may be directed to pay the debt to the judgment creditor (the successful party). When a party is in contempt for wilful or negligent failure to obey the court a writ of sequestration may issue, authorising the seizure and holding of all the

---

[56] *Davis* v. *Shepstone* (1886) 11 App.Cas. at 191 (jury); *Davies* v. *Powell Duffryn* [1942] A.C. 601, 616 (judge alone).
[57] See *Donald Campbell* v. *Pollak* [1927] A.C. 732.
[58] Administration of Justice (Appeals) Act 1934.
[59] See above, p. 95 and Administration of Justice Act 1969.
[60] Supreme Court Act 1981, s.15.
[61] *Mechanical Inventions* v. *Austin* [1935] A.C. 346.
[62] *Knight* v. *Clifton* [1971] Ch. 700. But see *Heaton's Transport* v. *T.G.W.U.* [1973] A.C. 15.
[63] Administration of Justice Act 1970; Debtors Act 1869. Imprisonment is only available in the High Court for non-payment of maintenance orders. Thus it is not found in the Queen's Bench Division but in the Family Division.

party's property until the order of the court has been obeyed. A charge may be imposed on certain types of property owned by the judgment debtor, and a receiver may be appointed by way of equitable execution to receive rents and profits. Insolvency proceedings may also be taken. A High Court judgment for the payment of money may be registered in the county court for enforcement there. This allows an order to be made for payment by instalments and the attachment of the future earnings of the judgment debtor.

Originating Summons

When a case in the High Court does not involve disputed questions of fact or is primarily a question of law or construction of statutes or documents, it may be commenced by originating summons instead of by writ. Since 1962 this procedure, always well known in the Chancery Division, has become more widely used in the Queen's Bench Division.

Chancery Division

Procedure in an action commenced by writ in the Chancery Division is in many respects similar to proceedings in the Queen's Bench Division. The principal difference is that more complex interlocutory relief before the trial is available in the Chancery Division.[64] It has been seen that several types of action must be commenced in the Chancery Division,[65] but in many cases parties are able to choose between the Divisions. This will be a matter of tactics. Cases raising questions of fact and involving the examination of many witnesses will be more appropriate for the Queen's Bench Division, whereas cases primarily raising questions of law or construction of documents could well go to the Chancery Division.[65a]

County Courts

County court proceedings are subject to both financial and geographic limits. For example, in contract and tort the amount in issue must be under £5,000 if the defendant is to be compelled to accept the jurisdiction of the court.[66] Parties may agree to

---

[64] See Odgers, *Pleadings and Practice* (22nd ed.), pp. 306, 311 and 313.
[65] See above, p. 77.
[65a] But transfer between Divisions is a matter of judicial rather than litigant management. A party requiring expedited trial should apply for that rather than a transfer. *Barclays Bank* v. *Bemister* (1987) *The Times*, December 15.
[66] County Courts Act 1984, s.15. But see now Practice Statement (Listings) (1988) *The Times*, January 13, above, p. 70.

waive these limits.[67] Proceedings must be commenced in the county court for the district in which the defendant resides or carries on business or in which the cause of action arose.

Proceedings are commenced by the plaintiff filing in the county court office a request for a summons and particulars of the claim. The Registrar of the county court will then issue a plaint note and summons. The summons and particulars, together with forms of admission, defence and counterclaim, must then be served on the defendant. This may be done by the bailiff of the court and may be done by post. The defendant may within a further fourteen days admit the claim, pay into court or file a defence and, if necessary, a counterclaim. He can, however, appear on the return day without having filed a defence and contest the plaintiff's claim, but he may be ordered to pay costs resulting from this.

Since 1972 there has been a "pre-trial review" before the Registrar which resembles the summons for directions in the High Court.

The County Court Rules make provision for the settlement of actions, and payment into court has the same effect as in the High Court.

Trial may be before the Judge or Registrar, the latter having compulsory jurisdiction up to £500. The Registrar also has an arbitral jurisdiction intended to deal with small claims. Very rarely trial may be with a jury of eight. Trial procedure resembles that in the High Court, but solicitors as well as barristers have a right of audience. There are complex rules governing the transfer of proceedings between the High Court and the county court. Rules as to costs are designed to ensure that cases within the jurisdiction of the county court are taken there instead of in the High Court. Enforcement of judgments follows the same pattern as in the High Court but, as was seen with the enforcement of High Court judgments by the county court, procedure in the county court is in some respects more efficient since orders may be made for payment by instalments or for the attachment of future earnings.

Appeal from the county court normally lies directly to the Court of Appeal (Civil Division).[68] Appeals from the Registrar lie to the Judge.

---

[67] See above, p. 72 of proposed limit of £50,000.
[68] Administration of Justice (Appeals) Act 1934. See above, p. 72.

INDEX